Lecture Notes in Computer Science 7261

Commenced Publication in 1973
Founding and Former Series Editors:
Gerhard Goos, Juris Hartmanis, and Jan van Leeuwen

Kerstin Eder   João Lourenço
Onn Shehory (Eds.)

Hardware and Software: Verification and Testing

7th International
Haifa Verification Conference, HVC 2011
Haifa, Israel, December 6-8, 2011
Revised Selected Papers

 Springer

Volume Editors

Kerstin Eder
University of Bristol, Department of Computer Science
Merchant Venturers Building 3.25, Woodland Road, Bristol BS8 1UB, UK
E-mail: kerstin.eder@bristol.ac.uk

João Lourenço
NOVA University of Lisbon, Department of Computer Science and Engineering
FCT-UNL, Quinta da Tore, 2829-516 Caparica, Portugal
E-mail: joao.lourenco@fct.unl.pt

Onn Shehory
IBM Research Labs at Haifa
Haifa University Campus, Mount Carmel, Haifa 31905, Israel
E-mail: onn@il.ibm.com

ISSN 0302-9743   e-ISSN 1611-3349
ISBN 978-3-642-34187-8   e-ISBN 978-3-642-34188-5
DOI 10.1007/978-3-642-34188-5
Springer Heidelberg Dordrecht London New York

Library of Congress Control Number: 2012950042

CR Subject Classification (1998): D.2.4-5, D.3.1, F.3.1-2, D.2.11, I.2.2-3

LNCS Sublibrary: SL 2 – Programming and Software Engineering

Typesetting: Camera-ready by author, data conversion by Scientific Publishing Services, Chennai, India

Printed on acid-free paper

Springer is part of Springer Science+Business Media (www.springer.com)

Preface

This volume contains the papers presented at the Haifa Verification Conference 2011, the 7th in the series of annual conferences dedicated to advancing the state of the art and state of the practice in verification and testing of hardware and software. HVC provides a forum for researchers and practitioners from both academia and industry to share their work, exchange ideas, and discuss challenges and future directions of testing and verification for hardware, software, and hybrid systems.

Academic research in system verification and testing is roughly divided into two major paradigms: formal verification and dynamic verification (testing). Within each paradigm, algorithms, techniques and even terminology may differ considerably between hardware-related solutions and software-related solutions. However, the common underlying goal of verification, across paradigms and system types, is to gain confidence in a system meeting its functional as well as its non-functional requirements. HVC is the only conference that brings together researchers and practitioners from all verification and testing sub-fields, thereby encouraging the migration of methods and ideas among domains. One key asset of HVC is the strong participation from industry. HVC provides a platform for the academic and industrial research communities to mix and mingle, thereby creating new opportunities for collaborative research. We are particularly proud to say that the papers selected for presentation at HVC 2011 covered a wide range of sub-fields related to testing and verification applicable to software, hardware, and hybrid systems, thus stimulating discussion within the wider verification community.

From a total of 43 submissions, the Program Committee selected 15 regular papers for full presentation, three tools papers for short presentation, and four posters for the student poster session on day one of the conference. HVC 2011 was organized in five technical sessions devoted to topics including synthesis, formal verification, software quality, testing, and coverage. The best paper selection jury considered both the quality of the technical paper as well as the presentation at the conference. The best paper prize was awarded to Marijn Heule, Oliver Kullmann, Siert Wieringa, and Armin Biere for their paper entitled "Cube and Conquer: Guiding CDCL SAT Solvers by Lookaheads."

Granted since 2007, the HVC award recognizes the most promising academic and industrial contribution to the fields of testing and software and hardware verification from the last five years. The HVC 2011 award went to Daniel Kroening from Oxford for his contribution of CBMC, a bounded model checker for C programs. CBMC is the first and most influential industrial-strength verification engine for a non-academic programming language, and hence a major milestone in automated verification. To date, CBMC is the only verification engine that supports the full functionality of C, including precise modeling of floating-point operations and bit-precise arithmetic. CBMC promotes the industrial adoption of formal software verification more than any other tool in existence and is therefore a significant contribution to the verification community.

The conference was hosted by IBM at the IBM Research Labs in Haifa. We would like to thank all who made HVC 2011 run smoothly and gratefully acknowledge the invaluable support by many on the IBM administrative team, without which this event could not meet its goals and match the high standards established over the years. We would like to thank the Program Committee, the HVC Award Committee, the Best Paper Prize Jury, the authors of all submissions to HVC 2011 and, of course, the presenters of the papers and posters accepted. All these contributed toward making HVC 2011 another success in the HVC conference series. We would also like to thank the tutorial presenters Avner Engel, Ofer Strichman, and Rachel Tzoref-Brill for an informative first day prior to the main conference. Special thanks are due to our invited speakers who enriched the program with insightful and inspiring presentations: Kathryn Kranen, Jasper Design Automation, Ben Liblit, University of Wisconsin-Madison, Klaus-Dieter Schubert, IBM Deutschland Research and Development GmbH, and Armin Biere, Johannes Kepler University, Linz.

Finally, we would like to thank our sponsors, IBM, Cadence, Mentor Graphics, and Jasper Design Automation, for their generous support in preparation and throughout the event.

July 2012   Kerstin Eder
                                                                João Lourenço
                                                                Onn Shehory

Organization

General Chair

Onn Shehory   IBM Haifa Labs, Israel

Program Chairs

Kerstin Eder   University of Bristol, UK   (Verification Track)
João Lourenço   New University of Lisbon,   (Software Testing Track)
                              Portugal

Tutorials Chair

Oz Hershkovitz   IBM Haifa Labs, Israel

Local Organization

Yair Harry   IBM Haifa Labs, Israel   (Webmaster)
Shirley Namer   IBM Haifa Labs, Israel   (Local Logistics)
Onn Shehory   IBM Haifa Labs, Israel   (Coordinator)

Program Committee

Sharon Barner   IBM Haifa Labs, Israel
Geoff Barrett   Broadcom, UK
Armin Biere   Institute for Formal Models and Verification, Austria
Eyal Bin   IBM Haifa Labs, Israel
Roderick Bloem   Graz University of Technology, Austria
Michael Browne   IBM, USA
Michael Butler   University of Southampton, UK
Radu Calinescu   University of Aston, UK
Hana Chockler   IBM Haifa Labs, Israel
Kerstin Eder   University of Bristol, UK
Eitan Farchi   IBM Haifa Labs, Israel
Harry Foster   Mentor Graphics, USA
Franco Fummi   University of Verona, Italy
Ian G. Harris   University of California Irvine, USA
Ziyad Hanna   Jasper DA, USA
Klaus Havelund   JPL, USA
Alan Hu   University of British Columbia, USA
Mika Katara   Tampere University of Technology, Finland
Zurab Khasidashvili   Intel, Israel

Tsvi Kuflik	University of Haifa, Israel
Mark Last	Ben Gurion University, Israel
João Lourenço	New University of Lisbon, Portugal
Tom Melham	Oxford University, UK
Amir Nahir	IBM Haifa Labs, Israel
Mauro Pezze	University of Lugano, Switzerland, and
	University of Milano Bicocca, Italy
Orna Raz	IBM Haifa Labs, Israel
Michael S. Hsiao	VirginiaTech, USA
Wolfram Schulte	Microsoft Research,USA
Onn Shehory	IBM Haifa Labs, Israel
Armando Tacchella	University of Genova, Italy
Helen Treharne	University of Surrey, UK
Shmuel Ur	Innovations Ltd., Israel
Helmut Veith	Vienna University of Technology, Austria
Heike Wehrheim	Paderborn University, Germany

HVC Award Committee

Shmuel Ur	Innovations Ltd., Israel (Chair)
Ian G. Harris	University of California Irvine, USA
Klaus Havelund	JPL, USA
Mika Katara	Tampere University of Technology, Finland
Ofer Strichman	Technion, Israel

Additional Referees

Sam Bayless	Yael Meller
Christian Bird	Madanlal Musuvathi
John Colley	Ziv Nevo
Chris Derobertis	Avigail Orni
Ricardo Dias	Andrey Rybalchenko
Andrew Edmunds	Alexander Schremmer
Cindy Eisner	Carl Seger
Ranan Fraer	Martina Seidl
Jim Grundy	Dominik Steenken
Georg Hofferek	Dorian Thomas
Andreas Holzer	Rachel Tzoref-Brill
Alexander Ivrii	Heikki Virtanen
Kenneth Johnson	Matti Vuori
Antti Jääskeläinen	Sven Walther
Robert Koenighofer	Nick Wiggins
Dmitry Korchemny	Chao Yan
Anatoly Koyfman	

Table of Contents

Software Quality

Testing and Coverage

Experience and Tools

Posters – Student Event

Preprocessing and Inprocessing Techniques in SAT

Armin Biere

Johannes Kepler University
Altenbergerstr. 69
4040 Linz
Austria

Abstract. SAT solvers are used in many applications in and outside of Computer Science. The success of SAT is based on the use of good decision heuristics, learning, restarts, and compact data structures with fast algorithms. But also efficient and effective encoding, preprocessing and inprocessing techniques are important in practice. In this talk we give an overview of old and more recent inprocessing and preprocessing techniques starting with ancient pure literal reasoning and failed literal probing. Hyper-binary resolution and variable elimination are more recent techniques of this century. We discuss blocked-clause elimination, which gives a nice connection to optimizing encodings and conclude with our recent results on unhiding redundancy fast.

Speaker Bio

Since 2004 Prof. Armin Biere chairs the Institute for Formal Models and Verification at the Johannes Kepler University in Linz, Austria. Between 2000 and 2004 he held a position as Assistant Professor within the Department of Computer Science at ETH Zürich, Switzerland. In 1999 Biere was working for a start-up company in electronic design automation after one year as Post-Doc with Edmund Clarke at CMU, Pittsburgh, USA. In 1997 Biere received a Ph.D. in Computer Science from the University of Karlsruhe, Germany.

His primary research interests are applied formal methods, more specifically formal verification of hardware and software, using model checking, propositional and related techniques. He is the author and co-author of more than 60 papers and served on the program committee of more than 45 international workshops and conferences. His highest influential work is the contribution to Bounded Model Checking. Decision procedures for SAT, QBF and SMT, developed by him or under his guidance rank at the top of many international competitions. Besides organizing several workshops Armin Biere was co-chair of SAT'06 and FMCAD'09. He is on the editorial board of the Journal on Satisfiability, Boolean Modeling and Computation (JSAT), and is one of the editors of the Handbook of Satisfiability. He also organizes the Hardware Model Checking Competition.

K. Eder, J. Lourenço, and O. Shehory (Eds.): HVC 2011, LNCS 7261, p. 1, 2012.

Pioneering the Future of Verification: A Spiral of Technological and Business Innovation

Kathryn Kranen

Jasper Design Automation
100 View St., Suite 101
Mountain View
94041
United States

Abstract. Changing the way the world verifies semiconductors and systems takes far more than algorithmic or methodological breakthroughs. Over the past two decades, there have been four or five great verification breakthroughs, while many other promising technologies have been relegated to the dust bin. Bringing a nascent EDA technology to mainstream use and commercial success requires alternating technological and business innovations to accelerate adoption.

In this session, you'll learn key concepts about bringing a disruptive technology to widespread adoption. Kathryn Kranen will share insights gained as a market pioneer of three technologies that have become the major pillars of today's mainstream system-on-chip verification: hardware emulation, constrained-random simulation, and formal property verification. You will also hear some of her visions of what the future of design and verification may hold.

Speaker Bio

Kathryn Kranen is responsible for leading Jasper's team in successfully bringing the company's pioneering technology to the mainstream design verification market. She has more than 20 years EDA industry experience and a proven management track record. While serving as president and CEO of Verisity Design, Inc., US headquarters of Verisity Ltd., Kathryn and the team she built created an entirely new market in design verification. (Verisity later became a public company, and was the top-performing IPO of 2001.) Prior to Verisity, Kathryn was vice president of North American sales at Quickturn Systems. She started her career as a design engineer at Rockwell International, and later joined Daisy Systems, an early EDA company. Kathryn graduated Summa cum Laude from Texas A&M University with a B.S. in Electrical Engineering. Kathryn is serving her fifth term on the EDA Consortium board of directors, and was elected its vice chairperson. In 2005, Kathryn was recipient of the prestigious Marie R. Pistilli Women in Electronic Design Automation (EDA) Achievement Award. In 2009, EE Times listed Kathryn as one of the "Top 10 Women in Microelectronics".

K. Eder, J. Lourenço, and O. Shehory (Eds.): HVC 2011, LNCS 7261, p. 2, 2012.

Automated Detection and Repair of Concurrency Bugs

Ben Liblit

Computer Sciences Department
University of Wisconsin–Madison
1210 West Dayton Street
Madison, WI 53706-1685
United States

Abstract. Finding and fixing concurrency bugs is critical in modern software systems. This talk examines two recent efforts to automate both the detection and the repair of certain types of concurrency bugs using a mixture of static, dynamic, and statistical methods.

First, we present a low-overhead instrumentation framework to diagnose production-run failures caused by concurrency bugs. We track specific thread interleavings at run-time, using sparse random sampling to limit overhead. Methods drawn from work in statistical debugging let us identify strong failure predictors among the sampled concurrent behaviors. Our approach offers a spectrum of performance and diagnosis capabilities suitable for wide deployment to real user desktops.

Second, we describe a strategy for automatically fixing one of the most common types of concurrency bugs in real-world code. Starting with descriptions of bad interleavings, our tool automatically inserts synchronization operations to steer future executions away from danger. Static analyses help us maintain good performance while reducing the risk of deadlocks. Dynamic monitoring allows for run-time recovery from deadlocks that could not be statically avoided.

Overall, our approach yields overheads too low to reliably measure; produces small, simple, understandable patches; and completely eliminates detected bugs in the targeted class across a variety of complex, real-world applications.

Speaker Bio

Ben Liblit is an associate professor in the Computer Sciences Department of the University of Wisconsin–Madison, with research interests in programming languages and software engineering. Professor Liblit worked as a professional software engineer for four years before beginning graduate study. His experience has inspired a research style that emphasizes practical, best-effort solutions that bring formal methods to bear against the ugly complexities of real-world software development.

Professor Liblit completed his Ph.D. in 2004 at UC Berkeley with advisor Alex Aiken. He earned the 2005 ACM Doctoral Dissertation Award for his work on post-deployment statistical debugging, and has received AFOSR Young Investigator and NSF CAREER awards in support of his research.

K. Eder, J. Lourenço, and O. Shehory (Eds.): HVC 2011, LNCS 7261, p. 3, 2012.

Verification Challenges of Workload Optimized Hardware Systems

Klaus-Dieter Schubert

IBM Deutschland Research and Development GmbH
Systems & Technology Group
71032 Böblingen
Germany

Abstract. Over the last couple of years it became more and more obvious that improvements in chip technology get smaller and smaller with each generation. Processor frequency is stagnating for some time now and single thread performance of general purpose processor cores is only increasing very slowly from generation to generation despite the fact that designers have more and more transistors they can utilize.

However, to stay competitive in the Compute Server business it is necessary to follow Moore's law and provide significant performance improvements to the customer every year. This begs the question how this can be achieved when traditional ways like cycle time improvements and the usage of more transistors are not yielding the desired results. The answer has to be a combination of logic, system and software design.

This talk will first describe why continuing with "business as usual" will fail going forward. It will then discuss a number of scenarios for workload optimized systems to overcome these hurdles before the focus will shift to the question: What challenges will that present to the area of hardware verification?

Speaker Bio

Klaus-Dieter Schubert received the Dipl.-Ing. degree in electrical engineering in 1990 from Stuttgart University (Germany). Subsequently, he joined IBM in Boeblingen and has been responsible for hardware verification of various IBM mainframe systems and its components. He was the technical lead for the hardware verification of the z900 2064 system before he moved to the field of hardware and software co-verification where he established the concept of virtual power-on (VPO) for zSeries and pSeries systems. From 2006 to 2008, Mr. Schubert was on a work assignment in Austin, Texas, where he has led the verification team for the POWER7 microprocessor. Today he is an IBM Distinguished Engineer and the technical leader for the hardware verification of future POWER processors. He has received two IBM Outstanding Achievement Awards for his contributions in the field of hardware verification.

K. Eder, J. Lourenço, and O. Shehory (Eds.): HVC 2011, LNCS 7261, p. 4, 2012.

Synthesis with Clairvoyance*

Orna Kupferman[1], Dorsa Sadigh[2], and Sanjit A. Seshia[2]

[1] Hebrew University, School of Engineering and Computer Science, Jerusalem, Israel
[2] UC Berkeley, EECS Department, Berkeley CA, USA

Abstract. We consider the problem of automatically synthesizing, from a linear temporal logic (LTL) specification, a system that is guaranteed to satisfy the specification with respect to all environments. Algorithms for solving the synthesis problem reduce it to the solution of a game played between the system and its environment, in which the system and environment alternate between generating outputs and inputs respectively. Typically, the system is required to generate an output right after receiving the current input. If a solution to the game exists, the specification is said to be realizable.

In this paper, we consider the role of clairvoyance in synthesis, in which the system can "look into the future," basing its output upon future inputs. An infinite look-ahead transforms the realizability problem into a problem known as universal satisfiability. A thesis we explore in this paper is that the notion of clairvoyance is useful as a heuristic even in the general case of synthesis, when there is no lookahead. Specifically, we suggest a heuristic in which we search for strategies where the system and the environment try to force each other into hopeless states in the game — states from which they cannot win, no matter how large the lookahead. The classification to hopeful and hopeless states is thus based on a modified notion of universal satisfiability where the output prefix is constrained. Our approach uses the automata for the specification in the process of classification into hopeful and hopeless states, and uses the structure of the automata in order to construct the game graph, but the important point is that the game itself is a reachability game. We demonstrate the efficiency of our approach with examples, and outline some directions for future work exploring the proposed approach.

1 Introduction

A frequent criticism against verification methods is that verification is done after significant resources have already been invested in the development of the system. The critics argue that the desired goal is to use the specification in the system development process in order to guarantee the design of correct systems. This is called *automatic synthesis*. Formally, given a specification to a reactive system, typically by means of an LTL formula, the goal in automatic synthesis is to transform it into a system that is guaranteed to satisfy the specification.[1]

---

* This research was supported in part by NSF grant CNS-0644436 and the Gigascale Systems Research Center, one of six research centers funded under the Focus Center Research Program (FCRP), a Semiconductor Research Corporation entity.

[1] To make life interesting, several different methodologies in system design are all termed "synthesis". The automatic synthesis we study should not be confused with *logic synthesis*, which is a process by which an abstract form of a desired circuit behavior (typically, register transfer level, which by itself may be the outcome of yet another synthesis procedure, termed *high-level synthesis*) is turned into a design implementation by means of logic gates.

K. Eder, J. Lourenço, and O. Shehory (Eds.): HVC 2011, LNCS 7261, pp. 5–19, 2012.
© Springer-Verlag Berlin Heidelberg 2012

In the late 1980s, several researchers realized that the classical approach to system synthesis, where a system is extracted from a proof that the specification is satisfiable, is well suited to *closed* systems, but not to *open* (also called *reactive* [10]) systems [1,4,21]. A reactive system interacts with its environment, and a correct system should satisfy the specification with respect to all environments. The right way to approach synthesis of reactive systems is to consider the situation as a (possibly infinite) game between the environment and the system. More formally, a strategy for a system with inputs in I and outputs in O maps finite sequences of inputs — words in $(2^I)^*$, which correspond to the actions of the environment so far, to an output in 2^O — a suggested action for the system. A specification ψ over $I \cup O$ is then *realizable* iff there is a strategy all of whose computations satisfy ψ, whre the computation of a strategy $f : (2^I)^* \to 2^O$ on a infinite sequence $i_0, i_1, i_2, \ldots \in (2^I)^\omega$ is $i_0 \cup f(\epsilon), i_1 \cup f(i_0), i_2 \cup f(i_0 \cdot i_1), \ldots$. The *synthesis problem* for ψ is to return a finite-state transducer that realizes it (or an answer that ψ is not realizable).

While model-checking theory has led to industrial development and use of formal-verification tools, the integration of synthesis in the industry is slow. This has to do with *theoretical limitations*, like the complexity of the problem (the synthesis problem for linear temporal logic (LTL) is 2EXPTIME-complete [21]), methodological reasons (the traditional solutions to the synthesis problem require the determinization of automata on infinite words [23] and the solution of parity games [15]), and *practical reasons*: the difficulty of writing complete specifications and environment assumptions, the lack of satisfactory compositional synthesis algorithms, and suboptimal results (current algorithms produce systems that satisfy the specification, but may be larger or less well-structured than systems constructed manually, and may satisfy the specification in a peculiar way).

In the last decade there has been a significant advances in the development of practical algorithms for synthesis. In the theoretical fronts, researchers have suggested LTL synthesis algorithms that circumvent determinization and parity games [17], algorithms for fragments of LTL that can be implemented symbolically [20], and algorithms that reduce LTL synthesis to the solution of safety games [6]. These algorithms have been implemented [7,13,14,20], and they also support basic compositional synthesis [7,16]. Synthesis tools that are based on them give encouraging recent results (c.f., synthesis of an arbiter for RAM's on-chip AMBA advanced high-performance bus from temporal specifications [9], an electronic voting machine [5], and more). Work has also been done on generating environment assumptions to reduce the specification burden for synthesis [18].

In this paper we describe a new approach for solving LTL synthesis. Consider an LTL formula ψ. Like earlier approaches, our main goal is to circumvent the determinization of the automaton for ψ and the solution of parity games. Unlike earlier approaches, our algorithm is based on reducing the synthesis problem to a solution of a reachability game, played between the system and the environment on a graph obtained by combining the subset constructions of the automata for ψ and $\neg\psi$. Our algorithm is a heuristic – the goals of the system and the environment in the reachability game are not dual, and it may be that no player can force the opponent to its target states. Even in that case, the information obtained from the game enables us to restrict standard synthesis algorithms to a subset of the game, which is often much smaller. In addition, as we elaborate below, our algorithm involves theoretical issues at the heart of the synthesis problem that we believe should get more attention. In particular, we study *synthesis with clairvoyance (look-ahead)*, which is strongly related to the need to work with deterministic automata [11,12].

Let us now explain the idea behind our algorithm. Recall that satisfiability of an LTL formula ψ only guarantees that there is a collaborative input sequence $x \in (2^I)^\omega$ with which the system can interact and generate an output sequence $y \in (2^O)^\omega$ such that the composition of x and y into a computation in $(2^{I \cup O})^\omega$ satisfies ψ. On the other hand, in realizability, the system should have a strategy that satisfies the specification with respect to all possible environments. Between the satisfiability and the realizability problems, one can consider *universal satisfiability*, where for every input sequence $x \in (2^I)^\omega$, there is an output sequence $y \in (2^O)^\omega$ such that the composition of x and y satisfies ψ. Clearly, not all satisfiable specifications are universally satisfiable. Also, it is not hard to see that while universal satisfaction is a necessary condition for realizability, it is not a sufficient condition. A good way to understand the difference between realizability and universal satisfiability is to consider *realizability with look-ahead* – a notion that generalizes both of them. In realizability with look-ahead k, for $k \geq 0$, we also seek a strategy for the system. Here, however, the system generates the output at position j only after seeing the input in all positions up to $j + k$. It is easy to see that realizability coincides with realizability with look-ahead 0, whereas universal satisfiability coincides with realizability with look-ahead ∞.

Look-ahead helps the system in two ways. First, when the ability to satisfy the specification depends on information from the future, the look-ahead reveals the future. Second, when different futures with the same prefix require different outputs, look-ahead postpones the need to commit to the same output for both futures. One may wonder if these two ways are not two different interpretation of the same extra burden that realizability poses on universal satisfiability, and indeed this is the case. In fact, this is exactly the same burden that requires us to determinize the specification automaton in the process of solving the realizability problem: different input sequences that share the same prefix may need to follow different runs of the nondeterministic automaton, and the run may differ already in the joint prefix. A look-ahead enables us to follow different runs in the joint prefix, as long as the difference between the sequences is "in the range of visibility" of the strategy. [2]

With all this in mind, our algorithm works as follows. First, we try our luck and check whether ψ is universally satisfiable. If it is not, then clearly ψ is also non-realizable and we are done. If it is, then we again try our luck and check whether $\neg\psi$ is strongly satisfiable by the environment. If it is not, then again we are done, as we can conclude that $\neg\psi$ is not realizable by the environment, making ψ realizable by the system, and in fact it is easy to find a transducer for it – the transducer can ignore the input and just generates the output that witnesses the fact $\neg\psi$ is not universally satisfiable by the environment. Note that checking universal satisfaction is much simpler than checking realizability, not just from a theoretical point of view (the problem is EXPSPACE-complete [24]), but also in practice – universal satisfaction amounts to checking universality of a non-

---

[2] This is similar to the link between online/offline algorithms and deterministic/nondeterministic automata [2].

deterministic Büchi word automaton. Our experiments show that we may actually be lucky quite often.

Our algorithm becomes more interesting when both ψ and $\neg\psi$ are universally satisfiable. Then, we know that with an infinite look-ahead, both the system and the environment can satisfy their dual goals, and it is only the nature of the interaction, which requires both of them to proceed on-line, that makes only one of ψ and $\neg\psi$ realizable.[3] Consider a prefix $w \in (2^{I \cup O})^*$ of a computation. We can say that the system is *hopeful after* w if ψ stays universally satisfiable even when the interaction is restricted to start with w. Note that in the definition of universal satisfaction, the outputs are existentially quantified. Thus, fixing the outputs in w may indeed prevent ψ from being universally satisfiable. Dually, the environment is hopeful after w if $\neg\psi$ stays universally satisfiable. Our algorithm checks whether the system has a strategy to force the environment to a prefix of a computation after which only the system is hopeful, and dually for the environment. In the first case, we can conclude that ψ is realizable, and we also get a transducer for it. In the second, we know that $\neg\psi$ is realizable by the environment. The good news is that the classification of prefixes can be reduced to a sequence of checks for universal satisfaction, and is needed only for prefixes the lead to different states in the subset construction of the automata for ψ and $\neg\psi$, with no determinization needed. Also, as noted above, in case neither the system nor the environment have a strategy to make the opponent hopeless, we can restrict traditional synthesis algorithms to take into an account the need of the system and the environment to stay in a hopeful set of states. As our examples show, our algorithm often terminates with a definite answer, and it may also leads to a significant reduction in the state space. In Section 6, we also point to other advantages of our algorithm.

Finally, we study synthesis with look-ahead and describe an algorithm for solving it. A solution for the problem is described already in [12] in the context of sequential calculus, Here, we adjust the solution to the modern setting of LTL and parity games, and relate it to our heuristic. Beyond the theoretical interest in realizability with look-ahead as a notion between universal satisfiabaility and realizability, look-ahead is interesting also from a practical point of view. As we demonstrate in the paper (see also [3,11]), look-ahead can make the difference between a specification being realizable and not being realizable. Since in practice we often do have a look-ahead (say, when the environment buffers its actions), it makes sense to use it.

2 Preliminaries

2.1 Satisfiability, Universal Satisfiability, and Realizability

Let I and O be finite sets of input and output signals, respectively. For an input sequence $x = i_0, i_1, \ldots \in (2^I)^\omega$ and an output sequence $y = o_0, o_1, \ldots \in (2^O)^\omega$, the *computation* $x \oplus y$ is the interleaved sequence $i_0 \cup o_0, i_1 \cup o_1, \ldots \in (2^{I \cup O})^\omega$.

Consider an LTL formula ψ over $I \cup O$. We consider three levels of satisfaction of ψ.

– The formula ψ is *satisfiable* if there is a computation that satisfies ψ.

---

[3] An orthogonal research direction is to study the cases in which this happens, and the setting in which a bounded lookahead is sufficient. As shown in [11], such problems are decidable.

– The formula ψ is *universally satisfiable* if for every input sequence $x \in (2^I)^\omega$, there is an output sequence $y \in (2^O)^\omega$ such that $x \oplus y$ satisfies ψ.
– The formula ψ is *realizable* if there is a strategy $f : (2^I)^* \rightarrow 2^O$ such that for every input sequence $x = i_0, i_1, i_2, \ldots \in (2^I)^\omega$, the computation of f on x, that is $i_0 \cup f(\epsilon), i_1 \cup f(i_0), i_2 \cup f(i_0 \cdot i_1), \ldots$ satisfies ψ.

It is not hard to see that realizability implies universal satisfiability, which implies satisfiability, but not the other way around. For example, let $I = \{q\}$ and $O = \{p\}$. It is easy to see that the formula Gq is satisfiable but not universally satisfiable. Also, the formula $G(p \leftrightarrow q)$ is universally satisfiable but not realizable. Indeed, if, by way of contradiction, f is a strategy that realizes it, then an input sequence x that starts with q if $f(\epsilon) = \emptyset$ and starts with $\{\emptyset\}$ if $f(\epsilon) = \{p\}$ is such that the computation of f on x does not satisfy $p \leftrightarrow q$, and hence does not satisfy $G(p \leftrightarrow q)$.

We note that in our definition of realizability, we did not require the strategy f to be finite state. Since LTL formulas induce regular languages, adding such a requirement would result in an equivalent definition [22]. Formally, a strategy $f : (2^I)^* \rightarrow 2^O$ is finite state if for every $o \in 2^O$, the language $f^{-1}(o)$, which is a subset of $(2^I)^*$, is regular. Equivalently, f is finite state if it is induced by a finite-state transducer – a deterministic automaton over the alphabet 2^I in which each state is labeled by a letter in 2^O. Then, given a sequence $w \in (2^I)^*$, the strategy f induced by the transducer is such that $f(w)$ is the label of the state that the transducer visits after reading w.

2.2 Automata on Infinite Words

A specification over $I \cup O$ can be viewed as a language over the alphabet $2^{I \cup O}$. The decision procedures for the three levels of satisfaction discussed above follow this view, and are based on automata on infinite words.

A *nondeterministic automaton* is a tuple $\mathcal{A} = \langle \Sigma, Q, Q_0, \delta, \alpha \rangle$, where Σ is a finite nonempty alphabet, Q is a finite nonempty set of states, $Q_0 \subseteq Q$ is a nonempty set of initial states, $\delta : Q \times \Sigma \rightarrow 2^Q$ is a transition function, and α is an acceptance condition. The automaton $\mathcal{A}$ is *deterministic* if $|Q_0| = 1$ and $|\delta(q, \sigma)| \leq 1$ for all states $q \in Q$ and symbols $\sigma \in \Sigma$.

A *run* r of $\mathcal{A}$ on an infinite word $w = \sigma_1 \cdot \sigma_2 \cdots \in \Sigma^\omega$ is an infinite sequence $q_0, q_1, \ldots$ of states such that $q_0 \in Q_0$, and for all $i \geq 0$, we have $q_{i+1} \in \delta(q_i, \sigma_{i+1})$. The acceptance condition α determines which runs are accepting. In the *Büchi* acceptance condition, $\alpha \subseteq Q$, and a run r is accepting if it visits some state in α infinitely often. Formally, let $inf(r) = \{q : q_i = q$ for infinitely many i's $\}$. Then, r is *accepting* iff $inf(r) \cap \alpha \neq \emptyset$. A word w is accepted by an automaton $\mathcal{A}$ if there is an accepting run of $\mathcal{A}$ on w. The *language* of $\mathcal{A}$, denoted $L(\mathcal{A})$, is the set of words that $\mathcal{A}$ accepts. We say that $\mathcal{A}$ is *empty* if $L(\mathcal{A}) = \emptyset$ and that $\mathcal{A}$ is *universal* if $L(\mathcal{A}) = \Sigma^\omega$. A *pre-automaton* is an automaton without an acceptance condition. We use NBW and DBW to abbreviate nondeterministic and deterministic Büchi automata, respectively.

We are going to mention also the *co-Büchi* and the *parity* acceptance conditions. The condition co-Büchi is dual to Büchi, thus a run is accepting if it visits α only finitely often. The parity is more complicated and for our purposes here it is enough to note that determistic parity automata (DPWs) are sufficiently expressive to recognize all the languages recognized by nondeterministic Büchi automata. Thus, NBWs can be translated to DPWs [19,23].

Theorem 1. [25] *For every LTL formula ψ, there is an NBW $\mathcal{A}_\psi$ with $2^{O(|\psi|)}$ states such that $L(\mathcal{A}_\psi) = \{w : w \models \psi\}$.*

2.3 Traditional Decision Procedures

In this section we briefly review the traditional algorithms for solving satisfiability, universal satisfiability, and realizability.

Deciding satisfiability is PSPACE-complete: given ψ, one can follow Theorem 1 and constructs the NBW $\mathcal{A}_\psi$. Clearly, ψ is satisfiable iff $L(\mathcal{A}_\psi)$ is not empty. Since the size of $\mathcal{A}_\psi$ is exponential in the length of ψ and checking its nonemptiness can be done on-the-fly in NLOGSPACE, the PSPACE complexity follows.

Deciding universal satisfiability is more complicated and is EXPSPACE-complete: Starting with $\mathcal{A}_\psi$, we construct an NBW $\mathcal{A}_\psi^{\exists O}$, obtained from $\mathcal{A}_\psi$ by taking its projection on I. That is, if $\mathcal{A} = \langle 2^{I \cup O}, Q, Q_0, \delta, \alpha \rangle$, then $\mathcal{A}_\psi^{\exists O} = \langle 2^I, Q, Q_0, \delta^{\exists O}, \alpha \rangle$, where for a state $q \in Q$ and input $i \in 2^I$, we have that $\delta^{\exists O}(q, i) = \{s : \exists o \in 2^O \text{ such that } s = \delta(q, i \cup o)\}$. It is not hard to see that a word $x \in (2^I)^\omega$ is accepted by $\mathcal{A}_\psi^{\exists O}$ iff there is a word $y \in (2^O)^\omega$ such that $x \oplus y$ is accepted by $\mathcal{A}$. Hence, $\mathcal{A}_\psi^{\exists O}$ is universal iff ψ is strongly satisfiable. Checking the universality of $\mathcal{A}_\psi^{\exists O}$ can be done by checking the emptiness of its complement. Since the size of $\mathcal{A}_\psi$, and hence also of $\mathcal{A}_\psi^{\exists O}$ is exponential in the length of ψ, complementation involves an exponential blow-up, and emptiness can be checked in NLOGSPACE, the EXPSPACE complexity follows.

Finally, deciding realizability is even more complicated, and is 2EXPTIME-complete. The traditional algorithm determinizes $\mathcal{A}_\psi$, and transforms the obtained DPW into a two-player game between the system and the environment. Formally, let $\mathcal{D}_\psi = \langle 2^{I \cup O}, Q, q_0, \delta, \alpha \rangle$ be the DPW for ψ. Then, the game is $G_\psi = \langle V, E \rangle$, where the set of vertices $V = V_{sys} \cup V_{env}$ is such that $V_{sys} = Q$ and $V_{env} \subseteq 2^Q$. For $S \in 2^Q$, we have that $S \in V_{env}$ iff there is $q \in Q$ and $o \in 2^O$ such that $S = \delta^{\exists I}(q, o)$, in which case $E(q, S)$. Also, $E(S, q')$ iff $q' \in S$. Deciding the realizability problem then amounts to deciding the winner in the game G_ψ with winning objective α. Intuitively, each transition of $\mathcal{D}_\psi$ is partitioned in the game G_ψ into two transitions: consider a vertex $q \in V_{sys}$. First, the system chooses an output $o \in 2^O$, and the game moves to the vertex $\delta^{\exists I}(q, o) \in V_{env}$. Then, the environment chooses an input $i \in 2^I$ and the game continues to the state in $\delta^{\exists I}(q, o)$ that i leads to, namely to $\delta(q, i \cup o) \in V_{sys}$.

It is sometimes convenient to refine G_ψ to include more information, which enables a labeling of the edges by the actions taken by the players. Thus, here $E \subseteq (V_{sys} \times 2^O \times V_{env}) \cup (V_{env} \times 2^I \times V_{sys})$. For that, we define, $V_{sys} = Q$ and $V_{env} \subseteq Q \times 2^O \times 2^Q$ is such that $\langle q, o, S \rangle \in V_{env}$ iff $S = \delta^{\exists I}(q, o)$. Then, we also have $E(q, o, \langle q, o, S \rangle)$. In addition, for all vertices $\langle q, o, S \rangle \in V_{env}$ and $q' \in V_{sys}$, we have that $E(\langle q, o, S \rangle, i, q')$ iff $q' = \delta(q, i \cup o)$. Note that $q' \in S$.

The system and the environment are dual, in the sense that we can view the setting as one in which the environment is trying to satisfy $\neg \psi$ when it interacts with all systems. Thus, the roles of the system and the environment may be switched, and we can talk about a formula ψ being universally satisfied by the environment, meaning that for every output sequence $y \in (2^O)^\omega$, there is an input sequence $x \in (2^I)^\omega$ such that $x \oplus y$ satisfies ψ. We can also talk about ψ being realizable by the environment, meaning that there is a finite-state strategy $g : (2^O)^* \rightarrow 2^I$ such that for every output sequence $y = o_0, o_1, o_2, \ldots \in (2^O)^\omega$, the computation of g on y, that is $o_0 \cup g(o_0), o_1 \cup g(i_0 \cdot o_1), o_2 \cup g(o_0 \cdot o_1 \cdot o_2), \ldots$ satisfies ψ. Note that in both types of realizability (by the system and by the environment), the system moves first. Thus, the settings are not completely dual. For universal satisfiability, the identity of the player that moves first is irrelevant, and the definitions are completely dual.[4] From determinancy of games, we know that either ψ is realizable by the system or $\neg\psi$ is realizable by the environment.

3 Using Universal Satisfiability

In this section we describe the first steps in our methodology for using universal satisfiability in the process of checking realizability. We also point to realizability with look-ahead as a notion between universal satisfiability and realizability.

Given a property ψ over I and O, we proceed as follows.

(1) Check universal satisfiability of ψ.
  (1.1) If the answer is negative, we are done. Indeed, if ψ is not universally satisfiable, then clearly ψ is also not realizable.
  (1.2) If the answer is positive, proceed to (2).
(2) Check universal satisfiability of $\neg\psi$ by the environment.
  (2.1) If the answer is negative, we are done. Indeed, if $\neg\psi$ is not universally satisfiable by the environment, then clearly $\neg\psi$ is also not realizable by the environment, implying that ψ is realizable by the system. Moreover, a transducer for ψ can simply generate the output sequence $y \in (2^O)^\omega$ for which for all $x \in (2^I)^\omega$ we have that $x \oplus y \models \psi$.
  (2.2) If the answer is positive, proceed to (3).
(3) This is the interesting case: both ψ and $\neg\psi$ are universally satisfiable. Note that while it cannot be that both ψ and $\neg\psi$ are realizable, they can both be universally satisfiable. When this happens, we know that one of the players, the system or the environment, cannot arrange the responses that work for the universal satisfiability in the form of the strategy that is needed for realizablity. For example, consider the formula $\psi = G(p \leftrightarrow q)$, with $I = \{q\}$ and $O = \{p\}$. Note that $\neg\psi = F(\neg(p \leftrightarrow q))$. While both ψ and $\neg\psi$ are universally satisfiable, only $\neg\psi$ is realizable by the environment.

The example of a robotic vehicle controller from [18], demonstrates how our heuristic detects that the system is not realizable when sufficient assumptions are not provided. The example of the robotic vehicle controller aims to synthesize a discrete planner that allows an autonomous robot to move in a rectangular grid, while avoiding obstacles. The obstacles are put and cleared by the environment at arbitrary times and squares. In this example, the specification ψ is of the form $\mathbf{A} \rightarrow \mathbf{G}$, where $\mathbf{A}$ is a conjunction of

---

[4] The cleanest way to handle this lack of duality is to parameterize the synthesis problem with a "who moves first" flag. We decided to keep the setting simpler and let the system move first in both settings.

assumptions on the environment, and **G** is a conjunction of guarnatees. The guarantees require the car to start at the initial square, and in each step to move to an adjacent square or to stay in the current one. The car cannot move to an occupied square, and it eventually have to reach the destination square. The assumptions on the environment require that there are no obstacles at the initial and destination squares. With this weak assumption, ψ is not universally satisfied and our heuristic terminates at Step **(1.1)**. In order to make the specification realizble, we need to add stronger assumptions to **A**. Adding the assumption that "all the squares must be clear of obstacles infinitely often" resolves the problem, and makes ψ realizable. Here too, out heuristic is helpful, as with the stronger assumption we get that $\neg\psi$ is not universally satisfied by the environment, thus our heuristic terminates at Step **(1.2)**.

Before we proceed to describe how our algorithm continues in Step (3), let us discuss the situation in more detail. Consider again the formula $\psi = G(p \leftrightarrow q)$. As noted above, ψ is not realizable. Intuitively, once the system generates an output, the environment can generate an input that does not agree with the polarity of the output, thus violating the specification. But what if the system can generate its output only after seeing the next input? Then, the specification is realizable. In general, the difference between universal satisfiability and realizability is the fact that in universal satisfiability the system knows the whole sequence of inputs before generating the output, whereas in realizability, the system has to react online and generate the next output without knowing the inputs yet to come. Between these two extreme cases, we can talk about *realizability with look-ahead*, where the system has to generate the next output after seeing a prefix of the inputs yet to arrive.

Definition 1. [realizable with look-ahead] *An LTL formula ψ over $I \cup O$ is realizable with look-ahead k (k-realizable, for short), if there is a strategy $f : (2^I)^{\geq k} \to 2^O$ such that for every input sequence $w = i_0, i_1, i_2, \ldots \in (2^I)^{\omega}$, the computation of f on w, that is $i_0 \cup f(i_0, i_1, \ldots, i_{k-1}), i_1 \cup f(i_0, i_1, \ldots, i_k), i_2 \cup f(i_0, i_1, \ldots, i_{k+1}), \ldots, i_j \cup f(i_0, i_1, \ldots, i_{k+j-1}), \ldots$ satisfies ψ.*

As explained in Section 1, both universal satisfiability and realizability are a special cases of k-realizability; the first with $k = \infty$ and the second with $k = 0$. Also, realizability with look-ahead is interesting also in practice, as it corresponds to realistic settings and can make specifications realizable [11,12].

4   When Both ψ and $\neg\psi$ Are Universally Satisfiable

In this section we continue the description of our algorithm, namely what to do when we get to Step (3). Let $\mathcal{A}_{\psi} = \langle 2^{I \cup O}, S, S_0, \rho, \alpha \rangle$ and $\mathcal{A}_{\neg\psi} = \langle 2^{I \cup O}, S', S_0', \rho', \alpha' \rangle$ be NBWs for ψ and $\neg\psi$, respectively. Let $\mathcal{U}_{\psi}$ be the pre-automaton obtained by applying the subset construction to $\mathcal{A}_{\psi}$ and $\mathcal{A}_{\neg\psi}$. Thus, $\mathcal{U}_{\psi} = \langle 2^{I \cup O}, 2^S \times 2^{S'}, \langle S_0, S_0' \rangle, \delta \rangle$, where for all $\langle P, P' \rangle \in 2^S \times 2^{S'}$ and $\sigma \in 2^{I \cup O}$, we have that $\delta(\langle P, P' \rangle, \sigma) = \langle \rho(P, \sigma), \rho'(P', \sigma) \rangle$. For a state $\langle P, P' \rangle$ of $\mathcal{U}_{\psi}$, let $L(\mathcal{A}_{\psi}^P)$ and $L(\mathcal{A}_{\neg\psi}^{P'})$ be the languages of $\mathcal{A}_{\psi}$ and $\mathcal{A}_{\neg\psi}$ with initial sets P and P', respectively. We say that a set $P \in 2^S$ is *system hopeful* (sys-hopeful, for short) if for all $x \in (2^I)^{\omega}$ there is $y \in (2^O)^{\omega}$ such that $x \oplus y \in L(\mathcal{A}_{\psi}^P)$. We say that a set $P' \in 2^{S'}$ is *environment hopeful* (env-hopeful, for short) if for all $y \in (2^O)^\omega$ there is $x \in (2^I)^\omega$ such that $x \oplus y \in L(\mathcal{A}_{\neg\psi}^{P'})$. Thus, system hopefulness coincides with universal satisfaction, except that instead of talking about satisfaction of an LTL formula we talk about the membership in the language of $\mathcal{A}_\psi^P$. Dually, environment hopefulness refer to membership in $\mathcal{A}_{\neg\psi}^{P'}$.

Consider a state $\langle P, P' \rangle \in 2^S \times 2^{S'}$ of $\mathcal{U}_\psi$. It is possible to decide in space exponential in the length of ψ whether P is system hopeful and whether P' is environment hopeful. Indeed, the check is similar to the check for universal satisfaction described in Section 2. For the case of system hopefulness, we project $\mathcal{A}_\psi^P$ on 2^I and check that the obtained NBW is universal. For environment hopefulness we do the same, with $\mathcal{A}_{\neg\psi}^{P'}$ and a projection on 2^O.

Remark 1. In case we start with a deterministic automaton $\mathcal{D}_\psi$ for the specification, we do not have to apply the subset construction, and we can work directly with $\mathcal{D}_\psi$. Then, the notion of system and environment hopefulness applies to single states, and checking whether a state s is env-hopeful is done by dualizing $\mathcal{D}_\psi$, thus getting a deterministic co-Büchi automaton for the negation of ψ. We can then project the co-Büchi automaton existentially on 2^O, and check whether the result is universal (see Example 1).

We can now describe the continuation of the algorithm:

(3) Consider the game induced by the pre-automaton $\mathcal{U}_\psi$.
(3.1) If the system has a strategy to reach a state $\langle P, P' \rangle$ such that P is sys-hopeful and P' is not env-hopeful, then we are done. Indeed, ψ is realizable, and we can also have a transducer for it.
(3.2) If the environment has a strategy to reach a state $\langle P, P' \rangle$ such that P' is env-hopeful and P is not sys-hopeful, then we are done. Indeed, in a manner dual to the one above, $\neg\psi$ is realizable by the environment.
(3.3) If we got here, both the system and the environment have strategies to stay forever in the region of states that are both sys-hopeful and env-hopeful. At this point we give up and turn to solve the realizability problem using one of the traditional algorithms. The information gathered during our algorithm is still useful and enables us to restrict the realizability game to states in the region of hopeful states (all the other states are replaced by two states – one is winning for the system and one is winning for the environment).

We conclude the description of the algorithm with the following theorem.

Theorem 2. *Consider an LTL specification ψ over $I \cup O$.*

1. *If the algorithm reaches Step (3), then all the states $\langle P, P' \rangle$ that are reachable in $\mathcal{U}_\psi$ are such that at least one of the sets P and P' is hopeful.*
2. *If the algorithm terminates in Steps (2.1) or (3.1), then ψ is realizable and the checks done by the algorithm induce a transducer for the system that satisfies ψ.*
3. *If the algorithm terminates in Steps (1.1) or (3.2), then ψ is not realizable and the check done induce a transducer for the environment that satisfies $\neg\psi$.*

Proof: We start with the first point. Consider a state $\langle P, P' \rangle$ that is reachable in $\mathcal{U}_\psi$. Let w be a word that leads to $\langle P, P' \rangle$. Consider now the parity game that corresponds to the realizability problem for ψ and the vertex v_w that the game reaches after the system and the environment proceeds according to w. Since parity games are determined, v_w is a winning vertex for either the system (in which case P must be hopeful) or the environment (in which case P' must be hopeful).

Now, if the algorithm terminates Step (2.1), then ψ is realizable as a transducer for it can simply generate the output sequence $y \in (2^O)^\omega$ for which for all $x \in (2^I)^\omega$ we have that $x \oplus y \models \psi$; the fact $\neg\psi$ is not universally realizable by the environment guarantees that such a sequence y exists, and we know how to find it: this is the sequence that witnesses the nonemptiness of the complement of $\mathcal{A}^{\exists I}_{\neg\psi}$.

Finally, when the algorithm terminates in Step (3.2), then ψ is realizable as a transducer for it can start with the strategy that reaches $\langle P, P' \rangle$ such that P is sys-hopeful and P' is not env-hopeful. It is guaranteed that when we apply Steps (1+2) of the algorithm with $\mathcal{A}^P_\psi$ instead of ψ and $\mathcal{A}^{P'}_{\neg\psi}$ instead of $\neg\psi$, we would end up end up in Step (2.1), thus once generating the prefix that leads to $\langle P, P' \rangle$, the transducer can continue with a fixed output sequence, as described above. The case ψ is not realizable is dual. □

We now demonstrate our algorithm with three examples. In all of them, we have for $I = \{q\}$ and $O = \{p\}$.

Example 1. We start with an example in which the NBW for the specification is deterministic. Let $\psi = G(p \leftrightarrow Fq)$. Note that ψ is equivalent to $G(p \rightarrow Fq) \wedge G(\neg p \rightarrow G\neg q)$. The specification is universally satisfiable: given a sequence $x \in (q, \neg q)^\omega$, it is not hard to see that the sequence $y \in (p, \neg p)^\omega$ in which p holds in position j iff q holds in a position grater than j is such that $x \oplus y \models \psi$. Consider the negation of the specification, that is $\neg\psi = F(p \wedge G\neg q) \vee F(\neg p \wedge Fq)$. It is not hard to see that $\neg\psi$ is universally satisfiable by the environment. Indeed, given a sequence $y \in (p, \neg p)^\omega$, a sequence $x \in (q, \neg q)^\omega$ in which q holds exactly when p does not hold, is such that $x \oplus y \models \neg\psi$.

On the left of Figure 1 below we describe a DBW $\mathcal{D}_\psi$ for ψ. Since $\mathcal{D}_\psi$ is deterministic, we do not have to apply the subset construction on it. On the right, we describe the two projections of $\mathcal{D}_\psi$ on I and on O.

Note that in $\mathcal{D}^{\exists O}_\psi$, only s_0 is universal (the other states are not universal since, for example, q^ω is not accepted from them). Thus, only s_0 is sys-hopeful in $\mathcal{D}_\psi$. In order to

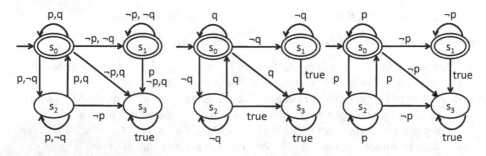

Fig. 1. A DBW $\mathcal{D}_\psi$ for $\psi = G(p \leftrightarrow Fq)$ (left), and its projections $\mathcal{D}^{\exists O}_\psi$ and $\mathcal{D}^{\exists I}_{\neg\psi}$ on I (middle) and O (right), respectively

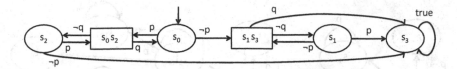

Fig. 2. The game induced by $\mathcal{D}_\psi$

find the env-hopeful states we consider the co-Büchi automaton $\mathcal{D}_{\neg\psi}^{\exists I}$. Here, all states are universal. Indeed, s_3 is an accepting sink, s_1 can get with both p and $\neg p$ to s_3 in one transition, s_2 can stay in s_2 forever with p^ω, and with all other words it can reach s_3, and finally, s_0 can reach s_2 and s_1 with p and $\neg p$, respectively. It follows that all the states in $\mathcal{D}_\psi$ are env-hopeful.

The game induced by $\mathcal{D}_\psi$ appears in Figure 2. The system states are ovals (and in them, the system chooses between p and $\neg p$), and the environment states are rectangles (the environment chooses q or $\neg q$). It is not hard to see that the environment has a strategy to force the system to a state that is not sys-hopeful while staying within env-hopeful states. Thus, we can conclude that ψ is not realizable.

Example 2. We now consider a case where $\mathcal{A}_\psi$ is nondeterministic, thus we proceed with NBWs for both ψ and $\neg\psi$. Consider the specification $\psi = (Gp \wedge Fq) \vee (G\neg p \wedge F\neg q)$. Thus, either the system always generates p and the environment generates q eventually, or the system always generates $\neg p$, and the environment generates $\neg q$ eventually. Note that $\neg\psi = (Fp \wedge F\neg p) \vee (G\neg q \wedge Fp) \vee (Gq \wedge F\neg p)$. It is not hard to see that ψ is universally satisfiable by the system and $\neg\psi$ is universally satisfiable by the environment.

In Figure 3, we describe the NBWs $\mathcal{A}_\psi$ (on the left, a union of two components) and $\mathcal{A}_{\neg\psi}$ (on the right, a union of three components).

We now check the system and environment hopefulness of sets that are reachable in the subset construction of the two NBWs. If we get to a set that is not hopeful, there is no need to continue the construction from it. In Figure 4 we describe the obtained deterministic pre-automata. In the figure, we indicate by dashed lines that the set is not hopeful. For example, the set $\{s_0\}$ is not sys-hopeful since there is no output sequence $y \in (p, \neg p)^\omega$ such that $x \oplus y$ is accepted from $\mathcal{A}_\psi^{\{s_0\}}$ for $x = (\neg q)^\omega$. Similarly, the set

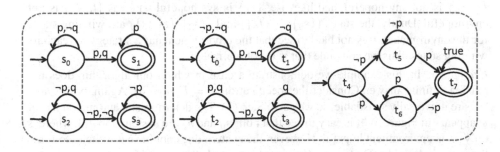

Fig. 3. The NBWs $\mathcal{A}_\psi$ (left) and $\mathcal{A}_{\neg\psi}$ (right)

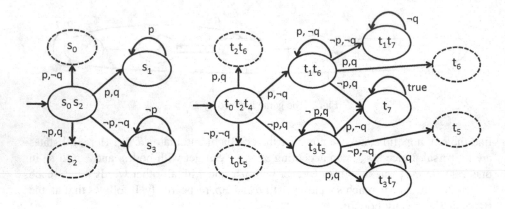

Fig. 4. The pre-automata obtained by applying the subset construction to $\mathcal{A}_\psi$ (left) and $\mathcal{A}_{\neg\psi}$ (right)

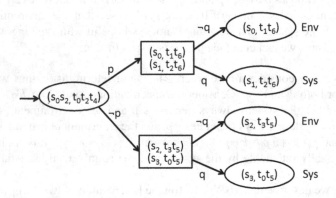

Fig. 5. The game corresponding to $\mathcal{U}_\psi$

$\{t_0, t_5\}$ is not env-hopeful since there is no input sequence $x \in (q, \neg q)^\omega$ such that $x \oplus y$ is accepted from $\mathcal{A}_{\neg\psi}^{\{t_0,t_5\}}$ for $y = (\neg q)^\omega$.

In Figure 5 we describe the game corresponding to $\mathcal{U}_\psi$, obtained by combining the two pre-automata. As indicated in the figure, the states $(\{s_1\}, \{t_2, t_6\})$ and $(\{s_3\}, \{t_0, t_5\})$ are winning states for the system. Indeed, $\{s_1\}$ is sys-hopeful whereas $\{t_2, t_6\}$ is not env-hopeful, and likewise, $\{s_3\}$ is sys-hopeful whereas $\{t_0, t_5\}$ is not env-hopeful. Dually, the states $(\{s_0\}, \{t_1, t_6\})$ and $(\{s_2\}, \{t_3, t_5\})$ are winning states for the environment. It is not hard to see that the environment has a strategy to reach its winning states, thus we conclude that ψ is not realizable.

Example 3. In this example we demonstrate a case in which our algorithm does not reach a definite answer. Consider the specification $\psi = F(p \leftrightarrow q)$. Again, both ψ and $\neg\psi$ are universally satisfiable, so we get to Step (3). The deterministic automaton $\mathcal{D}_\psi$ of ψ appears in Figure 6. It is easy to see that both s_0 and s_1 are system hopeful, whereas only s_0 is environment hopeful. However, the system does not have a strategy to force the game induced by $\mathcal{D}_\psi$ to s_1: if the system proceeds from s_0 with p, the environment will respond with $\neg q$, and if the system proceeds with $\neg p$, the environment will respond

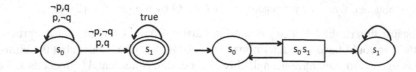

Fig. 6. A DBW for $\psi = F(p \leftrightarrow q)$ and the game corresponding to it

with q. Also, since both s_0 and s_1 are system hopeful, the environment does not have a strategy to force the game into states that are not system hopeful. So, we have to solve the realizability problem. We can use, however, the fact that game would get stuck in s_0, which would not satisfy the Büchi condition, thus ψ is not realizable.

5 LTL Realizability with Look-Ahead

In Section 3, we defined LTL realizability with look-ahead. This notion is not fundamentally new, and the problem of k-realizability was studied already in 1972, in the context of sequential calculus [12]. Here, we adjust the solution to the modern setting of LTL and DPWs, and describe how our algorithm can be adjusted to handle k-realizability too.

Theorem 3. *Consider an LTL formula ψ and an integer $k \geq 0$. Let $\mathcal{A}_\psi^k$ be such that $L(\mathcal{A}_\psi^k) = \{x \oplus y : x \oplus y^k \in L(\mathcal{A}_\psi)\}$, where y^k is the suffix of y from position k.*

- *We can construct an NBW $\mathcal{A}_\psi^k$ as above with number of states exponential in $|\psi|$ and k.*
- *We can construct an DPW $\mathcal{A}_\psi^k$ as above with number of states doubly-exponential in $|\psi|$ and exponential in k.*
- *Applying synthesis algorithms with respect to $\mathcal{A}_\psi^k$ rather than $\mathcal{A}_\psi$ solves the k-realizability problem.*

Proof: Let $\mathcal{A}_\psi = \langle 2^{I \cup O}, Q, \delta, q_0, \alpha \rangle$ be an NBW for ψ. We define $\mathcal{A}_\psi^k = \langle 2^{I \cup O}, Q', \epsilon, \delta', \alpha' \rangle$, where

- $Q' = (\bigcup_{0 \leq j < k} (2^I)^j) \cup (Q \times (2^I)^k)$. The first type of states is for accumulating the vector of the last $k - 1$ inputs. The second type is to be used after we have accumulated the first k inputs. Then, we follow the runs of $\mathcal{A}_\psi$, with the output being combined with the input read k letters earlier.
- The transition function is defined as follows.
  - For the first type of states, if $0 \leq j < k - 1$, we ignore the output component of the letter read (intuitively, since we shift the output by k, the output in the first $k - 1$ levels is not important) and only accumulate inputs in the vector. Accordingly, $\delta'(\langle i_1, \ldots, i_j \rangle, i \cup o) = \{\langle i_1, \ldots, i_j, i \rangle\}$.
  - In the last level of states from the first type, we still ignore the output read but get ready to start following the runs of $\mathcal{A}_\psi$. Accordingly, $\delta'(\langle i_1, \ldots, i_{k-1} \rangle, i \cup o) = Q_0 \times \{\langle i_1, \ldots, i_{k-1}, i \rangle\}$.
  - Then, we continue to follow the runs of $\mathcal{A}_\psi$, where o is combined with the input read k transitions earlier. Accordingly, $\delta'(\langle q, i_1, \ldots, i_k \rangle, i \cup o) = \delta(q, i_1 \cup o) \times \{\langle i_2, \ldots, i_k, i \rangle\}$.

– α' is obtained from α by replacing a set $F \subseteq Q$ by the set $F \times (2^I)^k$.

The construction of the DPW $\mathcal{A}^k_\psi$ is similar, starting from a DPW $\mathcal{A}_\psi$ for the property. Note that we could have also determinized the NBW described above, but the blow-up in terms of I could then have been doubly exponential. Note that $\mathcal{A}^k_\psi$ proceeds according to the input that was read k positions earlier, combined with the current output. This captures the fact that in k-realizability, the output is combined with the input only after knowing what the previous k inputs were. Accordingly, the game induced by the DPW $\mathcal{A}^k_\psi$ solves the k-realizability problem. □

Applying our algorithm in order to solve the k-realizability problem, we proceed with the game obtained from the subset construction applied on the the NBWs $\mathcal{A}^k_\psi$ and $\mathcal{A}^k_{\neg\psi}$. Note that in both automata, the O-component of a letters is combined with the I-component of the letter read k positions earlier. All the other details of the algorithm are the same.

6 Discussion

We described a simple heuristic that replaces the parity game corresponding to LTL synthesis with a game in which the system and the environment try to force each other into hopeless states in the game. Our definition of hopeless is based on universal satisfaction – the game-free variant of realizability, and is therefore easier to reason about.

Below we discuss some further advantages of our heuristic, and some directions for future research. First, several challenges in the context of realizability are easier to cope with using our approach. This includes compositional synthesis [16], mining for assumptions [18], and testing for inherent vacuity in specifications [8]. In all these problems, one can try to circumvent the need to work with parity games by using our heuristic that use instead hopeless finite prefixes.

Our definition of hopeful states can be replaced by other definitions, leading to looser (but even more efficient) or tighter (but more complex to achieve) heuristics. On the loose side, one can work with the nondeterministic automaton (rather than the subset construction on it). Under this definition, a prefix of a computation is hopeful if there is a single state s in $\mathcal{A}_\psi$ such that the prefix can lead to s and $\mathcal{A}^s_\psi$ is universally satisfiable. Note that now, states that are not hopeful may still be reachable by hopeful prefixes, thus the heuristic can be used in order to direct the subset construction to construct subsets only when such a construction is needed. On the tighter side, one can replace universal satisfaction by definitions that are game-based, but are easier to solve than parity.

Finally, in case our algorithm does not terminate with a definite answer, we suggested to continue with traditional synthesis algorithms, with actions being restricted to these that keep the system and the environment in their hopeful regions. We found this case very interesting: both the system and the environment can stay hopeful forever, yet only one of them can satisfy the acceptance condition of $\mathcal{A}_\psi$ (the system) or $\mathcal{A}_{\neg\psi}$ (the environment). We plan to study whether this special situation can be of help when we solve the parity game on the restricted region.

References

1. Abadi, M., Lamport, L., Wolper, P.: Realizable and Unrealizable Concurrent Program Specifications. In: Ausiello, G., Dezani-Ciancaglini, M., Ronchi Della Rocca, S. (eds.) ICALP 1989. LNCS, vol. 372, pp. 1–17. Springer, Heidelberg (1989)

2. Aminof, B., Kupferman, O., Lampert, R.: Reasoning about Online Algorithms with Weighted Automata. In: Proc. 20th SODA, pp. 835–844 (2009)
3. Breslauer, D.: On competitive on-line paging with lookahead. TCS 209(1–2), 365–375 (1998)
4. Dill, D.L.: Trace theory for automatic hierarchical verification of speed independent circuits. MIT Press (1989)
5. Dworkin, L., Li, W., Seshia, S.A.: Automatic synthesis of a voting machine design (2010) (Unpublished Manuscript)
6. Filiot, E., Jin, N., Raskin, J.-F.: An Antichain Algorithm for LTL Realizability. In: Bouajjani, A., Maler, O. (eds.) CAV 2009. LNCS, vol. 5643, pp. 263–277. Springer, Heidelberg (2009)
7. Filiot, E., Jin, N., Raskin, J.-F.: Compositional Algorithms for LTL Synthesis. In: Bouajjani, A., Chin, W.-N. (eds.) ATVA 2010. LNCS, vol. 6252, pp. 112–127. Springer, Heidelberg (2010)
8. Fisman, D., Kupferman, O., Sheinvald, S., Vardi, M.Y.: A Framework for Inherent Vacuity. In: Chockler, H., Hu, A.J. (eds.) HVC 2008. LNCS, vol. 5394, pp. 7–22. Springer, Heidelberg (2009)
9. Godhal, Y., Chatterjee, K., Henzinger, T.A.: Synthesis of AMBA AHB from formal specification. CoRR abs/1001.2811 (2010)
10. Harel, D., Pnueli, A.: On the development of reactive systems. In: NATO Advanced Science Institutes, vol. F-13, pp. 477–498. Springer (1985)
11. Holtmann, M., Kaiser, L., Thomas, W.: Degrees of Lookahead in Regular Infinite Games. In: Ong, L. (ed.) FOSSACS 2010. LNCS, vol. 6014, pp. 252–266. Springer, Heidelberg (2010)
12. Hosch, F., Landweber, L.: Finite delay solutions for sequential conditions. In: Proc. 1st ICALP, pp. 45–60 (1972)
13. Jobstmann, B., Bloem, R.: Game-based and simulation-based improvements for LTL synthesis. In: Proc. 3nd GDV (2006)
14. Jobstmann, B., Galler, S., Weiglhofer, M., Bloem, R.: Anzu: A Tool for Property Synthesis. In: Damm, W., Hermanns, H. (eds.) CAV 2007. LNCS, vol. 4590, pp. 258–262. Springer, Heidelberg (2007)
15. Jurdzinski, M., Paterson, M., Zwick, U.: A deterministic subexponential algorithm for solving parity games. SIAM Journal on Computing 38(4), 1519–1532 (2008)
16. Kupferman, O., Piterman, N., Vardi, M.Y.: Safraless Compositional Synthesis. In: Ball, T., Jones, R.B. (eds.) CAV 2006. LNCS, vol. 4144, pp. 31–44. Springer, Heidelberg (2006)
17. Kupferman, O., Vardi, M.Y.: Safraless decision procedures. In: Proc. 46th FOCS, pp. 531–540 (2005)
18. Li, W., Dworkin, L., Seshia, S.A.: Mining assumptions for synthesis. In: Proc. 9th MEMOCODE (July 2011)
19. Piterman, N.: From nondeterministic Büchi and Streett automata to deterministic parity automata. In: Proc. 21st LICS, pp. 255–264 (2006)
20. Piterman, N., Pnueli, A., Saar, Y.: Synthesis of Reactive(1) Designs. In: Emerson, E.A., Namjoshi, K.S. (eds.) VMCAI 2006. LNCS, vol. 3855, pp. 364–380. Springer, Heidelberg (2005)
21. Pnueli, A., Rosner, R.: On the synthesis of a reactive module. In: Proc. 16th POPL, pp. 179–190 (1989)
22. Rabin, M.O.: Automata on infinite objects and Church's problem. Amer. Mathematical Society (1972)
23. Safra, S.: On the complexity of ω-automata. In: Proc. 29th FOCS, pp. 319–327 (1988)
24. Sistla, A.P., Vardi, M.Y., Wolper, P.: The complementation problem for Büchi automata with applications to temporal logic. Theoretical Computer Science 49, 217–237 (1987)
25. Vardi, M.Y., Wolper, P.: Reasoning about infinite computations. Information and Computation 115(1), 1–37 (1994)

Generalized Reactivity(1) Synthesis without a Monolithic Strategy*

Matthias Schlaipfer, Georg Hofferek, and Roderick Bloem

Institute for Applied Information Processing and Communications (IAIK),
Graz University of Technology, Austria

Abstract. We present a new approach to synthesizing systems from Generalized Reactivity(1) specifications. Our method does not require a monolithic strategy, which can be prohibitively large. Instead, our approach constructs a circuit directly from the iterates of the fixpoint computation that computes the winning region. We build the overall system by combining these circuit parts. Our approach has generally lower memory requirements than previous GR(1) synthesis approaches, and is also faster. In addition to that, the circuits we build are eager, in the sense that they typically fulfill system guarantees faster than the circuits obtained with previous approaches, as experiments show.

1 Introduction

Formal methods have recently seen increased attention focused on synthesis techniques in which programs are created automatically from specifications. Such techniques may create full systems from a specification given, for instance, in temporal logic [7,17,16,10,11,4,19,15,8,18], or they may synthesize pieces of a program that are difficult to implement or were previously implemented incorrectly [20,22,14,23,12]. Synthesis promises to remove an important burden from the programmer, who only has to think about the specification and not about implementation details. The main drawback currently is the lack of capacity of synthesis tools — they are only applicable to small examples. Time and especially memory use of current tools are often prohibitive, keeping many realistic examples outside of the realm of synthesis.

In this paper we consider an alternative method to generate systems in GR(1) synthesis [16]. Our synthesis method is implemented in RATSY [4], a tool for synthesis of GR(1) properties. GR(1) properties can be viewed as an implication of deterministic Büchi automata. Let A_1 through A_n be the assumptions on the environment and let G_1 through G_m be the guarantees that the system has to fulfill. If $A_1, \ldots, A_n$ and $G_1, \ldots, G_m$ are expressed as deterministic Büchi automata, then the formula

$$\bigwedge_i A_i \implies \bigwedge_j G_j$$

* This work was supported in part by the European Commission through project DIAMOND (FP7-2009-IST-4-248613).

K. Eder, J. Lourenço, and O. Shehory (Eds.): HVC 2011, LNCS 7261, pp. 20–34, 2012.

is a GR(1) specification. Previous work [5,6] has shown that GR(1) is expressive, easy to use, and that it allows for a relatively efficient implementation of synthesis.

The time and memory use of RATSY is high. Moreover, it has the drawback of producing systems that are not very eager. The general strategy used by RATSY is to satisfy the guarantees one at a time in a round-robin fashion. Each of the guarantees is fulfilled using an attractor strategy in which the approach to the guarantee is enforced whenever all of the assumptions have been fulfilled. This formulation of the strategy is very general and allows significant freedom to choose a small implementation. However, since the attractor strategy only requires *some* progress to be made, this formulation allows for very lazy implementations that may take a long time to fulfill a goal.

In this paper we present an alternative to the round-robin strategy, which is *eager*: each goal is achieved as soon as possible. This gives us more desirable, responsive systems, which achieve some robustness against failure by the environment to achieve its liveness goals, at a fraction of the cost of other methods [2,3]. At the same time, our experimental results show that our new approach reduces time and memory use significantly at the expense of generating larger circuits.

The rest of the paper is organized as follows. In Section 2, we revisit some preliminaries necessary for our method and establish notation. In Section 3, we present our synthesis approach. Section 4 presents specific aspects of our implementation. In Section 5, we summarize our experimental results, and Section 6 concludes the paper.

2   Preliminaries

2.1   Generalized Reactivity

Generalized Reactivity(1) [16], GR(1) for short, is a syntactic restriction of Linear Temporal Logic (LTL). Let $\mathcal{I}$ and $\mathcal{O}$ be sets of (propositional) variables. A GR(1) specification φ is required to be of the form $\varphi = \varphi^e \rightarrow \varphi^s$ where φ^e and φ^s can be written as a conjunction of the following three parts [16]:

- A Boolean formula φ_i^e (φ_i^s, respectively) over $\mathcal{I}$ and $\mathcal{O}$, characterizing the initial states.
- An LTL formula φ_t^e (φ_t^s, respectively), characterizing the transitions of the environment (system, respectively). φ_t^e is of the form $\bigwedge_i \mathsf{G}(B_i)$, where each B_i is a Boolean combination of variables from $\mathcal{I}$ and $\mathcal{O}$, and expressions of the form $\mathsf{X}(v)$, where v is a variable from $\mathcal{I}$ for φ_t^e and from $\mathcal{I} \cup \mathcal{O}$ for φ_t^s.
- An LTL formula φ_f^e (φ_f^s, respectively), characterizing the fairness states for the environment (system, respectively). φ_f^e and φ_f^s are both of the form $\bigwedge_i \mathsf{G}\,\mathsf{F}\,B_i$ for a Boolean formulae B_i over $\mathcal{I} \cup \mathcal{O}$.

It is easiest to think about φ^e and φ^s as encoding the symbolic representation of the product of several Büchi automata. (Extra variables for encoding automata states can be modeled as extra state variables.) The goal of synthesis is to generate a Mealy machine that satisfies the GR(1) specification. The Mealy machine has inputs $\mathcal{I}$, state variables $\mathcal{I} \cup \mathcal{O}$, and the outputs coincide with (the next state values of) the state variables [16]. A Mealy machine satisfies a GR(1) specification if (1) φ_i^e and φ_i^s are satisfied initially, (2) as long as the environment fulfills φ_t^e, the system fulfills φ_t^s, and (3) if the environment fulfills φ_f^e, the system fulfills φ_f^s.

Synthesizing a correct system from its specification corresponds to finding a strategy in a *game* between the system (protagonist) and the environment (antagonist). Following [16], we define a *game structure* $\langle \mathcal{I}, \mathcal{O}, \Theta, \rho_e, \rho_s, \varphi \rangle$. Here, $\mathcal{I}$ is a set of (Boolean) input variables, which are under the environment's control. Similarly, $\mathcal{O}$ is a set of output variables, under the system's control. We define a *state* to be an interpretation of $\mathcal{I} \cup \mathcal{O}$, assigning to each variable either true or false. We will denote the set of all states with Q. Furthermore, Θ is the initial condition; in our case $\Theta = \varphi_i^e \wedge \varphi_i^s$. The transition relation of the environment is denoted by $\rho_e(\mathcal{I}, \mathcal{O}, \mathcal{I}')$, relating a present state $q \in Q$ to possible values for next inputs $I' \in \mathcal{I}'$, where $\mathcal{I}'$ contains primed copies of the elements in $\mathcal{I}$. In our case, $\rho_e = \varphi_t^e$, where we replace each occurrence of $\mathsf{X}v$ with v', representing the "next state" of v. Similarly, $\rho_s(\mathcal{I}, \mathcal{O}, \mathcal{I}', \mathcal{O}')$ is the transition relation of the system, relating a present state $q \in Q$ and a next input I' to possible values for next outputs $O' \in \mathcal{O}'$. We set $\rho_s = \varphi_t^s$, again replacing all occurrences of $\mathsf{X}v$ with v'. Finally, φ is the winning condition of the game. We use $\varphi = \varphi^e \rightarrow \varphi^s$. Furthermore, let J_j^G (for $j \in \{1, \dots, n\}$) and J_i^A (for $i \in \{1, \dots, m\}$) be the sets of fair states of the system and the environment, characterized by the conjuncts B_i in φ_f^s and φ_f^e, respectively. We will also refer to them as "guarantee states" and "assumption states" respectively.

One step of the game consists of the environment choosing values for the next inputs I', after which the system must choose values for the next outputs O'. The game is won by the system iff the resulting sequence of states in the game graph satisfies the winning condition φ. Informally speaking (and slightly simplified), the system wins the game if it is either able to ensure infinitely many visits to all sets of guarantee states, or if it can prevent the environment from visiting at least one of the sets of assumption states infinitely often.

A *strategy* is a (partial) function that maps the present state and next inputs to next outputs. It is called a *winning strategy* if every play that adheres to it is won by the system. A winning strategy can easily be turned into a correct implementation for the system [16,6].

2.2 μ-Calculus

For solving games, we use the propositional μ-calculus [13]. Formulae of the μ-calculus are defined recursively. Let Q be the set of all states of a game structure. Furthermore, let $\mathcal{V}$ be a set of variables. Every subset $S \subseteq Q$ and every variable $V \in \mathcal{V}$ is a μ-calculus formula. Let A, B be μ-calculus formulae. Then also $\neg A$, $A \cup B$, and $A \cap B$ are μ-calculus formulae, with the obvious semantics. Moreover, the μ-calculus comprises least and greatest fixpoint formulae, defined as follows.

For a μ-calculus formula P with a free variable $V \in \mathcal{V}$ the following are μ-calculus formulae:

$$\mu V . P(V) = \bigcup_i V_i, \quad \text{where } V_0 = \emptyset \text{ and } V_{i+1} = P(V_i) \text{ and} \tag{1}$$

$$\nu V . P(V) = \bigcap_i V_i, \quad \text{where } V_0 = Q \text{ and } V_{i+1} = P(V_i). \tag{2}$$

We extend the classical μ-calculus with a mixed-preimage operator MX, defined as follows:

$$\mathsf{MX}(V) = \{(i,o) \in Q \mid \forall i' . \exists o' . ((i,o,i') \models \rho_e \to (i,o,i',o') \models \rho_s) \wedge (i',o') \in V\}.$$

Semantically, $\mathsf{MX}(V)$ denotes the set of all states from which the system can force the play into a state in V, irrespective of the input i' chosen by the environment.

2.3 Computing the Winning Region of GR(1) Games

Piterman et al. [16] presented a μ-calculus formula for computing the *winning region* of a GR(1) game, i.e., the set of states from which the system can win the game by adhering to a winning strategy. The winning region of such a specification is given by the following triply-nested fixpoint formula [16]:

$$\mathsf{Win} = \nu Z . \bigwedge_{j=1}^{n} \mu Y . \bigvee_{i=1}^{m} \nu X . (J_j^G \wedge \mathsf{MX}(Z)) \vee \mathsf{MX}(Y) \vee (\neg J_i^A \wedge \mathsf{MX}(X)). \tag{3}$$

Piterman et al. [16] also show how to use the intermediate values of the fixpoint computations in Equation 3 to construct a strategy, consisting of the disjunction of three sub-strategies. These three sub-strategies correspond to the three disjuncts in Equation 3. Sub-strategy ρ_1 is applied when the game has reached a guarantee state in J_j^G. In this case, a counter jx that stores which guarantee should be fulfilled next is incremented (modulo n, the number of guarantees). Sub-strategy ρ_2 takes the play at least one step closer to a state in J_j^G. Sub-strategy ρ_3 ensures that the play stays in a region in which at least one of the sets of assumption states J_i^A is not visited.

Although systems that adhere to these sub-strategies are correct, they are not necessarily *eager*. The strategies only ensure that each step takes the play at least one step closer to a guarantee state, or even stay where they are as long as an assumption state is not reached. However, in many situations the system might have a choice of getting not only one, but several steps closer to a guarantee state. An eager system would always make the choice that takes it as close to the guarantee states as possible. It might even fulfil multiple guarantees at once.

2.4 Relation Determinization

The strategies computed according to [16] are relations, mapping a tuple (i,o,i') of present state inputs i, present state outputs o, and next state inputs i' to possible next state outputs o'. These relations can be represented by a characteristic function, usually in form of a Binary Decision Diagram (BDD). In order to build circuits, we need to extract completely specified functions for each of the Boolean output signals $o_i \in \mathcal{O}$ from this relation.

There are several ways to find functions compatible with a given relation [24,1,9,6,5]. We will use the approach presented in [6,5], as it integrates seamlessly with the symbolic algorithms we use. When given a BDD $b(\mathcal{I}, \mathcal{O}, \mathcal{I}', \mathcal{O}')$ we will write $\mathsf{FN}(b)$ to denote a circuit with inputs $\mathcal{I}, \mathcal{O}, \mathcal{I}'$ and outputs $\mathcal{O}'$, such that $\mathsf{FN}(b)(i, o, i') = o'$ only if $b(i, o, i', o') = \mathsf{true}$ or $\neg\exists o' . b(i, o, i', o')$. To emphasize that $\mathsf{FN}(b)$ is a (completely specified) function, we will sometimes write $\mathsf{FN}(b)(\mathcal{I}, \mathcal{O}, \mathcal{I}' \rightarrow \mathcal{O}')$.

3   Onion Rings Approach

Previous work [6,5] shows that tools implementing GR(1) synthesis spend a lot of time computing the strategy relation. While computing the winning region is comparatively fast, combining the intermediate results of the fixpoint computation to form a monolithic strategy requires a lot of CPU time and memory. We will demonstrate how to build a correct-by-construction circuit directly from the intermediate results of the winning region computation, without having to build a monolithic strategy relation first.

Our new synthesis approach is based on the intermediate results of fixpoint computations, which we call *onion rings*. The name stems from the form of the intermediate results of an attractor computation. Like in an onion, each iteration of the computation adds a layer of states "around" the previous results. We will show how to build two kinds of circuits. The first are *enable circuits* which detect whether we can reach a particular onion ring. The second are circuits that provide correct outputs for the case that we move to the particular enabled onion ring. Before that, however, we will introduce some simple auxiliary circuits that we will need to combine the other parts. In the following, we will denote circuits and combinational gates by upper-case sans-serif letters (e.g., circuit A, B, C, ..., gates AND, XOR). For "standard gates" such as AND and XOR, we will use infix notation (e.g. A AND B). BDDs will be denoted by lowercase letters (e.g. $a, b, c, \ldots$). Operations on BDDs will be denoted using the common logic operators such as $\wedge$ and $\exists$. Furthermore, we will write $\mathcal{C}(b)$ to denote a circuit equivalent to b. That is, a circuit having the variables of b as its inputs, and one output that is true if and only if the inputs are in the on-set of b.[1]

3.1   Auxiliary Circuits

The first auxiliary circuit we need is called SELECT. It has n one-bit selector inputs $S_1, \ldots, S_n$, and n data inputs $F_1, \ldots, F_n$, each m bits wide. Furthermore, SELECT$((S_1, \ldots, S_n), (F_1, \ldots, F_n))$ has an m bits wide data output, which is equal to F_1 if S_1 is true, equal to F_2 if S_1 is false and S_2 is true, equal to F_3 if

---

[1] Note that it is trivial to construct such a circuit by using one multiplexer for each BDD node.

S_1 and S_2 are false and S_3 is true, etc. I.e., the output equals the input with the lowest index for which the corresponding selector bit is true. If all selector signals $S_1, \ldots, S_n$ are false, the output of the SELECT circuit is arbitrary.

The second auxiliary circuit is a comparator. COMP(A, B) outputs true if and only if A and B are (bitwise) equal.

3.2   Enable Circuits for Onion Rings

From the computation of the winning region of a GR(1) game, we get a set of BDDs $x[j, r, i]$, each referring to variables in $\mathcal{I} \cup \mathcal{O}$ [16]. The indices i and j range over all the sets of assumption and guarantee states of the specification, respectively. The index r denotes iterations in the computation of the least fixpoint over Y in Equation 3. Each of these BDDs symbolically represents a set of states in the GR(1) game. The set represented by $x[j, r, i]$ denotes the set of states from which the system can either (1) enforce moving one step closer to one of the states in the j-th guarantee set (i.e., a state in $x[j, r', i']$ for $r' < r$ and arbitrary i'), or (2) stay in that part of $x[j, r, i]$, which does not share any states with the i-th set of assumption states. We will use primes to denote BDDs that represent sets of "next states" (i.e., referring to variables in $\mathcal{I}' \cup \mathcal{O}'$). For each BDD $x'[j, r, i]$, we build an enable circuit that detects whether a state described by $x'[j, r, i]$ is reachable by obeying the system transition relation ρ_s for some next state output O':

$$\text{EN}[j, r, i](\mathsf{I}, \mathsf{O}, \mathsf{I}') = \mathcal{C}(\exists \mathsf{O}' . \rho_s \wedge x'[j, r, i]) \tag{4}$$

A circuit EN[j, r, i] outputs true if and only if the tuple (I,O,I') at its input satisfies the system transition relation and gets the system into the set of states represented by $x'[j, r, i]$ under some output O'.

3.3   Function Circuits for Onion Rings

For each onion ring, as described in the previous section, we build a corresponding function circuit FN(I, O, I' → O') that computes the system's outputs for this particular case:

$$\text{FN}[j, r, i](\mathsf{I}, \mathsf{O}, \mathsf{I}' \to \mathsf{O}') = \text{FN}(\rho_s \wedge x'[j, r, i]) \tag{5}$$

The enable and function circuits are combined in a way to make maximum progress when approaching a guarantee state J_j^G. That means we want to choose the function corresponding to the minimal (r, i) whose enable circuit outputs true. I.e., we step to the innermost onion ring possible. We use SELECT circuits, as described in Section 3.1, to achieve this by ordering the selector (enable signals) and data inputs (function signals) lexicographically according to (r, i).

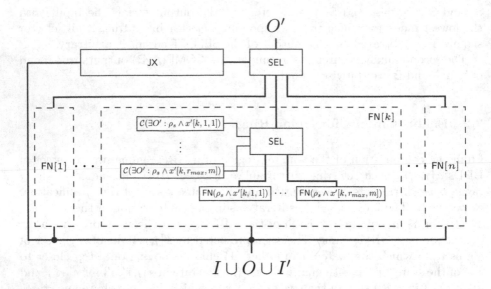

Fig. 1. Diagram of the whole circuit. Dashed boxes symbolize parts of the circuit that are built analogously to the neighboring parts drawn in detail.

$$
\begin{aligned}
\mathsf{FN}[j] = \mathsf{SELECT}(&(\mathsf{EN}[j,1,1],\ldots,\mathsf{EN}[j,1,m], \\
&\mathsf{EN}[j,2,1],\ldots,\mathsf{EN}[j,2,m],\ldots, \\
&\mathsf{EN}[j,r_{max},1],\ldots,\mathsf{EN}[j,r_{max},m]), \\
&(\mathsf{FN}[j,1,1],\ldots,\mathsf{FN}[j,1,m], \\
&\mathsf{FN}[j,2,1],\ldots,\mathsf{FN}[j,2,m],\ldots, \\
&\mathsf{FN}[j,r_{max},1],\ldots,\mathsf{FN}[j,r_{max},m]))
\end{aligned}
\tag{6}
$$

This gives us circuits for approaching each of the guarantee states eagerly. Each $\mathsf{FN}[j]$ corresponds to one of the dashed boxes in Fig. 1.

3.4   Bookkeeping Circuit for Guarantee Selection

Finally we have to choose which guarantee to approach next. In [16], this was done in a round-robin fashion using a modular counter jx. We present a new approach that satisfies each guarantee as quickly as possible without having to wait for a counter to match a guarantee's index j. We will first informally describe the principal idea behind the bookkeeping circuit we employ, and afterwards define it formally.

Our approach uses one bit of memory for each guarantee ($\mathsf{JX}[1],\ldots,\mathsf{JX}[n]$), plus one *master* bit (master). Initially, the master bit and all JX bits are all set to the same (arbitrary) value. The semantics of these bits is as follows:

JX[j] XOR master is true if and only if guarantee j has already been satisfied in the current round. A guarantee j will be satisfied when the play is about enter a state in the set represented by $J_j'^G$. When this happens, the corresponding bit JX[j] is flipped (if it was not already different from the master bit). As soon as all guarantees were satisfied in one round (i.e., all JX bits are different from the master bit), the master bit is flipped and the procedure starts another round. Thus, the JX bits together with the master bit allow us to determine which guarantees still have to be pursued at a given time.

Note that the sets J_j^G are not necessarily disjunct. Empirical evidence suggests that there are often states which belong to several (or even all) sets J_j^G. Imagine, for example, an arbiter with N request and grant signals, and N guarantees stating that every request must eventually be granted. Then the state in which no requests are made (and thus no grants are given) fulfills *all* N guarantees and thus belongs to all sets J_j^G. Our bookkeeping circuit can take advantage of that by flipping all the JX bits corresponding to (yet unfulfilled) guarantees that are fulfilled in a particular state. This leads to a much more eager systems compared to systems using a modular counter for bookkeeping. We will illustrate this with an example in Section 3.6.

We will now provide a formal definition of our bookkeeping circuit.

JX Flip Signal. We need *flip signals* to determine whether a guarantee is being satisfied or not. Guarantee j is being satisfied whenever we move to the states represented by $J_j'^G$.

$$\mathrm{JX}_{\mathsf{flip}}[j] = \mathcal{C}(J_j'^G) \tag{7}$$

JX Update. The value of a JX bit is updated (flipped) whenever the corresponding $\mathrm{JX}_{\mathsf{flip}}$ signal is true and the JX bit is still equal to the master bit. A diagram of this circuit is shown in Figure 2.

$$\mathrm{JX}'[j] = \mathrm{JX}[j] \text{ XOR } (\mathrm{JX}_{\mathsf{flip}}[j] \text{ AND COMP}(\mathrm{JX}[j], \text{ master})) \tag{8}$$

Master Update. The update of the master bit works as follows: The master bit is flipped when it is unequal to all next JX bits. I.e., the flip happens if and only if all guarantees have been satisfied in a round. A diagram of this circuit is shown in Figure 3.

$$\text{master}' = \text{master XOR } (\text{AND}_j \,(\text{NOT COMP}(\mathrm{JX}'[j], \text{ master}))) \tag{9}$$

Guarantee Selection. Finally, we need to select a guarantee that should be pursued at the moment. Candidates are all those guarantees whose JX bit equals the master bit, as these are the guarantees not yet fulfilled in the current

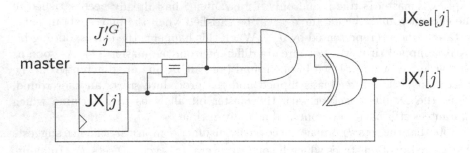

Fig. 2. Circuit for updating a JX bit with the signal for selecting a guarantee

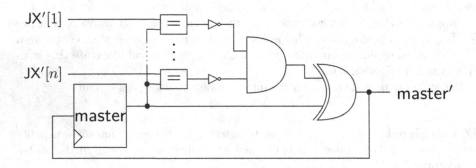

Fig. 3. Circuit for updating the master bit

round. The signal $JX_{sel}[j]$ tells whether or not guarantee j is a candidate for selection.

$$JX_{sel}[j] = COMP(master, JX[j]) \qquad (10)$$

3.5 Combining Functions with Guarantee Selection

To achieve eagerness, we use the signals $JX_{sel}[j]$ selector signals for the top-most SELECT circuit in Figure 1. I.e., we choose to make progress towards the lowest-numbered unsatisfied guarantee by choosing the corresponding function.[2]

$$FN(I, O, I' \to O') = SELECT((JX_{sel}[1], \ldots, JX_{sel}[n]), (FN[1], \ldots, FN[n])) \qquad (11)$$

Note that the outputs of the circuit in Equation 11 are also the primary outputs (O') of the overall system.

---

[2] This gives designers the possibility to prioritize guarantees by reordering them in the specification.

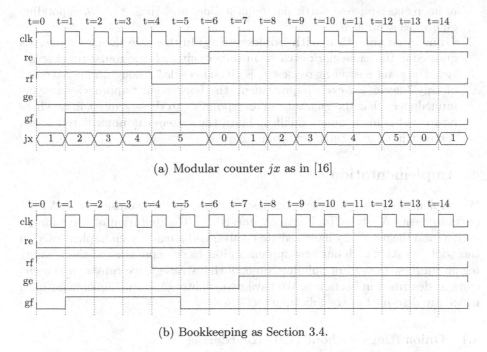

(a) Modular counter jx as in [16]

(b) Bookkeeping as Section 3.4.

Fig. 4. Timing diagram of a 6-input arbiter. The request and grant signals with indices $a, \ldots, d$ have been omitted, as they are all zero for the entire time shown.

3.6   Demonstration of Eagerness

To illustrate how the circuits synthesized according to our new method are more eager, we make the following comparison. We take a specification for a full-handshake arbiter with six request lines (ra to rf) and six corresponding grant lines (ga to gf). We synthesize circuits for this specification, once according to [16], and once according to the method presented in this paper. We simulate both circuits with the same input values. We set the request rf to 1 in clock cycles 0 to 4 and we set request re to 1 from cycle 6 on. The timing diagrams of our simulations are shown in Figures 4a and 4b. For increased readability, we have omitted some of the signals which are 0 the entire time in the waveform.

We observe a difference in the behavior of granting the requests by the two circuits in comparison:

1. **Round-robin strategy:** We see that the first request (rf) is immediately answered with grant gf. The second request (re), however, is only granted in cycle 11 (i.e., with a delay of 5 cycles), because the modular counter jx has to loop around first, in order to reach the value 4, which corresponds to ge. In each of the "wasted" 5 cycles, the implementation discovers that there

is no request on one particular request line, and thus, the corresponding guarantee is fulfilled.

2. **Guarantee selection with bookkeeping:** In this case the first request is granted in the same clock cycle as in the circuit with the round-robin strategy. The grant answering request *re* is given in cycle 7, though. This is a delay of only 1 cycle; a 4-cycle improvement: the bookkeeping approach discovers immediately that the guarantees corresponding to those request lines where no request is made are all fulfilled. Thus, the system can immediately fulfils the remaining guarantee concerning request *re*.

4   Implementation

We implemented the proposed synthesis method as an extension to RATSY (Requirements Analysis Tool with Synthesis) [4]. Computation of the winning region (and the necessary intermediate results) had already been implemented in this tool. We start with our new approach after the computation of the winning region finishes. Instead of building a monolithic strategy, we construct the circuits as described in Section 3. We have two slightly different implementations, which are described in the following sections.

4.1   Onion Rings without BDD Reordering

Our first approach is to create one sub-circuit after the other, immediately freeing any BDDs that are no longer required for subsequent computations. We keep a hash table of all BDD nodes for which we already constructed multiplexers. Since BDDs within the same manager may share internal nodes, we can reuse the corresponding multiplexers whenever necessary.

This advantage, however, comes at a price. We have to disable dynamic BDD reordering when we create the first circuit, because dynamic reordering may remove and/or reassign internal BDD nodes. Note, however, that reordering can of course be used before we create the first circuit. Thus, we enable dynamic reordering of BDDs during the computation of the winning region.

4.2   Onion Rings with BDD Reordering

As an alternative method, we first compute BDDs corresponding to all circuits without actually writing them out already. Thus, we can keep dynamic reordering enabled during all the computations.

Once we have computed all BDDs to be dumped, we perform a final (forced) reordering to reduce the size of the resulting multiplexer circuit, and then dump all BDDs at once, again taking advantage of node sharing.

5   Experimental Results

We used the specifications of the AMBA bus arbiter [5] for our experiments. We compared runtime, memory usage, and circuit size. We already had a working

Table 1. Experimental results for each test case and method

Circuit	Runtime [s]			Memory usage [GB]			Circuit Size [relative to Ref]	
	Ref	Onion_{RO}	Onion_{noRO}	Ref	Onion_{RO}	Onion_{noRO}	Onion_{RO}	Onion_{noRO}
amba02	3	6	11	0.55	0.57	0.57	18.3	31.9
amba03	53	27	44	0.67	0.62	0.66	4.5	8.0
amba04	176	517	846	0.99	1.55	1.19	40.5	66.6
amba05	492	885	846	1.41	1.13	1.49	23.6	62.7
amba06	1,059	723	1,370	1.55	1.45	1.18	16.9	42.9
amba07	1,960	1,532	1,592	1.63	1.56	1.50	12.3	22.5
amba08	13,390	19,800	36,433	7.45	16.62	16.89	X	X
amba09	5,394	4,011	4,578	2.45	2.63	2.41	16.9	28.4
amba10	12,673	5,413	8,941	7.20	3.11	2.67	25.4	46.7
amba11	10,685	7,609	11,277	4.24	4.41	2.68	13.2	23.9
amba12	55,997	7,831	11,585	9.18	4.79	2.79	19.2	28.5
amba13	40,229	14,787	15,825	13.81	5.05	4.39	10.8	25.7
amba14	41,538	17,077	14,287	8.92	5.77	2.98	21.1	30.3
amba15	43,173	17,721	19,646	14.98	8.10	4.24	16.7	24.7

synthesis implementation, based on cofactors [6] and used it as a reference point for our new technique. All experiments were conducted on a 64-bit Linux machine powered by a 2.66GHz Intel Xeon CPU with 64GB RAM. The 3 methods we have compared are as follows:

1. **Reference:** The cofactor-based approach described in [6]. This method serves as a reference point.
2. **Onion Rings without reordering:** The method described in Section 4.1.
3. **Onion Rings with reordering:** The method described in Section 4.2.

We will use the abbreviations Ref, Onion_{noRO} and Onion_{RO} to denote the methods. The results are presented in Table 1 and in Figures 5 and 6. We do not know why amba08 has a significantly higher time and memory consumption than amba09 in all three methods. A similar discrepancy has been observed before [6].

5.1 Runtime

We can see that for larger examples, method Onion_{RO} performs much better than the reference method. For smaller examples, the 3 methods perform similarly. We also see that finding a better BDD order pays off by improving the runtime. I.e., Onion_{RO} is typically faster than Onion_{noRO}.

5.2 Memory Usage

The memory requirements are taken from the Cudd_PrintInfo function of the CUDD [21] library and reflect the memory requirements of the BDD manager. Note that almost all memory used by RATSY is used by the BDD manager.

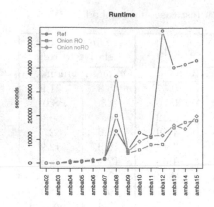
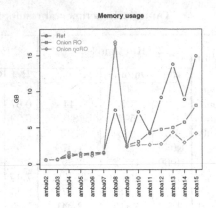

Fig. 5. Runtime for each approach and test case

Fig. 6. Memory usage for each approach and test case

We can see that the memory usage of our methods is better than the reference method. Again, smaller examples perform similarly, but for larger examples we gain an advantage. The method Onion$_{noRO}$ performs best, as it only needs to have the BDDs for creating a specific onion ring in memory. In contrast, Ref has to have the whole strategy BDD in memory, and Onion$_{RO}$ has to have the BDDs for all onion rings in memory to find a consistent BDD order before building the circuits.

5.3 Circuit Size

Circuit size was measured with abc[3]. Table 1 shows the relative circuit sizes with respect to the Reference method. For example, when synthesizing amba02 with method Onion$_{RO}$, the resulting circuit is 18.3 times the size of the circuit obtained when synthesizing amba02 with the Reference method. Note that factors have been rounded to one decimal. For amba08, abc runs into a timeout (marked with "X" in Table 1).

6   Conclusion and Future Work

We have presented a novel approach to GR(1) synthesis. Our technique builds upon [16], but circumvents the generation of a large, monolithic strategy relation. We have shown in our experiments that, using our technique, we can, in general, reduce the runtime and memory usage significantly. For larger examples, our method is able to synthesize results, where previous methods might have run out of memory, or run into timeouts. These results, however, come at the cost of larger circuits.

---

[3] http://www.eecs.berkeley.edu/~alanmi/abc/abc.htm

Apart from that, circuits built with our new method are *eager*, meaning that they fulfill the guarantees more quickly, whenever possible. First, we get as close as we can to the next guarantee state in every time step. Second, we check which guarantees are already fulfilled in parallel, instead of sequentially. This leads to more responsive, robust systems.

For future work, we will investigate different relation determinization techniques (cf. Section 2.4), which might improve circuit sizes. Also, we plan to investigate extensive "don't-care propagation". Whenever we have detected that we are in onion ring r, the output functions corresponding to all rings $s > r$ can actually be set to arbitrary values. Such optimizations might improve circuit size at the expense of additional CPU time.

References

1. Baneres, D., Cortadella, J., Kishinevsky, M.: A recursive paradigm to solve Boolean relations. In: Design Automation Conference, pp. 416–421 (2004)
2. Bloem, R., Chatterjee, K., Greimel, K., Henzinger, T., Jobstmann, B.: Robustness in the Presence of Liveness. In: Touili, T., Cook, B., Jackson, P. (eds.) CAV 2010. LNCS, vol. 6174, pp. 410–424. Springer, Heidelberg (2010)
3. Bloem, R., Chatterjee, K., Henzinger, T., Jobstmann, B.: Better Quality in Synthesis through Quantitative Objectives. In: Bouajjani, A., Maler, O. (eds.) CAV 2009. LNCS, vol. 5643, pp. 140–156. Springer, Heidelberg (2009)
4. Bloem, R., Cimatti, A., Greimel, K., Hofferek, G., Koenighofer, R., Roveri, M., Schuppan, V., Seeber, R.: RATSY – A New Requirements Analysis Tool with Synthesis. In: Touili, T., Cook, B., Jackson, P. (eds.) CAV 2010. LNCS, vol. 6174, pp. 425–429. Springer, Heidelberg (2010)
5. Bloem, R., Galler, S., Jobstmann, B., Piterman, N., Pnueli, A., Weiglhofer, M.: Automatic hardware synthesis from specifications: A case study. In: Proceedings of the Design, Automation and Test in Europe, pp. 1188–1193 (2007)
6. Bloem, R., Galler, S., Jobstmann, B., Piterman, N., Pnueli, A., Weiglhofer, M.: Specify, compile, run: Hardware form PSL. In: 6th International Workshop on Compiler Optimization Meets Compiler Verification (2007)
7. Church, A.: Logic, arithmetic and automata. In: Proceedings International Mathematical Congress (1962)
8. Filiot, E., Jin, N., Raskin, J.F.: An Antichain Algorithm for LTL Realizability. In: Bouajjani, A., Maler, O. (eds.) CAV 2009. LNCS, vol. 5643, pp. 263–277. Springer, Heidelberg (2009)
9. Jiang, J.H.R., Lin, H.P., Hung, W.L.: Interpolating functions from large Boolean relations. In: Proceedings of the 2009 International Conference on Computer-Aided Design, ICCAD 2009, pp. 779–784. ACM, New York (2009)
10. Jobstmann, B., Bloem, R.: Optimizations for LTL synthesis. In: 6th Conference on Formal Methods in Computer Aided Design (FMCAD 2006), pp. 117–124 (2006)
11. Jobstmann, B., Galler, S., Weiglhofer, M., Bloem, R.: Anzu: A Tool for Property Synthesis. In: Damm, W., Hermanns, H. (eds.) CAV 2007. LNCS, vol. 4590, pp. 258–262. Springer, Heidelberg (2007)
12. Jobstmann, B., Staber, S., Griesmayer, A., Bloem, R.: Finding and fixing faults. Journal of Computer and System Sciences 78(2), 441–460 (2012)
13. Kozen, D.: Results on the propositional μ-calculus. Theoretical Computer Science 27, 333–354 (1983)

14. Kuncak, V., Mayer, M., Piskac, R., Suter, P.: Complete functional synthesis. In: Proceedings of the 2010 ACM SIGPLAN Conference on Programming Language Design and Implementation, PLDI 2010 (2010)
15. Morgenstern, A., Schneider, K.: Exploiting the temporal logic hierarchy and the non-confluence property for efficient LTL synthesis. In: Montanari, A., Napoli, M., Parente, M. (eds.) Games, Automata, Logics, and Formal Verification (GandALF). Electronic Proceedings in Theoretical Computer Science (EPTCS), Minori, Italy, vol. 25, pp. 89–102 (2010)
16. Piterman, N., Pnueli, A., Sa'ar, Y.: Synthesis of Reactive(1) Designs. In: Emerson, E.A., Namjoshi, K.S. (eds.) VMCAI 2006. LNCS, vol. 3855, pp. 364–380. Springer, Heidelberg (2005)
17. Pnueli, A., Rosner, R.: On the synthesis of a reactive module. In: Proc. Symposium on Principles of Programming Languages (POPL 1989), pp. 179–190 (1989)
18. Schewe, S., Finkbeiner, B.: Bounded Synthesis. In: Namjoshi, K.S., Yoneda, T., Higashino, T., Okamura, Y. (eds.) ATVA 2007. LNCS, vol. 4762, pp. 474–488. Springer, Heidelberg (2007)
19. Sohail, S., Somenzi, F.: Safety first: A two-stage algorithm for LTL games. In: 9th Int. Conf. on Formal Methods in Computer Aided Design, pp. 77–84 (2009)
20. Solar-Lezama, A.: The Sketching Approach to Program Synthesis. In: Hu, Z. (ed.) APLAS 2009. LNCS, vol. 5904, pp. 4–13. Springer, Heidelberg (2009)
21. Somenzi, F.: CUDD: CU Decision Diagram Package. University of Colorado at Boulder, ftp://vlsi.colorado.edu/pub/
22. Staber, S., Jobstmann, B., Bloem, R.: Finding and Fixing Faults. In: Borrione, D., Paul, W. (eds.) CHARME 2005. LNCS, vol. 3725, pp. 35–49. Springer, Heidelberg (2005)
23. Vechev, M., Yahav, E., Yorsh, G.: Abstraction-guided synthesis of synchronization. In: Proc. Principles of Programming Languages, pp. 327–338. ACM (2010)
24. Watanabe, Y., Brayton, R.: Heuristic minimization of multiple-valued relations. IEEE Transactions on Computer-Aided Design of Integrated Circuits and Systems 12(10), 1458–1472 (1993)

IIS-Guided DFS for Efficient Bounded Reachability Analysis of Linear Hybrid Automata

Lei Bu, Yang Yang, and Xuandong Li

State Key Laboratory for Novel Software Technology,
Nanjing University, Nanjing, Jiangsu, P.R. China 210093
{bulei,lxd}@nju.edu.cn, yangyang@seg.nju.edu.cn

Abstract. In the authors' previous work, we proposed a linear programming (LP) based approach to check the reachability specification along one abstract path in a linear hybrid automaton (LHA) at a time by translating the reachability problem into the satisfiability problem of a linear constraint set. Then a depth-first-search (DFS) is deployed on the graph structure of the LHA to check all the paths with length in the threshold to answer the question of bounded reachability.

In this DFS-style bounded model checking (BMC) algorithm, once a path is found to be infeasible by the underlying LP solver, a backtracking on the graph structure will be conducted. Clearly, the efficiency of the algorithm depends on the accuracy of the backtracking. If the DFS can backtrack to the most reasonable location, the state space need to search and verify can be reduced significantly.

Fortunately, once a linear constraint set is judged to be unsatisfiable, the irreducible infeasible set (IIS) technique can be deployed on the unsatisfiable constraint set to give a quick analysis and find a small set of constraints which makes the whole program unsatisfiable. In this paper, we adopt this technique into our DFS-style BMC of LHA to locate the nodes and transitions which make the path under verification infeasible to guide the backtracking and answer the bounded reachability of LHA more efficiently.

1 Introduction

Hybrid automata [1] are well studied formal models for hybrid systems with both discrete and continuous state changes. However, the analysis of hybrid automata is very difficult. Even for the simple class of *linear hybrid automata (LHA)*, the reachability problem is undecidable [1–4]. The state-of-the-art symbolic model checking techniques for LHA try to compute the transitive closure of the state space of the system by geometric computation which is very expensive and not guaranteed to terminate. Several tools are designed and implemented in this style, like HYTECH [10] and its improvement PHAVer [11] but they do not scale well to the size of practical problems.

In recent years, bounded model checking (BMC) [5] has been presented as an alternative technique for BDD-based symbolic model checking, whose basic idea is to encode the next-state relation of a system as a propositional formula, and unroll this formula to some integer k, using SAT/SMT idea to search for a counterexample in the model executions whose length is bounded by k. These technique have been used to answer the reachability problem of LHA also. But, as these techniques require to encode the state space of LHA in threshold firstly, when the system size or the given step

K. Eder, J. Lourenço, and O. Shehory (Eds.): HVC 2011, LNCS 7261, pp. 35–49, 2012.
© Springer-Verlag Berlin Heidelberg 2012

threshold is large, the object problem could be very huge, which greatly restricts the size of the problem that can be solved [6, 7].

Both symbolic model checking and bounded model checking are facing the complete state space or the partly complete space under the threshold at one time which is always too large and complex for the solver to handle. In order to control the complexity of the verification of LHA, we proposed a linear programming (LP) based approach[8] to develop an efficient path-oriented reachability checker to check one abstract path in the graph structure of a LHA at a time to find whether there exists a behavior of the LHA along this abstract path and satisfy the given reachability specification. In such a manner, the length of the path and the size of the automaton being checked can be large enough to handle problems of practical interest. As a straightforward extension, all the abstract paths with length shorter than or equal to the threshold in the graph structure can be enumerated and checked one by one by depth-first-search(DFS) traversing to answer the question of bounded reachability analysis of the LHA.

The above DFS based BMC has shown good performance and scalability in our previous studies[9, 14]. Nevertheless, it has a lot of space to optimize:

- The simple DFS algorithm checks each path ρ in the given length threshold for the reachability by solving the corresponding linear program. Although the checking of a single path is very efficient, if the number of candidate path is large, it will still be time consuming. However, suppose we are checking whether location v is reachable in bound k, and v is not contained in ρ at all, we can simply falsify ρ for the reachability to save computation time.
- Once a path ρ is found to be infeasible, the DFS algorithm will only remove the last location in the path and backtrack to the location preceding the last one to search for the next candidate in a recursive manner. This backtracking method does not use any information of the infeasible path. If the infeasible cone in the linear constraint set related to ρ can be extracted, then the DFS procedure can backtrack to the exact place that makes the ongoing path infeasible. Then, the state space needed to search and verify can be pruned significantly.

Based on the above directions, we optimize our DFS-style BMC algorithm in the following ways:

- Only when the last location of the current visiting path ρ is contained in the reachability specification, the DFS procedure will call the underlying decision procedure to check the feasibility of ρ. Otherwise, the DFS will just go on traversing on the graph structure to reduce the time overhead.
- Once a linear constraint set is judged to be unsatisfiable, the irreducible infeasible set (IIS) technique[12] can be deployed to give quick analysis of the program and find a small set of constraints which makes the whole program unsatisfiable. We deploy this technique into our DFS-style BMC of LHA to locate the nodes and transitions which cause the path under verification infeasible to guide the backtracking and answer the bounded reachability of LHA more efficiently.

2   Linear Hybrid Automata and Reachability Verification

This section gives the formal definition of linear hybrid automata and presents the review of the path-oriented reachability analysis and bounded reachability analysis techniques that were proposed in our previous works[8, 9].

2.1   Linear Hybrid Automata

The linear hybrid automata (LHA) considered in this paper are defined in[13], which is a variation of the definition given in [1]. The flow conditions of variables in a linear hybrid automaton considered here can be given as a range of values for their derivatives.

Definition 1. An LHA H is a tuple $H = (X, \Sigma, V, V^0, E, \alpha, \beta, \gamma)$, where

- X is a finite set of real-valued variables; Σ is a finite set of event labels; V is a finite set of *locations*; $V^0 \subseteq V$ is a set of *initial locations*.
- E is a *transition relation* whose elements are of the form $(v, \sigma, \phi, \psi, v')$, where v, v' are in V, $\sigma \in \Sigma$ is a label, ϕ is a set of *transition guards* of the form $a \leq \sum_{i=0}^{l} c_i x_i \leq b$, and ψ is a set of *reset actions* of the form $x := c$ where $x_i \in X$, $x \in X$, a, b, c and c_i are real numbers (a, b may be ∞).
- α is a labeling function which maps each location in V to a *location invariant* which is a set of *variable constraints* of the form $a \leq \sum_{i=0}^{l} c_i x_i \leq b$ where $x_i \in X$, a, b and c_i are real numbers (a, b may be ∞).
- β is a labeling function which maps each location in V to a set of *flow conditions* which are of the form $\dot{x} \in [a, b]$ where $x \in X$, and a, b are real numbers ($a \leq b$). For any $v \in V$, for any $x \in X$, there is one and only one flow condition $\dot{x} \in [a, b] \in \beta(v)$.
- γ is a labeling function which maps each location in V^0 to a set of *initial conditions* which are of the form $x = a$ where $x \in X$ and a is a real number. For any $v \in V^0$, for any $x \in X$, there is at most one initial condition definition $x = a \in \gamma(v)$. □

Path and Behavior. We use the sequences of locations to represent the evolution of an LHA from location to location. For an LHA $H = (X, \Sigma, V, V^0, E, \alpha, \beta, \gamma)$, a *path segment* is a sequence of locations of the form $\langle v_0 \rangle \xrightarrow[\sigma_0]{(\phi_0, \psi_0)} \langle v_1 \rangle \xrightarrow[\sigma_1]{(\phi_1, \psi_1)} \ldots \xrightarrow[\sigma_{n-1}]{(\phi_{n-1}, \psi_{n-1})} \langle v_n \rangle$, which satisfies $(v_i, \sigma_i, \phi_i, \psi_i, v_{i+1}) \in E$ for each i ($0 \leq i < n$). A *path* in H is a path segment starting at an initial location in V^0.

For a path in H of the form $\langle v_0 \rangle \xrightarrow[\sigma_0]{(\phi_0, \psi_0)} \langle v_1 \rangle \xrightarrow[\sigma_1]{(\phi_1, \psi_1)} \ldots \xrightarrow[\sigma_{n-1}]{(\phi_{n-1}, \psi_{n-1})} \langle v_n \rangle$, by assigning each location v_i with a time delay stamp δ_i we get a *timed sequence* of the form $\begin{pmatrix} v_0 \\ \delta_0 \end{pmatrix} \xrightarrow[\sigma_0]{(\phi_0, \psi_0)} \begin{pmatrix} v_1 \\ \delta_1 \end{pmatrix} \xrightarrow[\sigma_1]{(\phi_1, \psi_1)} \ldots \xrightarrow[\sigma_{n-1}]{(\phi_{n-1}, \psi_{n-1})} \begin{pmatrix} v_n \\ \delta_n \end{pmatrix}$ where δ_i ($0 \leq i \leq n$) is a nonnegative real number, which represents a behavior of H such that the system starts at v_0, stays there for δ_0 time units, then jumps to v_1 and stays at v_1 for δ_1 time units, and so on.

The behavior of an LHA can be described informally as follows. The automaton starts at one of the initial locations with some variables initialized to their initial values. As time progresses, the values of all variables change continuously according to the flow condition associated with the current location. At any time, the system can change its current location from v to v' provided that there is a transition $(v, \sigma, \phi, \psi, v')$ from v to v' whose all transition guards in ϕ are satisfied by the current value of the variables. With a location change by a transition $(v, \sigma, \phi, \psi, v')$, some variables are reset to the new value accordingly to the reset actions in ψ. Transitions are assumed to be instantaneous.

Let $H = (X, \Sigma, V, V^0, E, \alpha, \beta, \gamma)$ be an LHA. Given a timed sequence ω of the form $\begin{pmatrix} v_0 \\ \delta_0 \end{pmatrix} \xrightarrow[\sigma_0]{(\phi_0, \psi_0)} \begin{pmatrix} v_1 \\ \delta_1 \end{pmatrix} \xrightarrow[\sigma_1]{(\phi_1, \psi_1)} \cdots \xrightarrow[\sigma_{n-1}]{(\phi_{n-1}, \psi_{n-1})} \begin{pmatrix} v_n \\ \delta_n \end{pmatrix}$, let $\zeta_i(x)$ represents the value of x ($x \in X$) when the automaton has stayed at v_i for delay δ_i along with ω ($0 \le i \le n$), and $\lambda_i(x)$ represents the value of x at the time the automaton reaches v_i along with ω. It follows that $\lambda_0(x) = a$ if $x = a \in \gamma(v_0)$, and $\lambda_{i+1}(x) = \begin{cases} d & \text{if } x := d \in \psi_i \\ \zeta_i(x) & \text{otherwise} \end{cases}$ $(0 \le i < n)$.

Definition 2. For an LHA $H = (X, \Sigma, V, V^0, E, \alpha, \beta, \gamma)$, a timed sequence of the form $\begin{pmatrix} v_0 \\ \delta_0 \end{pmatrix} \xrightarrow[\sigma_0]{(\phi_0, \psi_0)} \begin{pmatrix} v_1 \\ \delta_1 \end{pmatrix} \xrightarrow[\sigma_1]{(\phi_1, \psi_1)} \cdots \xrightarrow[\sigma_{n-1}]{(\phi_{n-1}, \psi_{n-1})} \begin{pmatrix} v_n \\ \delta_n \end{pmatrix}$ represents a behavior of H if and only if the following condition is satisfied:

- $\langle v_0 \rangle \xrightarrow[\sigma_0]{(\phi_0, \psi_0)} \langle v_1 \rangle \xrightarrow[\sigma_1]{(\phi_1, \psi_1)} \cdots \xrightarrow[\sigma_{n-1}]{(\phi_{n-1}, \psi_{n-1})} \langle v_n \rangle$ is a path;
- $\delta_1, \delta_2, \ldots, \delta_n$ ensure that each variable $x \in X$ evolves according to its flow condition in each location v_i ($0 \le i \le n$), i.e. $u_i \delta_i \le \zeta_i(x) - \lambda_i(x) \le u'_i \delta_i$ where $\dot{x} \in [u_i, u'_i] \in \beta(v_i)$;
- all the transition guards in ϕ_i ($1 \le i \le n-1$) are satisfied, i.e. for each transition guard $a \le c_0 x_0 + c_1 x_1 + \cdots + c_l x_l \le b$ in ϕ_i, $a \le c_0 \zeta_i(x_0) + c_1 \zeta_i(x_1) + \cdots + c_l \zeta_i(x_l) \le b$;
- the location invariant of each location v_i ($1 \le i \le n$) is satisfied, i.e.
  - at the time the automaton leaves v_i, each variable constraint $a \le c_0 x_0 + c_1 x_1 + \cdots + c_l x_l \le b$ in $\alpha(v_i)$ ($0 \le i \le n$) is satisfied, i.e. $a \le c_0 \zeta_i(x_0) + c_1 \zeta_i(x_1) + \cdots + c_l \zeta_i(x_l) \le b$, and
  - at the time the automaton reaches v_i, each variable constraint $a \le c_0 x_0 + c_1 x_1 + \cdots + c_l x_l \le b$ in $\alpha(v_i)$ ($0 \le i \le n$) is satisfied, i.e. $a \le c_0 \lambda_i(x_0) + c_1 \lambda_i(x_1) + \cdots + c_l \lambda_i(x_l) \le b$. □

Definition 3. For an LHA $H = (X, \Sigma, V, V^0, E, \alpha, \beta, \gamma)$, if a timed sequence of the form $\begin{pmatrix} v_0 \\ \delta_0 \end{pmatrix} \xrightarrow[\sigma_0]{(\phi_0, \psi_0)} \begin{pmatrix} v_1 \\ \delta_1 \end{pmatrix} \xrightarrow[\sigma_1]{(\phi_1, \psi_1)} \cdots \xrightarrow[\sigma_{n-1}]{(\phi_{n-1}, \psi_{n-1})} \begin{pmatrix} v_n \\ \delta_n \end{pmatrix}$ is a behavior of H, we say path $\rho = \langle v_0 \rangle \xrightarrow[\sigma_0]{(\phi_0, \psi_0)} \langle v_1 \rangle \xrightarrow[\sigma_1]{(\phi_1, \psi_1)} \cdots \xrightarrow[\sigma_{n-1}]{(\phi_{n-1}, \psi_{n-1})} \langle v_n \rangle$ is *feasible*, and location v_n is *reachable* along ρ. □

2.2 Reachability Specification and Verification

Reachability Specification. For an LHA $H = (X, \Sigma, V, V^0, E, \alpha, \beta, \gamma)$, a *reachability specification*, denoted as $\mathcal{R}(v, \varphi)$, consists of a location v in H and a set φ of variable constraints of the form $a \le c_0 x_0 + c_1 x_1 + \cdots + c_l x_l \le b$ where $x_i \in X$ for any i ($0 \le i \le l$), a, b and c_i ($0 \le i \le l$) are real numbers.

Definition 4. Let $H = (X, \Sigma, V, V^0, E, \alpha, \beta, \gamma)$ be an LHA, and $\mathcal{R}(v, \varphi)$ be a reachability specification. A behavior of H of the form $\begin{pmatrix} v_0 \\ \delta_0 \end{pmatrix} \xrightarrow[\sigma_0]{(\phi_0, \psi_0)} \begin{pmatrix} v_1 \\ \delta_1 \end{pmatrix} \xrightarrow[\sigma_1]{(\phi_1, \psi_1)} \cdots \xrightarrow[\sigma_{n-1}]{(\phi_{n-1}, \psi_{n-1})} \begin{pmatrix} v_n \\ \delta_n \end{pmatrix}$ *satisfies* $\mathcal{R}(v, \varphi)$ if and only if $v_n = v$ and each constraint in φ is satisfied when the automaton has stayed in v_n for delay δ_n, i.e. for each variable constraint $a \leq c_0 x_0 + c_1 x_1 + \cdots + c_l x_l \leq b$ in φ, $a \leq c_0 \zeta_n(x_0) + c_1 \zeta_n(x_1) + \cdots + c_m \zeta_n(x_l) \leq b$ where $\zeta_n(x_k)$ $(0 \leq k \leq l)$ represents the value of x_k when the automaton has stayed at v_n for the delay δ_n. H *satisfies* $\mathcal{R}(v, \varphi)$ if and only if there is a behavior of H which satisfies $\mathcal{R}(v, \varphi)$. □

Definition 5. Given LHA $H = (X, \Sigma, V, V^0, E, \alpha, \beta, \gamma)$, and reachability specification $\mathcal{R}(v, \varphi)$, by introducing a new sink location $v_\mathcal{R}$ and a sink transition $e_\mathcal{R}$ into H, which results a new LHA $H_\mathcal{R}$. The satisfiability of $\mathcal{R}(v, \varphi)$ on LHA H are equivalent to the reachability of $v_\mathcal{R}$ in $H_\mathcal{R}$ iff $\alpha(v_\mathcal{R}) = \emptyset$ and $e_\mathcal{R} = (v, \sigma, \phi, \psi, v_\mathcal{R})$, where $v = v \in \mathcal{R}(v, \varphi)$, $\phi = \mathcal{R}(v, \varphi)$, $\psi = \emptyset$. □

Based on the above definition, without loss of generality, in the following paragraph, we will only discuss the reachability problem of a given location in the LHA, which covers the verification of the reachability specification $\mathcal{R}(v, \varphi)$.

According to Definition.2, the reachability verification problem of location v_n along the path ρ can be translated into the satisfiability problem of a set of constraints on variables δ_i and $\zeta_i(x)$ where $(0 \leq i \leq n)$. If we use notation $\Theta(\rho, v_n)$ to represent this set of linear constraints, we can check whether ρ reaches location v_n by checking whether $\Theta(\rho, v_n)$ has a solution, which can be solved by linear programming (LP) efficiently.

Bounded Reachability Verification. The bounded reachability analysis is to look for a system trajectory in a given threshold which can satisfy the given specification. Last paragraph gives a technique to verify the reachability of an abstract path in the LHA. Based on that, we proposed a bounded reachability verification method in[9] to traverse the system structure directly by DFS and check all the potential paths one by one until a feasible path to the reachability target is found or the given threshold is reached.

The pseudocode for this algorithm is shown in Table.1. The main function is Verify($H, v, bound$) where H is the LHA, v is the reachability target location and *bound* is the value of the threshold. This function traverses the graph structure by calling function TRAVERSE($stack$) recursively, where the input parameter *stack* is the stack which contains the current visiting path. When the function finds a path which satisfies the specification, it returns 1, then the upper caller will be informed and the DFS will be terminated. If the return value is 0, the caller will remove the last location from the ongoing path and keep on traversing. Because whenever a new location is added into the ongoing path, the algorithm will check the feasibility of it, we call this algorithm the "Eager"-DFS based bounded reachability analysis algorithm.

Instead of encoding the whole problem space to a group of formulas like SAT-style solver, which suffers the state space explosion a lot when dealing with big problems, this plain DFS style approach only needs to keep the discrete structure and current visiting path in memory, and check each potential path one by one, which makes it possible to solve big problems as long as enough time is given. The case studies given in[9] give a demonstration of this approach which also supports our belief of this argument.

3 Pruning Algorithm For DFS Optimization

The DFS-based algorithm for bounded reachability analysis of LHA reviewed in the last section gives an intuitive method to traverse and check one path at a time[9]. As

Table 1. Eager-DFS Based Bounded Reachability Analysis of LHA

VERIFY $(H, v, bound)$
1. **for** each location $v_I \in V^0$:
2. **begin**
3.   new stack s;
4. s.push(v_I);
5.   int res=TRAVERSE(s);
6.   if (res==1) **return** true;
7. s.pop(v_I);
8. **end**
9. **return** false;

TRAVERSE $(stack\ s)$
1. Get the ongoing path $\rho = \langle v_0 \rangle \xrightarrow[\sigma_0]{(\phi_0, \psi_0)} \langle v_1 \rangle \xrightarrow[\sigma_1]{(\phi_1, \psi_1)} \ldots \xrightarrow[\sigma_{n-1}]{(\phi_{n-1}, \psi_{n-1})} \langle v_n \rangle$ from stack s;
2. check the feasibility of ρ;
3. **if** (infeasible) **return** 0;
4. **if** ((feasible)&&($v_n == v$)) **return** 1;
5. **if** (($s.depth == bound$)||(v_n doesn't have any successive location)) **return** 0;
6. **for** each successive location $sloc$ of v_n
7. **begin**
8. s.push($sloc$);
9.   boolean res=TRAVERSE(s);
10.   if (res==1) **return** res;
11. s.pop($sloc$);
12. **end**
13. **return** 0;

---

the number of paths under given bound are finite, this algorithm is guaranteed to terminate. Furthermore, the algorithm only checks the reachability of one path, therefore the memory usage will not blow up quickly without control.

3.1   Target Location-Guided Lazy-DFS

Basically, the above algorithm makes a tradeoff between space and time to handle problems with large size. Using our DFS-style BMC algorithm, we can solve a problem with practical size given enough time. As a result, we have a stable ground for the control of memory usage. Now let's turn our direction to time control, which means we want to give an algorithm to traverse the bounded behavior tree of a LHA more efficiently.

The current Eager-DFS algorithm checks all the paths under the given threshold. When the threshold is large and the graph structure is complex, there could be numerous candidate paths to check, which could consume a considerably large amount of computation time. Take the LHA in Fig.1 for example, suppose we want to check whether v_6 is reachable within bound 7, the related bounded behavior tree of this automaton is shown in Fig.2, which has 37 candidate paths, for example, $\langle v_1 \rangle \xrightarrow[e_1]{} \langle v_2 \rangle$ and so on. This means the DFS procedure could call the underlying LP solver 37 times in

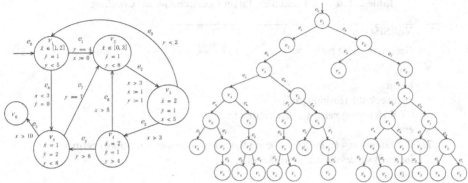

Fig. 1. Sample Automaton

Fig. 2. Behavior Tree With Bound 7

the worst case. If the size of bound is larger, the number of path segments need to check could blow up quickly, which will be the main bottleneck for the entire bounded verification. Therefore, if there is a method to decrease the number of paths need to check, then the efficiency of the above algorithm can be improved for sure.

By investigating the 37 paths, we can find that most of the paths are not even related with the reachability specification. As we are checking whether location v_6 is reachable in bound 7, path segments like $\langle v_1 \rangle \xrightarrow{e_1} \langle v_2 \rangle$, $\langle v_1 \rangle \xrightarrow{e_1} \langle v_2 \rangle \xrightarrow{e_2} \langle v_3 \rangle$ don't have location v_6 involved, therefore these paths can not satisfy the specification for sure and it could be a waste of time to check their feasibilities by calling a LP solver.

Based on this intuitive idea, we give the first straightforward optimization as follows: When checking whether location v is reachable along a path ρ, if the location v is not contained in ρ, the investigation of the feasibility of ρ will be postponed until v is traversed. Comparing with the Eager-DFS algorithm presented in the last section which checks the feasibility of the ongoing path whenever a new location is traversed, in this optimization, the calling of the LP solver will only be conducted once the new traversed location is specification related. Therefore, we name this algorithm as "Lazy"-DFS.

The pseudocode for the function TRAVERSE in Lazy-DFS algorithm is shown below in Table.2. The main difference between this algorithm and the algorithm in Table.1 is the checking of the feasibility of the ongoing path is moved into the branch with $v_n == v$. It is clear to see that only when the last location of the current visiting path ρ is the target location, the DFS procedure will call the underlying decision procedure to translate the feasibility of ρ into a linear constraint set and verify it by LP. Otherwise, the DFS will just go on traversing on the graph structure. Thus, the number of paths need to be checked can be reduced significantly to raise the efficiency. Again. let's take the automaton given in Fig.1 for example. Under Lazy-DFS, there are only 5 paths need to call the underlying decision procedure to check, e.g., $\langle v_1 \rangle \xrightarrow{e_1} \langle v_2 \rangle \xrightarrow{e_2} \langle v_3 \rangle \xrightarrow{e_3} \langle v_4 \rangle \xrightarrow{e_4} \langle v_5 \rangle \xrightarrow{e_5} \langle v_6 \rangle$, $\langle v_1 \rangle \xrightarrow{e_8} \langle v_5 \rangle \xrightarrow{e_5} \langle v_6 \rangle$ and so on.

Table 2. Lazy-DFS Based on Target Location-Guided Checking

TRAVERSE (*stack s*)

1 . Get the ongoing path $\rho = \langle v_0 \rangle \xrightarrow[\sigma_0]{(\phi_0, \psi_0)} \langle v_1 \rangle \xrightarrow[\sigma_1]{(\phi_1, \psi_1)} \ldots \xrightarrow[\sigma_{n-1}]{(\phi_{n-1}, \psi_{n-1})} \langle v_n \rangle$ from stack s;

2 . **if**($v_n == v$)

3 . **begin**

4 .   check the feasibility of ρ;

5 .   **if** (feasible) **return** 1 **else return** 0;

6 . **end**

7 . **if** (($s.depth == bound$)‖(v_n doesn't have any successive location)) **return** 0;

8 . **for** each successive location *sloc* of v_n

9 . **begin**

10.   s.push(*sloc*);

11.   int res=TRAVERSE(s);

12.   if (res==1) **return** res;

13.   s.pop(*sloc*);

14. **end**

15. **return** 0;

3.2 IIS-Based Infeasible Constraint Locating and Backtracking

In general, by only checking the paths which are specification related, the times of calling the underlying LP solver can be reduced greatly. But it is not always the case. Still take the automaton given in Fig.1 for example. Based on the Lazy-DFS algorithm given in Table.2, when checking the automaton according to target location v_6, the first path that the algorithm will call the underlying decision procedure is: $\rho = \langle v_1 \rangle \xrightarrow{e_1}$ $\langle v_2 \rangle \xrightarrow{e_2} \langle v_3 \rangle \xrightarrow{e_3} \langle v_4 \rangle \xrightarrow{e_4} \langle v_5 \rangle \xrightarrow{e_5} \langle v_6 \rangle$. Suppose it is proved that ρ is not feasible by calling the underlying LP solver, the algorithm will pop out the last location v_6 from the stack and visit the next branch from v_5. Suppose the path segment $\rho'' = \langle v_1 \rangle \xrightarrow{e_1} \langle v_2 \rangle \xrightarrow{e_2}$ $\langle v_3 \rangle \xrightarrow{e_3} \langle v_4 \rangle$ is already infeasible, as ρ'' is not related with the reachability target, under Lazy-DFS the feasibility of ρ'' will not be checked at all. But, if the algorithm deployed is the Eager-DFS which checks all the path segments as shown in Table.1, the feasibility of ρ'' will be checked right after location v_4 is added into the ongoing path. Once ρ'' is proved to be infeasible, then a backtracking will be conducted immediately, which means the subtree starting from location v_4 with prefix as ρ'' will not be traversed in Eager-DFS at all. But, in the Lazy-DFS algorithm, this subtree will still be traversed. So, is there a method which can reduce the times of solving LP problems as proposed by Lazy-DFS and also backtrack to the exact place where infeasibility happened to prune the behavior tree as Eager-DFS? The answer is yes!

Now, let's come back to the automaton given in Fig.1, in location v_3 we have $\dot{x} = 2$, $\dot{y} = 1$ and $x < 5$. According to definition 2, in the related constraint set $\mathbb{R}$, there are accordingly constrains: $\delta_{v_3} > 0$, $\zeta_{v_3}(x) - \lambda_{v_3}(x) = 2\delta_{v_3}$, $\zeta_{v_3}(y) - \lambda_{v_3}(y) = \delta_{v_3}$, $\zeta_{v_3}(x) < 5$, where $\lambda_{v_3}(x) = \lambda_{v_3}(y) = 1$ as x and y are reset to 1 on transition e_2. On transition e_3, there is guard $x > 3$. In location v_4, there is invariant $y > 4$. Therefore, we also have constraints $\zeta_{v_3}(x) > 3$ and $\zeta_{v_3}(y) > 4$ in $\mathbb{R}$. If we name this set of constraints as $\mathbb{R}_{\rho'}$, clearly it is unsatisfiable. As $\zeta_{v_3}(x) < 5$, $\zeta_{v_3}(x) > 3$, and $\zeta_{v_3}(x) - 1 = 2\delta_{v_3}$, we can get $1 < \delta_{v_3} < 2$. Because $\zeta_{v_3}(y) - 1 = \delta_{v_3}$, we can get $2 < \zeta_{v_3}(y) < 3$, which contradicts with $\zeta_{v_3}(y) > 4$. As these constraints are generated according to the invariants and guards from transition e_2, e_3, and location v_3, v_4, this implies the path segment $\langle v_2 \rangle \xrightarrow[e_2]{}$ $\langle v_3 \rangle \xrightarrow[e_3]{} \langle v_4 \rangle$ is infeasible, but $\langle v_2 \rangle \xrightarrow[e_2]{} \langle v_3 \rangle$ is an feasible one. Therefore, if the DFS algorithm is clever enough, it will backtrack to the location v_3 and traverse the next branch $\langle v_3 \rangle \xrightarrow[e_9]{} \langle v_1 \rangle$. So, now the problem is how to locate such a backtracking point?

The answer is the irreducible infeasible set (IIS) technique[12]. Generally speaking, a set of linear constraints $\mathbb{R}$ is said to be satisfiable, if there exists a valuation of all the variables which makes all the constraints in $\mathbb{R}$ to be true. Otherwise, $\mathbb{R}$ is unsatisfiable. If $\mathbb{R}$ is unsatisfiable, then IIS of $\mathbb{R}$ is a subset $\mathbb{R}' \subseteq \mathbb{R}$ that $\mathbb{R}'$ is unsatisfiable and for any $\mathbb{R}'' \subset \mathbb{R}'$, $\mathbb{R}''$ is satisfiable.

Intuitively speaking, the IIS of a linear constraint set is an unsatisfiable set of constraints that becomes satisfiable if any constraint is removed. Fortunately, quoted from[12], the algorithm to locate the IIS from a unsatisfiable set is "simple, relatively efficient and easily incorporation into standard LP solvers". Actually many software packages are available which supports the efficient analysis of a linear constraint set and locating of the minimal IIS, such as MINOS[16], IBM CPLEX[17] and LINDO[18]. Therefore, given an infeasible path ρ, we can simply analyze the constraint set $\mathbb{R}$ generated according to this path to locate the IIS $\mathbb{R}'$. Now, if there is a mapping function to map each constraint $\nabla \in \mathbb{R}'$ to the original elements in the path, we can manipulate the structure of the bounded depth behavior tree more efficiently.

Definition 6. Given LHA $H = (X, \Sigma, V, V^0, E, \alpha, \beta, \gamma)$, path $\rho = \langle v_0 \rangle \xrightarrow[\sigma_0]{(\phi_0, \psi_0)} \langle v_1 \rangle \xrightarrow[\sigma_1]{(\phi_1, \psi_1)}$ $\ldots \xrightarrow[\sigma_{n-1}]{(\phi_{n-1}, \psi_{n-1})} \langle v_n \rangle$, and linear constraint set $\mathbb{R}$ which is generated according to the feasibility of ρ. For constraint $\nabla \in \mathbb{R}$, the stem location set $\mathbb{V}_\nabla$ of ∇ in ρ is defined as follows:

- if ∇ is generated according to the time duration on location v_i ($0 \leq i \leq n$), $\delta_{v_i} \geq 0$, $v_i \in \mathbb{V}_\nabla$;
- if ∇ is generated according to the transition guard in ϕ_i on transition e_i ($0 \leq i \leq n - 1$), $v_{i+1} \in \mathbb{V}_\nabla$. If $i > 0$, $v_{i-1} \in \mathbb{V}_\nabla$ as well;
- if ∇ is generated according to the reset action in ψ_i on transition e_i ($0 \leq i \leq n - 1$), $v_{i+1} \in \mathbb{V}_\nabla$. If $i > 0$, $v_{i-1} \in \mathbb{V}_\nabla$ as well;
- if ∇ is generated according to the flow conditions in β_{v_i} location v_i ($0 \leq i \leq n$), $v_i \in \mathbb{V}_\nabla$. If $i > 0$, $v_{i+1} \in \mathbb{V}_\nabla$ as well;
- if ∇ is generated according to the invariants in α_{v_i} in location v_i ($0 \leq i \leq n$);
    - if ∇ is generated according to $\zeta_i(x)$, $v_i \in \mathbb{V}_\nabla$
    - if ∇ is generated according to $\lambda_i(x)$, $v_i \in \mathbb{V}_\nabla$, if $i > 0$, $v_{i-1} \in \mathbb{V}_\nabla$ as well. □

Definition 7. Given LHA $H = (X, \Sigma, V, V^0, E, \alpha, \beta, \gamma)$, path $\rho = \langle v_0 \rangle \xrightarrow[\sigma_0]{(\phi_0, \psi_0)} \langle v_1 \rangle \xrightarrow[\sigma_1]{(\phi_1, \psi_1)}$ $\ldots \xrightarrow[\sigma_{n-1}]{(\phi_{n-1}, \psi_{n-1})} \langle v_n \rangle$ and linear constraint set $\mathbb{R}$ which is generated according to the feasibility of ρ. For a set $\mathbb{R}' = \{\nabla_1, \nabla_2, \ldots, \nabla_m\} \subseteq \mathbb{R}$, the stem location set of $\mathbb{R}'$ is $V_{\mathbb{R}'} = V_{\nabla_1} \cup V_{\nabla_2} \cup \cdots \cup V_{\nabla_m}$.   □

Basically speaking, given a path ρ and the linear constraint $\mathbb{R}_\rho$, the above two definitions mark each constraints ϕ in $\mathbb{R}_\rho$ according to a location v in ρ. This means, ϕ will not be added into $\mathbb{R}_\rho$ until ρ travels to location v. Now, let's review the constraint set $\mathbb{R}_{\rho'}$ given in the beginning of this section again. $\mathbb{R}_{\rho'} = \{\delta_{v_3} > 0, \zeta_{v_3}(x) - \lambda_{v_3}(x) = 2\delta_{v_3}, \zeta_{v_3}(y) - \lambda_{v_3}(y) = \delta_{v_3}, \lambda_{v_3}(x) = 1, \lambda_{v_3}(y) = 1, \zeta_{v_3}(x) < 5, \zeta_{v_3}(x) > 3, \zeta_{v_3}(y) > 3\}$. Clearly the stem location set of $\mathbb{R}_{\rho'}$ is $V = \{v_2, v_3, v_4\}$.

Suppose $\mathbb{R}_{\rho'}$ is the only IIS in the constraint set of path $\rho = \langle v_1 \rangle \xrightarrow{e_1} \langle v_2 \rangle \xrightarrow{e_2} \langle v_3 \rangle \xrightarrow{e_3} \langle v_4 \rangle \xrightarrow{e_4} \langle v_5 \rangle \xrightarrow{e_5} \langle v_6 \rangle$, because if any constraint in $\mathbb{R}_{\rho'}$ is removed, the new constraint set is satisfiable. Then, it clearly implies that the path segment before reaching the location with the biggest index in the stem location set of $\mathbb{R}_{\rho'}$, which is v_4 in ρ, is feasible. So the sub tree starting from v_4 after $\langle v_1 \rangle \xrightarrow{e_1} \langle v_2 \rangle \xrightarrow{e_2} \langle v_3 \rangle$ doesn't need to be traversed.

Furthermore, as mentioned above, the constraint set that IIS technique located can be mapped back to a path segments ρ' in the path ρ. This path segment can be saved as a guideline for the future traversing, once a new traversed path ρ'' contains an exact path segment as ρ', we can simply falsify ρ'' for verification without call the underlying decision procedure, since the syntax elements in ρ' has already been proved to be infeasible in ρ, the occurrence of ρ' in ρ'' will just be translated into the same set of unsatisfiable constraints with just variable name changed.

Based on the above discussion, the optimized function TRAVERSE (*stack*) is given below in Table.3. A new function IIS (*stack*) is introduced in Table.3 as well. This function finds the IIS in the constraint set according to the ongoing path $\langle v_0 \rangle \xrightarrow[\sigma_0]{(\phi_0, \psi_0)} \langle v_1 \rangle \xrightarrow[\sigma_1]{(\phi_1, \psi_1)} \ldots \xrightarrow[\sigma_{m-1}]{(\phi_{m-1}, \psi_{m-1})} \langle v_m \rangle$ at first, then locates the stem location set from the IIS constraint set. By locating the node v_k in the set with the largest index, this function will inform the upper caller to backtrack to location v_{k-1} by indicating the distance between v_{k-1} and v_m.

Furthermore, once a path segment ρ' is located in the IIS, ρ' will be added into a global vector Ω as "bad examples". Then in the Traverse function, once a path is found to be specification related, the algorithm will check whether this path contains any "bad example". If any of the bad examples is hit, the Traverse function will directly return the backtracking step to the upper caller[1].

Based on the algorithm given in Table.3, once a path ρ is proved to be infeasible, an IIS based method will be called to locate the path segment which makes ρ infeasible. Then the DFS algorithm can backtrack to the right position to prune the bounded behavior tree efficiently. Besides that, the path segment will be saved to falsify the other new generated paths under checking to save the computation time.

---

[1] Generally speaking, the mapping with bad examples can be preformed once a new location is added to the path, but the matching will be time consuming if the size of example set is huge, so we decide to be lazy again to postpone the matching until the target is found.

Table 3. IIS-DFS Based On Infeasible Path Segment Localization

---

TRAVERSE (*stack s*)

1. Get the ongoing path $\rho = \langle v_0 \rangle \xrightarrow[\sigma_0]{(\phi_0,\psi_0)} \langle v_1 \rangle \xrightarrow[\sigma_1]{(\phi_1,\psi_1)} \ldots \xrightarrow[\sigma_{n-1}]{(\phi_{n-1},\psi_{n-1})} \langle v_n \rangle$ from stack s;

2. **if**($v_n == v$)
3. **begin**
4.   **if** ($\exists \omega \in \Omega$ && ω is a path segment in ρ)
5.   locate ω in ρ as $\rho_\omega = \langle v_i \rangle \xrightarrow[\sigma_i]{(\phi_i,\psi_i)} \langle v_{i+1} \rangle \xrightarrow[\sigma_{i+1}]{(\phi_{i+1},\psi_{i+1})} \ldots \xrightarrow[\sigma_{j-1}]{(\phi_{j-1},\psi_{j-1})} \langle v_j \rangle$;
6.   **return** j-n;
7.   check the feasibility of ρ;
8.   **if** (unfeasible)
9.   **return** IIS(s);
10. **end**
11. **if** ((*s.depth == bound*)$\|$(v_n doesn't have any successive location)) **return** 0;
12. **for** each successive location *sloc* of v_n
13. **begin**
14.   s.push(*sloc*);
15.   int res=TRAVERSE(s);
16.   if (res==1) **return** res;
17.   s.pop(*sloc*);
18.   if (res < 0) **return** res+1;
19. **end**
20. **return** 0;

IIS (*stack s*)

1. Get the ongoing path $\rho = \langle v_0 \rangle \xrightarrow[\sigma_0]{(\phi_0,\psi_0)} \langle v_1 \rangle \xrightarrow[\sigma_1]{(\phi_1,\psi_1)} \ldots \xrightarrow[\sigma_{m-1}]{(\phi_{m-1},\psi_{m-1})} \langle v_m \rangle$ from stack s;

2. Locate the stem location set $\mathbb{V}_\rho$ and the accordingly path segment ρ' of ρ;
3. Ω.add(ρ');
4. Get the location v_k in $\mathbb{V}_\rho$ with the largest index;
5. return k-m;

---

4   Case Studies

In order to evaluate the performance of the optimization methods presented in this paper, we upgrade our bounded reachability checker for LHA: BACH[9, 14] to a new version BACH 3 (http://seg.nju.edu.cn/BACH/). BACH 3 shares the graphical LHA Editor with BACH. As the LP solver underlying BACH is OR-objects[15] which does not support the functionality of IIS analysis. BACH 3 calls the IBM CPLEX[17] instead, which gives a nice support of IIS analysis.

In the experiments, we evaluate the performance of BACH 3 under three different settings according to the underlying DFS algorithm, which are Eager-DFS, Lazy-DFS and IIS-DFS respectively. The experiments are conducted on a DELL workstation (Intel Core2 Quad CPU 2.4GHz, 4GB RAM).

As the comparisons between Eager-DFS and other related tools are already reported in[9], in this section, we focus on the comparison between the three different DFS algorithms to show the performance of the optimization methods presented in this paper.

We use three benchmarks in the experiments. The first LHA is the sample automaton given in Fig.1 in this paper. The second one is the temperature control system used in our previous case studies in[9]. The third automaton is the automated highway example introduced in[19] with 5 cars included. These automata are shown in Fig.3. For the sample automaton, we are checking whether location v_6 is reachable. In the other two automata, the reachability of the target location under checking is v_4 for temperature control system, which stands for that no rod is available in the nuclear reactor; and v_6 for the automated highway which stands for that a car collision will happen.

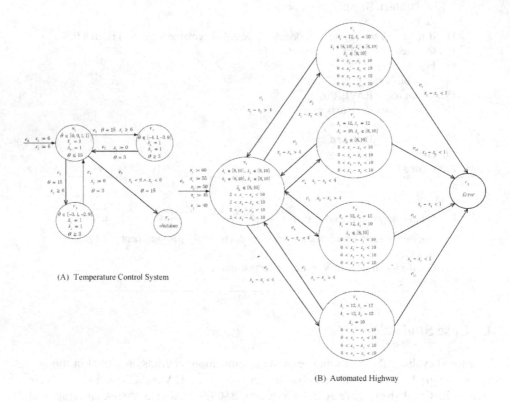

(A) Temperature Control System

(B) Automated Highway

Fig. 3. Experimental Automata

We conduct these three DFS algorithms on all of these three automata. The time limit is set as 2 hours in the experiments. The performance data for each benchmark are shown in Table.4,5,and 6 respectively. In these tables we show the total time spent for each problem w.r.t different bound size. Furthermore, in order to show the performance of the optimization techniques in decreasing the number of paths to check, we also collect and report the times BACH 3 calls the underlying LP solver -CPLEX, each call means a unique path is transformed into an LP constraint set and solved by CPLEX. To demonstrate these data more intuitively, we also show the plotted graphs in Fig.4.

Table 4. Performance Data On The Sample Automaton In 2 Hours

Tech. Bound	Eager-DFS		Lazy-DFS		IIS-DFS	
	Total Time (Sec.)	Call CPLEX	Total Time (Sec.)	Call CPLEX	Total Time (Sec.)	Call CPLEX
10	0.252	51	0.063	17	0.046	2
20	7.111	431	1.487	853	0.124	2
30	98.354	3223	44.610	46037	0.343	2
40	1036.987	23743	2784.989	2544981	1.322	2
50	N/A	N/A	N/A	N/A	10.729	2
70	N/A	N/A	N/A	N/A	1040.308	2

Table 5. Performance Data On The Temperature Control System Benchmark In 2 Hours

Tech. Bound	Eager-DFS		Lazy-DFS		IIS-DFS	
	Total Time (Sec.)	Call CPLEX	Total Time (Sec.)	Call CPLEX	Total Time (Sec.)	Call CPLEX
5	0.062	16	0.022	3	0.075	3
15	1.595	636	0.58	127	0.595	23
25	46.004	20476	9.669	4095	1.77	43
35	2256.519	655356	386.743	131071	19.867	63
40	N/A	N/A	3389.555	1048575	141.046	75
50	N/A	N/A	N/A	N/A	6470.308	95

Table 6. Performance Data On The Automated Highway System Benchmark In 2 Hours

Tech. Bound	Eager-DFS		Lazy-DFS		IIS-DFS	
	Total Time (Sec.)	Call CPLEX	Total Time (Sec.)	Call CPLEX	Total Time (Sec.)	Call CPLEX
5	1.115	61	0.113	20	0.383	20
10	27.877	2045	1.328	340	0.656	20
15	822.996	65533	79.611	21844	1.647	20
20	N/A	N/A	1689.658	349524	28.225	20
25	N/A	N/A	N/A	N/A	1242.241	20

We can see that with any of the optimizations deployed, the size of the problem that can be solved are increased significantly and the performance for the same question are clearly optimized. Furthermore, IIS-DFS outperforms Lazy-DFS substantially. Take the automated highway system as example, when bound is set as 15, it cost Eager-DFS 822.9 seconds to check 65533 paths. By using Lazy-DFS, the verification time is decreased to 79.6 seconds by only checking 21844 paths. Finally, when use IIS-DFS, the verification is finished in only 1.6 seconds, and only 20 paths are verified.

The reason is that in our DFS schema, each time a candidate path is found, the algorithm will call the underlying LP solver to reason the feasibility of the path. When the size of path and/or the number of candidate paths is large, the reasoning by LP will be very time consuming. By using optimization techniques presented in this paper, the number of paths need to check is reduced significantly, thus, it is possible to solve problem more quickly and to solve larger problems. In detail:

- By introducing Lazy-DFS, the number of candidate paths to check can be reduced in most of the cases, that's the reason that Lazy-DFS outperforms Eager-DFS.

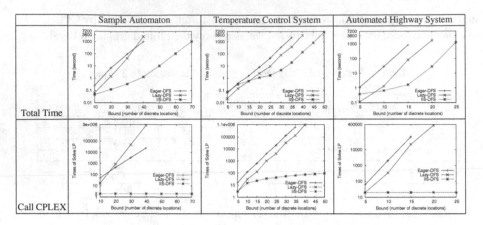

Fig. 4. Performance of Bounded Reachability Analysis in 2 Hours

- By introducing IIS-DFS, when a path is infeasible, IIS can locate the exact path segment where the infeasibility happens to guide the backtracking. Besides this, the infeasible path segment can be saved as a "bad example" that if any future candidate path has a same path segments as the "bad example", the candidate path can be falsified for the feasibility reasoning without call the underlying LP solver. That's the reason that IIS-DFS outperforms Lazy-DFS in almost all the experiments.
- Indeed, if a candidate path can be matched with a "bad example", then it can be falsified directly without call the underlying LP solver to save computation time. Nevertheless, when the size of the candidate path set is huge, the comparison between each of the candidate path and the "bad example" set will also be very time consuming, that's the reason that as shown in our data, the total time spent is not proportional to the times of calling CPLEX.

5 Conclusion

The bounded reachability analysis of hybrid automata is difficult. Even for the simple class of linear hybrid automata (LHA), the state-of-the-art tools can only analyze systems with few continuous variables, control nodes and small bound.

In this paper, we present an algorithm to check the bounded reachability of LHA in a DFS manner. Only the abstract path related with the reachability specification will be analyzed by the underlying LP solver. If the path is judged to be infeasible, the IIS technique will be deployed on the infeasible path to locate the path segment which makes this path infeasible to guide the backtracking of the DFS.

We implement the optimization techniques presented in this paper into BACH which is a bounded reachability checker for LHA. The experiments on BACH greatly strengthen our belief that with the help of the optimization methods presented in this paper, the size of the problem that BACH can solve is increased substantially while the time for solving the same problem is reduced significantly as well.

Acknowledgement. The authors are supported by the National 863 High-Tech Programme of China (No.2011AA010103), the National Natural Science Foundation of China (No.90818022, No.61100036) and by the Jiangsu Province Research Foundation (BK2011558).

References

1. Henzinger, T.A.: The theory of hybrid automata. In: Proceedings of LICS 1996, pp. 278–292. IEEE Computer Society (1996)
2. Henzinger, T.A., Kopke, P.W., Puri, A., Varaiya, P.: What's Decidable About Hybrid Automata? Journal of Computer and System Sciences 57, 94–124 (1998)
3. Henzinger, T.A., Ho, P.-H., Wong-Toi, H.: Algorithmic Analysis of Nonlinear Hybrid Systems. IEEE Transactions on Automatic Control, 540–554 (1998)
4. Alur, R., Courcoubetis, C., Halbwachs, N., Henzinger, T.A., Ho, P.-H., Nicollin, X., Olivero, A., Sifakis, J., Yovine, S.: The algorithmic analysis of hybrid systems. Theoretical Computer Science 138, 3–34 (1995)
5. Biere, A., Cimatti, A., Clarke, E., Strichman, O., Zhu, Y.: Bounded Model Checking. In: Advance in Computers, vol. 58, pp. 118–149. Academic Press (2003)
6. Fränzle, M., Herde, C., Ratschan, S., Schubert, T., Teige, T.: Efficient solving of large nonlinear arithmetic constraint systems with complex boolean structure. Journal on Satisfiability, Boolean Modeling and Computation 1, 209–236 (2007)
7. Audemard, G., Bozzano, M., Cimatti, A., Sebastiani, R.: Verifying Industrial Hybrid Systems with MathSAT. In: Proceedings of BMC 2004, ENTCS, vol. 119(2), pp. 17–32. Elsevier Science (2005)
8. Li, X., Jha, S.K., Bu, L.: Towards an Efficient Path-Oriented Tool for Bounded Reachability Analysis of Linear Hybrid Systems using Linear Programming. In: Proceedings of BMC 2006, ENTCS, vol. 174(3), pp. 57–70. Elsevier Science, 07 (2006)
9. Bu, L., Li, Y., Wang, L., Li, X.: BACH: Bounded Reachability Checker for Linear Hybrid Automata. In: Proceedings of the 8th International Conference on Formal Methods in Computer Aided Design, pp. 65–68. IEEE Computer Society (2008)
10. Henzinger, T.A., Ho, P.-H., Wong-Toi, H.: HYTECH: a model checker for hybrid systems. Software Tools for Technology Transfer 1, 110–122 (1997)
11. Frehse, G.: PHAVer: Algorithmic Verification of Hybrid Systems Past HyTech. In: Morari, M., Thiele, L. (eds.) HSCC 2005. LNCS, vol. 3414, pp. 258–273. Springer, Heidelberg (2005)
12. Chinneck, J., Dravnieks, E.: Locating minimal infeasible constraint sets in linear programs. ORSA Journal on Computing 3, 157–168 (1991)
13. Bu, L., Li, X.: Path-Oriented Bounded Reachability Analysis of Composed Linear Hybrid Systems. Software Tools Technology Transfer 13(4), 307–317 (2011)
14. Bu, L., Li, Y., Wang, L., Chen, X., Li, X.: BACH 2: Bounded ReachAbility CHecker for Compositional Linear Hybrid Systems. In: Proceedings of the 13th Design Automation & Test in Europe Conference, Dresden, Germany, pp. 1512–1517 (2010)
15. OR-Objects, http://OpsResearch.com/OR-Objects/index.html
16. Chinneck, J.: MINOS(IIS): Infeasibility analysis using MINOS. Computers and Operations Research 21(1), 1–9 (1994)
17. CPLEX, http://www-01.ibm.com/software/integration/optimization/cplex-optimizer/
18. L. Systems Inc., http://www.lindo.com/products/api/dllm.html
19. Jha, S., Krogh, B.H., Weimer, J.E., Clarke, E.M.: Reachability for Linear Hybrid Automata Using Iterative Relaxation Abstraction. In: Bemporad, A., Bicchi, A., Buttazzo, G. (eds.) HSCC 2007. LNCS, vol. 4416, pp. 287–300. Springer, Heidelberg (2007)

Cube and Conquer:
Guiding CDCL SAT Solvers by Lookaheads[*]

Marijn J.H. Heule[1,2], Oliver Kullmann[3], Siert Wieringa[4], and Armin Biere[2]

[1] Delft University of Technology, The Netherlands
[2] Johannes Kepler University Linz, Austria
[3] Swansea University, United Kingdom
[4] Aalto University Helsinki, Finland

Abstract. Satisfiability (SAT) is considered as one of the most important core technologies in formal verification and related areas. Even though there is steady progress in improving practical SAT solving, there are limits on scalability of SAT solvers. We address this issue and present a new approach, called *cube-and-conquer*, targeted at reducing solving time on hard instances. This two-phase approach partitions a problem into many thousands (or millions) of cubes using lookahead techniques. Afterwards, a conflict-driven solver tackles the problem, using the cubes to guide the search. On several hard competition benchmarks, our hybrid approach outperforms both lookahead and conflict-driven solvers. Moreover, because *cube-and-conquer* is natural to parallelize, it is a competitive alternative for solving SAT problems in parallel.

1 Introduction

Satisfiability (SAT) solvers have become very powerful tools to tackle problems ranging from industrial formal verification [4] to hard combinatorial challenges [27]. The most successful tools are known as *conflict-driven clause learning* (CDCL) solvers [24]. These solvers have data-structures optimized for huge instances and focus reasoning on learning new clauses from emerging conflicts. Although there exist several approaches to parallelize CDCL solvers [10], it appears hard to significantly improve performance on most industrial problems.

On the other hand, *lookahead* solvers [14] focus on small hard problems which require sophisticated heuristics to solve them efficiently. These solvers can be parallelized naturally and effectively. Yet, even with many cores at hand, they cannot compete with single core CDCL solvers on industrial problems.

While developing a method for computing van der Waerden numbers, Kullmann observed that CDCL and lookahead solvers can be interleaved in such a way that the combination outperforms both pure methods. In short, lookahead is used to assign a certain fraction of the variables, and afterwards CDCL tackles the reduced problem. For optimal performance the lookahead solver partitions the original problem into thousands (sometimes millions) of cubes. The CDCL solver iteratively assumes each cube to be true and solves the simplified instance.

In order to apply this method, called *cube-and-conquer*, on a large spectrum of problems, we present a mechanism that determines dynamically when to cut

---

[*] The first and the fourth author are supported by the Austrian Science Foundation (FWF) NFN Grant S11408-N23 (RiSE). The third author is supported by Academy of Finland project 139402.

K. Eder, J. Lourenço, and O. Shehory (Eds.): HVC 2011, LNCS 7261, pp. 50–65, 2012.
© Springer-Verlag Berlin Heidelberg 2012

off a branch in the search-tree of a lookahead solver to send it to a CDCL solver. Using this mechanism, several hard industrial problems can be solved more efficiently using the combination of solvers than with a stand-alone SAT solver. Additionally, the combined solving method can be parallelized naturally as well. Therefore, using a parallel implementation of our method, we are able to solve some hard instances faster than alternative methods.

Our approach is based on the following intuition. Obviously the reduced formulas, after applying some decisions, become easier to solve. Furthermore, at least empirically, CDCL solvers are effective on solving instances which are rather easy for their size, utilizing *local* heuristics including those based on variable activities. On the other hand, lookahead solvers are considered to be better at picking good decisions at the top-level, by using more global heuristics. There has to be a transition between hard and easy subproblems. So we try to switch from lookahead to CDCL solving when the subproblem seems to become easy.

The outline of this paper is as follows. After some preliminaries in Section 2, an overview of the cube-and-conquer method is provided in Section 3 as well as a description of both solver types. Section 4, discussing the above application to Ramsey theory, offers a motivating study of the method. Then a general methodology is developed. The details of the first phase, the "cube"-phase (partitioning the problem) are discussed in Section 5, and the details of the second phase, the "conquer"-phase (solving the sub-problems) in Section 6. Experimental results are presented in Section 7 and some conclusions are drawn in Section 8.

2 Preliminaries

For a Boolean variable x, there are two *literals*, the positive literal, denoted by x, and the negative literal, denoted by $\neg x$. A *clause* is a disjunction of literals, and a *CNF formula* is a conjunction of clauses. A clause can be seen as a finite set of literals, and a CNF formula as a finite set of clauses. A *unit clause* contains exactly one literal. A truth assignment for a CNF formula F is a function φ that maps variables in F to $\{\mathbf{t}, \mathbf{f}\}$. If $\varphi(x) = v$, then $\varphi(\neg x) = \neg v$, where $\neg \mathbf{t} = \mathbf{f}$ and $\neg \mathbf{f} = \mathbf{t}$. A clause C is satisfied by φ if $\varphi(l) = \mathbf{t}$ for some $l \in C$. An assignment φ satisfies F if it satisfies every clause in F. A *cube* is a conjunction of literals and a *DNF formula* a disjunction of cubes. A cube can be seen as a finite set of literals and a DNF formula as a finite set of cubes. If $c = (l_1 \wedge \ldots \wedge l_k)$ is a cube, then $\neg c = (\neg l_1 \vee \ldots \vee \neg l_k)$ is a clause. A truth assignment φ can be seen as the cube of literals l for which $\varphi(l) = \mathbf{t}$. A cube c is satisfied by φ if $\varphi(l) = \mathbf{t}$ for all $l \in c$. An assignment φ satisfies DNF formula D if it satisfies some cube in D. A DNF formula D is called a *tautology* if every full assignment φ satisfies D. For a CNF formula F, *Boolean constraint propagation* (BCP) (or *unit propagation*) propagates all unit clauses, i.e., repeats the following until fix-point: if there is a unit clause $(l) \in F$, remove from $F \setminus \{(l)\}$ all clauses that contain the literal l, and remove the literal $\neg l$ from all clauses in F. The resulting formula is referred to as BCP(F). If $\emptyset \in$ BCP(F), we say that BCP derives a conflict.

3 Combining CDCL and Lookahead

The main complete SAT solver types are *conflict-driven clause learning* (CDCL) solvers [24] and *lookahead* solvers [14]. In short, CDCL solvers are optimized for

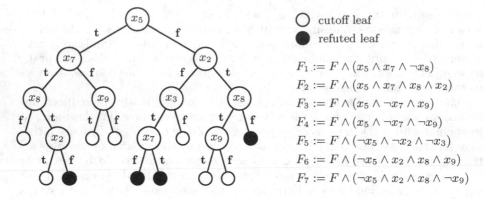

Fig. 1. A partition of a CNF formula F into seven subformulas F_i. The binary search tree on the left is constructed by a lookahead solver. It shows in the internal nodes the decision variable, and on the edges the truth value of a branch. Black leaves represent refuted leaves, while white leaves are cutoff leafs. The decisions of cutoff leaves yield a cube of assumptions that together with F forms a subformula F_i.

large industrial problems and consequently use inexpensive decision heuristics. In contrast, lookahead solvers focus on small hard problems on which it pays off to compute sophisticated decision heuristics. This section describes the main features of these solvers, and how we want to combine both types.

Overview. The central approach in this paper deals with a lookahead solver that partitions a formula into many subformulas which in turn are solved by a CDCL solver. The sophisticated decision heuristics of lookahead solvers are used to compute important decision variables. These decisions are provided to the CDCL solver to guide the search process.

Figure 1 illustrates this approach by an example. The left shows a binary search tree produced by a lookahead solver. Internal nodes contain a decision variable. On the edges the truth value is shown to which a decision variable is set to reach a child node. There are two possible leaf nodes. Either the lookahead solver refuted the branch because a conflict emerged, or the *cutoff heuristic* suggests that this branch should be solved by a CDCL solver. This heuristic (discussed in detail in Section 5) is crucial for the effectiveness of the approach.

The cutoff branches can be described as a cube of the decisions on the path to the leaf. A CDCL solver can solve the branch by either adding the decisions as unit clauses, or by adding them as *assumptions* (see the Incremental SAT solving paragraph below). In case one of the branches is satisfiable, the original formula is satisfiable (and hence remaining branches could be neglected). If all cutoff branches are unsatisfiable, the original formula is unsatisfiable.

The use of lookahead heuristics to partition a formula have been proposed by Hyvärinen *et al.* [15]. In [15] formulas are partitioned into dozens of subformulas which are distributed on a grid to be solved in parallel. The starting point of this paper is now the discovery, discussed in Section 4, that some hard combinatorial problems can be efficiently solved by partitioning them into many thousands of subformulas (millions for harder problems). Inspired by these results we focus on the latter approach. We also use more sophisticated lookahead techniques as employed in state-of-the-art lookahead solvers.

Lookahead Solvers. Since CDCL is currently the dominant approach in practical SAT solving, we assume the reader already knows how CDCL solvers work, and otherwise refer to [24] for more details.

Lookahead solvers combine the David-Putnam-Logemann-Loveland (DPLL) algorithm [7] with *lookaheads*; for a general discussion see [14,19], while we describe here an exemplary scheme. Given a CNF formula F, a lookahead on literal x works as follows: First, x is assigned to t, followed by BCP. Second, in case there was no conflict, the difference between F and the reduced formula F' is measured. The quality of lookahead techniques depends heavily on the used measurement. A frequently used method weighs the clauses in $F' \setminus F$ (the ones that are reduced but not satisfied). Third, all simplifications are reversed to get back to F. If a conflict was detected during the lookahead, then x is forced to f and is called a *failed literal*. The measurements are used to determine the decision variable in each node of the search tree. In general a variable x is chosen for which both the lookahead on x and $\neg x$ result in a large reduction of the formula. We remark that this scheme combines reduction (elimination of failed literals) and lookahead (estimating the quality of a branch by considering its development in the future), while in general these processes can be different.

State-of-the-art lookahead solvers are kcnfs [8], march [25], OKsolver [18], and satz [23]. These solvers show strong performances on hard random k-SAT formulas, but they cannot compete with CDCL solvers on large industrial instances. Apart from random instances, lookahead techniques are also useful for combinatorial problems; these problems have some form of structure to be exploited, and yield relatively small but typically very hard SAT problems.

While measuring the reduction of the formula F, most lookahead solvers also perform *local learning*. In contrast to the learning in CDCL solvers, local learning computes clauses (mostly unary and binary) that can be added to the formula for further reduction, but that have to be removed again during backtracking to the parent node in the search tree. An example of local learning is hyper binary resolution [2]. Current state-of-the-art lookahead solvers do not implement conflict clause learning as in CDCL solvers, and mostly not even backjumping (except of the OKsolver). For an overview of local learning we refer to [14].

Incremental SAT Solving. A frequently used feature of CDCL solvers is *incremental SAT solving* [9]. The solver provides an interface to (i) add clauses to the formula and (ii) to solve the formula under a cube of assumptions (decisions at level 0). Both techniques are very useful for tools that integrate SAT solvers. The input of an incremental solver can be seen as a sequence consisting of both clauses and cubes, where each cube defines a *job* which is the conjunction of that cube and all clauses preceding it in the sequence. In the context of cube-and-conquer we solve one formula under a set of cubes, thus all clauses precede all cubes in the solver input. A useful feature of incremental SAT solvers is that if a formula has no solutions under a given cube c, then the solver returns a subset $c' \subseteq c$ that was required to prove unsatisfiability. The clause $\neg c'$ can then be added to the formula to improve performance on other cubes.

As an example of the above, let us return to Figure 1. Now, consider a CDCL solver solving F_2, which is F assuming cube $(x_5 \wedge x_7 \wedge x_8 \wedge x_2)$. If however actually only $(x_8 \wedge x_2)$ is required to proof unsatisfiability, then we can add $(\neg x_8 \vee \neg x_2)$ to the formula. This binary clause is conflicting with F_6 and F_7, so by adding it, these cubes are immediately refuted.

4   Creating Cubes: The Basic Method

In this section we describe cube-and-conquer in its simplest form, as it came out of investigations into van-der-Waerden-like numbers ([21,1,22]). The principle aim is to solve extremely hard instances, which would take many years on a single machine. Thus a natural splitting of the problem into sub-problems is applied, and since lookahead solvers are competitive on these instances, it is natural to use lookahead for this task. The great surprise now is that on these (easy) sub-problems, conflict-driven solvers are very fast, and via this collaboration a *total speed-up* (regarding the *total running time*) of at least a factor of two (compared always to the best single solver available) is achieved. So even on a single machine the problems are solved at least twice as fast, and additionally the splitting is ideal for parallelization (via clusters for example; no communication is needed between the processes). This was the birth of "cube-and-conquer". The lookahead solver is the OKsolver, which participated successfully at the SAT 2002 competition and aims at being as "theoretically clean" as possible; see [18,19] for further information, and see the OKlibrary ([20]) for the renovated source code. It uses complete elimination of failed literals, and autarky reduction for the partial assignment at hand (see [17]). The distance along a branch is, as discussed above, a weighted sum of the number of new clauses, while the heuristics is the product of these values for the two branches (to be maximized); again (as for the reduction), all variables are (always) considered.

Computing the cubes is rather simple: cubes are partial assignments, corresponding to initial parts of the paths from the root to leaves in the splitting (branching) tree, and the task is to "cut off" these paths at the right place. Two methods are implemented, interpreting a depth parameter $D \geq 0$: either the branches are cut off when exactly D decisions have been made (method A), or when the total number of assigned variables (decisions, unit propagations, failed literals, autarkies) is at least D (method B).

The interface to the sub-solver is here as simple as possible: a complete decoupling is achieved by *applying* the partial assignments, and the sub-solver just gets the results. So each sub-instance is solved completely independent of each other, and the sub-solver only sees the sub-instance. For method A as well as for method B, the partial assignments contain everything: the decisions, the unit-propagation, the failed literals, the autarkies found (including pure literals).

On the implementation side, there are two simple data formats: either storing each partial assignment in its own file in DIMACS format (this is used for the experiments below), or creating an iCNF file[1], which here is basically just the concatenation of the instance and the partial assignments, put into one big file. Processing runs through the partial assignments, applies them to the original CNF, and calls the sub-solver on the sub-instance. Since only unsatisfiable instances are considered in this section, and the sub-instances are independent of each other, the order of the instances does not matter. All methods and all data are available in the OKlibrary, see [20]. The cutoff (the above parameter D) is determined ad-hoc such that sub-instances only take *a few seconds* (this seems to be around the optimum, but with less overhead, as achieved by the system discussed in Section 5, one can partition further — the more cubes the better).

---

[1] http://users.ics.tkk.fi/swiering/icnf/

We report here only on two instance classes, determining unsatisfiability of van-der-Waerden (vdW) instances and palindromic vdW instances, using in both cases two colors, and thus the instances have a canonical translation into boolean CNF. Such problems are explained (resp. introduced in the palindromic case) in [1], and they were also part of the SAT 2011 competition. The standard (boolean) vdW-problems are given by equations $\text{vdw}(k_1, k_2) = n$, for natural numbers $k_1 \leq k_2 \leq n$, meaning that whenever partitioning $\{1, \ldots, n\}$ into two parts, it holds that the first part contains an arithmetic progression (ap for short) of size k_1 or the second part contains an ap of size k_2 (and n is minimal with this property). This gives a CNF with n variables $v_1, \ldots, v_n$ and with two clause-sizes k_1, k_2, where the clauses of length k_1 are all the ap's of size k_1, as positive clauses, and the clauses of length k_2 are all the ap's of size k_2, as negative clauses. The *palindromic* (boolean) vdW-problems are given by equations $\text{vdw}^{\text{pd}}(k_1, k_2) = (n_1, n_2)$ $(n_1 < n_2)$, with a similar meaning, only that now only palindromic partitions are allowed, thus regarding the partition as a bit-string of length n, given by the values of $v_1, \ldots, v_n$, and requiring that $(v_1, \ldots, v_n) = (v_n, \ldots, v_1)$. By these equations, the number of variables is halved, replacing v_n by v_1 and so on, and shorter clauses are obtained. Subsumption elimination is performed on the instances. There are now two unsatisfiable problems, one using $\frac{n_1+1}{2}$ variables, with $n = n_1 + 1$ as the smallest n with unsatisfiable problem, and one with $\frac{n_2+1}{2}$ variables, based on the smallest $n = n_2$ such that *all* $n' \geq n$ yield unsatisfiable problems. For standard vdW-instances, lookahead solvers can perform better than conflict-driven solvers, while for palindromic vdW-instances conflict-driven solvers are much better (here we are not speaking about cube-and-conquer, but about standard SAT solving). Method (B) for determining the cutoff was vastly superior (diminishing the variability of the sub-instances enormously), and is only considered here. As the sub-solver, minisat-2.2.0 performed very well here and is used throughout. All times are on a single core with about 2 GHz (parallelization has not been used), and the times for the cube-and-conquer approach is the total time, including all computations (writing each sub-instance to file etc.). All solvers mentioned below for comparison seem best performing (as ordinary SAT solvers, on the original (full) instances).

For $\text{vdw}(3, 15) = 218$ (yielding 13362 clauses) the lookahead solver satz (version 215) needs about 20h, while with $D = 35$ (yielding 32331 cubes) it is solved in about 4h. The maximal time per job is 5 seconds, enabling trivial optimal parallelization with more than 2000 processors (by just distributing the jobs for the sub-problems to the first available processor). For $\text{vdw}(4, 8) = 146$ (yielding 4930 clauses) picosat (version 913) takes 8h. Setting $D = 20$ (yielding 65270 cubes), it is solved in 4h, with maximal job-time of 22s. picosat for $\text{vdw}(5, 6) = 206$ was aborted after a week, while with $D = 20$ (yielding 91001 cubes) it was solved in about one day. For $\text{vdw}^{\text{pd}}(3, 25) = (586, 607)$ (yielding 45779 resp. 49427 clauses), precosat (version 570) used in both cases about 13 days, while with $D = 45$ (yielding 9120 resp. 13462 cubes) the problems were solved in about 6.5h resp. 2 days. For $\text{vdw}^{\text{pd}}(4, 12) = (387, 394)$ (yielding 15544 resp. 15889 clauses) minisat version 2.2.0, was aborted after 2 weeks, while setting $D = 30$ resp. $D = 34$ (yielding 132131 resp. 147237 cubes) solved the problems in 2 days resp. 8h. Finally, for $\text{vdw}^{\text{pd}}(5, 8) = (312, 323)$ (yielding 9121 resp. 9973 clauses), minisat used 3 1/2 days resp. 53 days, while setting $D = 20$ in both cases (yielding 22482 resp. 87667 cubes) solved it in 5h resp. 40h.

5   Creating Cubes: A General Methodology

This section shows how to modify a lookahead solver into a partitioning tool. First, we explain where to modify the code, Section 5.1. Second, we present an adaptive mechanism to cut off branches in Section 5.2. We conclude with some important heuristics in Section 5.3. The automatic partitioning provided here essentially is able to simulate the splitting characteristics from Section 4.

5.1   General Framework

The procedure *CreateCubes*, a modified lookahead solver for partitioning, shown in Figure 2, takes as input a CNF formula F and outputs two sets. The first set $\mathcal{A}$ is a disjunction of cubes for which each cube represents a set of assumptions that describe a cutoff branch in the DPLL tree. The cubes in $\mathcal{A}$ cover all subproblems of F that have not been refuted during the partition procedure. The second set $\mathcal{C}$ is a conjunction of clauses. Each of these (learnt) clauses are implied by F and represent refuted branches in the DPLL tree. Hence the clauses in $\mathcal{C}$ can be added to F to obtain a logically equivalent formula $F' := F \cup \mathcal{C}$.

The recursive procedure has five inputs. Besides F, $\mathcal{A}$, and $\mathcal{C}$, it passes on the set of *decision literals* (denoted by φ_{dec}) and the set of *implied literals* (denoted φ_{imp}). Implied literals are assignments that were forced by BCP or some form of learning such as failed literal reasoning. Initially, *CreateCubes* is called with the input formula F and all the other parameters as empty sets.

In line 1 of the procedure, the method *LAsimplify_and_learn* is called. This method simplifies the formula by BCP and lookaheads, forcing some variables to certain truth values. All assigned variables are added to φ_{imp}. Additionally, it produces *local learnt clauses* which are added to F. In case the current assignment falsifies F then a conflict clause is learnt. This clause consists of the complements of the decisions and is added to $\mathcal{C}$ (line 2). Line 3 deals with cutting off branching which is further discussed in the next subsection. The procedure *LAdecide* on line 4 determines the next decision variable and preferred truth value based on lookaheads. There exists a vast body of work on these decision heuristics [19]. Section 5.3 offers the details of this produce.

After *CreateCubes* is terminated, $\mathcal{A}$ and $\mathcal{C}$ are optimized. First, the clauses in $\mathcal{C}$ are reduced in size by applying self-subsumption resolution. For instance, back to the example in Figure 1 with $(x_5 \lor x_2 \lor \neg x_3 \lor x_7), (x_5 \lor x_2 \lor \neg x_3 \lor \neg x_7) \in \mathcal{C}$, then the resolvent $(x_5 \lor x_2 \lor \neg x_3)$ replaces both antecedent clauses. When $\mathcal{C}$ is

CreateCubes (CNF F, DNF $\mathcal{A}$, CNF $\mathcal{C}$, dec. lits. φ_{dec}, imp. lits. φ_{imp})

1 $\langle F, \varphi_{\text{imp}} \rangle := $ *LAsimplify_and_learn* $(F, \varphi_{\text{dec}}, \varphi_{\text{imp}})$

2 **if** $\varphi_{\text{dec}} \cup \varphi_{\text{imp}}$ falsify a clause in F **then return** $\langle \mathcal{A}, \mathcal{C} \cup \{\neg\varphi_{\text{dec}}\} \rangle$

3 **if** cutoff heuristic is triggered **then return** $\langle \mathcal{A} \cup \{\varphi_{\text{dec}}\}, \mathcal{C} \rangle$

4 $l_{\text{dec}} := $ *LAdecide* $(F, \varphi_{\text{dec}}, \varphi_{\text{imp}})$

5 $\langle \mathcal{A}, \mathcal{C} \rangle := $ *CreateCubes* $(F, \mathcal{A}, \mathcal{C}, \varphi_{\text{dec}} \cup \{l_{\text{dec}}\}, \varphi_{\text{imp}})$

6 **return** *CreateCubes* $(F, \mathcal{A}, \mathcal{C}, \varphi_{\text{dec}} \cup \{\neg l_{\text{dec}}\}, \varphi_{\text{imp}})$

Fig. 2. The general framework of the recursive procedure *CreateCubes*

fully optimized, this set of conflict clauses is used to remove assumptions in $\mathcal{A}$. For instance if $(\neg x_5 \wedge x_2 \wedge x_8 \wedge x_9) \in \mathcal{A}$, and $(x_5 \vee \neg x_2 \vee x_8) \in \mathcal{C}$, then x_8 is removed as an assumption because it will be forced by BCP after $\mathcal{C}$ is added to F. After these optimizations until fix-point, $\mathcal{A}$ is a tautology.

5.2   Cutoff Heuristic

The heuristic that triggers the cutoff of a branch is of crucial importance to create an effective partition. Ideally, this heuristic partitions the original problem into several subproblems such that 1) the runtimes to solve each of the subproblems are comparable and 2) the sum of these runtimes (at least) does not exceed the runtime of solving the original instance.

A (simplifying) interpretation of the results discussed in Section 4 is that for some hard combinatorial problems both objectives can be achieved by cutting off a branch if a certain fraction (say 10%) of the variables is assigned — this measure is much easier to handle than the solution time for the sub-instances, which for the experiments reported in Section 4 was determined in an ad-hoc manner. There actually the total solution time for the subproblems was not just not bigger than the original solution time, but much smaller. So this metric is very useful for several small hard problems. However, for the larger industrial instances, the number of decisions appears to be also of important to determine the hardness of a subproblem. Additionally, for these formulas sometimes a single decision assigns 10% of the variables, while for other formulas it requires over 100 decisions. In the former case the number of partitions becomes too small, while in the latter case the number of partitions becomes too large.

An alternative approach by Hyvärinen *et al.* [15] cuts off a branch after k decisions have been made (this was called method A in Section 4). The advantage of this approach is that one can clearly upper-bound the number of partitions in advance. However, branches with the same number of decisions are rarely equally hard to solve. It is often the case, that assigning a decision literal x to $\mathbf{t}$ results in significantly more implied literals than assigning x to $\mathbf{f}$ or vice versa.

We combine both approaches by using the product of the number of decisions and the number of assigned variables, $|\varphi_{\text{dec}}| \cdot |\varphi_{\text{dec}} \cup \varphi_{\text{imp}}|$, as the cutoff metric. Furthermore, the refined procedure *CreateCubes**, Figure 3, includes a dynamic cutoff mechanism. It implements the cutoff of a branch (with the cutoff heuristic discussed above) as shown in line 5 using a threshold parameter θ. Two lines update the value of θ. The first, the *increment rule* on line 1, raises the value by 5% without a condition. This rule aims to restore the value in case it was reduced too much. The second, the *decrement rule* on line 3, lowers the value by 30%. This rule tries to avoid two unfavorable situations described below.

First and most importantly, the value is decreased if the lookahead solver hits a conflict, meaning that the current node is a refuted branch. The rationale of this update is as follows. If the lookahead solver was able to show that the current node is conflicting, then probably a CDCL solver could have found the conflict faster. Additionally, if the CDCL solver would have found the conflict, then it could have analyzed it and possibly computed a smaller reason of this conflict (than all decisions as computed by the lookahead solver). By lowering θ, the mechanism tries to cut off neighboring branches before a conflict emerges.

Secondly, the mechanism prevents the recursive procedure from going too deep into the DPLL tree. For most interesting instances, it appeared useful to

$CreateCubes^*$ (CNF F, DNF $\mathcal{A}$, CNF $\mathcal{C}$, dec. lits. φ_{dec}, imp. lits. φ_{imp})
1      $\theta := 1.05 \cdot \theta$
2      $\langle F, \varphi_{\text{imp}} \rangle := LAsimplify\_and\_learn\ (F, \varphi_{\text{dec}}, \varphi_{\text{imp}})$
3   **if** $\varphi_{\text{dec}} \cup \varphi_{\text{imp}}$ falsify a clause in F **or** $|\varphi_{\text{dec}}| > 20$ **then** $\theta := 0.7 \cdot \theta$
4   **if** $\varphi_{\text{dec}} \cup \varphi_{\text{imp}}$ falsify a clause in F **then return** $\langle \mathcal{A}, \mathcal{C} \cup \{\neg\varphi_{\text{dec}}\}\rangle$
5   **if** $|\varphi_{\text{dec}}| \cdot |\varphi_{\text{dec}} \cup \varphi_{\text{imp}}| > \theta \cdot |\text{vars}(F)|$ **then return** $\langle \mathcal{A} \cup \{\varphi_{\text{dec}}\}, \mathcal{C}\rangle$
6      $l_{\text{dec}} := LAdecide\ (F, \varphi_{\text{dec}}, \varphi_{\text{imp}})$
7      $\langle \mathcal{A}, \mathcal{C} \rangle := CreateCubes^*\ (F, \mathcal{A}, \mathcal{C}, \varphi_{\text{dec}} \cup \{l_{\text{dec}}\}, \varphi_{\text{imp}})$
8   **return** $CreateCubes^*\ (F, \mathcal{A}, \mathcal{C}, \varphi_{\text{dec}} \cup \{\neg l_{\text{dec}}\}, \varphi_{\text{imp}})$

Fig. 3. The recursive procedure $CreateCubes^*$ with the cutoff mechanism

decrease θ for all nodes with a depth larger than 20. In case one wants the mechanism to finish creating cubes within a few seconds, then the condition should be dependent on the size of the formula, such as $|\varphi_{\text{dec}}| + \log_2(|F|) > 30$.

Initially, θ should be large enough to ensure that the mechanism will cut off the tree at a reasonable depth. We used $\theta := 1000$ as initial value. Using a value which is a factor 10 larger or smaller hardly influences the resulting partition. Using this initial value, θ will first be decreased before cutting off a branch.

5.3   Heuristics for Splitting

Besides the development of the cutoff mechanism, the standard heuristics for lookahead solvers had to be tweaked in order to realize fast performance.

Decision Heuristics. The default and costly lookahead evaluation heuristic (measurement) in most lookahead solvers is based on the clauses that are reduced, but not satisfied during a lookahead. These clauses are weighted depending on their (new) length. In general, a clause of length k has a weight which is a factor five times larger compared to a clause of length $k + 1$. A more cheaply heuristic counts the number of variables that are assigned during the lookahead.

For an example of both heuristics, consider the formula F below. Because the longest clauses have length 3, all "new" clauses have length 2, so no weights are required. Let $\text{eval}_{\text{cls}}(x_i)$ denote the clause based heuristic being the (weighted) sum of the reduced, not satisfied clauses and $\text{eval}_{\text{var}}(x_i)$ the variable based heuristic being the number of assigned variables during the lookahead on $x_i = 1$. E.g., $\text{eval}_{\text{var}}(\neg x_6) = 1$ and $\text{eval}_{\text{cls}}(\neg x_6) = 2$ because the lookahead on $x_6 = 0$ reduces two clauses from ternary to binary, and only x_6 is assigned. Notice that the values of the two heuristics are not necessarily related. $\text{eval}_{\text{cls}}(x_i)$ may be much smaller than $\text{eval}_{\text{var}}(x_i)$. For instance $\text{eval}_{\text{cls}}(\neg x_2) = 1$, while $\text{eval}_{\text{var}}(\neg x_2) = 4$.

$$F = (\neg x_1 \vee \neg x_3 \vee x_4) \wedge (\neg x_1 \vee \neg x_2 \vee \neg x_3) \wedge (\neg x_1 \vee x_2) \wedge (x_1 \vee x_3 \vee x_6) \wedge$$
$$(\neg x_1 \vee x_4 \vee \neg x_5) \wedge (x_1 \vee \neg x_6) \wedge (x_4 \vee x_5 \vee x_6) \wedge (x_5 \vee \neg x_6)$$

In general, lookahead solvers rank variables x_i by $\text{eval}(x_i) \cdot \text{eval}(\neg x_i)$. Ties are broken by $\text{eval}(x_i) + \text{eval}(\neg x_i)$. The decision heuristics select in each node of the DPLL tree the variable with the highest rank.

The default heuristics $\mathsf{eval}_{\mathsf{cls}}$ appeared to be quite effective on instances that had none or few binary clauses. This is frequently the case for random and crafted instances used in the SAT competitions. However, we noticed that $\mathsf{eval}_{\mathsf{var}}$ was more effective on industrial instances. An advantage of $\mathsf{eval}_{\mathsf{var}}$ is that it does not require the eager data-structures used in lookahead SAT solvers. Hence, this heuristic can relatively easy be implemented in CDCL solvers.

Direction Heuristics. Given a decision variable x, *direction heuristics* decide which branch (x to t or x to f) to explore first; see Section 5.3.2 in [14] for more information. Direction heuristics in lookahead solvers aim to improve performance on satisfiable formulas. Therefore, the solver prefers the branch that is most "likely" to be satisfiable. For methods how to estimate such probabilities see Section 7.9 in [19], and see Subsection 4.6.2 in [3] for some discussions in the CSP context. As a cheap approximation one can take the least constraint branch first. This is the complementary strategy of the *first fail principle* [12] which is often used in Constraint Satisfaction. In case $\mathsf{eval}(x) < \mathsf{eval}(\neg x)$, x to t is explored first. Otherwise x to f is preferred. For a certain node with decision variable x, we refer to the branch with $\mathsf{eval}(x) < \mathsf{eval}(\neg x)$ as its *left branch*. The other branch we call its *right branch*.

The partition mechanism as described in Section 5.2 seems to be quite robust regarding the direction heuristics. The number of cubes and the average size of the cubes is hardly influenced by exploring the left or the right branch first. However the order in which partitions are visited has a clear impact on performance related to the left and right branches, when considering how the *sub-problems* are solved; see Section 6.1.

6   Solving Cubes

A CDCL solver deals with the second phase of the cube-and-conquer method. The solver takes as input the original formula F, optionally extended with the learnt clauses C, and the set of assumption cubes $\mathcal{A}$. The latter is ordered based on some heuristic. For each cube $c \in \mathcal{A}$ based on this order, the CDCL solver solves $F \wedge c(\wedge C)$. First, we present how to solve the cubes sequentially (Section 6.1). Second, we discuss a parallel solving approach (Section 6.2).

6.1   Sequential Solving

The sequential solving procedure is rather straightforward and shown in Figure 4. Iteratively, a cube $c \in \mathcal{A}$ is selected (line 3) and assumed to be true followed by solving the simplified formula (line 4). In case the result is satisfiable, the original formula is satisfiable and hence the procedure ends. After all cubes have been refuted, the formula is found to be unsatisfiable.

After refuting a cube, most CDCL solvers provide a technique, known as *AnalyzeFinal*, to extract a subset of the cube that was required to proof unsatisfiability. It can be useful to add the clause –the complement of this subset– to the formula (line 5). Adding it can help refuting another cube more easily and the CDCL solver cannot remove it (in contrast to learnt clauses). However, if $|\mathcal{A}|$ is much larger than $|F|$, the addition may significantly slow down performance.

```
SolveCubes (CDCL solver S, CNF F, DNF A)
1      S.Load (F)
2      while A is not empty do
3          get a cube c from A and remove c from A
4          if S.SolveWithAssumptions (c) = satisfiable then return satisfiable
5          S.AnalyzeFinal ()                                          // optional
6          S.ResetClauseDeletionPolicy ()
7      return unsatisfiable
```

Fig. 4. The pseudo-code of the sequential solver using the partition

Last, but not least, we observed that removing some learnt clauses after refuting a cube can significantly improve performance of cube-and-conquer. This can be explained by the intuition that the subproblems are relatively independent and hence the learnt clauses of one subproblem can hardly be reused for another subproblem. Removal of learnt clauses is realized by reseting the clause deletion policy after solving a cube (line 6). So the size of the clause database is reduced to its initial size and the least important clauses are kicked out.

Describing the Cubes. In the partition procedure CreateCubes, the cube consists only of all decisions (φ_{dec}) from the root to the cutoff. Alternatively, one could describe a cube by all the assigned variables ($\varphi_{dec} \cup \varphi_{imp}$). The latter may include several assignments that a CDCL solver cannot reconstruct by BCP, for instance the failed literals. Recall that this approach is used is Section 4 and by Hyvärinen et al. [15,16]. However, it seems that communicating implied variables to a CDCL solver does not improve runtime. Throughout our experiments, using cubes consisting of only decision literals resulted in stronger performance.

The order in which the decision literals are assumed in the CDCL solver influence the size of conflict clauses. The natural order –the order in which the decisions were made– appears to be the best alternative.

Ordering the Cubes. During the experiments, we observed a relation between the time it requires to refute a cube and the number of right branches between the root and the cutoff of that cube: the more right branches (also known as *discrepancies*), the easier the corresponding subformula. On the other hand, for satisfiable formulas, cubes that cover a solution tend to have *few right branches*. Although we focused mostly on unsatisfiable formulas, we observed that for satisfiable benchmarks it pays off to solve the cubes with few right branches first. This strategy is known as *limited discrepancy search* [13].

There is also another reasoning for preferring this order, namely when solving cubes in parallel (see Section 6.2). In case CreateCubes produces an unbalanced tree, then frequently one or a few cubes will consume most of the computation costs to solve a formula. Therefore, one should solve the hard cubes first: a few cores attack these cubes, while others solve the easy ones. Otherwise, if a hard cube needs to be solved in the end, there would no cubes left for the other cores.

6.2 Parallel Solving

A natural extension of the approach in the prior section is to consider solving the partitions in parallel. In existing work on parallel SAT solving [10] two main approaches are distinguishable. The first aims to partition the formula in an attempt to divide the total workload evenly over multiple computation nodes, the second are so called *portfolio* approaches [11]. Rather than partitioning the formula, *portfolio* systems run multiple solvers in parallel, each attempting to solve the same formula, and the system finishes whenever the fastest solver finishes. Often such portfolios consist simply of multiple instances of the same CDCL solver, as those can be made to all traverse the search space in a different order by as little as using different random seeds. Such parallel solvers thus mostly exploit the lack of robustness of SAT solvers, and can be surprisingly effective. Parallel SAT solvers of both types can be extended with exchange of learnt clauses between computation nodes.

In the solving phase of cube-and-conquer many partitions are independently solved and thus it can be easily parallelized. However as we make use of incremental SAT, so one can also think of this phase as one single incremental problem. In [26] two different job assignment strategies for parallel incremental SAT were discussed and implemented in a tool called Tarmo. That work was focused on Bounded Model Checking (BMC) but it can be seen as a general framework for parallel incremental SAT solving with clause sharing. The first strategy implemented is the *multijob* approach in which an idle node is assigned the first job that is not already assigned to any other node. When two nodes are idle at the same time the job assignment order is undefined but it is guaranteed that no two nodes ever work on the same job. The second strategy called *multiconv* is inspired by portfolio solvers, and it simply runs a conventional incremental SAT solver on all jobs on all nodes. The latter can be effective for BMC where jobs are difficult and job order is relevant. For cube-and-conquer however we deal with a huge number of jobs, most of which are very easy, which means there are no large deviations in single job run times for the *multiconv* strategy to exploit. For this application *multijob* is a natural choice, although it is not ideal. If the partitioning is uneven a small number of the jobs may make up a large fraction of the run time. Thus using *multijob* nodes given only easy jobs may end up sitting idle waiting for a small number of nodes with hard jobs to finish. In Tarmo we experimented also with an extended strategy, *multijob+*, which is like *multijob* except that it will assign a job that is already being solved by some node to nodes that would otherwise become idle. This modified strategy appeared to beneficial for performance of the cube-and-conquer solving phase.

Another feature of Tarmo is its ability to share learnt clauses between solver threads. As discussed in [26] different settings are possible for the amount of clauses shared. Tarmo's default setting which shares learnt clauses that have a length which is below average appeared the most effective for this application.

After studying the parallelization of cube-and-conquer's solving phase using various versions of Tarmo, a special purpose multithreaded version of the fast SAT solver lingeling was created, which uses the basic *multijob* strategy. This special purpose solver called iLingeling is faster than Tarmo for this application although it does not use clause sharing or the *multijob+* strategy yet.

7   Experimental Results

The experiments focus on the strength of cube-and-conquer on hard application benchmarks. For this paper we used instances from the SAT 09 application category that were not solved during the competition (within the given timeout of 10,000 seconds) – the same set as used in [16]. We modified two existing SAT solvers according to the general method of cube-and-conquer. First, the look-ahead SAT solver march [25] was converted into a splitting tool called march_cc. Second, the CDCL solver lingeling was extended to deal with iCNF files. This version called iLingeling also supports solving cubes in parallel. The sources of both tools are available on http://fmv.jku.at/cnc/.

Phase I of our cube-and-conquer implementation consists of A) simplifying the formula using the preprocessor of lingeling (option -s) and B) calling march_cc on the result. The cutoff mechanism in march_cc is implemented as shown in Figure 3. Three benchmarks in the SAT09 suite (9dlx* and sortnet*) remained too large after simplifying and caused memory problems for march_cc. Therefore, we replaced $|\varphi_{dec}| > 20$ by $|\varphi_{dec}| > 10$ in the decrement rule for these instances. We used the cheap $eval_{var}$ lookahead evaluation, because it resulted in improved performance compared to $eval_{cls}$. The reported runtimes in Table 1 for phase I include both preprocessing and partitioning – the latter consuming most of the time. Notice that partitioning is based on lookahead. Hence, this part can relatively easy be parallelized. Since solving cubes requires more time than creating them, this optimization is left for future work. march_cc outputs an iCNF file which concatenates the simplified formula and a line for each cube.

For phase II of cube-and-conquer, the iCNF file is provided to iLingeling. We used a 12-core-machine during this phase. On such a machine, iLingeling starts 12 worker threads using separate lingeling solvers. Idle threads ask for the first cube that has not been dealt with by another thread. After receiving a cube, lingeling solves the reduced formula of the first phase with the cube as assumptions. After a cube is refuted, the clause database of the corresponding lingeling is reduced as discussed in Section 6.1. A thread terminates either when a solution is found by one of the 12 solvers or when no new cube is available. iLingeling terminates when all threads are terminated.

Table 1 shows the results of our cube-and-conquer implementation on hard SAT 2009 application instances. The experiments are run on a two 6-core AMD Opteron 2435 machine from 2009. This machine, part of a cluster, has 32GB main memory and each job had a memory limit of 2.5GB per core. Additionally it shows the results of three alternative solvers, which we obtained from [16]:

- Plingeling 276, a multi-core portfolio solver using 12 cores [5].
- ManySAT 1.5, multi-core portfolio solver using 4 cores [11].
- PT-Learn, an iterative partitioning solver with learning running on a grid [16].

The portfolio solvers Plingeling and ManySAT were run on exactly the same hardware as our implementation, while PT-Learn was run on the M-grid environment consisting of nine clusters with CPU's from 2006 to 2009.

When we compare our approach with the two portfolio solvers Plingeling and ManySAT, then cube-and-conquer solves several more of these hard instances. Portfolio solvers are stronger on the three huge instances 9dlx* and sortnet*.

Table 1. Results on benchmarks of the SAT 2009 application suite that were not solved during that competition. S denotes satisfiable, U denotes unsatisfiable. Phase I uses `lingeling` for preprocessing and `march_cc` for partitioning. The column I shows the total time (in seconds) of both tools on a single core. Phase II uses `iLingeling` to solve the cubes. Both the total time (sum of all threads) and the real time are listed. For the other solvers only the real time is provided which originate from [16]. — denotes that the timeout of 4 hours (14400 seconds) was reached.

Benchmark	S U	number of cubes	I total	II total	II real	Plingeling real	ManySAT real	PT-Learn real
9dlx_vliw_at_b_iq8	U	84	284	—	—	3256	2750	—
9dlx_vliw_at_b_iq9	U	40	314	—	—	5164	3731	—
AProVE07-25	U	98320	168	81513	6858	—	—	9967
dated-5-19-u	U	28547	478	5601	2538	4465	18080	2522
eq.atree.braun.12	U	86583	115	3218	269	—	—	4691
eq.atree.braun.13	U	83079	106	17546	1466	—	—	9972
gss-24-s100	S	339398	1853	14265	1191	2930	6575	3492
gss-26-s100	S	493870	1517	66489	5547	18173	—	10347
gus-md5-14	U	78488	649	—	—	—	—	13890
ndhf_xits_09_UNS	U	39351	128	—	—	—	—	9583
rbcl_xits_09_UNK	U	61653	210	132788	16900	—	—	9819
rpoc_xits_09_UNS	U	36733	255	104552	20665	—	—	8635
sortnet-8-ipc5-h19	S	583	271	48147	4023	2700	79010	4304
total-10-17-u	U	19773	948	5927	5561	3672	10755	4447
total-5-15-u	U	7865	192	—	—	—	—	18670

A possible explanation could be that these instances must be "easy" relative to their size. Therefore, lookahead techniques can not really help the CDCL solvers.

The PT-Learn solver shows on most instances comparable performance to cube-and-conquer – although the latter is an order of magnitude faster on the eq.atree.braun* and gss* benchmarks. The comparison of both solvers in Table 1 however is biased towards PT-Learn: the experiments are run on similar hardware, but PT-Learn runs up to 60 jobs at the same time, while cube-and-conquer runs at most 12 jobs. PT-Learn suffers a bit from delays, while our solver runs on one machine. So, the presented results are suggesting that cube-and-conquer is actually the strongest solver on these hard application benchmarks.

Additional experiments suggest that our current implementation of cube-and-conquer is not optimal yet. For several instances, we observed improved real time using less than 12 cores. E.g., our 4 core cube-and-conquer experiments dated-5-19-u in 901 seconds. Also, total-10-17-u was solved in 2632 seconds using a single core. This time is almost half the 12 core real time and faster than the other parallel SAT solvers. Notice that for both instances the real time is relatively close to the total time, indicating that solving a certain cube requires most of the computational cost.

8 Conclusions

We presented the novel SAT solving approach cube-and-conquer which is a very powerful method to solve hard CNF formulas. Our approach combines sophisticated lookahead decision heuristics with the efficiency of CDCL solvers. Results on hard van der Waerden benchmarks using our basic method show reduced computational costs up to a factor 20 compared to the fastest "pure" SAT solver. Moreover, using our cutoff mechanism, we were able to apply cube-and-conquer on hard application instances of the SAT competition. As a result, we outperform on most of these benchmarks the state-of-the-art parallel SAT solvers.

While this paper focused on the *offline* version of cube-and-conquer (i.e., a strict separation between both phases), we plan to implement an *online* version in the future. By integrating the method into a single solver, the phases can communicate with each other. For instance, the cube creation phase may select more effective decision literals if it knows which variables were frequently part of *AnalyzeFinal*. Also, if a cube appears hard to solve, the conquer phase can request additional assumptions.

References

1. Ahmed, T., Kullmann, O., Snevily, H.: On the van der Waerden numbers $w(2; 3, t)$. Tech. Rep. arXiv:1102.5433 [math.CO], arXiv (February 2011)
2. Bacchus, F.: Enhancing Davis Putnam with extended binary clause reasoning. In: AAAI 2002, pp. 613–619 (2002)
3. van Beek, P.: Backtracking search algorithms. In: Rossi, F., van Beek, P., Walsh, T. (eds.) Handbook of Constraint Programming, ch. 4, pp. 85–134 (2006)
4. Biere, A.: Bounded model checking. In: Biere, et al. (eds.) [6], ch. 14, pp. 455–481
5. Biere, A.: Lingeling, Plingeling, Picosat and Precosat at SAT race 2010 (2010)
6. Biere, A., Heule, M.J.H., van Maaren, H., Walsh, T. (eds.): Handbook of Satisfiability. FAIA, vol. 185. IOS Press (February 2009)
7. Davis, M., Logemann, G., Loveland, D.: A machine program for theorem-proving. Commun. ACM 5(7), 394–397 (1962)
8. Dubois, O., Dequen, G.: A backbone-search heuristic for efficient solving of hard 3-SAT formulae. In: Nebel, B. (ed.) IJCAI, pp. 248–253. Morgan Kaufmann (2001)
9. Eén, N., Sörensson, N.: Temporal induction by incremental SAT solving. Electr. Notes Theor. Comput. Sci. 89(4), 543–560 (2003)
10. Hamadi, Y.: Conclusion to the special issue on parallel SAT solving. JSAT 6(4), 263 (2009)
11. Hamadi, Y., Jabbour, S., Sais, L.: ManySAT: a parallel SAT solver. JSAT 6(4), 245–262 (2009)
12. Haralick, R.M., Elliott, G.L.: Increasing tree search efficiency for constraint satisfaction problems. Artif. Intell. 14(3), 263–313 (1980)
13. Harvey, W.D., Ginsberg, M.L.: Limited discrepancy search. In: IJCAI 1995, pp. 607–613 (1995)
14. Heule, M.J.H., van Maaren, H.: Look-Ahead Based SAT Solvers. In: Biere, et al. (eds.) [6], ch. 5, vol. 185, pp. 155–184 (2009)
15. Hyvärinen, A.E.J., Junttila, T., Niemelä, I.: Partitioning SAT Instances for Distributed Solving. In: Fermüller, C.G., Voronkov, A. (eds.) LPAR-17. LNCS, vol. 6397, pp. 372–386. Springer, Heidelberg (2010)
16. Hyvärinen, A.E.J., Junttila, T., Niemelä, I.: Grid-Based SAT Solving with Iterative Partitioning and Clause Learning. In: Lee, J. (ed.) CP 2011. LNCS, vol. 6876, pp. 385–399. Springer, Heidelberg (2011)
17. Kleine Büning, H., Kullmann, O.: Minimal Unsatisfiability and Autarkies. In: Biere, et al. (eds.) [6], ch. 11, vol. 185, pp. 339–401 (February 2009)
18. Kullmann, O.: Investigating the behaviour of a SAT solver on random formulas. Tech. Rep. CSR 23-2002, University of Wales Swansea, Computer Science Report Series, 119 pages (2002), http://www-compsci.swan.ac.uk/reports/2002.html

19. Kullmann, O.: Fundaments of Branching Heuristics. In: Biere, et al. (eds.) [6], ch. 7, vol. 185, pp. 205–244 (February 2009)
20. Kullmann, O.: The OKlibrary: Introducing a "holistic" research platform for (generalised) SAT solving. Studies in Logic 2(1), 20–53 (2009)
21. Kullmann, O.: Green-Tao Numbers and SAT. In: Strichman, O., Szeider, S. (eds.) SAT 2010. LNCS, vol. 6175, pp. 352–362. Springer, Heidelberg (2010)
22. Kullmann, O.: Computing ordinary and palindromic van der Waerden numbers via collaboration between look-ahead and conflict-driven SAT solvers (in preparation, February 2012)
23. Li, C.M.: Anbulagan: Heuristics based on unit propagation for satisfiability problems. In: IJCAI, vol. (1), pp. 366–371 (1997)
24. Marques-Silva, J.P., Lynce, I., Malik, S.: Conflict-Driven Clause Learning SAT Solvers. In: Biere, et al. (eds.) [6], ch. 4, vol. 185, pp. 131–153 (February 2009)
25. Mijnders, S., de Wilde, B., Heule, M.J.H.: Symbiosis of search and heuristics for random 3-SAT. In: Mitchell, D., Ternovska, E. (eds.) LaSh 2010 (2010)
26. Wieringa, S., Niemenmaa, M., Heljanko, K.: Tarmo: A framework for parallelized bounded model checking. In: Brim, L., van de Pol, J. (eds.) PDMC. EPTCS, vol. 14, pp. 62–76 (2009)
27. Zhang, H.: Combinatorial designs by SAT solvers. In: Biere, et al. (eds.) [6], ch. 17, pp. 533–568

Implicative Simultaneous Satisfiability and Applications

Zurab Khasidashvili and Alexander Nadel

Intel Corporation, P.O. Box 1659, Haifa 31015 Israel
{zurab.khasidashvili,alexander.nadel}@intel.com

Abstract. This paper proposes an efficient algorithm for the systematic learning of implications. This is done as part of a new search and restart strategy in the SAT solver. We evaluate the new algorithm within a number of applications, including BMC and induction with invariant strengthening for equivalence checking. We provide extensive experimental evidence attesting to a speedup of one and often two orders of magnitude with our algorithm, on a representative set of industrial and publicly available test suites, as compared to a basic version of invariant strengthening. Moreover, we show that the new invariant strengthening algorithm alone performs better than induction and interpolation, and that the absolutely best result is achieved when it is combined with interpolation. In addition, we experimentally demonstrate the superiority of an application of our new algorithm to BMC.

1 Introduction

The need to efficiently solve many closely related problems arises in numerous applications of model checking [8] and equivalence checking [12]. Various automatic invariant strengthening algorithms fall into this class of applications. In such algorithms one has to guess the missing invariants that strengthen the target property, thereby making it easier to prove. However, for the guessing to succeed, many potential invariants must be tried out, and therefore for overall efficiency it is very important that the evaluation of potential invariants be very fast.

In the domain of SAT solving [3,14], several efficient approaches to solving multiple related objectives *incrementally* [26,27] or *simultaneously* [13] have been developed in the past, and due to its increasing importance this is an active research area. The two approaches are closely related, yet there are subtle fundamental differences between the two. Their relative performance depends on the nature of the benchmarks.

In this work we focus on improving and refining the *Simultaneous SATisfiability* (or *SSAT*) approach to solving multiple closely related SAT tasks. Recall that the *SSAT* algorithm aims at proving a number of related objectives (called *proof objectives*, or POs) in *one* backtrack search. The algorithm receives a CNF instance and a number of literals that occur in the CNF. These literals represent the POs. If there is a satisfying assignment to the CNF where a PO is

K. Eder, J. Lourenço, and O. Shehory (Eds.): HVC 2011, LNCS 7261, pp. 66–79, 2012.

assigned false, then the PO is not a logical consequence of the CNF instance and is therefore called *falsifiable*; otherwise it is *valid*. For *each* PO, the $SSAT$ algorithm returns one of the following statuses: *valid*, *falsifiable*, or *indeterminate* (in case the algorithm is interrupted). This is different from solving the satisfiability status of the conjunction of all POs.

As an example, consider the problem of combinational or sequential equivalence checking of circuits. By the nature of the problem, and in particular, by the nature of the design or synthesis of an implementation model based on a specification model, there are many internal nodes in the circuits that are equivalent. Exploiting these internal equivalences often helps enormously in proving the functional equivalence of the corresponding outputs of the two circuit designs. The POs are then equivalences of the form $x \leftrightarrow y$ or $x \leftrightarrow \neg y$ between internal nodes x and y of the specification and implementation circuits. On a large set of Intel and academic benchmarks, we found that $SSAT$ is more efficient within the invariant-strengthening algorithms than saturation or multiple incremental calls to the SAT solver. Still, there is an inefficiency caused by the fact that the definitions of many (sometimes tens or hundreds of thousands) of the POs corresponding to the candidate invariants must be added to the CNF instance: an equivalence of the form $x \leftrightarrow y$ or $x \leftrightarrow \neg y$ is translated into four clauses (with the standard Tseitin encoding), and these extra clauses noticeably slow down the SAT solver.

We introduce a novel DPLL-based approach, called implicative $SSAT$ (or $SSAT^{\rightarrow}$), that leverages from the fact that the POs are equivalences consisting of two implications, e.g., $x \rightarrow y$ and $y \rightarrow x$. The $SSAT^{\rightarrow}$ algorithm learns these implications and equivalences *without encoding them into the CNF*. Instead, it deals with them during the search using a dedicated algorithm. This leads to a speedup of up to two orders of magnitude as compared to other approaches to invariant strengthening that also try to prove a maximal number of candidate invariants at a given induction depth. Our algorithm can solve any number of user-given properties simultaneously. The algorithm is discussed in Section 2.

We propose two new applications of $SSAT$ and $SSAT^{\rightarrow}$ (Sections 3 and 4, respectively). One is *in-depth BMC*, which uses simultaneous solving in a BMC [2] scheme where unrolling happens with intervals [11,28] (the SAT solver is not called after each unrolling step). The other application is an invariant strengthening algorithm for equivalence checking known as van Eijk's method [10]. Both Sections 3 and 4 present a rich collection of experiential results demonstrating the efficiency of our algorithms. In Section 5 we provide an extensive overview of related work, in order to make it clear how our research advances to the state of the art. Conclusions and discussion of future work appear in Section 6.

2   Implicative $SSAT$

Recall that $SSAT$ modifies the modern SAT solver's algorithm in a way that allows it to solve multiple proof objectives in one search ([13], Section 5). The $SSAT$ algorithm always maintains a PO literal, called the currently watched

PO (CWPO), that the SAT search tries to falsify. At the beginning of the search CWPO is set to be any PO literal. At every stage of the search, prior to invoking a generic decision heuristic, CWPO is assigned false. The CWPO ceases to be the currently watched PO in two circumstances:

(1) When a model containing CWPO = false is discovered, in which case we mark as falsifiable the CWPO as well as all the POs that are assigned false (or are don't care literals) in the model;
(2) When the CWPO is discovered to be globally true, in which case we mark the CWPO as valid.

In either of these circumstances, we check whether there exists an *unresolved* PO l – a PO that has not been found valid or falsifiable. If such an unresolved PO l exists, we set the CWPO to l, otherwise the algorithm halts. The algorithm returns the pair $(vPOs, fPOs)$ consisting of POs proved valid and POs proved falsifiable.

We found it very useful to frequently reschedule POs in the $SSAT$ algorithm: each CWPO ceases to be a CWPO after a given number of restarts, and the next PO in a sorted list of POs is selected as the CWPO. In other words, the list of unresolved POs is rotated. This is different from the original $SSAT$ algorithm (where a CWPO ceases to be a CWPO only after it gets resolved), and often prevents wasting search effort in irrelevant search space: the learning gained resolving other POs often makes it easier to resolve the once problematic CWPO later. In particular, thanks to frequent rescheduling, simpler invariants are discovered easily and solved first; rescheduling can thus be seen as an improved version of the widely used method according to which candidate invariants are sorted in a bottom-up fashion and solved in that order.

As discussed earlier, in applications where the POs are equivalences of the form $PO = o_s \leftrightarrow o_i$, and there are many POs, translating them all into the CNF instance can be a significant overhead for the solver. Therefore, we propose implicative $SSAT$, or $SSAT^{\rightarrow}$, as an algorithm that takes a number of pairs (o_s^j, o_i^j) as input and reports the status of each equivalence $o_s^j \leftrightarrow o_i^j$ for each j: if there is a satisfying assignment with $\neg o_s^j \wedge o_i^j$ or $o_s^j \wedge \neg o_i^j$, then the equivalence is false and $PO^j = o_s^j \leftrightarrow o_i^j$ is *falsifiable*; otherwise it is *valid*.

For deciding the validity of an equivalence $PO = o_s \leftrightarrow o_i$, the algorithm checks the satisfiability status of two implications $PO^{\rightarrow} : o_s \rightarrow o_i$ and $PO^{\leftarrow} : o_s \leftarrow o_i$. A pseudo algorithm for $SSAT^{\rightarrow}$ is described in Figure 1. For simplicity of presentation, we do not treat the circumstance where there are initial unit clauses, in which case some POs might be found valid before the loop at line 2. The algorithm's structure is similar to that of SSAT. The main difference is that the $SSAT^{\rightarrow}$ algorithm needs to track the status of implications, rather than single literals. Consequently, the treatment of the CWPO in lines 8 – 19 becomes more complex, since each PO has two implications and each implication has two literals. Consider line 25, which is supposed to find globally valid PO implications. Our algorithm (not specified in Figure 1) returns that a PO implication $PO^{\rightarrow} : o_s \rightarrow o_i$ is valid if one of the following conditions holds:

(1) o_s is globally false (false at decision level 0);
(2) o_i is globally true;
(3) At decision level 1: both o_s and o_i are true, where o_s is the decision literal and o_i is an implied literal.

3   In-Depth BMC with $SSAT^\rightarrow$

In this section we discuss a variant of the BMC algorithm that employs $SSAT^\rightarrow$ in a way that differs from the known usages of incremental SAT with assumptions in BMC [9]. Besides the maximal bound k, *BMC with intervals* [11] takes an argument i that denotes the length of the bound intervals in which SAT checks for falsification of the property are performed. For instance, with $i = 10$ and $k = 100$, bound intervals $0-9, 10-19, \ldots, 90-99, 100$ are checked consecutively and incrementally. More precisely, given a safety property P and a state s, assume that $P(s)$ is a variable denoting P in state s. Then in the interval $0-9$, BMC with intervals calls the SAT solver to check the satisfiability of the following formulas, where Tr and I denote the transition and initial state relations, and $P_{0-9} = P(s_0) \wedge \ldots \wedge P(s_9)$.

$$I(s_0) \wedge path(s_0, \ldots, s_9) \wedge \neg P_{0-9}$$
$$path(s_0, \ldots, s_k) = Tr(s_0, s_1) \wedge \ldots \wedge Tr(s_{k-1}, s_k)$$

In the *in-depth BMC* algorithm that we propose, in each interval such as $0-9$, we call $SSAT^\rightarrow$ with POs $P(s_0), \ldots, P(s_9)$, on the unrolled instance.

Tables 1 and 2 compare our implementations of incremental BMC [9] (column BMC), incremental BMC with intervals (BMC10, BMC25), and in-depth BMC (BMC10$^\rightarrow$, BMC25$^\rightarrow$), for the maximal bound $k = 100$ and intervals $10, 25$, on 417 problems from several families of HWMCC'10 benchmarks. We also compare our results with ABC-BMC3, which is ABC's implementation of incremental BMC, and ABC-BMC2, which is similar to BMC with intervals but whose unrolling intervals are determined based on the extra gate count [19]. We selected the problems that were unsatisfiable for both the ABC-BMC2 strategy in the competition and our BMC implementation, since most of the falsifiable instances in the HWMCC'10 set are too easy. The first table shows 115 problem instances for which a 900-second time-out occurred for at least one of the strategies before the maximal bound was reached; for each group the sum of the reached bounds is shown. The second table shows the run-times per group and per strategy for the remaining 302 problem instances.

The tables show that in-depth BMC reaches higher bounds than any other version of BMC. Implication learning was disabled in these experiments, since for BMC these techniques are useful only for very difficult instances. The advantage of in-depth BMC over BMC can be explained as follows: In the interval $0-9$, while trying to falsify, say, $P(s_3)$, the $SSAT^\rightarrow$ solver has a view of the cones of $P(s_4), \ldots, P(s_9)$ as well; this allows the solver to infer and use useful correlations among signals at bounds up-to 3 from the definitions, user constraints (possibly

$SSAT^{\rightarrow}$ $(cnf, [PO_1 = (o_s^1, o_i^1), \ldots, PO_n = (o_s^n, o_i^n)])$
1: CWPO = any PO pair;
2: **while** (true) **do**
3:    **if** CWPO is marked valid or falsifiable **then**
4:       **if** all the POs are marked valid or falsifiable **then**
5:          **return** $(vPOs, fPOs)$;
6:       **end if**
7:       CWPO = any PO pair (o_s^j, o_i^j) that is yet unresolved;
8:       **if** $PO^{\rightarrow}$ is unresolved **then**
9:          σ = true
10:       **else**
11:          σ = false
12:       **end if**
13:       **if** o_s is unassigned **then**
14:          Assign $o_s = \sigma$
15:       **else**
16:          **if** o_i is unassigned **then**
17:             Assign $o_i = \neg\sigma$
18:          **end if**
19:       **end if**
20:    **else**
21:       Assign choose-decision-literal();
22:    **end if**
23:    **while** (status == local-conflict) **do**
24:       status = BCP();
25:       Mark any PO implication $PO^{\rightarrow}$ or $PO^{\leftarrow}$ that is discovered to be globally true as valid;
26:       If for an unresolved PO both $PO^{\rightarrow}$ and $PO^{\leftarrow}$ are marked valid, mark the PO valid;
27:       **if** status == global-conflict **then**
28:          Mark all unmarked POs valid;
29:          **return** $(vPOs, fPOs)$;
30:       **end if**
31:       **if** (status == model) **then**
32:          Mark any falsified PO implication $PO^{\rightarrow}$ or $PO^{\leftarrow}$ falsifiable;
33:          If for an unresolved PO one of the implications $PO^{\rightarrow}$ and $PO^{\leftarrow}$ is marked falsifiable, mark the PO falsifiable;
34:          Unassign all the literals that are not globally true;
35:       **end if**
36:       **if** (status == local-conflict) **then**
37:          Add a conflict clause; Backtrack;
38:          Assign literal that must be flipped following conflict analysis;
39:       **end if**
40:    **end while**
41: **end while**

Fig. 1. Pseudo algorithm for implicative $SSAT$ (or $SSAT^{\rightarrow}$)

Table 1. Comparing the bound for 115 timed-out instances

Family	BMC	BMC10	BMC10$^{\rightarrow}$	BMC25	BMC25$^{\rightarrow}$	ABC-BMC2	ABC-BMC3
bj	405	393	461	328	462	485	553
bob	674	645	736	427	697	706	710
cmu	137	140	138	150	143	158	174
eij	785	765	846	551	848	585	730
nus	283	301	301	301	355	225	385
pdt	3393	3504	3963	2957	3983	3430	3673
pj	300	312	331	252	347	404	404
texas	202	202	168	176	199	202	202
Total (bound)	6179	6262	6944	5142	**7034**	6195	6831

Table 2. Comparing the run-time for 302 completed instances

Family	BMC	BMC10	BMC10$^{\rightarrow}$	BMC25	BMC25$^{\rightarrow}$	ABC-BMC2	ABC-BMC3
bj	215.8	324.9	190.6	341.4	103.3	407.07	51.08
bob	116.7	853.1	648.9	1622	1176	186.99	174.61
cmu	203.4	21.1	14.6	21.9	17.3	3.9	3.38
eij	678.2	513.1	190.2	1446.1	141.4	62.38	171.58
nus	2609.1	747.5	617	933.4	883.8	311.87	396.16
pdt	4202	2837.1	1981.8	4230.3	1884.8	1350.72	955.41
pj	513.2	911.1	449	829.4	555.8	569.72	940.1
texas	8.4	22.4	142.1	33.7	37.7	25.67	25.06
vis	311.9	238	138.7	406.3	147.6	94.7	169.52
Total (cpu time)	9614.6	8049.7	5187.5	12336.5	5697.9	4458.19	**3108.8**

sequential), and PO assignments at higher bounds. While BMC with intervals also has the view of the cones of all the POs $P(s_o), \ldots, P(s_9)$, in contrast to in-depth BMC, it can either solve them all together (by proving that $\neg P_{0-9}$ is unsatisfiable) or solve none of them. Solving all the POs is more complex than only proving valid POs up to $P(s_3)$.

4 $SSAT^{\rightarrow}$ and Strengthening Inductive Invariants

A basic scheme combining invariant strengthening and temporal induction is depicted in Figure 2. This scheme was proposed in [4]. The induction and invariant strengthening algorithms in [23,10], as well as the algorithms that we propose, can be seen as instances of this algorithm scheme. Recall that, according to the temporal induction scheme [23], a property P is valid if for some m, the formulas $base(P, k)$ and $step(P, m)$ defined below are unsatisfiable for all $0 \leq k \leq m$ (for simplicity, we omit discussion of the loop-free condition for the induction step).

$$base(P, k) = I(s_0) \wedge path(s_0, \ldots, s_k) \wedge P(s_0) \wedge \ldots \wedge P(s_{k-1}) \wedge \neg P(s_k)$$
$$step(P, k) = path(s_0, \ldots, s_{k+1}) \wedge P(s_0) \wedge \ldots \wedge P(s_k) \wedge \neg P(s_{k+1})$$

To interface the base and step formulas $base(P, k)$ and $step(P, k)$ for a property $P = l \leftrightarrow r$ with $SSAT^{\rightarrow}$, we change them as follows, where $l(s_i) \leftrightarrow r(s_i)$ represents P at state s_i:

Induction with invariant strengthening $(P, nMaxDepth)$

```
k = 0;
POs = Create_candidate_invariants() (where P ∈ POs);
while (k <= nMaxDepth ) do
  POs = BASE(POs, k);
  if (POs ≠ [ ]) then
    POs = STEP(POs, k);
  end if
  if (POs ≠ [ ]) then
    k + +;
  end if
end while
```

Fig. 2. Pseudo algorithm for induction with invariant strengthening

$$base\_cnf(k) = I(s_0) \wedge path(s_0, \ldots, s_k)$$
$$base\_PO\_pairs(P, k) = [(l(s_k), r(s_k))]$$
$$step\_assumption(P, k) = P(s_0) \wedge \ldots \wedge P(s_k)$$
$$step\_cnf(k) = path(s_0, \ldots, s_{k+1})$$
$$step\_assum\_cnf(P, k) = step\_cnf(k) \wedge step\_assumption(P, k)$$
$$step\_PO\_pairs(P, k) = [(l(s_{k+1}), r(s_{k+1}))]$$

Then, $base(P, k)$ is satisfiable iff

$$SSAT^{\rightarrow}(base\_cnf(k), base\_PO\_pairs(P, k))$$

returns P as falsifiable; similarly $step(P, k)$ is unsatisfiable iff

$$SSAT^{\rightarrow}(step\_assum\_cnf(P, k), step\_PO\_pairs(P, k))$$

returns P as valid. Thus the above formulas define a sound way of using $SSAT^{\rightarrow}$ in temporal induction.

Now, if we want to perform the base and step checks simultaneously for a number of POs $PO_0, \ldots, PO_n$, the definitions of $base\_cnf(k)$ and $step\_cnf(k)$ remain unchanged – they do not depend on the properties that one is interested in. The step assumption is the conjunction of formulas $step\_assumption(PO_i, k)$ for $0 \le i \le n$, and the base and step PO lists are defined as follows:

$$base\_PO\_pairs(POs, k) = [(l_0(s_k), r_0(s_k)), \ldots, (l_n(s_k), r_n(s_k))]$$
$$step\_PO\_pairs(POs, k) = [(l_0(s_{k+1}), r_0(s_{k+1})), \ldots, (l_n(s_{k+1}), r_n(s_{k+1}))]$$
$$step\_assumption(POs, k) = \wedge_{i=0}^{i=n} step\_assumption(PO_i, k)$$
$$step\_assum\_cnf(POs, k) = step\_cnf(k) \wedge step\_assumption(POs, k)$$

The $BASE(POs, k)$ procedure employing $SSAT^{\rightarrow}$, called $base\_issat$, is depicted in Figure 3.(a). $vPOs$ denote the POs whose corresponding base formulas are valid in state s_k. Similarly, Figure 3.(b) depicts the $STEP(POs, k)$ procedure employing $SSAT^{\rightarrow}$, called $step\_issat$.

(a) **base_issat** (POs, k)

$(vPOs, fPOs) = SSAT^{\rightarrow}(base\_cnf(k), base\_PO\_pairs(POs, k));$

report $fPOs$ as falsifiable;

return vPos;

(b) **step_issat** (POs, k)

$i = 0;$

$POs^0 = POs;$

while (true) **do**

$(vPOs^i, fPOs^i) = SSAT^{\rightarrow}(step\_assum\_cnf(POs^i, k), step\_PO\_pairs(POs^i, k));$

$POs^{i+1} = vPOs^i;$

if $(fPOs^i = [\,])$ **then**

break;

end if

$i = i + 1;$

end while

report POs^i as valid;

return $POs \setminus POs^i;$

Fig. 3. $BASE(POs, k)$ and $STEP(POs, k)$ for invariant strengthening with $SSAT^{\rightarrow}$

We call the invariant strengthening algorithm just described $invSSAT^{\rightarrow}$. In the same vein, we refer to the similar invariant strengthening algorithm employing $SSAT$ as $invSSAT$. Further, in the experiments reported below, we use $invSATURk$ to denote the invariant strengthening scheme of [4], where k-saturation is used as combinational reasoning engine. By $invCONJ$, we refer to the invariant strengthening scheme where saturation is replaced by SAT. That is, in $invCONJ$, the candidate invariants are proven using the conjunction approach to verifying multiple properties presented in [11].

Table 3. Comparing invariant strengthening algorithms as well as strategy combinations with induction and interpolation

Algorithm	Fam. 1		Fam. 2		Fam. 3		Fam. 4		Fam 5		Fam. 6		Fam. 7		Total	
	time	solv	time	solv	time	solv	time	solv	time	solv	time	solv	time	solv	time	solv
invSSAT$^{\rightarrow}$ & interp.	8	132	366	574	39	659	1	142	475	147	513	3775	2983	230	**4387**	**5659**
invSSAT$^{\rightarrow}$	9	132	365	574	36	659	1	142	16	147	512	3775	3686	230	4627	5659
invSSAT	6	132	418	574	45	659	1	142	14	147	258	3775	21311	218	22055	5647
invSATUR0 & interp.	94	132	4345	529	115	659	2	142	221	147	1841	3774	683	230	7304	5613
invSATUR0 & induction	5	132	10390	532	675	654	1000	140	1000	145	55	3773	26059	217	39186	5593
invCONJ	97	132	1233	574	3783	659	10	142	61	147	2077	3775	229856	1	237120	5430
interp.	4018	128	21171	494	20487	548	38	142	3943	45	4526	3774	19349	217	73535	5348
induction	18020	43	24836	478	52737	185	1000	133	2037	131	70159	184	60053	187	228845	1341
invSATUR1	11	40	283	19	44	408	2	13	12	18	305	53	752	28	1413	579

In Table 3 we report experimental results for 7 families of equivalence checking problems from recent microprocessor designs at Intel. Each family corresponds to a functional module. These 7 families together contain 5659 sequential equivalence checking problem instances. The designs are non-state-matching, therefore provable internal equivalences form a very small portion of all potential equivalences (the number of provable equivalences is typically a few hundreds, and many of them are very simple.) The timeout used in our experiments was 1000 seconds (in combined algorithms, the timeout was divided between the strategies). The maximal unrolling bound in all algorithms was 100. In the columns named *solv* we report the number of problem instances solved by each algorithm per family and in total. In the columns named *time* we report the time spent on each family and in total. We compare the different versions of invariant strengthening algorithms discussed in this section, as well as combinations of the best invariant strengthening algorithms with temporal induction [23] and interpolation [18]. We used a rescheduling rate of 5 in the experiments for $invSSAT^{\rightarrow}$.

$invSATUR0$ and $invSATUR2$ could not solve any of the problem instances, and therefore these algorithms do not appear in the table. Compared to the SAT-based conjunction method $invCONJ$, employing $SSAT$ in $invSSAT$ yields an order of magnitude speedup, and an additional 217 problem instances were solved. Employing $SSAT^{\rightarrow}$ in $invSSAT^{\rightarrow}$ yields an average $52.6x$ speedup compared to $invCONJ$, and an additional 229 problems were solved. The additional gain in $invSSAT^{\rightarrow}$ compared to $invSSAT$ is due to quick processing of candidate implications in $SSAT^{\rightarrow}$, which was our main motivation for introducing $SSAT^{\rightarrow}$. While $invSATUR0$ is too weak to solve any of the problem instances, it can very quickly prove important equivalences which might help the induction [23] and interpolation [18] algorithms. Similarly, invariants proven by $invSSAT^{\rightarrow}$ can significantly improve the runtime of interpolation. The results show that $invSSAT^{\rightarrow}$ outperforms both the induction and interpolation algorithms, and that $invSSAT^{\rightarrow}$ combined with interpolation is the winning algorithm overall: it solves all 5659 problem instances, and is faster than any other single or combined algorithm.

We also ran several strategy combinations on the 417 problems discussed in Section 3, and compared them with their counterparts in ABC (ABC-scorr denotes ABC's scorr algorithm with unrolling bound 100; scorr is the algorithm within ABC that is the closest to our invariant strengthening algorithms). The summary of these results is presented in Table 4: as one can see, the results, both

Table 4. Comparing strategy combinations on 417 HWMCC'10 problem instances

Algorithm	time	solv
$invSSAT^{\rightarrow}$ & interp.	**78106**	**319**
ABC-interpolation	109166	310
$invSSAT^{\rightarrow}$	133266	296
invCONJ	135519	294
invSSAT	135774	294
invSATUR0 & interp.	141619	283
interpolation	144131	282
ABC-scorr & ABC-interp	149540	281
invSATUR0 & induction	147645	265
ABC-scorr	146685	242
induction	176056	231

in terms of solved problems and runtimes, are similar to what was observed on Intel benchmark families, although the impact of combining invariant strengthening strategies with induction and interpolation algorithms is even greater. The combination of $invSSAT^{\rightarrow}$ followed by interpolation (which reuses the learning) remains the best combination.

5   Related Work

The CNF and the POs for an $SSAT^{\rightarrow}$ instance are often produced by translating a circuit ckt into CNF. Following [22], in our model-checking tool, a circuit is represented as a collection of *triplets* of the form $x := y \rightarrow z$ or $x := y \leftrightarrow z$, where x, y, and z are literals. This is close to the widely used And-Inverter Graph (AIG) representation [16], where the triplets are of the form $x := y \wedge z$. Besides the structural information recorded as triplets, our representation of ckt maintains its variables in equivalence classes (E-classes, for short) [22]; each class has a representative variable, and all the variables in an equivalence class are known to be (logically) equivalent to the representative or its negation. When converting ckt into an $SSAT$ instance, only the representative variables and the relations between them are reflected in the resulting CNF. The unit and two-literal clauses learned during the $SSAT$ search are added to ckt. Saturation [24] on the enhanced ckt may yield additional learning, including the learning of equivalences and inverse equivalences among the representative variables of E-classes; this in turn enables merging E-classes and reducing the number of representative variables.

The aim of $SSAT^{\rightarrow}$ is to solve *closely related* objectives in at most one complete search. The $SSAT^{\rightarrow}$ solver has a view of the *entire problem instance*, and has the freedom to focus on resolving a particular objective and to switch between the objectives *as part of the search strategy*. Furthermore, again as part of the search strategy, $SSAT^{\rightarrow}$ tries to learn the entire instance by learning the implications between all pairs of variable assignments. These implications are recorded as two-literal clauses (which are known to be very important learnings). Equivalences derived from them enable merging variables by merging their equivalence clauses.

The idea of learning the implications between circuit signal values was introduced in the *recursive learning* algorithm [17], in the context of circuit ATPG [1]. There implications are learned iteratively using a dedicated constant propagation algorithm, with increasing effort at each iteration. The learned implications are used to speedup the backward justification process (which is the main routine of ATPG). $SSAT^{\rightarrow}$ can be seen as a SAT-based implementation of recursive learning, where the learning of implications happens as part of the SAT search rather than as a separate routine. Indeed, $SSAT^{\rightarrow}$ introduces a new dimension to restart strategies. Traditionally, a restart strategy refers to *when* to restart, not *how* to restart. $SSAT$ introduces *fairness* into the how-to-restart strategy: the first two variable assignments after a restart do not follow the default search heuristic of the SAT solver; instead, every pair of variables in the candidate equivalences list is considered with four possible value assignments. We note that the *when* part of the restart strategy in our $SSAT^{\rightarrow}$ solver is the same in all the reported experiments; and our SAT solver is implemented as a special case of $SSAT^{\rightarrow}$ since the latter has more generic (incremental) interface (API).

The crucial idea of simplifying equivalence checking by proving (observable) internal equivalences and merging equivalent nodes was introduced in [6]. The AIGs data structure and BDD and SAT sweeping [16,15] allow for very efficient implementation of this idea. The triplet and equivalence classes data structure is closely related to the AIGs data structure, however it is no longer a DAG. In addition we work with constraints explicitly, a fact which entangles the cones of the objectives even more tightly. Finally, we do not use local BDDs [16] or AIG rewriting [5] to optimize the problem instance; instead we rely on saturation [24] and on learning from $SSAT^{\rightarrow}$ to achieve a compact representation.

An incremental version of SAT sweeping was proposed in [19], where, in addition, rescheduling of candidate equivalences was first considered. In that paper the authors work incrementally with a *SAT-with-assumptions* interface [9]. The idea behind $SSAT^{\rightarrow}$ could be used to extend SAT-with-assumptions, so that it could treat assumptions that are implications rather than literals.

Unlike $SSAT^{\rightarrow}$, in [19] each CWPO is targeted for falsification in its *cone of influence*; this is achieved by an API that allows the SAT solver to work with a subset of relevant variables (computed based upon the circuit), and Boolean Constraint Propagation (BCP) needs to be modified accordingly. This modified search procedure is not described in detail in [19], we therefore couldn't re-implement it for a fair comparison (moreover, recall that we use a very different circuit representation). Our early experience with simultaneous solving of multiple POs by solving each PO in its cone of influence and re-using *pervasive* learned clauses compared to $SSAT$ is reported in [13], and is negative. In fact, one of the main original motivations for introducing $SSAT$ was to eliminate the overhead of computing the cones of each objective and managing the conflict clauses. The relative performance of these two methods certainly depends on the nature of the problems at hand; Overall, our experience (within our implementation) is that $SSAT$ performs much better when the POs that are solved simultaneously are closely related (and their cones have a high percentage of overlap). As observed in [15], *modern SAT solvers are efficient in focusing on relevant parts of the problem*. This saves us the effort of *forcing* the SAT solver to work exclusively with the cone-of-influence of the CWPO. Furthermore, when working with the entire instance, one has a greater freedom in deciding assignments for other PO implications (that might not be in the cone), thereby increasing the chance of solving them as a side-effect of the search. For example, in $SSAT^{\rightarrow}$, the default behavior is that after assigning the CWPO, the other yet unresolved user POs are assigned next, with false. Experimental evaluation of the in-depth BMC strategy clearly demonstrates that giving a solver a wider view of the problem instance and letting it decide how to perform the search is beneficial.

Since in $SSAT^{\rightarrow}$, unlike in previous work, solving candidate equivalences is a by-product of the search heuristic, in our approach it becomes much less important to reduce candidate equivalences by quick falsification methods such as simulation with random or biased input patterns or satisfying-assignments [6,15,19]. Since we work with user constraints explicitly, as part of the E-classes data structure, we cannot use random simulation of inputs for quick falsification (the constraints need not hold for arbitrary input assignments). We have experimented with multiple methods of diverse satisfying assignment generation [21] in order to use them as simulation patterns for quick falsification of candidate equivalences, and while they can significantly reduce the number of candidate equivalences, this didn't noticeably affect overall runtime, because $SSAT^{\rightarrow}$ typically generates many satisfying assignments during the search (biased towards the falsification of as many POs as possible) and they filter out false candidate equivalences very efficiently.

The basic idea of invariant strengthening for sequential equivalence checking was proposed by van Eijk in [10]. The transition invariants were computed using BDDs. This idea was further generalized in [4], in two ways: the basic transition invariant scheme was enhanced by the temporal induction scheme [23], and saturation [24] replaced the usage of BDDs. Numerous circuit-level optimizations were proposed in [7]; the main differences with our approach has been discussed above. The *speculative reduction* technique [20] further advances van Eijk's method by strengthening the inductive assumptions within refinement iterations of candidate invariant set; this is done by creating copies of the current set of candidate invariants and assuming them (*in all reachable states*) when proving other candidates.

6   Conclusions

The main contribution of this paper is the introduction of a highly scalable and efficient DPLL-based algorithm $SSAT^{\rightarrow}$ that can decide the satisfiability of a large number of (user-given and automatically generated) proof objectives in a single DPLL search, where each proof objective can be either a single literal or an implication between two literals.

We have presented a number of applications of $SSAT^{\rightarrow}$ in bounded and unbounded model checking. The experimental results on academic as well as Intel benchmarks for in-depth BMC and for induction with invariant strengthening fully support the usefulness of these new algorithms compared to the state-of the art.

The $SSAT^{\rightarrow}$ algorithm has already been used as an efficient core DPLL-based engine in many other verification applications at Intel.

Our implication learning algorithms can be viewed as advanced techniques for simplifying combinational problems by systematically learning 2-literal clauses. An interesting future work would be to investigate how to deal with more complex relations between pairs or triplets of literals using a dedicated DPLL-based algorithm. In particular, an immediate generalization of the idea of $SSAT^{\rightarrow}$ would be to designate an algorithm that would efficiently learn 3-literal clauses as part of the SAT search: for example, if no implications have been learned between variables a, b, c, a clause $a \wedge \neg b \wedge c$ can be learned if any other combination of the assignments leads to a global conflict.

Acknowledgements. We thank the ABC developers for help in running the ABC experiments reported in the paper. Baruch Sterin contributed to the ideas and the implementation of some of the reported algorithms.

References

1. Abramovici, A., Breuer, M.A., Friedman, A.D.: Digital Systems Testing and Testable Design. Computer Science Press (1990)
2. Biere, A., Cimatti, A., Clarke, E., Zhu, Y.: Symbolic Model Checking without BDDs. In: Cleaveland, W.R. (ed.) TACAS 1999. LNCS, vol. 1579, pp. 193–207. Springer, Heidelberg (1999)
3. Biere, A., Heule, M., Van Maaren, H., Walsh, T.: Handbook of Satisfiability. IOS Press (2009)
4. Bjesse, P., Claessen, K.: SAT-Based Verification without State Space Traversal. In: Hunt, W.A., Johnson, S.D. (eds.) FMCAD 2000. LNCS, vol. 1954, pp. 372–389. Springer, Heidelberg (2000)
5. Bjesse, P., Boralv, A.: DAG-aware circuit compression for formal verification. In: ICCAD 2004 (2004)
6. Brand, D.: Verification of large synthesized designs. In: ICCAD 1993 (1993)
7. Case, M.L., Mishchenko, A., Brayton, R.K., Baumgartner, J., Mony, H.: Invariant-strengthened elimination of dependent state elements. In: FMCAD 2008 (2008)
8. Clarke, E.M., Grumberg, O., Peled, D.A.: Model Checking. MIT Press (1999)
9. Eén, N., Sörensson, N.: Temporal induction by incremental SAT solving. ENTCS 89(4) (2003)
10. van Eijk, C.A.J.: Sequential equivalence checking without state space traversal. In: DATE 1998 (1998)
11. Fraer, R., Ikram, S., Kamhi, G., Leonard, T., Mokkedem, A.: Accelerated verification of RTL assertions based on satisfiability solvers. In: HLDVT 2002 (2002)
12. Huang, S.-Y., Cheng, K.-T.: Formal Equivalence Checking and Design Debugging. Kluwer (1998)
13. Khasidashvili, Z., Nadel, A., Palti, A., Hanna, Z.: Simultaneous SAT-Based Model Checking of Safety Properties. In: Ur, S., Bin, E., Wolfsthal, Y. (eds.) HVC 2005. LNCS, vol. 3875, pp. 56–75. Springer, Heidelberg (2006)
14. Kroening, D., Strichman, O.: Decision Procedures. EATCS. Springer (2008)
15. Kuehlmann, A.: Dynamic Transition Relation Simplification for Bounded Property Checking. In: ICCAD 2004 (2004)
16. Kuehlmann, A., Krohm, F.: Equivalence checking using cuts and heaps. In: DAC 1997 (1997)
17. Kunz, W., Pradhan, D.K.: Recursive learning: An attractive alternative to the decesion tree for test generation in digital circuits. In: ITC 1992 (1992)
18. McMillan, K.L.: Interpolation and SAT-Based Model Checking. In: Hunt Jr., W.A., Somenzi, F. (eds.) CAV 2003. LNCS, vol. 2725, pp. 1–13. Springer, Heidelberg (2003)
19. Mishchenko, A., Chatterjee, S., Brayton, R., Een, N.: Improvements to combinational equivalence checking. In: ICCAD 2006 (2006)

20. Mony, H., Baumgartner, J., Mishchenko, A., Brayton, R.: Speculative reduction-based scalable redundancy identification. In: DTAE 2009 (2009)
21. Nadel, A.: Generating Diverse Solutions in SAT. In: Sakallah, K.A., Simon, L. (eds.) SAT 2011. LNCS, vol. 6695, pp. 287–301. Springer, Heidelberg (2011)
22. Nordström, J.: Stålmarck's Method Versus Resolution: A Comparative Theoretical Study. Stockholm University (2001)
23. Sheeran, M., Singh, S., Stålmarck, G.: Checking Safety Properties Using Induction and a SAT-Solver. In: Hunt, W.A., Johnson, S.D. (eds.) FMCAD 2000. LNCS, vol. 1954, pp. 108–125. Springer, Heidelberg (2000)
24. Sheeran, M., Stålmarck, G.: A tutorial on Stålmarck's method of propositional proof. Formal Methods In System Design 16(1) (2000)
25. Silva, P.M., Sakallah, K.: Robust search algorithms for test pattern generation. In: FTCS (1997)
26. Strichman, O.: Accelerating bounded model checking of safety properties. Formal Methods in System Design 24 (2004)
27. Whittemore, J., Kim, K., Sakallah, K.: SATIRE: A new incremental satisfiability engine. In: DAC (2001)
28. Wieringa, S.: On incremental satisfiability and bounded model checking. In: DIFTS (2011)

Liveness vs Safety – A Practical Viewpoint

B.A. Krishna[1], Jonathan Michelson[2], Vigyan Singhal[3], and Alok Jain[4]

[1] Chelsio Communications
[2] NVIDIA
[3] Oski Technology
[4] Cadence Design Systems

Abstract. Within the formal verification community, choosing between liveness and safety approaches has long been a subject of debate. This paper applies both approaches to a common design in the networking industry, a Deficit Weighted Round Robin (DWRR) arbiter. It then presents the tradeoffs we encountered while applying both approaches and also describes how we overcame state space explosion. We also describe two real post-silicon design bugs that we found, which were missed by all simulation methods.

1   Introduction

Correctness properties that define a system take the form of safety and liveness assertions [1]. Computer scientists have long debated the merits of safety and liveness approaches while casting these correctness properties. For example, consider the following contrasting manifestos from a liveness workshop [2]:

Moshe Vardi: *"Liveness properties are used to abstract away from messy safety properties."*

Leslie Lamport: *"Since the inherent complexity of checking liveness is greater than that of checking safety, engineers can check more complicated and therefore more useful models by checking only safety properties."*

In this paper, we will use a real design to put these theories to a practical test, taking advantage of various proof-engines at our disposal, including one that implements the known automated approach to transform liveness into safety properties [3].

Our design implements a DWRR arbiter [4], a practical scheme to implement fair queuing. Traffic at the inputs of the arbiter arrives on various ports. Each port has an associated weight. These weights determine the bandwidth distribution across the various ports. If we consider an n-port DWRR, with the ports having weights $W0$, $W1$, ..., $Wn-1$ respectively, then the averaged fractional bandwidth given to port(i) will be $Wi/(W0+W1+...+Wn-1)$.

Hardware implementations of DWRRs typically have per-port counters that maintain a notion of currently available credits. These counters enforce the bandwidth distribution. Ports request arbitration from DWRR, and the credit counter of the

K. Eder, J. Lourenço, and O. Shehory (Eds.): HVC 2011, LNCS 7261, pp. 80–94, 2012.

winning port is reduced by a cost charged by the port. The cost represents the amount of bandwidth consumed by the port. When a port has negative credits, it will not win arbitration, provided that a port with positive credits is requesting arbitration. Every time the sum of the credit counters goes to 0 or below, each counter is refreshed by its weight.

Two properties are paramount for such a DWRR: (a) the fairness property that the average bandwidth distribution is equal to the configured weights; and (b) the liveness property that states: *If port i arbitrates at time t, then it will always eventually be given a grant at some time t'>=t, regardless of the weight distribution across ports.* In this paper, we focus on this latter liveness property, which is one of the classical liveness properties [5].

Given the importance of this property, we applied formal verification techniques to validate the design. Unfortunately, the cones of influence of such liveness properties tend to have very large sequential depths because of the numerous internal counters implementing the arbitration decision making logic. This arbitration logic relies upon the integrity of these counters, and abstracting them away as purely nondeterministic signals yields bogus counterexamples. Therefore, other techniques were needed to make the proofs tractable.

Very few people in the industry apply formal verification on complex designs, largely because difficult problems are intractable without the use of a suitable abstraction methodology. Unfortunately, there is a woeful lack of case studies and discussion of practical, applicable abstraction methods in the published literature. Through this paper, we want to contribute two approaches to verify forward progress in DWRR arbiters, given how prevalent they are in the networking ASIC industry.

The paper first describes the operational details associated with our 4 port DWRR and then focuses on our experiences in obtaining liveness property proofs for this circuit both with and without certain manual abstractions. It then describes how we recast our recalcitrant liveness property in terms of safety properties.
Next, we compare and contrast liveness and safety-based approaches to evaluate the merits and demerits of each. We then describe two post-silicon bugs that were found during the formal verification process.

The Cadence IFV [6] model checker was used over the course of this project. For the purposes of this discussion, we limit ourselves to languages supported by commercial tools like PSL and SVA (System Verilog Assertions). These languages all happen to be LTL-based. We also limit this discussion to the 1800-2005 SV standard [7] where strong liveness is the default.

All our properties were run on a machine with two dual core AMD Opteron processors running at 2.6Ghz, with 1 Mbyte cache each and 16 Gbyte of main memory.

2   Operational Details

In this section, we describe our DWRR's interface and the associated handshaking protocol that governs the behavior of each port. The design maintains per-port credit counters, initialized to configured port Weights, and a priority queue of port numbers.

Each port presents an arbitration request until a grant is handed to it by the DWRR. Once a grant is obtained, the port in question utilizes this grant for an arbitrary number of cycles. During any cycle of this occupancy, the port can specify a *cost*. The port holding the grant is allowed to specify a non-zero *cost* multiple times while holding on to a grant.

This *cost* determines the bandwidth utilized. When a non-zero *cost* is specified, the per-port credit counter is decremented by the specified *cost*. When the grant is relinquished, the priority of this port is made the lowest, in order to ensure arbitration fairness across ports. If the sum of the per-port counters reaches 0 or goes negative, each per-port counter is refreshed by its Weight. A new "DRR round" starts whenever the per-port counters are refreshed.

For timing purposes, our design maintains another counter called the global counter. It is always added and subtracted by the same amounts as the per-port counters. In fact, we verified in a separate exercise that it always equals the sum of the per-port counters. The design uses it to determine when new DRR rounds start.

Configuration (Static) Inputs:

- $Wi[1:0]$ Port i's Weight (legal values: 1, 2, and 3)

Per-port arb/grant interface:

- Pi_Req (input)   port(i) asserts this signal to request a grant.
- Pi_Gnt (output) DWRR asserts this signal to give port(i) a grant.
- Pi_Vld (input) grant holder asserts this to qualify $Pi\_\{Cost,Eop\}$
- Pi_Cost (input) grant holder specifies cost provided Pi_Vld is asserted
- Pi_Eop (input) grant holder asserts this with Pi_Vld to relinquish grant.

The interface signals conform to the following protocol rules:

1. Pi_Req should be asserted until Pi_Gnt is asserted.
2. When port(i) does not have a grant, it should not assert Pi_Vld.
3. Once port(i) has a grant, it can charge a cost against its per-port credit counter by asserting: Pi_Vld & Pi_Cost. This will cause the per port credit counter to be subtracted by the specified amount. If Pi_Vld is not asserted, Pi_Cost will be ignored by the DWRR.
4. Once port(i) has a grant, it can choose to relinquish this grant by asserting: Pi_Vld & Pi_Eop. If Pi_Vld is not asserted, Pi_Eop will be ignored by the DWRR.
5. Each port must charge a non-zero cost before relinquishing its grant.

The credit counter of each port(i) is initialized to the configuration weight Wi. The arbiter examines the per-port counters associated with all arbitrating ports. A grant is given to the highest priority arbitrating port with positive credits. If there is no port arbitrating with positive credits, then the highest priority arbitrating port with zero or negative credits receives a grant. In all cases, once a grant is given, the granted port is deprecated to the end of the priority queue.

When a cost is subtracted from the per-port credits, the resulting credit value could be negative. To accommodate negative credits, a separate sign bit is maintained alongside each per-port counter. Further, ports with negative credits can win grants and continue to drive the credits more negative. The design avoids wrap by defining a maximum negative value at which the per-port counters saturate.

Counter refresh happens when the global counter value goes from a positive to either a negative or zero value. During a refresh, the per-port counters are incremented by a value limited by their original configuration weight. If a per-port counter was 0 or negative, it is incremented by its configuration weight. If a per-port counter was positive, it is set to a value equal to the configuration weight.

3   Formal Verification Strategy

In order to model the constraints for the FV of the DWRR, we used a 3-state FSM. Each port's inputs were driven by signals that were combinationally generated from a state variable, *Pi_state*, whose state transitions are described in Figure 1.

Pi_state FSM

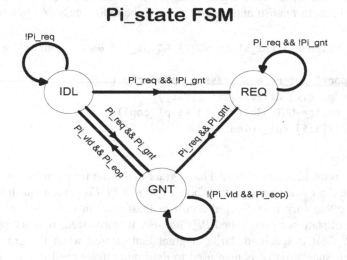

Fig. 1. Pi_state

The state variable *Pi_state*, has 3 possible states, namely IDL, REQ and GNT. The significance of each state is as follows:

- *Pi_state==IDL*: The port has not yet started arbitrating for a grant and may or may not be asserting *Pi_Req*. In this state, *Pi_Req* is non-deterministically driven to 0 or 1 while *Pi_Vld, Pi_Eop* and *Pi_Cost* are driven to 0.
- *Pi_state==REQ*: The port was arbitrating in the previous cycle, but did not possess a grant. Therefore, in this cycle, it should continue arbitrating, so *Pi_Req* should be asserted, and *Pi_Vld, Pi_Eop* and *Pi_Cost* are driven to 0.

- *Pi_state*==GNT: The port has already secured a grant. In this cycle, the port a) may or may not relinquish the grant by asserting *Pi_Vld && Pi_Eop* and b) may or may not charge a *cost* to its credit counter by asserting *Pi_Vld && Pi_Cost*.

This state variable was then utilized to generate inputs *Pi_Req, Pi_Vld, Pi_Cost,* and *Pi_Eop*. In addition, the per-port configuration weight inputs *W1, W2, W3, W4,* were driven by *rigid* variables that were non-deterministically set to {1,2,3} at the time of reset, and preserved constant throughout.

In order to eliminate bogus counter-examples, we added the below constraints:

- Once a port acquires a grant, it will always eventually relinquish it *(fairness constraint)*.
- Once a port acquires a grant, it will always charge a non-zero cost at least once *(safety constraint)*. This constraint was required as per the design specifications.

Both these constraints were specified as SVA assumptions to eliminate false negative paths where either a port holds a grant forever or relinquishes a grant without charging a cost. The former constraint was coded using the following SVA code snippet:

```
wire pi_release = (pi_state==GNT) && pi_vld && pi_eop;

assume_porti_gnt_release: assume property (
  @(posedge clk) disable iff (!rst_)(
    (pi_state==GNT && !(pi_vld && pi_eop))
    |-> ##[1:$] (pi_release)
  )
);
```

In other words, if, at time t, port(i) has a grant and is not relinquishing it, then there will be some t' > t when port(i) asserts both *Pi_Vld & Pi_Eop* to relinquish the grant.

To ensure that each port charged a *cost* at least once in the course of holding a grant, 1 bit of state per port, called *Pi_Charged*, is introduced. It is set whenever a non-zero *Pi_Cost* is specified during a grant and cleared when the grant is relinquished. This state variable is then used to determine if we need to post a non-zero cost at the time of grant relinquishment.

With all these constraints in place, we cast the liveness property in SVA as follows:

```
assert_propi_liveness: assert property (
  @(posedge clk) disable iff (!rst_)
    (pi_state==REQ) |-> ##[0:$] (pi_gnt)
  )
);
```

If, at time t, port(i) is arbitrating, then there will always be some t' >= t when port(i) gets a grant.

An intuitive attempt to cast this as a safety property that applies a cycle bound on the maximum number of cycles that can elapse before a requesting port gets a grant, will fail. Unfortunately, for our DWRR arbiter, there is no such cycle bound. We will explore safety based alternatives in a later section.

4 Liveness

Once the FV scaffolding was built, numerous attempts were made to converge on proofs without deploying any abstractions. We utilized all possible proof engines, but none succeeded in converging over an 8+ hour window.

Despite having relatively few state bits in the cone of influence, the proofs were not tractable because the sequential depths associated with these proofs were inordinately large. Consequently, we studied the cone of influence associated with the liveness property in order to reduce it. Simplistic attempts to abstract away the per-port credit counters entirely resulted in counterexamples that were bogus, consisting of paths that never occurred in the real implementation. These paths consisted of scenarios where the internal counters exhibited values that would never occur in the real design.

It became clear to us that if we are to abstract away per-port credit counters, we need an abstraction that places constraints on the permissible range of values. While thinking through counter abstractions, we realized that simpler abstractions are possible elsewhere. We will start with the simpler abstractions and later revisit a counter abstraction.

Abstraction(I). The following interface assumptions helped us gain insights into possible abstraction techniques:

- Each port required a non-deterministic variable to generate a "random" cost (*Pi_Cost*), possibly multiple times in the course of holding a grant.
- Each port additionally required a state variable, *Pi_charged*, to ensure that during a grant, a non-zero cost would be specified at least once.

We observed that, as per the port specifications, since *Pi_Cost* and *Pi_Charged* can be posted if and only if this port was in possession of a grant, it seemed unnecessarily onerous to maintain these state variables on a per-port basis.

Rather, since only one port can be in possession of a grant, and since only that particular port can charge a cost or relinquish, we realized that the DWRR would internally have a mux, which had various per-port cost inputs and a single set of outputs, "Vld" and "Cost" that pertains to the port in possession of a grant. The DWRR internally does maintain such a multiplexer whose outputs were: *sel_vld, sel_cost* & *sel_port={0,1,2,3}*. This mux appeared to be relatively trivial to verify separately.

The first abstraction we deployed did the following: We introduced cutpoints at *sel_vld* & *sel_cost*. The FV framework directly posted cost values on this interface, keeping in mind the DUT's requirement that a non-zero cost has to be posted by a port at least once while it is holding a grant (and not necessarily at the time the grant is relinquished). This abstraction therefore eliminated 4 per-port state bits and replaced it with a single bit state variable, for the purposes of generating cost.

The single state bit is cleared upon a new grant and set whenever a cost is posted. It is consulted during EOP. If no cost has been posted before EOP, a cost is posted at EOP. If a cost has already been posted, then another cost may be optionally posted at EOP. It was possible to trivially establish that this abstraction scheme was sound through visual inspection of the RTL.

Abstraction (II). The second manual abstraction that we used stemmed from another design insight: There should still be arbitration fairness even if refresh never occurs. Without any refreshes, the credit counters of all ports that win grants and post costs will be driven negative. At this point, the DWRR should simply hand out grants in a "round-robin" fashion, provided the behaviors of the per-port counters and priority list are preserved.

The global credit counter, which is the sum of the various per-port credit counters, serves a sole purpose: To trigger refresh. The second abstraction eliminated the global counter by introducing a cutpoint directly at the internal RTL signal *wt_refresh*, which was responsible for generating per-port counter refreshes. There was no need to impose fairness constraints on the behavior of *wt_refresh*.

Results with Abstractions (I) & (II)

Once these two manual abstractions were deployed, we tried multiple different BDD [8] and SAT [9] based engines. The BDD based engines used the Emerson and Lei algorithm [10] to natively check liveness properties

With Abstractions (I) & (II), *assert_propi_liveness* ran to completion within ~ 25 minutes. Our lowest runtime was obtained with a SAT based engine that used Property Directed Reachability (PDR [11]) and employed a filter to automatically translate liveness properties into safety properties [3].

Abstraction (III). In an attempt to further reduce proof runtimes, we then gave thought to more sophisticated abstraction techniques. We observed that per-port counter values are manipulated in the course of two events: 1) *decrements* when costs are posted, and 2) *increments* during refresh. We further observed that the RTL's arbitration grant logic only discriminated between *{positive, 0, negative}* per-port counter values and did not care about the actual values. This insight led us to believe that it would be possible to abstract each per-port counter as 2 bits.

The DUT internally maintains 4 per-port counters within state variables: *wt_cur0*, *wt_cur1*, *wt_cur2* and *wt_cur3*. These RTL registers are updated every cycle from "next" state variables: *wt_nxt0*, *wt_nxt1*, *wt_nxt2* and *wt_nxt3*. To deploy Abstraction (III), we preserved the per-port counter for the port under liveness consideration and then introduced cutpoints at *wt_nxt* for all the other three ports' credit counters. These cutpointed signals are then driven by abstraction code described in Table 1.

Table 1. Non-deterministic per-port counter abstraction for wt_nxt

```
always @(*) begin
  wt_nxt = wt_cur;
   if (decrement && wt_refresh) /* subtract && add */
      wt_nxt = rnd0 ? WT_POS: rnd1 ? WT_ZERO: WT_NEG;
   else
   if (decrement && !wt_refresh) /* subtract only */
      if (wt_cur==WT_POS)
         wt_nxt = rnd0 ? WT_POS: rnd1 ? WT_ZERO: WT_NEG;
      else
      if (wt_cur==WT_ZERO)
         wt_nxt = WT_NEG;
   else
   if (!decrement && wt_refresh) /* add only */
      if (wt_cur==WT_ZERO)
         wt_nxt = WT_POS;
      else
      if (wt_cur==WT_NEG)
         wt_nxt = rnd0 ? WT_POS: rnd1 ? WT_ZERO: WT_NEG;
end
```

In the course of deploying Abstraction(III), we found the need to assume a new fairness constraint. This constraint was needed for subtle reasons.

Fairness constraint: If we see new arbitration requests infinitely often, then we will always eventually see a refresh.

In the absence of this fairness constraint, the model checker can construct counterexamples where the liveness port under consideration remains forever at deficit credit values (and is therefore disadvantaged) while others, even after being given grants, do not go negative and remain eternally advantaged because of our abstraction's nondeterminism. This is an artificial scenario, since in reality, these other ports will eventually use enough credits to cause a refresh. Sufficient refreshes will replenish the disadvantaged port's credits and raise its arbitration priority. To avoid this unrealistic scenario, we use the fairness constraint which states that there will always eventually be a refresh allowing our deficit port to recover credits over time.

Results with Abstractions(I), (II) & (III)
When all 3 abstractions were deployed, this liveness property ran to completion, passing in ~ 100 seconds, when we used a SAT (PDR based) engine [11]. Our next step was to ensure the soundness of Abstraction (III). We were able to establish trivially through visual inspection that this abstraction is sound. However, we also had to prove our fairness constraint.

In order to prove our fairness constraint, we removed Abstractions (II) & (III) and expressed this constraint in SVA as:

```
assert_liveness_refresh: assert property (
  @(posedge Clk) disable iff (!rst_)(
    ##[0:$] (wt_refresh)
  )
);
```

The above liveness property was falsified by the model checker, which generated a counterexample exposing a design anomaly. Within the counterexample, *port0* was the only arbitrating port. It had an initial credit counter value of *3*. It then proceeded to issue requests and was given grants. For each grant, it posted a cost of 1 credit. This caused *port0*'s credit counter to become negatively saturated at -4. *port0* continued to infinitely get grants, but the posted costs were not applied to either the global credit counter or *port0's* credit counter. Consequently, *wt_refresh* was forever deasserted.

We classify this behavior as a bug. If a port with negative credits is in possession of a grant and posts a cost while no positive port is arbitrating, then this event should force *wt_refresh* to be asserted, triggering a refresh of all per-port credit counters. Such new semantics would ensure that (a) all grants result in modification of per-port/global counters and (b) If we see new requests infinitely often, we will be assured of eventually seeing a refresh.

This bug does not affect the validity of the earlier proof that used Abstractions (I) & (II) because it prevents refresh only when ports with negative credits are arbitrating. As previously stated, the arbiter degrades to round robin at this point, thereby maintaining fairness. In fact, the first liveness proof with Abstractions (I) & (II) shows that forward progress does not require any refreshes.

After fixing this bug, *assert_liveness_refresh* ran to completion, passing in ~120 seconds using the same SAT (PDR based) engine[11]]. The cumulative runtime for our counter abstraction based proofs was ~ 3.5 minutes, constituting a significant improvement over our earlier approach which resulted in a runtime of ~ 25 minutes.

5   Safety (Bounded Forward Progress)

Since the inherent complexity of proving liveness is much higher than that of proving safety, we wondered if safety-based approaches would converge without abstractions. Consequently, we began exploring ways to verify this circuit with safety properties. We found that we could do so by answering the question, "If a particular port is arbitrating for a grant, what is the *maximum* number of grants (N) that can be given to others after which point this port *will* be given a grant?"

We identified a set of two safety properties that implies the liveness property under consideration. These safety properties are:

- *If port(i) is arbitrating for a grant, no more than a total of N grants can be given to other ports.*
- *If no port is currently holding a grant and at least one port arbitrates at time t, then a grant will be given to one of them at t+1.*

The first property only verifies that less than or equal to N grants are given to other ports. This, by itself, is insufficient. A faulty DUT that halts before issuing N+1 grants to other ports would still pass this metric but fail the original liveness property. Therefore we needed the second property as well.

All starvation scenarios involve one of two things:

1. Other ports keep getting grants forever (or)
2. No port gets grants in the future

Both scenarios described above will result in a violation of our safety property set.

Composing the exact safety property set required to imply forward progress, that can be used in lieu of our liveness property, was non-trivial. We iterated through many different sets of safety assertions before agreeing upon the ones outlined above. Our next task was to compute N (max. grants given to others while a port is arbitrating).

Computation of N

Consider a 4 port DWRR with each port having an n bit credit counter. We consider an implementation where the global counter is always equal to the sum of the various per-port counters. Each n bit per-port credit counter is in the range: $\{-2^{(n-1)}...2^{(n-1)}-1\}$.

If we have n-bit wide per-port credit counters, we find that the configuration weights required for this worst case scenario will consist of: $port(i)$'s $Wi = 1$ and $port(j!=i)$'s $Wj = 2^{(n-1)}-1$. This configuration maximally disadvantages $port(i)$ and maximally advantages all $port(j!=i)$.

The total number of credits, T, available at the beginning of round #1 will be equal to the sum of the configuration weights. That is, $T = 1+3*(2^{(n-1)}-1)$.

In the first round, $port(i)$ will get a grant and proceed to drive himself into the worst deficit possible. In other words, $port(i)$ will go from $+1$ to $-2^{(n-1)}$. That is, $port(i)$ will consume a total of C credits, $C = 2^{(n-1)}+1$. The remaining credits in this round, R, expands to $R = T-C = 3*2^{(n-1)}-2 - (2^{(n-1)}+1) = 2*2^{(n-1)}-3$.

These remaining credits will be handed out to other ports, i.e., $port(j!=i)$, and during each grant, only one credit will be consumed by these ports, in the worst case path.

During subsequent rounds, $port(i)$ will be replenished only with 1 new credit, and $port(i)$ will slowly work its way out of its deficit value. Meanwhile, other ports, never having gone deficit, will be fully replenished to their original configuration weight.

The total number of credits available for arbitration, during the round #2, will be $R+1$. The "$+1$" comes about because $port(i)$'s credit counter, which was at a deficit, got incremented by its Weight $Wi = 1$. During the second round, $port(i)$ will receive one credit, but still be in deficit mode. Therefore *port(i)* will not receive a grant and all *R+1* credits will be given to *ports(j!=i)*, with each of them utilizing *1* credit per grant.

The total number of credits available for arbitration, during the round #3, will be *R+2*. During the third round, *port(i)* will receive one credit, but still be in deficit mode. Therefore *port(i)* will not receive a grant and all *R+2* credits will be given to *port(j!=i)*, with each of them utilizing *1* credit per grant.

The number of rounds of arbitration required for *port(i)* to go from his deficit to a positive credit level works out to: $M = C = 2^{(n-1)}+1$. A total of *M* rounds of arbitration will be required for *port(i)* to recover from deficit and win a grant where

$$M = 2^{(n-1)}+1.$$

The grand total number of grants given to other *port(j!=i)* across all rounds of arbitration, while *port(i)* is waiting, works out to be an arithmetic progression of the form: *{{ R }, { R+1 }, {R+2}, ..., {R+(M-1)}}*, so *N* will therefore be equal to the sum of this progression, which works out to be $= N = M/2*(2*R+(M-1))$.

For our DUT's configuration, we have

$$M = 2^{(n-1)}+1 = 2^{(3-1)}+1 = 2^2+1 = 5 \text{ and } R = 2*2^{(n-1)}-3 = 2*2^{(3-1)}-3 = 2*2^{(2)}-3 = 5.$$

So our sum, $N = 5/2*(2*5+(5-1)) = 5/2*(10+4) = 5/2*14 = 35$. This is the answer to our question: "If *port(i)* is arbitrating, what is the maximum number of grants that can be given to *port(j!=i)* after which point *port(i)* is guaranteed to be given a grant".

This analysis was not done entirely upfront. Based on our knowledge of the design, we attempted to compute *N*, verified this computation using a model checker, and found counterexamples which we then analyzed. After refining our understanding of the subtleties in the design, we recomputed *N*. We iteratively repeated this process until our manual computation matched the behavior observed with the model checker. This was a very laborious and time consuming process. As it turned out, minor design details played a major role in the computation, more so than any of us had anticipated.

Note that the bug previously disclosed does not impact the maximum N because it causes the arbiter to degrade to round robin. The worst-case N for a 4 port round robin arbiter is 3.

A simple finite state machine, shown in Table II, was written to count the number of grants given to port (j!=i) while port(i) is arbitrating without having obtained a grant. Here, *N* is equal to *MAX_CNTi*.

Table 2. Implementation of per port grant counter

```
// pi_gnt_ctr: counts gnts to port(j!=i) while port(i) waits
always @(posedge Clk) begin
  if (!rst_ || pi_granting)
    pi_gnt_ctr <= 7'd0; // rst or got our grant; clear ctr
  else begin
   if (pi_requesting && non_pi_granting)
     // pi requesting but !pi getting grants; incr. ctr
     pi_gnt_ctr <= pi_gnt_ctr+7'd1;
  end
 end
end

// We should never see MAX_CNTi+1 grants given to others
assert_propi_req: assert property (
  @(posedge Clk) disable iff (!rst_)(
    (pi_gnt_ctr!=(MAX_CNTi+7'd1))
 )
```

The state variable *pi_gnt_ctr* is initialized to 0. Whenever port(i) is requesting grants, if some other port(j!=i) wins a grant, we increment *pi_gnt_ctr*. Whenever port(i) wins a grant, we clear *pi_gnt_ctr*. Our safety property ensures that *pi_gnt_ctr* will never have a value of *MAX_CNTi+1*, which would indicate *N+1* grants given to other ports.

Stating *N* in such a concrete fashion (as 35 for a 4-port DWRR) gives us tighter bounds than our liveness property specification.

We observe that as the per-port counter widths increase, this *N* goes up exponentially, making the safety properties much more computationally intensive.

There are some pitfalls associated with "guestimating" N. The designer was unable to precisely compute N upfront and provide it in the specification. Were we to guess a value and find a failure, in the absence of us knowing what N is precisely, we would not know whether this failure is a real bug, or simply a case where our safety property has not waited for enough grants. It is likely that the designer will not view such a failure as compelling evidence of design malfunction.

The best cumulative runtime of our safety property proofs was ~ 5 minutes using the BDD[8]-based engines which is greater than the runtime observed with our liveness based approach, i.e. the counter abstraction liveness proofs. However, unlike the liveness-based approach, here we required no manual abstractions to render our proofs tractable.

We further note that the liveness formulation is more portable than the safety equivalent. The safety invariants tend to be more design specific than the more general liveness properties. We found that seemingly trivial design changes yielded large changes in N while the liveness properties remained valid unchanged regardless of the design's implementation details.

6   Property Results

Formal verification of this block took place after the design was taped-out. The liveness properties passed. For experimental purposes, we artificially inserted a couple of starvation type bugs. These bugs manifested themselves as liveness property failures.

During the liveness-based effort, we identified a design bug pertaining to the behavior of *wt_refresh*. During the safety-based effort, we encountered a non-critical bug that did not affect the liveness proofs. Following is the description of this bug:

In DWRR configurations that have a cost input wider than 1 bit, it is possible that 1 cycle *after* a refresh, the global counter will still be zero, leading to a new round of arbitration with 0 credits, causing yet another refresh during the next cycle. This bug exposes a non-critical design sub-optimality.

This second bug does not invalidate the liveness or the safety proofs because it just lengthens the duration of refresh from 1 cycle to 2 cycles. The design does not hand out grants during refresh, so this bug does not add additional counter manipulation corner cases. Furthermore, none of our proofs depend upon the length of refresh.

This second bug was not found as a direct consequence of failing the safety properties outlined above. The "computation of N" safety approach forced us to examine several microscopic details relating to the arbiter's grant mechanism, which in turn led us to cast a secondary safety property that eventually identified our second bug. Had we exclusively used a liveness approach, we would not have cast other detailed properties pertaining to the internal grant mechanism. As a consequence of using a safety-based approach, we were forced to ask previously unidentified questions about the design. If we had simply "guestimated" an appropriate N until we found a passing value, we also would not have cast secondary questions or found this second bug.

7   Conclusions and Limitations

We have compared and contrasted liveness and safety-based approaches while proving forward progress in our DWRR circuit. We invested roughly equal effort on both approaches with a view to characterizing each in terms of abstractions required, proof runtimes and suitability of proof-engines.

There is a dearth of papers that describe (a) the applicability of well-known abstraction techniques to industrial designs and (b) the advantages and disadvantages of liveness and safety-based approaches in proving forward progress for such designs. In narrating our experiences, we aspire to fill both voids.

The Liveness proofs exhibited better runtimes with the right sort of abstraction techniques (including but not limited to counter abstractions), in conjunction with the SAT (PDR based) engine[11]. This makes liveness an attractive option for us, particularly since we did not have a forward progress definition, in the form of a precise safety event bound, *a priori*.

Our liveness-based approach required considerable effort in experimenting with various abstractions and proof-engines as well as in identifying design insights that made application of these abstractions possible.

Our safety based approach required no abstractions and had a slightly higher runtime than the liveness runtime. The safety-based approach required us to expend a lot of effort in (a) identifying a precise set of safety properties that implied forward progress and (b) computing an exact bound on the number of grants that could be given to others while a port is arbitrating for a grant.

If we had to choose one approach over the other, it would be based on the following criterion: Has the designer specified and endorsed a precise event bound (for the max. number of grants that can be given to other ports)? Is this bound stable? If the answer to either of those questions is "no", we conclude that a liveness based approach is preferable. On the other hand, if the answer to both those questions is "yes", we conclude that a safety based approach is viable and practical.

We also conclude that both approaches are viable, but have their downsides. Liveness may be preferred by users comfortable with making abstractions to reduce larger runtimes, and safety might be preferred by users who can work more closely with the designers to come up with precise, design-specific safety properties. Engineers with sufficient time might prefer both - liveness for simpler property formulation with easier portability if design changes occur, and safety for more precise specification that can find additional bugs.

By formally verifying our DWRR circuit, we also gained subtle insights into the current design, which include but are not limited to the following:

1. We have arrived at a precise formula that determines the number of grants that can be given to other ports while a particular port is arbitrating.
2. We observe that if per-port counters are preserved intact and the refresh logic is abstracted away entirely, then we are guaranteed forward progress.
3. We observe that if per-port counters are carefully abstracted and we are always eventually assured of a refresh, then we are guaranteed forward progress.

We view these insights as a valuable by-product of the overall FV effort since they constitute a more rigorous specification of our existing design and can help influence future design changes.

References

1. Lamport, L.: Proving the Correctness of Multiprocess Programs. IEEE Transactions on Software Engineering SE-3(2) (March 1977)
2. Liveness Manifestoes. In: Beyond Safety International Workshop, Schloss Ringberg, Germany (April 2004), http://cs.nyu.edu/acsys/brond-safety/
3. Biere, A., Artho, C., Schuppan, V.: Liveness Checking as Safety Checking. Electronic Notes in Theoretical Computer Science 66(2) (2002)

4. Shreedar, M., Varghese, G.: Efficient Fair Queing using Deficit Round Robin. IEEE/ACM Trans. Networking 4(3) (June 1996)
5. Manna, Z., Pnueli, A.: Adequate proof principles for invariance and liveness properties of concurrent programs. Science of Computer Programming 4(3) (December 1984)
6. Incisive Formal Verifier User Guide, Cadence Design Systems
7. IEEE Standard for System Verilog – Unified Hardware Design, Specification and Verfication Language, IEEE Standards Board (November 2005)
8. Bryant, R.E.: Graph Based Algorithms for Boolean Function Manipulation. IEEE Transactions on Computers C-35(8) (1986)
9. Moskewicz, M.W., Madigan, C.F., Zhao, Y., Zhang, L., Malik, M.: Chaff: Engineering an Efficient SAT solver. In: Proceedings of the 38th Design Automaton Conference (2001)
10. Emerson, E.A., Lei, C.L.: Efficient Model Checking in Fragments of the Proposition Mu-Calculus. In: Proceedings of the 1st Symposium on Logic in Computer Science (1986)
11. Bradley, A.R., Manna, Z.: Checking safety by inductive generalization of counterexamples to induction. In: Proc. FMCAD (2007)

Predicting Serializability Violations: SMT-Based Search vs. DPOR-Based Search

Arnab Sinha[1], Sharad Malik[1], Chao Wang[2], and Aarti Gupta[3]

[1] Princeton University
[2] Virginia Polytechnic Institute
[3] NEC Laboratories America

Abstract. In our recent work, we addressed the problem of detecting serializability violations in a concurrent program using predictive analysis,
where we used a graph-based method to derive a predictive model from a
given test execution. The exploration of the predictive model to check alternate interleavings of events in the execution was performed explicitly,
based on stateless model checking using dynamic partial order reduction
(DPOR). Although this was effective on some benchmarks, the explicit
enumeration was too expensive on other examples. This motivated us to
examine alternatives based on symbolic exploration using SMT solvers.
In this paper, we propose an SMT-based encoding for detecting serializability violations in our predictive model. SMT-based encodings for
detecting simpler atomicity violations (with two threads and a single
variable) have been used before, but to our knowledge, our work is the
first to use them for serializability violations with any number of threads
and variables. We also describe details of our DPOR-based explicit search
and pruning, and present an experimental evaluation comparing the two
search techniques. This provides some insight into the characteristics of
the instances when one of these is superior to the other. These characteristics can then be used to predict the preferred technique for a given
instance.

1 Introduction

The atomicity of a set of operations is a desired correctness condition for concurrent programs. There exist many different notions of atomicity, useful in various
contexts [22,11,4]. In this paper, we address conflict-serializability [22], a widely
used notion. Informally, an execution is conflict-serializable if it is equivalent,
in some sense, to a serial execution where the individual atomic regions are
executed sequentially. In general, atomicity violations can be detected by observing a particular trace, called the *monitoring problem* [5,27], or by exploring
alternate interleavings of events in a given trace, called the *predictive analysis
problem* [7,26,28,33,37,25,6,17].

The existing predictive analysis methods are broadly classified into two categories based on their precision. Methods in the first category detect *must-
violations*, i.e. the reported violation must be a real violation [26,37,33]. Methods

K. Eder, J. Lourenço, and O. Shehory (Eds.): HVC 2011, LNCS 7261, pp. 95–114, 2012.

in the second category detect *may-violations*, i.e. the reported violation may be a real violation [25,6,17]. Due to higher precision, the methods in the first category are usually expensive. Therefore, effort is needed to improve performance and scale better on long traces.

In our recent prior work on predictive analysis [28], we proposed a method in the first category, where we used a graph-based technique to derive a predictive model called a TAS (Trace Atomicity Segment) that is based on read-write and synchronization events in the observed trace. The TAS is used to generate alternate interleavings, called *Almost View Preserving (AVP)* interleavings, that are guaranteed to be feasible executions of the concurrent program. Therefore, any serializability violations detected on AVP interleavings are also guaranteed to be real violations. The basic idea is to consider alternate interleavings where any thread is allowed to *break* its read-coupling, i.e. it reads from a different write event than what was observed in the given trace, but to *skip* all subsequent dependent events in this and other threads (since they can no longer be guaranteed to be feasible). Essentially, AVP interleavings preserve the view in each thread upto some prefix, and only the prefixes and broken read events are allowed to appear in a serializability violation.

1.1   Motivating Example

To motivate the issue of feasible executions, consider a program execution shown in Figure 1, with events numbered in the order of execution in the given trace. It has four concurrent threads $(T_1 \ldots T_4)$ and four shared variables $(x, y, z$ and $t)$. The rectangular boxes (in threads T_2 and T_4) denote pre-specified atomic blocks (e.g. using `begin_atomic` and `end_atomic` labels in the trace). The inter-thread edges represent read-after-write (RaW) orders. Suppose that event e_9 in T_1 is conditional on the value of z in e_5, which gets its value from e_4. Note that the given trace is a serializable execu-

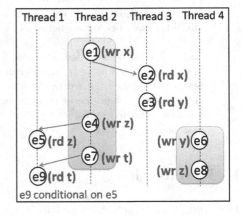

Fig. 1. This is a serializable program execution trace

tion since the events can be ordered as $(e_1, e_4, e_7), e_2, e_3, e_5, e_9, (e_6, e_8)$ without violating atomicity of the blocks. In Figure 2, we show two other possible interleavings of the same events, where the atomicity of the atomic block in thread T_2 is violated.

Although both interleavings shown in Figure 2 are unserializable, the violation in (a) is real, while the violation in (b) may be bogus. Specifically, in execution (b), event e_8 happens between e_4 and e_5, thereby assigning a different value to the shared variable z in event e_5 than in the original trace. Therefore, the value read by event e_5 may not be the same (we call this a *broken-read*), which may affect the occurrence of event e_9 down the line.

1.2 Overview and Contributions

In our prior work [28], we used an explicit state traversal technique based on Dynamic Partial Order Reduction (DPOR) [8] to generate AVP interleavings from our predictive model, and each interleaving was checked by looking for a cycle in the corresponding D-serializable (DSR) graph [22,27]. Although use of dynamic partial order reduction ensures that no redundant interleavings (with respect to

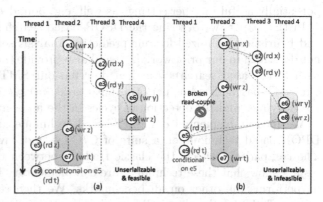

Fig. 2. The interleaving (a) is unserializable and feasible. However, the interleaving (b) is unserializable but not guaranteed to be feasible. (The broken arrow represents serializability violation path defined in Section 2.)

the conflict-based partial order) are generated, the number of interleavings was still quite high for many benchmarks in our experiments. This motivated us to examine symbolic search techniques, that avoid an explicit enumeration of the AVP interleavings.

Note that symbolic encodings of interleavings in a concurrent program have been studied earlier [32,33,29,30]. However, their focus is on read-write consistency constraints to ensure feasible interleavings, and suitable interference abstractions and refinement to weaken/strengthen these constraints for modular analysis. These encodings (capturing a concurrent trace) can be utilized with a suitable encoding of any target property for verification. In this paper, we use a similar encoding of read-write consistency (adapted to our predictive model), and combine it with an encoding for checking serializability violations (for any number of variables, for any number of threads) based on cycle detection. This general serializability property has not been addressed in any of the earlier symbolic efforts, which handled only data races, deadlocks, and simple atomicity/serializability violations (involving a single variable and two threads). Indeed, our symbolic encoding of serializability violations based on cycle detection can be potentially combined with other SMT-based encodings of interleavings in a concurrent program.

In recent years, the advancements in SAT and SMT solvers [19,21] have been leveraged in many areas of automated software verification, including symbolic exploration for concurrent programs, e.g. symbolic partial order reduction [35], symbolic predictive analysis [34,33], datarace detection [24]. Therefore, it is natural to examine whether SMT-based search can be useful in our method for predictive analysis. Although previous methods have used SMT-based encodings for detecting simple serializability violations involving two threads and a single variable [33], to the best of our knowledge, our method proposed here is the first SMT-based technique for detecting general serializability violations involving any number of threads and variables. Our SMT-based encoding can be potentially useful in other settings as well, e.g. bounded model checking [1,9].

In this paper, we describe the DPOR-based search with additional pruning and heuristics optimized for our predictive analysis setting (these details were not described in our prior work [28], and also provide the context for comparison with SMT-based search). We then describe our SMT-based search in detail. Our SMT-based encoding performs both tasks: (a) symbolic exploration of AVP interleavings, and (b) detection of cycles in the associated DSR graph.

We have implemented our SMT-based technique and compare it with our DPOR-based technique on a suite of C/C++ and Java benchmark programs. The comparison reflects the classic tradeoff between time and space, and our results show that these techniques are complementary in the sense that neither outperforms the other on all benchmarks. We then consider some features of our predictive model that indicate which technique is likely to perform better (based on our current experiments). Specifically, we consider the relative TAS size (how big is the TAS model, relative to the trace) and coupling between threads (number of inter-thread edges, relative to number of all events) that seem to be good predictors.

Contributions: To summarize, this work makes the following contributions.

- We describe details of a DPOR-based explicit technique for exploration of interleavings, with additional pruning and heuristics optimized for finding serializability violations.
- We propose an SMT-based technique for detecting serializability violations using predictive analysis, suitable for modern SMT-solvers.
- We provide experimental results for the SMT-based technique, using two state-of-the-art SMT-solvers – Yices [15] and Z3 [31].
- Finally, we present the comparative results between DPOR-based and SMT-based techniques in our predictive analysis, and identify some characteristics of instances that can be used to select between them.

2   Preliminaries

In this section, we summarize the needed background on our prior work. We omit the detailed formal discourse (available online in [28]), and describe the main aspects. We consider a concurrent program consisting of a set of *threads* $T_1, \ldots, T_k$ and a set of *shared variables*. Let $tid = \{1, \ldots, k\}$ be the set of thread indices. The remaining aspects of the program, including the control flow and the expression syntax, are intentionally left unspecified for generality.

Program Trace Model: An execution trace $\rho = e_1, e_2, \ldots e_n$ is a sequence of events, each of which is an instance of a *visible* operation (read/write accesses to shared variables and synchronization operations are regarded as visible operations) during the execution of the concurrent program. An event is represented as a 5-tuple $(tid, eid, type, var, child)$, where tid is the thread index, eid is the event index (that starts from 1 and increases sequentially within a thread), $type$ is the event type, var is either a shared variable (in read/write operations) or a synchronization object, $child$ is the child thread index (in thread create/join). The event type is one of $\{read, write, fork, join, acquire, release, wait, notify, notifyall, atomic\_begin, atomic\_end\}$.

An execution trace ρ provides a total order on the events appearing in ρ. We derive a partial order by retaining only the set of must-happen-before constraints, which collectively are sufficient to guarantee feasibility of the serializations of this partial order.

Partial Order Graph: Let $G(V, E)$ be a partial order graph such that $V(G)$ is the set of vertices, each of which represents an event in the trace (we use vertices and events interchangeably when the context is clear). A directed edge in $E(G)$ (the set of edges) is either a program order (PO), or a read-after-write (RaW), or a synchronization (Sync.) edge. If there is a RaW edge from a to b in G, then the pair (a, b) is defined as a *read-couple*. In a different interleaving, if b reads from a different event c, we say that the read-couple for b in G is *broken*.

We assign clock-vectors to each vertex in G, following the idea of Lamport's Logical Clock [18] in order to check the causality order between any two events. An example of a partial order graph with 3 threads is shown in Figure 3. The rectangular block in this figure represents an atomic block denoted by $\mathcal{A}$. $V(\mathcal{A})$ denotes the vertices in $\mathcal{A}$. The number inside each vertex is the eid. The vectors are shown in square brackets next to the vertices. For convenience, we shall refer to vertex 1 in the 2nd thread as vertex 2.1.

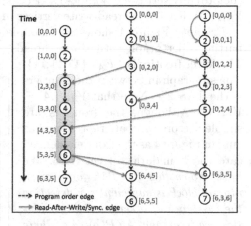

Fig. 3. The PO graph with vectors. Vertices represent events from the trace. The dashed and solid edges are PO and RaW/Sync. edges respectively. Note that RaW edges can both be inter- and intra-thread edges.

Almost View Preserving (AVP) Interleavings: Let G' be a partial order graph derived from ρ similar to G, except that it has only the program order and sync. edges. Let $t \in T$, where T be the set of all interleavings consistent with G'. Let v be a read event in t. For each read event v in t, if the read couple for v in ρ is broken in t, then all vertices w, such that v must-happen-before w in G, are deleted from t resulting in t'. $AVP(\rho)$ is the set of all t' s.t. $t \in T$. **Serializability Violation Path**: It is well-known that there is a conflict-serializability violation if there exists a cycle in the D-serializable (DSR) graph [22,27]. In our setting, for any alternate interleaving we *conceptually* construct a conflict graph G_C (similar to a DSR graph), where the vertices are the read/write events and edges represent conflicting accesses and program order. There is an atomicity violation if we can find a path that starts and terminates within the atomic block, and visits at least one vertex outside the atomic block in G_C.

Trace Atomicity Segment (TAS): For each atomic block $\mathcal{A}$, we identify a TAS as a subgraph $\mathcal{Z}_\mathcal{A} \subseteq G$ that is sufficient for the purpose of detecting all serializability violations among $AVP(\rho)$. Intuitively, the TAS captures all events that *may happen in parallel with events in $\mathcal{A}$*, until broken reads are encountered. Our overall technique derives a TAS for each atomic block in the given trace. In effect, this considers a sliding window over the trace, where each window looks at alternate interleavings among events that can happen in parallel with an atomic block.

A *frontier* is a k-tuple, i.e. a vector, where the ith integer represents the *eid* of some event in i^{th} thread. A TAS is bounded by two frontiers: *upper* and *lower*, with respect to G (see Figure 4). Events that must happen before the first event within $\mathcal{A}$ are above the upper frontier. Analogously, events that must happen after the last event in $\mathcal{A}$ are below the lower frontier. The subgraph of G between the upper frontier and the lower frontier is called the TAS $\mathcal{Z}_\mathcal{A}$. The usefulness of frontiers is that no vertex above the upper frontier (below the lower frontier) may appear after (before) any vertex $v \in V_{RW}(\mathcal{A}) \subseteq V(\mathcal{Z}_\mathcal{A})$ in any interleaving in $AVP(\rho)$ (where $V_{RW}(\mathcal{A})$ denotes the read-write vertices in the given atomic block).

Example: Figure 4 shows an example of a TAS for the atomic region in a partial order graph with three threads. The upper frontier is $UF_\mathcal{A}=\{8,5,6\}$. The lower frontier is $LF_\mathcal{A}=\{17,11,11\}$.

The subgraph in between the frontiers is the TAS $\mathcal{Z}_\mathcal{A}$. Note that $V_{RW}(\mathcal{A}) \subseteq V(\mathcal{Z}_\mathcal{A})$. Although, the frontiers are simple vectors, they are represented as cuts in Figure 4 as the frontiers demarcate the boundaries of the TAS. *We have shown that the TAS for a given atomic block is sufficient for detecting the existence of a serializability violation path among $AVP(\rho)$, i.e. there exists no violation path that includes vertices outside $\mathcal{Z}_\mathcal{A}$.* In effect, the TAS serves as our predictive model, and we search over all AVP interleavings over events in the TAS.

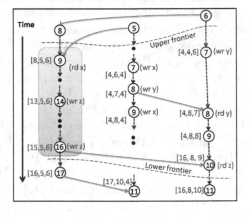

Fig. 4. The TAS in a partial order graph G, with respect to the atomic block (shaded rectangular region). The upper and lower frontiers are given by $\{8,5,6\}$ and $\{17,11,11\}$, respectively.

Note that for a violation path, there must exist at least two events within the atomic block that conflict with other access(es) outside the atomic block but within the TAS. Although such events may exist across a long trace, they may not occur within a relatively small TAS. This provides a static check: If such events do not exist in a TAS, then no violation is possible among $AVP(\rho)$. In practice, this static check is frequently successful.

3   Explicit Search within the TAS

If the TAS $\mathcal{Z}_{\mathcal{A}}$ fails the above simple static check, i.e. a serializability violation may be possible, we search among all the interleavings within $\mathcal{Z}_{\mathcal{A}}$ to find the unserializable one. In this section, we use a Dynamic Partial Order Reduction (DPOR [8,36]) based explicit search algorithm. We also improve this DPOR search with several sound pruning techniques and search heuristics.

3.1   Overview of DPOR Algorithm

An interleaving prefix $\pi = e_1, e_2, \ldots e_k$ is a sequence of a subset of the events in ρ; that is, $\forall i$, event e_i belongs to ρ, $|\pi| \leq |\rho|$, and events in π are not necessarily in the same order as in ρ. Two interleaving prefixes comprised of the same subset of events are *conflict-equivalent* iff the relative order of all pairs of conflicting events is same. The DPOR algorithm can be used to generate one representative interleaving from each conflict-equivalent class, by avoiding the other (redundant) interleavings.

In the DPOR algorithm, an interleaving prefix π is represented as a sequence $s_1, s_2, \ldots s_k$ of program states, where event e_i is executed during the transition from s_i to s_{i+1}, for all $i = 1, 2, \ldots k$. At each state s, we use $s.enabled$ to record the set of threads that are ready to execute. The next event in any thread $\tau \in s.enabled$ is referred to as the *ready-transition*. We also use $s.backtrack \subseteq s.enabled$ to record a subset of the enabled threads, where each thread $\tau \in s.backtrack$ represents a possible scheduling choice at s in some future runs. Note that $\tau \notin s.backtrack$ means that, according to the partial order reduction theory, executing thread τ at state s would have led to a redundant interleaving [8].

Two mutually independent transitions (t_i, t_j) whose events are both ready for execution are referred to as *co-enabled* transitions. For instance, if a lock is acquired by one thread, it must be released before another thread can acquire it. Therefore, the transition that releases the lock and the transition that acquires it are mutually dependent, and hence are not co-enabled transitions.

Although DPOR is efficient in testing concurrent programs, it is not geared toward enumeration of interleavings in a predictive model such as ours. More specifically, it does not take TAS and the read-write coupling requirements into consideration. Therefore, we have customized the original DPOR for TAS, and our new algorithm is presented in Figures 5& 6. (Our modifications are lines marked with a '⋆'.) In the pseudo-code, we use symbol S to denote the state stack $(s_0 s_1 \ldots s_d \ldots s_n)$, and use $s.stack\_depth$ to denote the depth of state s in stack S. We start search with the first event in an atomic region $\mathcal{A}$ (say u_0) (lines 1-3, procedure **Init**). At each state s, we first find a set of preceding states (whose next events are mutually dependent with the enabled events at s) and update their *backtrack* sets (lines 2-12, procedure **Explore**). Here, in order to properly

```
Init {
1:   if(u_0.type = read or write)
         computeEnabledRaW(s_0, s_0, u_0);
2:   else computeEnabled(s_0, s_0, u_0);
3:   S.push(s_0);
4:   Explore(S);
5: }

Explore(S) {
1:   let s = S.top_of_stack();
2:   for each thread h{
3:       let t_n be a transition such that t_n.tid ∈ s.enabled and t_n.tid = h
             and t_n is not a coupled read in the atomic block;
4:       for all transitions t_d in the current explored path dependent with
             t_n and it may be co-enabled with t_n{
5:           let s_d be the state in S from which t_d is executed;
★ 6:         if (s_d.cs ≥ CS_max or
               (bt_tag.isTrue ? (bt_tag.stack_depth< s_d.stack_depth):false))
★ 7:             continue;
8:           let E = {q.tid ∈ s_d.enabled | (q.tid = h ∧ q is not a coupled
                 read from the atomic block) ∨ (t_d ≺ q ≺ t_n and q is
                 dependent with some t' such that, q ≺ t' ≺ t_n &
                 t'.tid = h)};
9:           if (E ≠ {}) then
                 choose any member of E and add to s_d.backtrack;
10:          else
                 add {q.tid | q.tid ∈ s_d.enabled and q is not a coupled
                 read from the atomic block} to s_d.backtrack;
11:      }
12: }
13:  if (s.enabled is not empty) {
★ 14:    heuristically, pick t.tid from s.enabled;
15:      s.backtrack ← {t.tid};
16:      let done = {};
17:      while (∃t such that t.tid ∈ s.backtrack \done){
18:          add t to done;
19:          let, s' ← next(s, t);
★ 20:        computeContextSwitch(s, s', t); // compute cs for s'
★ 21:        if(t.type = read or write) computeEnabledRaW(s, s', t);
22:          else computeEnabled(s, s', t); // compute s'.enabled
23:          S.push(s');
24:          Explore(S);
25:          S.pop();
26:      }
27:  }
28: }
```

Fig. 5. Generating and checking the non-interfering runs

update the *backtrack* sets and avoid redundant interleavings, we need to track the conflicting pairs of transitions within the interleaving prefix. After finding and updating the backtrack sets of dependent preceding states, we need to pick an enabled thread at state *s* to execute. Rather than randomly picking (as in the original DPOR), we heuristically pick a thread, insert it in *s.backtrack* (lines 14-15, procedure **Explore**), and continue. We continue exploring the enabled threads in *s.backtrack* by calling **Explore** recursively, until all threads in this backtrack set are explored (lines 17-27). At this point, we insert the thread into the *done* set (line 18).

In this DPOR search, deciding whether any of the read-couples is broken in the current prefix is crucial. We use a map called *active_couple* to store the mapping from the 'written but not read' shared variables to the last coupled-reader in ρ (a written value can be read by multiple readers). Once the last reader reads the variable, the map is removed from *active_couple* (line 12, procedure **computeEnabledRaW**).

The set *enabled* is computed by procedure **computeEnabledRaW** if the current transition is a read/write access (Figure 6) and by the standard procedure **computeEnabled** otherwise (pseudo-code omitted for brevity). Procedure **computeEnabledRaW** is designed specifically to handle constraints from the RaW edges (or couples), while procedure **computeEnabled** deals with the standard synchronization primitives. It is worth pointing out that the original DPOR does not have or need procedure **computeEnabledRaW**. In our case, if a coupled read is mismatched, i.e. the read event is not reading the value it is supposed to read, the following events in the thread are skipped (line 6-7, procedure **computeEnabledRaW**).

Several helper procedures such as **preProcess** and **postProcess** (lines 1 and 16, respectively) are also called. We omit their pseudo code, but provide a brief description as follows. Procedure **preProcess** helps in initializing the various data-structures of a state (except for s_0, the current state inherits those data-structures from the previous state). Procedure **postProcess** helps in eliminating or inserting thread-ids into the *enabled* of the current state depending on certain conditions related to the ready-transitions and the data-structures of the current state.

```
computeEnabledRaW (states: s_p, s_c, transition: t) {
    // s_p: previous state; s_c: current state;
1:   preProcess (s_p, s_c);
2:   if (t.type = write and this write is coupled) {
3:     s_c.active_couple ← s_c.active_couple ∪ {(t.var, last reader of t)};
4:   } else if (t.type = read and this read is coupled) {
5:     if (t.var ∈ s_c.active_couple){
6:       if (read-couple is broken)
7:         s_c.next(t.tid) ← null; // thread virtually terminates
8:       if (t = s_c.active_couple[t.var]) //t is the last reader
9:         s_c.active_couple ← s_c.active_couple.erase(t.var);
10:    }
11:  }
12:  if(read-couple is broken and t is the broken read within the atomic region) {
13:    bt_tag.isTrue ← true;
14:    bt_tag.stack_depth ← s_p.stack_depth;
15:  }
16:  postProcess (s_p, s_c);
17: }
```

Fig. 6. Computing *enabled* using RaW edges

Although we are performing a restricted search (by using RaW edges to reduce the number of interleavings), the explicit search overhead is still not practical in most of our initial experiments. These unrealistic run-times pushed us to look for smarter prunings and heuristics. In order to further reduce the number of interleavings, we propose several sound pruning techniques (Section 3.2) and search heuristics (Section 3.3).

3.2   Pruning TAS Search Space

Consider the scenario in Figure 7 (a), where $t_{lastInAB}$ is the last transition in the atomic region (from state s_d) and t is the current transition in the interleaving prefix. Assume that t_i, t_j and t_k are the predecessor transitions from states s_i, s_j and s_k respectively, conflicting with t. Our observation is that, if the atomicity property is not violated in the interleaving prefix until $t_{lastInAB}$, then updating the backtrack set of any successor state after s_d cannot generate any viola-tion path. This claim can be justified as follows. First, updating the backtrack set of successors of s_d will not change the interleaving prefix until $t_{lastInAB}$. Second, there is no transition within the atomic block after $t_{lastInAB}$, and no vio-lation exists in the prefix until $t_{lastInAB}$. Hence there does not exist a serializ-ability violation path in the interleavings with fixed pre-fix until $t_{lastInAB}$. There-fore, in Figure 7 (a), we update the backtrack sets of s_i and s_j only (and leave the backtrack set of s_k unchanged).

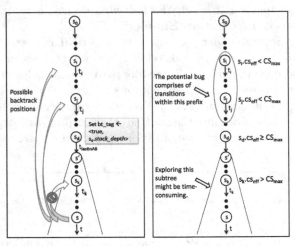

Fig. 7. (a) Setting a marker when the last transition ($t_{lastInAB}$) from the atomic region appears in the pre-fix helps in pruning the interleavings. (b) Tuning the parameter CS_{max} can help in carrying out localized search.

We implement this sound pruning technique in line 6 of procedure **Explore**, by introducing the global data-structure bt_tag (read as *backtrack-tag*). This data-structure has two fields: a Boolean variable $isTrue$ and an integer variable $stack\_depth$. The data-structure is set in line 13-14 in procedure **computeEnabledRaW**, if current transition t is a mismatched read in $\mathcal{A}$ and the following events within $\mathcal{A}$ are skipped. The field $stack\_depth$ records the depth of s_d in the state-stack S such that, subsequent updates of the backtrack set of s can be ignored if $bt\_tag.isTrue$ is true and $bt\_tag.stack\_depth < s.stack\_depth$ (lines 6-7, Fig. 5).

3.3   Heuristics for TAS Search

We also use context bounding (i.e. limiting the number of context-switches) as a search heuristic to reduce cost. However, this is an unsound reduction technique because it may miss real bugs. We call a context switch *significant* when it is either inevitable (i.e. the previous transition is the last event of its thread) or needed to facilitate read-after-write or wait-notify couples. All other context-switches are referred to as *insignificant*. Our definition of *insignificant* context switches differs from the *preemptive* context switches in CHESS [20] since we also consider the RaW constraints.

We assign a counter $s.cs$ to record the number of insignificant context switches in the interleaving prefix up to state s. Let CS_{max} be the maximum number of insignificant context-switches permitted by the user. Observe that in line 6 of procedure **Explore**, for a state s_d, if $s_d.cs \geq CS_{max}$, we will skip the update of its backtrack set. The intuition behind this conditional update is as follows. Assume that there is a potential violation path comprising of fewer insignificant context-switches, then it will be detected by our algorithm with a small predetermined CS_{max}. In line 14, procedure **Explore**, the thread is heuristically picked from $s.enabled$ to efficiently utilize this budget. In practice, we can broaden the search space incrementally, by first exploring the interleavings with fewer context switches, and then gradually increasing the maximum number of insignificant context switches. In other words, the insignificant context-switch bounding enables a localized search within a fixed prefix length.

The complexity of this clock-vector based algorithm, as derived in [8], is $O(kdr)$, where k is number of threads, d is the maximum size of the search stack and r is the number of transitions explored.

4   Implicit Search within the TAS

As discussed earlier, an alternate framework for systematic exploration of events within the TAS is SMT-based implicit exploration. We now show how to encode the problem as an SMT instance using difference logic. This instance can then be analyzed by state of the art SMT solvers.

4.1   Encoding of the Violation Path Reachability

Consider the example in Figure 8. All the vertices shown in the figure (u, v, v' and w) write to variable x. The path $u \rightarrow v \rightarrow v' \rightarrow w$ is a violation path. We encode this violation path which may be present in some alternate interleaving $\rho' \in AVP(\rho)$. Although, an alternate interleaving ρ' may contain one or many broken read-couples (as any thread is allowed to break its read-coupling), for ease of understanding, we first consider the case which does not allow broken read-couples. This assumption will be subsequently relaxed to include the possibility of broken read couples.

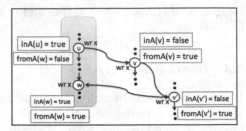

Atomic Block Membership Condition: The violation path always begins in an atomic block. We define the following function $inA(u)$ for a vertex u.

Fig. 8. The function $inA(u)$ denotes whether vertex u belongs to the atomic block, while function $fromA(u)$ denotes if u is reachable from some vertex within $\mathcal{A}$ via a violation path

$$inA(u) = \begin{cases} \text{true} & \text{if } u \in V(\mathcal{A}) \\ \text{false} & \text{otherwise} \end{cases} \tag{1}$$

Consider edge (u, v) such that v is a conflicting access in a different thread from u. In the interleaving ρ', u happens before v. Let $x(u)$ be a function that assigns an integer value to the vertex u. This is used to provide ordering constraints between vertices in the violation path. $x(u) < x(v)$ iff in ρ', u happens before v.

We define function $fromA(v)$ to be true if vertex v is reachable from $\mathcal{A}$ along a possible violation path. Let the function $edgeFromA(u,v)$ be true if v is reachable from $\mathcal{A}$ through u. There are two cases.
Case 1 $(u \in V(\mathcal{A}))$: In ρ', $x(u) < x(v)$ and v should be outside the atomic block (i. e. $inA(v) = \text{false}$) ensuring that the path leaves the atomic block. Then,

$$edgeFromA(u,v) = (\neg inA(v) \ \wedge \ (x(u) < x(v))) \quad \text{if } u \in V(\mathcal{A}) \tag{2}$$

In Fig. 8, $edgeFromA(u,v)$ is true.
Case 2 $(u \notin V(\mathcal{A}))$: Vertex u happens before v and u is already on a violation path (i.e. $fromA(u) = \text{true}$). Then,

$$edgeFromA(u,v) = (fromA(u) \ \wedge \ (x(u) < x(v))) \quad \text{if } u \notin V(\mathcal{A}) \tag{3}$$

In Fig. 8, $(x(v) < x(v'))$ and $fromA(v) = \text{true}$ imply $edgeFromA(v,v') = \text{true}$.

We refer to the set of eligible (u, v) pairs that need to be considered in the $edgeFromA$ computation defined above as EP_Set. There are two possibilities for edges in this set. Either, (i) the vertices u and v conflict or (ii) they belong to the same thread.

$$EP\_Set = \{(u,v) \mid ((u.type = write \vee v.type = write)$$
$$\wedge \ (u.var = v.var)) \vee (u.tid = v.tid), \text{where } u,v \in V_{RW}\}$$

Thus, combining Eq. 2 and Eq. 3 we can define function $fromA(v)$.

$$fromA(v) = \bigvee_{\forall (u,v) \in EP\_Set} edgeFromA(u,v) \tag{4}$$

4.2   Encoding of the Violation Path

Finally, there exists a violation path iff there exists at least one vertex u within $\mathcal{A}$ such that $fromA(u)$ is true implying that u is reachable from some vertex in $\mathcal{A}$ via a violation path that visits vertices outside $\mathcal{A}$. So the following condition (Φ) is satisfied if the interleaving contains a violation path.

$$\Phi_{VP} = \bigvee_{\forall u \in V(\mathcal{A})} fromA(u) \tag{5}$$

4.3   Encoding of the Program Order

For each edge $(u,v) \in E(G)$ except for the RaW edges (since the RaW edges denote read-couples which can be broken), the following constraint is introduced in the encoding.

$$HB(u,v) = (x(u) < x(v)) \tag{6}$$

Let,

$$\Phi_{PO\_Sync} = \bigwedge_{\forall (u,v) \in PO\_Sync\_Set} HB(u,v) \tag{7}$$

where,

$$PO\_Sync\_Set = \{(u,v) \mid (u,v) \in E(G) \text{ and } (u,v)$$
$$\text{is not a RaW edge.}\}$$

Moreover, for each conflicting pair (u,v) such that u may happen in parallel with v, denoted by $u \mid v$,

$$\phi_{Par}(u,v) = (x(u) < x(v)) \vee (x(v) < x(u)) \tag{8}$$

Let,

$$\Phi_{Par} = \bigwedge_{\forall (u,v) \in Par\_EP\_Set} \phi_{Par}(u,v) \tag{9}$$

where,

$$Par\_EP\_Set = \{(u,v) \mid (u,v) \in EP\_Set \text{ and } (u \mid v)\}$$

4.4   Encoding of Synchronizations

The synchronization events like lock-unlock and wait-notify also need to be encoded to get an alternate feasible interleaving. First, we encode the lock-unlocks. Let $lk_1 = (u_{lk1}, u_{unlk1})$ and $lk_2 = (u_{lk2}, u_{unlk2})$ are two pairs of vertices that operate on the same lock-variable. As the locked regions cannot overlap, there are two possibilities (1) $x(u_{unlk1}) < x(u_{lk2})$, or (2) $x(u_{unlk2}) < x(u_{lk1})$. Therefore, for each pair of lock-unlock events operating on the same lock,

$$\phi_{LK}(lk_1, lk_2) = (x(u_{unlk1}) < x(u_{lk2})) \vee (x(u_{unlk2}) < x(u_{lk1})) \tag{10}$$

Let,

$$\Phi_{LK} = \bigwedge_{\forall (lk_1, lk_2)} \phi_{LK}(lk_1, lk_2) \tag{11}$$

The wait-notify events are encoded similarly. Let, (u_w, u_n) be a wait-notify couple and u'_n be another notify event operating on the same variable. Therefore, u'_n should not come in between u_w and u_n in any interleaving. Therefore,

$$\phi_{WN}(u_w, u_n, u'_n) = (x(u'_n) < x(u_w)) \vee (x(u_n) < x(u'_n)) \tag{12}$$

Let,

$$\Phi_{WN} = \bigwedge_{\forall (u_w, u_n, u'_n)} \phi_{WN}(u_w, u_n, u'_n) \tag{13}$$

4.5   Encoding of Broken Read-Couples

For a given trace ρ, the set $AVP(\rho)$ contains interleavings where one or many read-couples are broken. Next, we encode these broken read-couples. We introduce two new related functions - $Broken$ and $Skip$. Intuitively, whenever a read-couple is broken, $Broken(u)$ is true where u is the reader and $Skip(v)$ is true for all the following vertices v. These two functions are defined using mutual recursion. Consider the read-couple (u, v) in Figure 10. The read-couple can be broken under three circumstances.

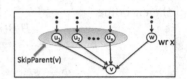

Fig. 9. Let $u_1, u_2, \ldots, u_n$ be the parents of v in G such that none of them writes. The set $\{u_1, u_2, \ldots, u_n\}$ is denoted as $SkipParent(v)$.

1. Some other write event u' happens between u and v (i.e., $HB(u, u') \wedge HB(u', v)$), where $HB(u, v)$ stands for $(x(u) < x(v)))$ and none of u, v and u' are skipped (i.e., $\neg(Skip(u) \vee Skip(v) \vee Skip(u')))$. We refer to u' as "challenger" as it challenges the read-couple (u, v). This condition is denoted as $\phi_{B1}(u, v)$.

2. Vertex v appears before u (i.e., $HB(v, u)$ is true) and none of u and v are skipped (i.e., $\neg(Skip(u) \vee Skip(v)))$. This condition is denoted as $\phi_{B2}(u, v)$.

3. The writer u is skipped while reader v is not skipped (i.e., $Skip(u) \wedge \neg Skip(v)$). This condition is denoted as $\phi_{B3}(u, v)$.

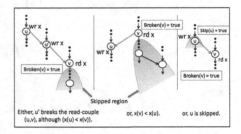

Fig. 10. Let (u, v) be a read-couple and u' writes the same variable. The read-couple can be broken in three ways in an alternate interleaving ρ'. (1) u' happens between u and v, or, (2) v happens before u, or, (3) u is skipped.

Further, if some write u' happens before v, where v is initially not read-coupled and none of u' and v are skipped, then $Broken(v)$ is true.

Thus, we define $Broken(v)$ as follows.

$$Broken(v) = \begin{cases} \begin{aligned} &\phi_{B1}(u,v) \vee \phi_{B2}(u,v) \\ &\qquad \vee \phi_{B3}(u,v) \\ &\bigvee_{\forall u'}(HB(u',v) \quad \wedge \quad \neg(Skip(u') \vee Skip(v))) \end{aligned} \\ \\ false \end{cases}$$

(u,v) is a read-couple and u' is challenger,

v reads but not read-coupled within the TAS and u' is a challenger,

otherwise.
(14)

where,

$$\phi_{B1}(u,v) = \neg(Skip(u) \vee Skip(v)) \wedge \left(\bigvee_{\forall u'}(HB(u,u') \wedge HB(u',v) \wedge \neg Skip(u')) \right)$$

$$\phi_{B2}(u,v) = \neg(Skip(u) \vee Skip(v)) \wedge HB(v,u)$$

$$\phi_{B3}(u,v) = Skip(u) \wedge \neg Skip(v)$$

The intuitive idea behind the condition for a vertex v being skipped is as follows: (c.f. Figure 9): when any of the parents of v in G is skipped or broken, except when the parent is a conflicting write from a different thread (only possible in case of read-couples), v is also skipped. When a parent that writes in a different thread is skipped, v must be the coupled read which gets broken (but not skipped) and the events following v are skipped. The set $SkipParent(v)$ is defined as follows.

$$SkipParent(v) = \{u \mid (u,v) \in E(G) \text{ except when } u \text{ is a write from a different thread}\}$$

Next we define $Skip(v)$. We skip a vertex v when one of the members of $SkipParent(v)$ is skipped or broken.

$$Skip(v) = \begin{cases} false & \text{if } SkipParent(v)=\{\} \\ \bigvee_{u \in SkipParent(v)} Skip(u) \vee Broken(u) & \\ & \text{otherwise.} \end{cases}$$
(15)

Note that although we have used mutual recursion in the definitions of $Skip$ and $Broken$, the definitions are not cyclic. The reason for this is as follows. The definition of $Skip(v)$ depends on the values of $Skip(u)$ and $Broken(u)$, where u is one of the parents of v. Therefore, the definition of $Skip$ is not cyclic. The function $Broken(v)$ is also acyclic since it refers to $Skip$ function and we have already argued that $Skip$ is acyclic.

4.6   Encoding Allowing the Broken Read-Couples

We now state the modified constraints that allow the broken reads. The modifications in the constraints are underlined.

- **The atomic block membership constraints**: If a vertex within $\mathcal{A}$ is skipped, the violation path cannot start from the vertex. Therefore, we modify Eq. 1 to account for the broken read-couples in the following equation,

$$inA(u) = \begin{cases} \underline{\neg Skip(u)} & \text{if } u \in V(\mathcal{A}) \\ \text{false} & \text{otherwise} \end{cases}, \tag{16}$$

- **The encoding of the reachability of the violation path**: The function $edgeFromA$ is meaningless when either u or v is skipped. Thus, we add a new conjunctive clause $(\neg(Skip(u) \lor Skip(v)))$ to the original definition of $edgeFromA$.

$$edgeFromA(u,v) = \begin{cases} (\neg inA(v) \land (x(u) < x(v)) \\ \quad \underline{\land \neg(Skip(u) \lor Skip(v)))}, \\ \quad\quad \text{if } u \in V(\mathcal{A}) \\ (fromA(u) \land (x(u) < x(v)) \\ \quad \underline{\land \neg(Skip(u) \lor Skip(v)))}, \\ \quad\quad \text{otherwise} \end{cases} \tag{17}$$

Finally, we combine Equations 5, 7, 9, 11 and 13 to get the complete encoding

$$\Phi = (\Phi_{VP} \land \Phi_{PO\_Sync} \land \Phi_{Par} \land \Phi_{LK} \land \Phi_{WN}) \tag{18}$$

where, the functions inA, $fromA$, $Broken$, $Skip$ are defined in Equations 16, 4, 14 and 15 respectively.

4.7   Complexity

The number of constraints is bounded by $O(N + mpq^2 + l_{ev}^2 l)$, where N, m, p, q, l_{ev} and l represent: number of events, number of variables, maximum number of reads per variable, maximum number of writes per variable, maximum number of events per lock variable and number of lock variables respectively.

5   Results

We have implemented our technique in a prototype tool. This tool is capable of logging/analyzing execution traces generated by both Java programs and multithreaded C/C++ programs using Pthreads. The program traces used are all available online [14]. The C++ benchmark is available online [12]. All the Java benchmarks are publicly available [3,10,13,16,23].

The tool logs execution traces at runtime from C++ source code instrumented using the commercial front end from Edison Design Group (EDG). For Java programs, we use execution traces logged at runtime by a modified Java Virtual Machine (JVM). For each test case, we first execute the program using the default OS thread scheduling and log the execution trace. Next we apply our algorithm to detect the serializability violations. For Java traces, we assume that all synchronized blocks are intended to be atomic, unless the synchronized block has a wait. For the C++ application, we assume that all blocks using scoped locks (monitors implemented using Pthreads locks and condition variables) are intended to be atomic.

All our experiments were conducted on an Intel i7 machine (2.67 GHz, 3 GB memory) running Ubuntu 2.6.31-14-generic. Our experiments are designed to study how implicit interleaving enumeration using SMT compares against explicit enumeration using DPOR. As part of this, we consider two different SMT-solvers (Yices [15] & Z3 [31]). However, a fair comparison of Yices and Z3 is not possible as we can use the Yices API, but need to call Z3 using

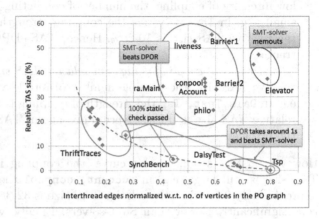

Fig. 11. It is our intuition, although not validated over large set of programs, that the winner among DPOR vs SMT can be predicted given the relative TAS size and the strength of the coupling (these can be determined statically) between the threads in a trace

the SMT instance in a file as the Z3 API library is not available for Unix [2]. Further, we have also considered bit-blasting of the order variables (the x variables) in the SMT encoding rather than using difference logic. However, the results with bit-blasting are not significantly different from those without it.

We found that when the number of constraints generated in symbolic exploration (i.e. SMT) largely exceeds the interleavings explored in explicit exploration (i.e. DPOR), the DPOR-based strategy runs faster compared to the SMT-solvers. This observation has been validated for both the SMT solvers - Yices and Z3.

In Figure 11, we present an interesting observation made from our experimental results. We define *coupling strength* as the ratio of the inter-thread edges and the number of vertices in the graph. A low (high) number represents loosely (strongly)-coupled threads. (These indicators can be derived & generalized over all available traces.) We characterized the traces with respect to their relative TAS sizes (ratio of number of vertices within the TAS and in the entire trace) (Y-axis) and coupling strength (X-axis). We found that traces where DPOR beats SMT-solvers lie around the curve indicated in Figure 11. We classify the traces that lie further away from this curve into two sub-groups: (1) Those for which SMT-solvers beat DPOR, and (2) Those for which SMT-solvers run out of memory. Observe that, the traces belonging to sub-group 2 lie further away from the curve compared to those belonging to sub-group 1. We offer the following explanation for this observation. The curve contains traces for which one of the following is true.

1. *The strength of coupling is very low but relative TAS size is large* - due to low intensity of coupling, the number of conflicting accesses is probably very small, e.g. in `ThriftTraces` the coupling strength is between 0.1-0.3, and the relative TAS size is 10-26%. Hence, TAS+DPOR is effective for these traces.

2. *The strength of coupling is high but relative TAS size is small* - due to small relative TAS size, the possible number of interleavings is again very small, e.g. in `DaisyTest, Tsp` the strength of coupling is between 0.65-0.8 and the relative TAS size is 0-2%. Hence, once again, TAS+DPOR is effective for these traces.

However, in traces outside this curve, the coupling is such that the relative TAS size is still large, e.g. in `account, conpool` the strength of coupling is approximately 0.56 while the relative TAS size is 32-38%. In such cases, DPOR runs significantly slower than SMT-solvers. Finally, when both the coupling-strength and relative TAS size are both high the SMT-solvers run out of memory, e.g. in traces from `Elevator`, the strength of coupling is 0.7-0.8 and relative TAS size is 36-48% and SMT-solvers run out of memory. We would like to clarify that while this explanation seems to fit this limited data set, further experimentation is needed with a larger data set to draw general conclusions.

6   Conclusion

This paper builds on our previous work on predictive analysis using trace-atomicity-segments for almost-view-preserving interleavings [28]. It first provides details of an explicit search algorithm that explores possible interleavings using specialized heuristics in a DPOR based search. (This was not described in [28]). Next, it shows how this problem may be encoded as an SMT instance, thus leveraging modern SMT solvers. Finally, based on experimental evaluation, it provides some insight into the characteristics of the instances when one of these techniques is superior to the other. These characteristic can be used to predict the preferred technique for a given problem instance.

References

[1] Biere, A., Cimatti, A., Clarke, E.M., Zhu, Y.: Symbolic Model Checking without BDDs. In: Cleaveland, W.R. (ed.) TACAS 1999. LNCS, vol. 1579, p. 193. Springer, Heidelberg (1999)

[2] Z3: Linux binary, http://research.microsoft.com/enus/um/redmond/
     projects/z3/download.html
[3] Farchi, E., Nir, Y., Ur, S.: Concurrent Bug Patterns and How to Test Them. In:
     IPDPS, p. 286 (2003)
[4] Farzan, A., Madhusudan, P.: Causal Atomicity. In: Ball, T., Jones, R.B. (eds.)
     CAV 2006. LNCS, vol. 4144, pp. 315–328. Springer, Heidelberg (2006)
[5] Farzan, A., Madhusudan, P.: Monitoring Atomicity in Concurrent Programs. In:
     Gupta, A., Malik, S. (eds.) CAV 2008. LNCS, vol. 5123, pp. 52–65. Springer,
     Heidelberg (2008)
[6] Farzan, A., Madhusudan, P.: Meta-analysis for Atomicity Violations under Nested
     Locking. In: Bouajjani, A., Maler, O. (eds.) CAV 2009. LNCS, vol. 5643, pp. 248–
     262. Springer, Heidelberg (2009)
[7] Farzan, A., Madhusudan, P.: The Complexity of Predicting Atomicity Violations.
     In: Kowalewski, S., Philippou, A. (eds.) TACAS 2009. LNCS, vol. 5505, pp. 155–
     169. Springer, Heidelberg (2009)
[8] Flanagan, C., Godefroid, P.: Dynamic Partial-Order Reduction for Model Check-
     ing Software. In: POPL 2005, pp. 110–121 (2005)
[9] Ganai, M.K., Gupta, A.: Accelerating High-Level Bounded Model Checking. In:
     ICCAD 2006, pp. 794–801 (2006)
[10] Havelund, K.: Using Runtime Analysis to Guide Model Checking of Java Pro-
     grams. In: Havelund, K., Penix, J., Visser, W. (eds.) SPIN 2000. LNCS, vol. 1885,
     pp. 245–264. Springer, Heidelberg (2000)
[11] Herlihy, M.P., Wing, J.M.: Linearizability: A Correctness Condition for Concur-
     rent Objects. ACM Trans. Program. Lang. Syst. 12, 463–492 (1990)
[12] http://incubator.apache.org/thrift/
[13] Joint CAV/ISSTA special event on specification, verification, and testing of con-
     current software, http://research.microsoft.com/qadeer/cav_issta.html
[14] http://www.princeton.edu/~sinha/CAV12_Traces.zip
[15] Yices: An SMT solver, http://yices.csl.sri.com
[16] Java grande forum benchmark suite, http://www2.epcc.ed.ac.uk/computing/
     research_activities/java_grande/index_1.html
[17] Kahlon, V., Wang, C.: Universal Causality Graphs: A Precise Happens-Before
     Model for Detecting Bugs in Concurrent Programs. In: Touili, T., Cook, B., Jack-
     son, P. (eds.) CAV 2010. LNCS, vol. 6174, pp. 434–449. Springer, Heidelberg
     (2010)
[18] Lamport, L.: Time, Clocks, and the Ordering of Events in a Distributed System.
     Commun. ACM 21(7) (1978)
[19] Moskewicz, M.W., Madigan, C.F., Zhao, Y., Zhang, L., Malik, S.: Chaff: Engineer-
     ing An Efficient SAT Solver. In: DAC 2001, New York, NY, USA, pp. 530–535
     (2001)
[20] Musuvathi, M., Qadeer, S., Ball, T., Basler, G., Nainar, P.A., Neamtiu, I.: Finding
     and Reproducing Heisenbugs in Concurrent Programs. In: OSDI 2008, pp. 267–280
     (2008)
[21] Nieuwenhuis, R., Oliveras, A., Tinelli, C.: Solving SAT and SAT Modulo Theories:
     From an Abstract Davis–Putnam–Logemann–Loveland Procedure to DPLL(T). J.
     ACM 53, 937–977 (2006)
[22] Papadimitriou, C.H.: The Serializability of Concurrent Database Updates. J.
     ACM 26(4), 631–653 (1979)
[23] von Praun, C., Gross, T.R.: Static Detection of Atomicity Violations in Object-
     Oriented Programs. Object Technology 3(6) (2004)

[24] Said, M., Wang, C., Sakalla, K., Yang, Z.: Generating Data Race Witnesses by an SMT-Based Analysis. In: NFMS (2011)

[25] Savage, S., Burrows, M., Nelson, G., Sobalvarro, P., Anderson, T.: Eraser: A Dynamic Data Race Detector for Multithreaded Programs. ACM Trans. Comput. Syst. 15(4), 391–411 (1997)

[26] Serbănută, T.F., Chen, F., Rosu, G.: Maximal Causal Models for Multithreaded Systems. Tech. Rep. UIUCDCS-R-2008-3017, UIUC

[27] Sinha, A., Malik, S.: Runtime Checking of Serializability in Software Transactional Memory. In: IPDPS, pp. 1–12 (2010)

[28] Sinha, A., Malik, S., Wang, C., Gupta, A.: Predictive Analysis for Detecting Serializability Errors through Trace Segmentation. In: MEMOCODE (2011)

[29] Sinha, N., Wang, C.: Staged Concurrent Program Analysis. In: Foundations of Software Engineering, FSE (2010)

[30] Sinha, N., Wang, C.: On interference abstractions. In: POPL 2011, pp. 423–434 (2011)

[31] http://research.microsoft.com/enus/um/redmond/projects/z3/

[32] Wang, C., Chaudhuri, S., Gupta, A., Yang, Y.: Symbolic Pruning of Concurrent Program Executions. In: Foundations of Software Engineering (FSE), pp. 23–32 (2009)

[33] Wang, C., Limaye, R., Ganai, M., Gupta, A.: Trace-Based Symbolic Analysis for Atomicity Violations. In: Esparza, J., Majumdar, R. (eds.) TACAS 2010. LNCS, vol. 6015, pp. 328–342. Springer, Heidelberg (2010)

[34] Wang, C., Kundu, S., Ganai, M.K., Gupta, A.: Symbolic Predictive Analysis for Concurrent Programs. In: Cavalcanti, A., Dams, D.R. (eds.) FM 2009. LNCS, vol. 5850, pp. 256–272. Springer, Heidelberg (2009)

[35] Wang, C., Yang, Z., Kahlon, V., Gupta, A.: Peephole Partial Order Reduction. In: Ramakrishnan, C.R., Rehof, J. (eds.) TACAS 2008. LNCS, vol. 4963, pp. 382–396. Springer, Heidelberg (2008)

[36] Yang, Y., Chen, X., Gopalakrishnan, G.: Inspect: A Runtime Model Checker for Multithreaded C Programs. Tech. Rep. UUCS-08-004, University of Utah (2008)

[37] Yi, J., Sadowski, C., Flanagan, C.: SideTrack: Generalizing Dynamic Atomicity Analysis. In: PADTAD, pp. 1–10 (2009)

SAM: Self-adaptive Dynamic Analysis for Multithreaded Programs*

Qichang Chen[1], Liqiang Wang[1], and Zijiang Yang[2]

[1] Dept. of Computer Science, University of Wyoming, WY, USA
{qchen2,wang}@cs.uwyo.edu
[2] Dept. of Computer Science, Western Michigan University, MI, USA
zijiang.yang@wmich.edu

Abstract. Many dynamic analysis techniques have been proposed to detect incorrect program behaviors resulted from faulty code. However, the huge overhead incurred by such dynamic analysis prevents thorough testing of large-scale software systems. In this paper, we propose a novel framework using compile-time and run-time optimizations on instrumentation and monitoring that aim to significantly reduce the overhead of dynamic analysis on multithreaded programs. We implemented a tool called SAM (Self-Adaptive Monitoring) that can selectively turn off excessive monitoring on repeated code region invocations if the current program context has been determined to be redundant, which may assist many existing dynamic detection tools to improve their performance. Specifically, we approximate the program context for a code region invocation as a set of variables, which include path-critical variables and shared variables accessed in that region. The path-critical variables are inferred using a use-definition dataflow analysis, and the shared variables are identified using a hybrid thread-based escape analysis. We have implemented the tool in Java and evaluated it on a set of real-world programs. Our experimental results show that it can significantly reduce the runtime overhead of the baseline atomicity violation and data race analyses by an average of 50% and 20%, respectively, while roughly keeping the accuracy of the underlying runtime detection tools.

1 Introduction

Dynamic analysis often suffers from the expensive runtime overhead which prevents it from scaling up to large-scale enterprise software systems. Despite its superior accuracy on error reporting compared to static analysis, the dynamic monitoring overhead has been an issue that prevents many runtime approaches from being adopted practically. According to our and other researchers' experiences [4,8,6,19,11,1,2], the runtime overhead is largely due to repetitive monitoring on code blocks' executions with the same or similar context. For the programs with intensive memory accesses, the problem is more severe. In our

---

* The work was supported in part by ONR N000140910740 and NSF CAREER 1054834.

K. Eder, J. Lourenço, and O. Shehory (Eds.): HVC 2011, LNCS 7261, pp. 115–129, 2012.
© Springer-Verlag Berlin Heidelberg 2012

experiment with the benchmark `tsp` [10], the executions produce as many as 20 million memory access events even under a small input dataset with only 3 threads. With the further investigation, we found that most of these events are generated from a certain number of code blocks and involve many objects created from the same class.

Faced to these issues, we are motivated to design a more efficient and scalable approach to speed up the widely-used dynamic analysis on multithreaded programs. In this paper, we propose a novel framework using compile-time and run-time instrumentation and monitoring optimizations that aim to significantly reduce the overhead of dynamic analysis on multithreaded programs. We implemented a tool called SAM (Self-Adaptive Monitoring) in Java, which can selectively turn off excessive monitoring on a repeated code region invocation if the program context of the current thread has been determined to be redundant. For any code region that has been monitored before, we do not monitor it again as long as the code region is executed with the same thread context previously visited, because this usually will not contribute additional information to dynamic analysis of multithreaded programs. An important observation is that for concurrency error detection, where the primary goal is to reveal the bugs resulted from incorrectly using synchronization and accessing shared variables, we are concerned about the accessing order of shared memory locations rather than their contents.

To demonstrate its effectiveness, we evaluated SAM over a set of multithreaded Java programs in conjunction with two baseline analysis tools, the Eraser for detecting data race [15] and the DAVE for detecting atomicity violation [18]. The experimental results show that this approach is more effective in reducing the subsequent analyses' performance overhead and better in preserving the baseline tools' accuracy than the prior approach [8].

This paper makes the following contributions:

- Our approach uses a refined program context approximation to check program state equivalence and avoid repeated monitoring, which results in more precise context approximation. The program context for a code region invocation is approximated as a set of path-critical variables and shared variables accessed in that region. We extend use-definition dataflow analysis to infer the path-critical variables, and design a hybrid thread-based escape analysis to identify the shared variables.
- SAM is specially designed for multithreaded programs by taking into account the synchronization information and shared variables when approximating the program contexts for each thread. Specifically, SAM considers the lockset held by the current thread.
- SAM can be easily integrated with dynamic analysis tools, which allows developers to focus on the dynamic analysis design rather than be distracted on tuning overhead and optimizing performance.

The rest of this paper is organized as follows. Section 2 reviews the literature and discusses how SAM differs from the related work. Section 3 introduces the motivations and key insights in SAM, and describes our extended use-def dataflow analysis. Section 4 covers SAM's implementation details. Section 5 presents our experimental evaluation on SAM and demonstrate its performance improvement. Section 6 concludes this paper and discusses the future work.

2 Related Works

Different optimization techniques for dynamic analysis have been designed. Fei *et al.* [8] present a tool called Artemis, which is the most related work to our tool SAM. Artemis is a dynamic tool implemented in C and helps reduce the runtime overhead of the dynamic analysis tools. The code region analyzed by Artemis is based on the function level. Our current implementation of SAM follows this approach and also works on the method/function level. All prior observed contexts for a code region are recorded in a table. The currently observed context is compared with the previously preserved contexts to determine whether the monitoring on the function can be safely turned off. The context in Artemis at the entry point of each function invocation contains all global variables and function parameter variables. If a variable in the context is in primitive type, its value is checked when comparing contexts; if a variable in the context is in complex type (*e.g.*, pointer to a data structure), its type, instead of its value, is checked when comparing contexts. Note the context of Artemis is an approximation. While it reduces monitoring overhead, certainly, it will also cause the underlying tools to miss information, which further affects the accuracy of the baseline tools. In addition, Artemis does not consider synchronization operation and concurrent accessing, hence cannot handle multithreaded programs. Our tool SAM utilizes a more accurate context approximation approach and supports multithreaded programs.

Arnold *et al.* [1] design a similar framework that also duplicates code into two versions: original and instrumented, and inserts counter-based sampling code to allow statistically turning on/off the monitoring. SAM differs from it in that it focuses on multithreaded programs, and its context approximation is more precise.

Sampling is another popular technique to reduce the runtime overhead of dynamic analysis. This approach is suitable for the scenarios when multiple runs of the sampled program yield complementary information. However, it suffers from under-reporting problem hence may miss errors. Moreover, the need of multiple runs in the sampling-based monitoring further limits its applicability. Liblit *et al.* [11] use the sampling technique to reduce the frequency of code monitoring for long running programs. Hauswirth and Chilimbi [9] sample the code for possible memory leak error at a sampling rate that is inversely proportional to the frequency of code segment execution.

Many other runtime monitoring tools [16,5] have resorted to static analysis to reduce the overhead of dynamic analysis. Yong *et al.* [19] proposes several techniques that rely on the results of static analysis to remove unnecessary instrumentation from the code, which in turns reduces the subsequent dynamic analysis overhead. The techniques specifically designed to reduce the overhead of runtime type-checking can also be adopted for other similar dynamic analysis systems. Although static analysis can guide dynamic analysis to avoid monitoring some code executions, its effect on reducing overhead is usually limited and quite ad-hoc to applications.

There are also research work in the area of parallelizing runtime checking to reduce overhead. Patil *et al.* [14] suggest to use shadow process to check pointer and array accesses in C program. Oplinger *et al.* [13] spawn a speculative thread to execute the checking code. Although these techniques use parallelism to reduce the checking overhead, they also introduce additional communication overhead that is usually not negligible.

3   The Design of SAM

3.1   An Overview

The insight for the overhead of dynamic analysis is that monitoring and analyzing many repeated events inevitably slows down the program's execution. To avoid repeated monitoring, SAM relies on checking program context to direct the baseline tool to avoid monitoring repeated events. As we mentioned before, the execution of the benchmark `tsp` contains as many as 20 million access events on shared variables. Without optimization, such huge number of events will prevent any dynamic analysis from finishing within reasonable time.

The tool Artemis [8] is a step toward this goal. It adopts a method level context checking scheme. Artemis keeps track of the method contexts prior to the entrance of every method. However, besides its inaccurate context, Artemis is targeted for serial code and cannot handle multithreaded programs. For example, Artemis does not consider any synchronization state or the currently held locks when computing the context, which leads to under-approximation of the context. In contrast, our tool SAM is designed to assist the dynamic tools to analyze multithreaded programs. It considers the current synchronization state when computing the context and takes into account the path-critical variables and shared (escaped) objects accessed in the current method, while Artemis considers all global variables for the context. For example, if a method $f()$ is invoked by a thread that holds the locks l_1 and l_2, then the two acquired locks l_1 and l_2 will be included in the context.

Let m be a method, Θ_m be the program context prior to the execution of m. The context Θ_m consists of the following three kinds of variables:

$$\Theta_m : \begin{cases} R_m : \text{all references to shared (escaped) objects that that are accessed in} \\ \quad m, \text{including "this" and locking objects accessed in } m. \\ PCCV_m : \begin{cases} \text{If } R_m = \emptyset, PCCV_m \text{ is } \emptyset. \\ \text{If } R_m \neq \emptyset, PCCV_m \text{ is a set of path-critical context variables,} \\ \quad i.e., \text{ the variables that are not defined inside } m \ (e.g., \\ \quad \text{method parameters, fields of escaped objects) and could} \\ \quad \text{directly or indirectly affect the execution path of } m. \end{cases} \\ O_m^{lck} : \begin{cases} \text{If } R_m = \emptyset, O_m^{lck} \text{ is } \emptyset. \\ \text{If } R_m \neq \emptyset, O_m^{lck} \text{ is all locking objects held at the entrance of } m. \end{cases} \end{cases}$$

Thus, Θ_m is represented by $\langle R_m, PCCV_m, O_m^{lck} \rangle$. A variable v in Θ_m is denoted by $\langle v, val(v) \rangle$. If v is an object reference, $val(v)$ is its hash code obtained in runtime. If v is in a primitive type, $val(v)$ is its runtime value.

Figure 1 illustrates how the context check works and the difference between our tool SAM and Artemis. The code in the **then** branch of the **if** statement is the original code. The deposited value is added to account **a1** then **allBalance** is updated. In this example, Artemis's context contains **a1**, **a** (method arguments), and **allBalance** (global variable), whereas SAM's context contains only **a1** (an object accessed in the method) and **allBalance** (global variable), because **a** is not a path-critical variable, and **allBalance** is a global variable that is shared among multiple threads. Here, Artemis does not consider the address of object **a1** but only its class type. The approximation of the object type would cause the underlying baseline tool to miss some important information if the method **deposit** is invoked twice with two distinct objects of **Account**, as the second invocation would be deemed by Artemis as redundant and thus not monitored by the underlying error detection tool. Therefore, the underlying baseline tool's accuracy suffers in this case.

```
public class Account{
    public static int allBalance = 0;
    private int bal = 0;
    void deposit(Account a1, int a){
    if(artemisCheck(a1, a, allBalance)){
        // original version
        a1.bal += a;
        allBalance += a;
    }{
        // instrumented version
        ...
    }
    }
}
```

```
public class Account{
    public static int allBalance = 0;
    private int bal = 0;
    void deposit(Account a1, int a){
    if(samCheck(a1)){
        // original version
        a1.bal += a;
        allBalance += a;
    }{
        // instrumented version
        ...
    }
    }
}
```

Fig. 1. Code snippets that illustrate the context check in Artemis and SAM

There are trade-offs between accuracy and efficiency for the approach of SAM. SAM is subject to the thread scheduling nondeterminism that might cause shared variables or path-critical context variables to be changed during the method invocation, which may invalidate the initial context checking. Intuitively, such scenarios happen very rarely. In addition, SAM's context does not include the newly created objects within the current method. Usually, the escaping of these objects, if happens, will occur in the following invocations of other methods, which will be analyzed when these methods are invoked. Certainly, an object may escape within the method where it is created (*e.g.*, is assigned to a static field). However, such possibility is rare. In our experiment shown in Section 5, all these scenarios affecting inaccuracy did not appear. Note that each thread has its own context profiles in SAM does not include any information from other threads to compute the method context for current thread because they will not affect monitoring events except for the two cases mentioned before.

Algorithm 1 shows the algorithm of SAM's context check. We conduct an intraprocedural analysis to generate a symbolic context for each method. The symbolic context is similar to the runtime context, except that the symbolic context contains all object references accessed in the method, and the values of the context variables are null. In the runtime context, all references to unescaped objects are removed, and the context variables are updated by the corresponding runtime values. At the same time, each method is expanded with two versions of the code: one version consists of the original code, and the other version is the instrumented code by the baseline tool. A context check is inserted at the beginning of each method. When a method is invoked, we first call "Remove-UnescapedObjects (C_m)" to get rid of all non-escaped objects in the symbolic context C_m. Then "RuntimeValueUpdate(C'_m, P_m)" is called to update all symbolic names with their runtime values. Then we check whether the current context has ever been contained in the context table CT_m that stores all previous visited contexts. If the current context Θ_m has been encountered before, we call the uninstrumented code directly; otherwise, we call the instrumented code and save Θ_m into CT_m.

```
Input:
Cm: the symbolic context for method m generated from static analysis;
Pm: the program runtime state at the entrance of method m;
CTm: the runtime context table storing previously visited contexts for m;

SAM-ContextCheck(Cm, Pm, CTm){
C'm = RemoveUnescapedObjects(Cm);
Θm = RuntimeValueUpdate(C'm, Pm);
for each ctm ∈ CTm do
    if Θm == ctm then
        execute the uninstrumented version of code of m;
        return;
    end
    continue;
end
CTm = CTm ∪ {Θm};
execute the instrumented version of code of m;
}
```

Algorithm 1. The SAM context check algorithm.

3.2   Context Checking for Multithreaded Programs

Given a method m, a variable v is a *branching variable* if v is included in a branching expression of m(*e.g.*, the conditional expression in `if/for/while/switch` statements). A variable u is a *path-critical context variable* (*PCCV*) if u is not defined inside m (*e.g.*, method parameters or fields of escaped objects) could directly or indirectly affect the value of a branching variable.

To infer *PCCV* according to branching variables, we use an extended use-def dataflow analysis. Use-def analysis [12] identifies and tracks a variable's definition and usage sites inside a function. The DU (*i.e.*, def-use) and UD (*i.e.*, use-def) chains are a concise representation of the dataflow information about a given variable. The DU chain of a variable starts from the definition site of the variable and connects it to all the variable use sites where the defined variable can flow to. In contrast, the UD chain for a variable connects a variable's use site to all its definition sites.

Algorithm 2 illustrates how to compute the set of *PCCV*. We iteratively apply a use-def intraprocedural dataflow analysis (*i.e.*, UD chain) to identify and track the path-critical context variables that indirectly affect the program's execution path. Specifically, given a branching variable's use site, we track its definition statements. For any local variable on the assignment statement's right-hand-side (RHS), we continuously track its definition recursively. This search is repeated till we identify all non locally defined variables whose values directly or indirectly affect the branching variables. These non-local variables, which may be object references, fields, or parameter variables, are *PCCV* for the given branching variables.

4 Implementation and Optimization

We use the Eclipse JDT [7] to instrument program source code. To simplify the instrumentation, SAM first duplicates each method in the original program source into two methods with different suffix names. The method with the suffix name "_original" represents the original method that will not be instrumented by the baseline analysis tool. The method with the suffix "_instrumented" is the method that will be instrumented by the baseline tool. This allows the baseline tool to easily instrument program source code without resorting to complex tagging or structure identification mechanism. At each method entrance, SAM inserts an `if` statement for the context check and places the function calls to the original or the instrumented methods into the `then` and `else` branches, respectively. If the context has been observed before, the original code is chosen. Otherwise, the instrumented version will be activated in the execution.

Escape analysis plays an important role in our context checking. Thread escape analysis is to determine whether and when a variable becomes shared by multiple threads. We utilize our thread-based escape analysis to identify escaped objects, which is based on our previous work [3]. When an object *o* is created, *o* is owned by its creating thread. Object *o* is said to be *thread-escaped* or *shared* when it becomes accessible by two or more threads. When an object *o* becomes accessible by multiple threads, its fields are vulnerable to concurrent accessing, hence may result in concurrency errors such as data races and atomicity violations. Thus, it is important to know whether (even when) an object escapes from its creating thread during the program's execution. During the program's execution, the dynamic thread escape analysis is complemented and refined with the thread escape information from the context-sensitive flow-insensitive interprocedural static analysis for each unexecuted code block to produce the final

Input: $\mathcal{AST}_\mathcal{M}$: the abstract syntax tree of a method $\mathcal{M}$.
Output: $\mathcal{PCCV}$: the set of symbolic path-critical context variables.

```
ComputePCCV(M){
BV = ∅; // the set of branching variables.
PCCV = ∅;
for each statement S in AST_M do
    if S contains branching expression, say expr then
        for each variable v in expr do
            BV = BV ∪ {v};
        end
    end
end
for each v ∈ BV do
    ComputeUseDef(v);
end
}

ComputeUseDef(v) {
compute the definition sites DS_v of v;
for each definition site ds_v ∈ DS_v do
    if ds_v is on a field of locally created object then
        continue;
    end
    if ds_v is out of the scope of M then
        PCCV = PCCV ∪ {v};
    end
    Let RHS_V be the list of variables on the RHS of ds_v;
    for each variable rhs_v in RHS_V do
        ComputeUseDef(rhs_v);
    end
end
}
```

Algorithm 2. The algorithm for computing path-critical context variables.

hybrid thread escape analysis results. The thread-based escape analysis results are used to identify the shared objects.

To further reduce the context checking overhead incurred by SAM, we design the following optimization technique. To avoid maintaining a huge context table and reduce the memory usage in SAM, we insert an array field to store the contexts in different threads for each method in the class, which can be indexed by the thread ID in runtime. These context tables are initialized with empty content. When a context check is encountered in runtime, the accessing thread will use its thread ID as index to retrieve the current context table and compare the newly computed context against the ones saved in current table. This approach avoids maintaining a multi-level hierarchical context table for each thread and reduces the lookup frequency and overhead.

5   Experiments

We present three sets of experimental results over the benchmarks including Elevator, Tsp, Sor, and Hedc from [17], and Vector, Stack, and Hashtable from JDK 1.6. For the Elevator benchmark, we tested it with 2 threads using the provided input data and instrumented a timer that forces the program to terminate after a wall-clock time of 10 seconds. For the benchmark Tsp, we tested it with 3 threads using the provided input datasets map13, map14, and map15. For the benchmark Sor, we tested it with 2 threads and 50 iterations. For the benchmarks Vector, Stack, and HashTable, we tested them using 2 threads to concurrently insert, update, and remove elements.

The first experiment measures the performance overhead and effectiveness of SAM's context checking without the baseline monitoring tool. The second and third experiments aim to illustrate the SAM's performance improvement and accuracy preservation on the dynamic analysis. Specifically, we evaluate SAM using our dynamic atomicity violation detector DAVE [18] and the Eraser race detector [15].

To compare SAM with Artemis, we also implement a revised version of Artemis [8] that can work for multithreaded Java programs context checking. Specifically, in the enhanced Artemis_C (C stands for Concurrent), each thread rather than the whole program maintains its own context profiles and the context of a method consists of the method parameters and global variables (static fields) that are accessed in the method.

The experiments are performed on a machine with 1.6 GHz Intel Core Duo dual-core CPU with 4 GB memory, Windows XP SP3, and Sun JDK 1.6.

5.1   Artemis_C and SAM's Context Checking Overhead

To measure the context check overhead and effectiveness of Artemis_C and SAM, we evaluate Artemis_C and SAM over the aforementioned benchmarks without the baseline monitoring instrumentation. The experimental results are shown in Figure 2 and Figure 3. The runtime overhead introduced by the context check in SAM itself is around 270% on average and thus is not significant compared to the huge overhead (typically in the order of 10x or more) incurred by the baseline tool for the memory-intensive benchmarks. In addition, SAM filters 67% of all observed contexts in the benchmarks, which is very effective in filtering out the redundant monitoring for reducing the subsequent baseline tool's monitoring overhead. The runtime overhead introduced by the context check in Artemis_C is about 370% and 72% of the observed contexts are deemed redundant by Artemis_C. Although Artemis_C has a higher context filtering rate than SAM, it does not preserve baseline tool's accuracy as well as SAM, which is discussed in the following sections.

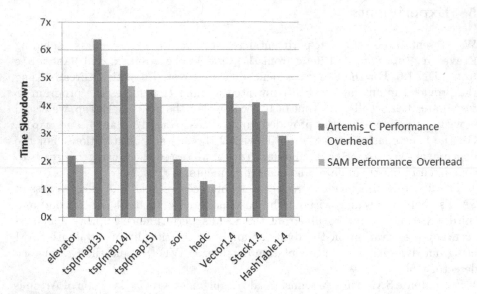

Fig. 2. The performance overheads of Artemis_C and SAM's context checking

Program	LOC	threads	number of redundant contexts (Artemis_C)	number of total context checks performed (Artemis_C)	effectiveness	number of redundant contexts (SAM)	number of total context checks performed (SAM)	effectiveness
elevator	339	3	9513	9829	96.79%	9615	9723	98.89%
tsp(map13)	519	3	151689	151875	99.88%	151363	151875	99.66%
tsp(map14)	519	3	226687	227097	99.82%	210643	211869	99.42%
tsp(map15)	519	3	145664	146035	99.75%	144025	145028	99.31%
sor	8253	3	396	402	98.51%	198	402	49.25%
hedc	4267	3	9903	9921	99.82%	9898	9921	99.77%
Vector1.4	383	2	4	27	14.81%	4	27	14.81%
Stack1.4	418	2	0	33	0.00%	0	33	0.00%
HashTable1.4	597	2	4	11	36.36%	4	11	36.36%

Fig. 3. The effectiveness of Artemis_C and SAM's context checking

5.2 SAM + DAVE vs. Artemis_C + DAVE

In the second experiment, we evaluate SAM with our atomicity violation detector DAVE. DAVE is a dynamic analysis [18] that detects atomicity violations in multi-threaded Java programs.

The experimental results are shown in Figures 4 and 5. As we can see from Figure 5, our baseline tool DAVE with SAM has experienced an average 43% performance improvement, whereas the performance improvement of Artemis_C over DAVE is about 20%.

In addition, we can see from Figure 4 that SAM outperforms Artemis_C in preserving the baseline tool DAVE's atomicity violation coverage in the benchmarks **elevator, tsp(map13), tsp(map14)** and **hedc**. Note that the atomicity violation coverage is not the number of atomicity violation errors revealed by

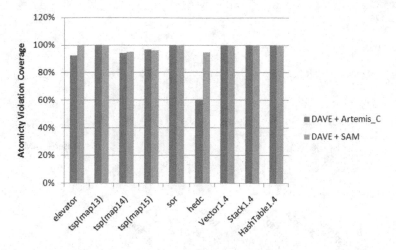

Fig. 4. DAVE's atomicity violation coverage when it is integrated with Artemis and SAM

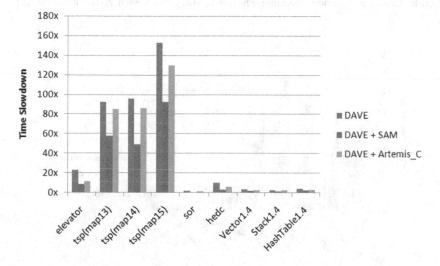

Fig. 5. DAVE's monitoring overhead using Artemis and SAM

the tool in the source program. For example, a program might have only 2 locations that are involved in an atomicity violation which may occur repeatedly for 1,000 times in the execution. If the dynamic analysis observes the repeated 900 atomicity violations occurred in the execution, we say it has a 90% violation coverage. If the dynamic analysis identifies all the two locations in the source code that are involved in the atomicity violations, it has no accuracy loss. Figure 8 compares the DAVE's accuracy loss when using Artemis_C and SAM, respectively. It can be seen that SAM keeps the accuracy on all benchmarks except for Tsp(map14), whereas Artemis_C loses accuracy on both Elevator

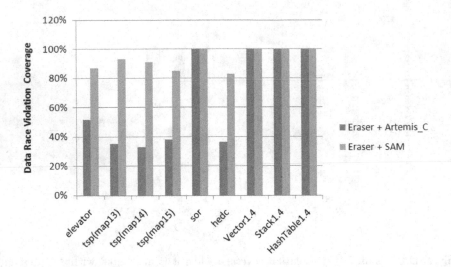

Fig. 6. Eraser's violation coverage when it is integrated with Artemis and SAM

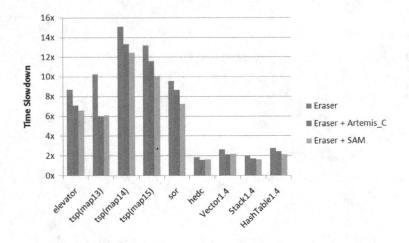

Fig. 7. Eraser's monitoring overhead using Artemis and SAM

and Tsp(map14). In addition, SAM also outperforms Artemis_C on accuracy
on Elevator. One of the main reasons incurs loss of accuracy for SAM and
Artemis_C is that they failed to feed some non-redundant events to the baseline
analysis tools due to the context approximation and filtering. Certainly, in order to improve accuracy, we can incorporate more information when computing
the context, but it will lead to a much higher context checking overhead which
might offset the performance benefits brought about by turning off the repeated
monitoring.

5.3   SAM + Eraser vs. Artemis_C + Eraser

The Eraser [15] is a dynamic analysis tool for detecting data races. Eraser checks race conditions based on a simple locking policy, *i.e.*, all accesses to a shared variable should be protected by a common lock. To simplify experimental setup, our Eraser implementation does not classify the benign data races and false positives from the real data race bugs.

Figures 6 and 7 show the violation coverage and performance slowdown of Eraser using Artemis_C and SAM, respectively. As we can see, Eraser+SAM has about 93% violation coverage on average while Eraser+Artemis_C has only about 66%. In addition, Eraser+SAM has better violation coverage than Eraser+Artemis_C (90% violation coverage) on most benchmarks except for `sor`, `Vector`, `Stack`, and `Hashtable`, on which the baseline tool Eraser does not report any data race warnings. However, SAM and Artemis_C does not reduce the Eraser's monitoring time by a large portion, which is due to the simple on-the-fly analysis algorithm used in Eraser. As shown in Figure 7, Eraser+SAM has less performance slowdown than Eraser+Artemis_C on most benchmarks except for `tsp(map13)`, `hedc` and `Vector 1.4`. Figure 8 compares the Eraser's data race accuracy when using Artemis_C and SAM, respectively. It can be seen that SAM also outperforms Artemis_C in preserving the Eraser's accuracy in the benchmarks `elevator`, `tsp(map13)`, `tsp(map14)` and `hedc` with only an average accuracy loss of 5%.

Program	Base(s)	Dummy(s)	DAVE		DAVE with SAM		DAVE with Artemis_C		Eraser		Eraser with SAM		Eraser with Artemis_C	
			time(s)	nAV	time(s)	nAV	time(s)	nAV	time(s)	nDR	time(s)	nDR	time(s)	nDR
elevator	0.25	0.95	5.73	18	2.16	18	2.96	16	2.18	43	1.65	41	1.78	3
tsp(map13)	0.33	4.63	30.57	0	19.18	0	28.13	0	3.38	11	2.02	11	1.98	5
tsp(map14)	0.43	5.78	41.46	14	21.13	12	37.13	12	6.48	12	5.35	10	5.72	5
tsp(map15)	0.41	5.62	52.12	26	31.42	26	44.21	26	4.48	13	3.43	11	3.94	7
sor	0.6	0.92	2.20	0	0.72	0	1.54	0	10.35	0	7.83	0	9.37	0
hedc	1.64	3.65	8.50	7	2.79	7	5.21	7	1.57	27	1.37	25	1.34	15
Vector1.4	0.1	0.2	0.80	6	0.4	6	0.61	6	0.58	0	0.48	0	0.47	0
Stack1.4	0.1	0.2	0.82	6	0.51	6	0.72	6	0.6	0	0.49	0	0.52	0
HashTable1.4	0.2	0.3	0.92	2	0.55	2	0.71	2	0.61	0	0.47	0	0.54	0

Fig. 8. Comparison of the performance and accuracy of the DAVE, DAVE+SAM, DAVE+Artemis_C, Eraser, Eraser+SAM, and Eraser+Artemis_C. "Base" is the original program's running time without instrumentation. "Dummy" is the instrumented program's running time without any analysis (intercepting events only). The column "nAV" denotes the number of atomicity violations, which are counted based on the places in source code involved in atomicity violations. The column "nDR" denotes the number of data races, which are counted based on the source code locations involved in data races. All execution times are measured in seconds.

6   Conclusions and Future Work

In this paper, we propose a self-adaptive monitoring scheme for reducing the runtime overhead of dynamic program analysis. Our experiments show that this approach significantly reduces the overhead of the baseline dynamic analysis tools with slight accuracy loss. It can be utilized by the general dynamic analyses to improve their runtime performance, reduce the analysis turnaround time, and scale up to large memory-intensive programs.

Our future work includes integrating it and evaluating its effectiveness with other dynamic analysis tools, establishing context checking's cost model, and investigating more fine-grained block-level context checking scheme.

References

1. Arnold, M., Ryder, B.G.: A framework for reducing the cost of instrumented code. SIGPLAN Not. 36(5), 168–179 (2001)
2. Callanan, S.: Flexible debugging with controllable overhead. Ph.D. Dissertation, Stony Brook University (2009)
3. Chen, Q., Wang, L., Yang, Z.: HEAT: A Combined Static and Dynamic Approach for Escape Analysis. In: 33rd Annual IEEE International Computer Software and Applications Conference (COMPSAC 2009). IEEE Press, Seattle (2009)
4. Chen, Q., Wang, L., Yang, Z., Stoller, S.: HAVE: Detecting Atomicity Violations via Integrated Dynamic and Static Analysis. In: Chechik, M., Wirsing, M. (eds.) FASE 2009. LNCS, vol. 5503, pp. 425–439. Springer, Heidelberg (2009)
5. Choi, J.-D., Lee, K., Loginov, A., O'Callahan, R., Sarkar, V., Sridharan, M.: Efficient and precise datarace detection for multithreaded object-oriented programs. In: Proceedings of the ACM SIGPLAN 2002 Conference on Programming Language Design and Implementation, PLDI 2002, pp. 258–269. ACM, New York (2002)
6. Dwyer, M.B., Kinneer, A., Elbaum, S.: Adaptive online program analysis. In: ICSE 2007: Proceedings of the 29th International Conference on Software Engineering, pp. 220–229. IEEE Computer Society, Washington, DC (2007)
7. Eclipse, http://www.eclipse.org/
8. Fei, L., Midkiff, S.P.: Artemis: practical runtime monitoring of applications for execution anomalies. SIGPLAN Not. 41(6), 84–95 (2006)
9. Hauswirth, M., Chilimbi, T.M.: Low-overhead memory leak detection using adaptive statistical profiling. SIGPLAN Not. 39(11), 156–164 (2004)
10. Java Grande Forum. Java Grande Multi-threaded Benchmark Suite. version 1.0, http://www.javagrande.org/
11. Liblit, B., Aiken, A., Zheng, A.X., Jordan, M.I.: Bug isolation via remote program sampling. SIGPLAN Not. 38(5), 141–154 (2003)
12. Muchnick, S.S.: Advanced compiler design and implementation. Morgan Kaufmann Publishers Inc., San Francisco (1997)
13. Oplinger, J., Lam, M.S.: Enhancing software reliability with speculative threads. SIGARCH Comput. Archit. News 30, 184–196 (2002)
14. Patil, H., Fischer, C.: Low-cost, concurrent checking of pointer and array accesses in c programs. Softw. Pract. Exper. 27, 87–110 (1997)
15. Savage, S., Burrows, M., Nelson, G., Sobalvarro, P., Anderson, T.E.: Eraser: A dynamic data race detector for multi-threaded programs. ACM Transactions on Computer Systems 15(4), 391–411 (1997)

16. Vakkalanka, S., Szubzda, G., Vo, A., Gopalakrishnan, G., Kirby, R.M., Thakur, R.: Static-Analysis Assisted Dynamic Verification of MPI Waitany Programs (Poster Abstract). In: Ropo, M., Westerholm, J., Dongarra, J. (eds.) PVM/MPI. LNCS, vol. 5759, pp. 329–330. Springer, Heidelberg (2009)

17. von Praun, C., Gross, T.R.: Object race detection. In: Proc. 16th ACM Conference on Object-Oriented Programming, Systems, Languages and Applications (OOPSLA). SIGPLAN Notices, vol. 36(11), pp. 70–82. ACM Press (October 2001)

18. Wang, L., Stoller, S.D.: Accurate and efficient runtime detection of atomicity errors in concurrent programs. In: Proc. ACM SIGPLAN 2006 Symposium on Principles and Practice of Parallel Programming (PPoPP). ACM Press (March 2006)

19. Yong, S.H., Horwitz, S.: Using static analysis to reduce dynamic analysis overhead. Form. Methods Syst. Des. 27, 313–334 (2005)

Concurrent Small Progress Measures

Michael Huth[1], Jim Huan-Pu Kuo[1], and Nir Piterman[2]

[1] Department of Computing
Imperial College London
London, SW7 2AZ, United Kingdom
{m.huth,jimhkuo}@imperial.ac.uk
[2] Department of Computer Science
University of Leicester
Leicester, LE1 7RH, United Kingdom
nir.piterman@leicester.ac.uk

Abstract. We report on multi-core implementations of parity game solvers based on Small Progress Measures. We revisit a known implementation of multi-core machines (PW solver), and change, in what we call the PW_e solver, the way it computes progress measures. We then suggest an alternative implementation (CSPM), that reduces logical dependency on configuration state and makes performance less dependent on configuration details. In experimental evaluation, both PW_e and CSPM out-perform PW. On most benchmarks, especially larger ones, CSPM performs better than PW_e. The observed linear speed-up of parallelization shows great promise for parallel implementations of game solvers.

1 Introduction

Parity games are an important foundational concept in formal methods. Structurally, parity games are graph-based, zero-sum, two-person games with infinite plays. Such games are determined [12]: either player 0 or player 1 wins a given node in the game, and each player has some memoryless, pure strategy that wins from all nodes which that player wins, her so called winning region.

One reason for the importance of these games is that a variety of applications reduce to the solution of parity games. We briefly discuss a few of these problems and how parity games address them.

The *modal μ-calculus* [7] is an important temporal logic with least and greatest fixed point operators. In practice, one considers its local model checking problem: given a state in a Kripke structure and a formula of the modal μ-calculus, decide whether that state satisfies that formula. It is known that this problem is equivalent to that of deciding whether a particular node in a parity game is won by a particular player [10]. *Design synthesis* is the process of automatically producing controllers from temporal logic specifications [9]. Synthesis has been used, e.g., for the production of robot controllers [8]. Parity games and their solution can complete a key step in design synthesis. Parity games also play an important role in *decision procedures* for the satisfiability for formulas written in the temporal logic CTL* (see e.g. [4]).

K. Eder, J. Lourenço, and O. Shehory (Eds.): HVC 2011, LNCS 7261, pp. 130–144, 2012.
© Springer-Verlag Berlin Heidelberg 2012

Solving parity games is generally hard. The decision problem of which player wins a node is in UP ∩ coUP [6]. The best known deterministic algorithms for solving parity games have sub-exponential running time. The tool PGSolver [2] supports a host of such deterministic, sequential algorithms and can often solve games with millions of nodes in reasonable time.

Yet, not much research has been done on the parallelization of parity game solvers. This is somewhat surprising, given the shift to multi-core computing. We are only aware of the work in [11], which implements and evaluates a solver based on small progress measures [5] (SPM) on a multi-core architecture.

The approach taken in that paper has a fairly complex configuration space (e.g. a partition of the node set into pools of nodes) and the performance of the parallel solver appears to depend significantly on the configuration state.

We therefore want to research how one can implement concurrent versions of SPM in a more generic manner, with less configuration space, and with more robust performance gains. In this paper we therefore make the following two contributions. Firstly, we change the way the algorithm in [11] accesses shared data and thereby improve considerably its run time. Secondly, we develop an alternative concurrent implementation of SPM that

- has less logical dependency on configuration state,
- exhibits a performance less dependent on configuration details, and
- has an experimentally observed linear speed-up in the parallelization.

Each of our new implementations performs better than the other on some of the benchmarks and both outperform the original implementation of [11].

Outline of paper. Parity games, and the SPM solver are presented in Section 2. Prior work on parallelizing this solver on multi-core machines features in Section 3, as does a presentation of our improvement to it. The design and rationale of our concurrent implementation of this solver is found in Section 4. Our experimental results, and comparison to prior work are in Section 5. The correctness of our solver is stated in Section 6. The paper concludes in Section 7.

2   Background

A parity game $G = (V_0, V_1, E, c)$ is a two-player game (player 0 and 1) played on a directed graph (V, E) with a finite set of nodes $V = V_0 \cup V_1$ and edges $E \subseteq V \times V$. The disjoint sets of nodes V_0 and V_1 are owned by player 0 and 1, respectively. We assume that for all $v \in V$, there exists $w \in V$ with (v, w) in E.

The coloring function $c \colon V \to \mathbb{N}$ returns the color $c(v)$ of the node v in V. Let d be $\max_{v \in V} c(v)$. We say that $d + 1$ is the index of G.

A play λ in G starts from some node $v_0 \in V$ and results in an infinite path of nodes $v_0 v_1 v_2...$, where the owner of v_i chooses the successor v_{i+1} such that (v_i, v_{i+1}) is in E. Let $\mathsf{Inf}(\lambda)$ be the set of colors that occur in λ infinitely often: $\mathsf{Inf}(\lambda) = \{k \in \mathbb{N} \mid \exists I \subseteq \mathbb{N} \text{ infinite} \colon \forall i \in I \colon k = c(v_i)\}$. Player 0 wins play λ iff $\min \mathsf{Inf}(\lambda)$ is even; otherwise player 1 wins play λ.

A strategy for player s (where $s = 0$ or 1) is a total function $\tau_s \colon V_s \to V$, such that $(v, \tau_s(v))$ is in E, whenever v is in V_s. From node v_0, a pair of strategies

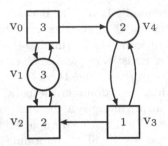

Fig. 1. Parity game G with index 4

τ_0 and τ_1 induce a unique play $(\tau_0, \tau_1)(v_0) = v_0, v_1, \ldots$, where if s is the owner of node v_i then $v_{i+1} = \tau_s(v_i)$. Strategy τ_{w0} is winning from node v_0 if for every τ_1 we have $(\tau_{w0}, \tau_1)(v_0)$ is won by player 0. A winning strategy for player 1 is defined similarly. Parity games are determined [12]: the set of nodes in a parity game G can be divided into disjoint winning regions W_0 and W_1, where player s has a strategy τ_{ws} that is winning in W_s, as it guarantees that player s wins all plays beginning in W_s regardless of the strategy chosen by s's adversary.

Jurdziński's small progress measures (SPM) algorithm [5] solves a parity game through the computation of a least fixed point for a monotone function in a finite lattice. The algorithm extracts the winning regions for both players and the winning strategy for player 0. Thus, the extraction of a winning strategy for the other player requires a second run of that solver on a dual game.

We now define the finite lattice that the SPM solver uses.

Definition 1. *Let G be a parity game of index $d + 1$.*
1. *For each color i, let m_i be the number of nodes v in G with color i.*
2. *For a color i in G, set $M_i = \{0, \ldots, m_i\}$ if i is odd and $M_i = \{0\}$ otherwise.*
3. *Define $M_G = M_0 \times M_1 \times \ldots \times M_d$ and $M_G^\top = M_G \cup \{\top\}$.*
4. *A progress measure is an element of $M_G^\top$.*

For an example, consider the parity game G in Fig. 1. We have $m_1 = 1$, $m_3 = 2$, and $M_G^\top = \{(0,0,0,0), (0,0,0,1), (0,0,0,2), (0,1,0,0), (0,1,0,1), (0,1,0,2), \top\}$.

The SPM solver modifies a progress measure function $\rho : V \to M_G^\top$, which for every node v returns the progress measure of v. The value of $\rho(v)$ has to relate to all or some $\rho(w)$, where (v, w) is in E, according to a set of SPM stability rules defined below. If one of these rules is broken, $\rho(v)$ is updated to satisfy the rule again. If no rule is broken, the algorithm stops.

Operators $>_n$, $<_n$, and $=_n$ compare progress measures lexicographically from the 0th up to the nth tuple position. Also, for every n and every α in $M_G^\top$ we have $\top >_n \alpha$, $\top >_n \top$, and $\top \geq_n \top$. For example, $(0,1,0,2) =_1 (0,1,0,0)$, $(0,1,0,2) =_2 (0,1,0,0)$, and $\top >_3 \top >_3 (0,1,0,2) >_3 (0,1,0,0) >_3 (0,0,0,2)$.

Progress measure ρ is modified by SPM stability rules, shown in Fig. 2. If for some v in V, $\rho(v)$ does not satisfy all SPM stability rules, we say $\rho(v)$ is unstable. By abuse of language we then also call node v unstable. Also, we call a progress measure function ρ stable if there is no v for which $\rho(v)$ is unstable.

1. If v is in V_0 and $c(v)$ is even, then $\rho(v) \geq_{c(v)} \rho(w)$ for some (v, w) in E.
2. If v is in V_0 and $c(v)$ is odd, then $\rho(v) >_{c(v)} \rho(w)$ for some (v, w) in E.
3. If v is in V_1 and $c(v)$ is even, then $\rho(v) \geq_{c(v)} \rho(w)$ for all (v, w) in E.
4. If v is in V_1 and $c(v)$ is odd, then $\rho(v) >_{c(v)} \rho(w)$ for all (v, w) in E.

Fig. 2. SPM stability rules for progress measure functions $\rho\colon V \to M_G^\top$

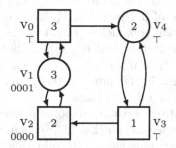

Fig. 3. Parity game G annotated with stable progress measure written next to nodes

In the SPM algorithm, the initial value of ρ is $v \mapsto \mathbf{0}\colon V \to M_G^\top$, which maps all nodes to the constant 0 vector – the least element of $(M_G^\top, \leq_d)$. If for some v in V, v is unstable, then the algorithm updates $\rho(v)$ to the minimal progress measure in the lattice $M_G^\top$ such that v is no longer a reason for ρ being unstable. The algorithm terminates when ρ is stable.

For all v in V, value $\rho(v)$ thus monotonically increases in $(M_G^\top, \leq_d)$. If $\rho(v)$ increases so that some component is strictly greater than its possible maximum value, an "overflow" occurs, and $\rho(v)$ becomes $\top$. The intuition is then that player 1 wins node v. We record the formal results from [5] for this solver.

Theorem 1. [5] *For parity game G with index $d+1$ and ρ the least-fixed point, and stable progress measure computed by SPM in lattice $(M_G^\top, \leq_d)$ we have:*
- *The winning regions of G are $W_0 = \{v \in V \mid \rho(v) \neq \top\}$ and $W_1 = V \setminus W_0$.*
- *A winning strategy for player 0 in W_0 is some $\tau_{w0}\colon V_0 \to V$ such that $\rho(v) = w^*$ for every (v, w^*) in E with $\rho(w^*) = \min_{(v,w) \in E} \rho(w)$.*

Thus we can extract both winning regions and a winning strategy for player 0 from the progress measure that is the output of the SPM solver on that game. The progress measure for G in Fig. 1, computed by SPM, is shown in Fig. 3: so $W_0 = \{v_1, v_2\}$, $W_1 = \{v_0, v_3, v_4\}$, and a winning strategy of player 0 is $v_1 \to v_2$.

The SPM algorithm in [5] iterates through the entire node set until the progress measure function is stable. In [1], a modified algorithm reprocesses only nodes that require update. Technically, this requires a counter value and a value for a node's "best" successor node. In a parallel implementation, though, synchronization of the logic of these values is required to ensure correctness, and has detrimental effect on the performance. We, therefore, strive to find a better balance between thread contention and computational complexity.

3   PW Solver: The Concurrent State of the Art

In [11], van de Pol and Weber introduced a concurrent implementation of a parity game solver based on SPM (called PW here). The PW solver partitions the set of nodes of parity game G into N partitions $V = P_1 \cup P_2 \cup \cdots \cup P_n$, where each P_i is controlled by a different worker ω in $\{1, 2, \ldots, n\}$.

The pseudocode of the PW algorithm is shown in Fig. 4. Each worker ω iterates through all nodes v of her partition P_ω in an ordering specified by one of the suggested permutation approaches [11]. A worker ω calculates a progress measure value $\rho'(v)$ for all such v ($update(\rho(v))$ on line 6) such that $\rho'(v)$ satisfies the SPM rules (Fig. 2). If $\rho'(v) >_{c(v)} \rho(v)$, then $\rho(v)$ is updated to $\rho'(v)$, otherwise, $\rho'(v)$ is discarded. This requires worker ω to read values of ρ for nodes from partitions controlled by *other* workers.

The PW solver computes a least fixed point ρ where in each iteration all workers work on their respective portion of ρ concurrently. The solver stops when no worker modifies her portion of ρ (terminating condition on line 11), as then no worker will obtain new work to do.

The implementation of the PW solver requires little modification from the sequential SPM solver, and is thus a simple and elegant solution for utilizing processing resources of multi-core environments. But the performance of the PW solver can be affected by configuration options, which we discuss next.

Each iteration in the PW solver can decide whether another iteration is required only once all workers have finished their partition scans. We thus want a fairly uniform balance of computational loads across workers so as to minimize idling. But partitioning V into sets P_i of roughly equal size, as done in [11], does not recognize that the computational loads for individual workers depend also on the number of successor nodes. Also, the workload of individual workers should reduce as computation progresses towards the least fixed point. But even if $\rho(v)$ has reached its least fixed point in partition P_i, an iteration of PW would still require worker i to calculate a new and now redundant progress measure $\rho'(v)$. Further, the permutation approaches suggested in [11] either rely on the heuristics of the parity game generation, or trade off (either way) the computational complexity with higher lock contention. There is no obvious method for deciding which of these approaches is best in terms of overall performance, without prior analysis of the structure of the parity game.

To resolve some of these issues we devise an improved version of the PW algorithm, which we call PW_e. We add an if statement that governs the execution of lines 6-9 in the PW code. The condition of this if statement is that method $stable(v)$ from Fig. 6 returns `false`. That method checks whether SPM rules are broken for v and whether $\rho(v)$ requires an update. It is computationally cheaper than $update(v)$, so we expect to see some performance gain from PW to PW_e.

4   CSPM: Our Concurrent Solution

We report on our design of a concurrent SPM solver, denoted as CSPM henceforth. The objectives of our design are to optimally utilize the resources and

```
 1    Partition V to P₁, P₂, ..., Pₙ
 2    repeat
 3        changed = false
 4        do in parallel n times
 5            for each v ∈ Pᵢ ordered by selected permutation approach
 6                ρ'(v) = update(ρ(v))
 7                if ρ'(v) >_c(v) ρ(v) then
 8                    ρ(v) = ρ'(v)
 9                    changed = true
10        await all terminate
11    until !changed
```

Fig. 4. The PW algorithm

processing power offered by the modern computing hardware, to minimize idling of threads, and to ensure all threads are doing "useful" work as much as possible.

The implementation of our CSPM solver is shown in Fig. 5. It exploits the local nature of updating progress measure functions via the SPM stability rules: a new value of $\rho(v)$ is solely determined by current values of ρ at successor nodes of v in (V, E). Clearly, this means that one can process sets of nodes concurrently without interference if these sets are not connected by edges in (V, E).

```
 1    insert all v ∈ V to pendingQueue
 2    repeat N times in parallel
 3        let v = pendingQueue.remove(0)
 4        if stable(v) is not true then
 5            parallelLift(v)
 6            add all nodes from {w ∈ V | (w, v) ∈ E} to pendingQueue
 7    until pendingQueue = ∅
```

Fig. 5. Main loop of the CSPM algorithm

But even if (v, w) is in E, then updates to $\rho(v)$ and $\rho(w)$ cannot lead to genuine interference. To see this, we consider two cases:

1. If $\rho(w)$ is updated before $\rho(v)$, then the update of $\rho(v)$ takes the new value of $\rho(w)$ into consideration, which is sound.
2. If $\rho(v)$ is updated before $\rho(w)$, then the update of $\rho(v)$ is based on stale data at w. But a subsequent update of $\rho(w)$ causes another iteration, at which point in time v has the current value of $\rho(w)$. So this is sound as well.

Our design of CSPM is informed by these insights in order to minimize thread blocking so as to maximize total throughput. The code for CSPM has only two synchronized sections in its main loop (see Fig. 5). The first one is the *pendingQueue*, which contains a list of nodes that need to be processed. The second one is the access to $\rho(v)$, which is protected by a multiple-readers/single-writer lock. Other node properties such as owner and color, are immutable, and so can be read by multiple threads safely without the need for locking.

Therefore, our design of CPSM reduces critical sections to finer synchronized segments, and lets multiple workers process nodes without blocking each other until the actual update of the value $\rho(v)$, see the code $parallelLift(v)$ in Fig. 7.

We now discuss our CSPM solver in detail. In its main loop (Fig. 5), the queue $pendingQueue$ holds the nodes which *may* require processing, thus it initially contains all nodes. For a predefined number N of worker threads, each worker thread ω removes the first node v from the queue, and processes v as follows:

On line 4, worker thread ω examines whether the value of $\rho(v)$ is stable for all w according to the SPM stability rules by method call $stable(v)$ (see Fig. 6). If so, nothing is modified. Otherwise, $parallelLift$ (see Fig. 7) is performed on v to update the value of $\rho(v)$. All the predecessors of v now *may* be subject to modifications of their progress measures, and so they are all added to the $pendingQueue$. This process repeats until $pendingQueue$ is empty.

```
1  synchronized on ρ(v):
2     if  ρ(v) = ⊤ then return true
3  for all  w ∈ {u ∈ V | (v,u) ∈ E}
4     synchronized on ρ(w):
5           let  ϱ(w) = ρ(w)
6     synchronized on ρ(v): {
7           if  ρ(v) >c(v) ϱ(w) then
8                 if v ∈ V₀ then return true
9           else if  c(v) is even and  ρ(v) =c(v) ϱ(w) then
10                if v ∈ V₀ then return true
11          else if v ∈ V₁ then return false
12    }
13 if  v ∈ V₁ then return true
14 else return false
```

Fig. 6. *stable(v)*

Method $stable(v)$ (see Fig. 6) checks whether $\rho(v)$ satisfies the SPM stability rules. It contains finer synchronized segments to avoid lengthy blocking. As mentioned, the mutable part $\rho(v)$ of node v is protected by multiple-read/single-write locks to ensure thread safety. This is sound as method $stable(v)$ only needs read access, and so minimal blocking of concurrently running threads is achieved.

Access to mutable parts has been marked by *synchronized on* symbols, and unmarked lines are safe for concurrent access. Progress measure comparisons are performed lexicographically up to the position that is the color of the left-hand side node, e.g., the comparison of $\rho(v)$ and $\rho(w)$ is done up to the $c(v)$th position.

On line 2, if $\rho(v)$ is already $\top$, it can not be incremented further, therefore, $\rho(v)$ is considered stable. The remainder of method $stable(v)$ implements the SPM stability rules in Fig. 2, relying on a local copy $\varrho(w)$ of the current value of $\rho(w)$, so that $\rho(w)$ is accessed only once. The rules are implemented as follows:
- If $\rho(v)$ is greater than $\varrho(w)$ and $v \in V_0$, the SPM stability rules for V_0 are met and $\rho(v)$ is deemed stable.

- If $c(v)$ is even, v is in V_0, and $\rho(v)$ is equal to $\varrho(w)$, it means $\rho(v)$ is equal to at least one of $\{\rho(w) \mid (v,w) \in E\}$. This makes $\rho(v)$ stable also.
- If $c(v)$ is even, v is in V_1, and $\rho(v)$ is equal to $\varrho(w)$, the stability of $\rho(v)$ is not yet decided. Since stability requires that $\rho(v) \geq \rho(w)$ for all (v,w) in E, we have to iterate through all successors of v.
- If v is in V_1 and $\rho(v)$ is less than $\varrho(w)$, then $\rho(v)$ is unstable.
- Finally, the code only reaches line 13/14 if
  - either $\rho(v)$ is greater than all values $\varrho(w)$ and v is in V_1, so $\rho(v)$ is stable.
  - Or v is in V_0 with $\rho(v)$ less than all values of $\varrho(w)$, hence, $\rho(v)$ is unstable.

```
1   synchronized on ρ(v):
2       if ρ(v) = ⊤ then return
3   let ρ_new(v) = 0
4   for all w ∈ {y ∈ V | (v,y) ∈ E}
5       let ρ'_new(v) = prog(v,w)
6       if ρ_new(v) = 0 then  ρ_new(v) = ρ'_new(v)
7       else
8               if  (v ∈ V_1 and ρ'_new(v) >_c(v) ρ_new(v))
9               or  (v ∈ V_0 and ρ'_new(v) <_c(v) ρ_new(v))
10                  then ρ_new(v) = ρ'_new(v)
11  synchronized on ρ(v):
12      if ρ(v) <_c(v) ρ_new(v) then  ρ(v) = ρ_new(v)
```

Fig. 7. $parallelLift(v)$

Fig. 7 shows the pseudocode of method $parallelLift(v)$. Its design ensures the correct, concurrent calculation of the potentially new value $\rho_{new}(v)$ of $\rho(v)$. On line 2, if $\rho(v)$ is already $\top$, the method simply returns without any action. The temporary progress measure $\rho_{new}(v)$ holds the potential value for $\rho(v)$. Line 3 initializes $\rho_{new}(v)$ to value $\mathbf{0}$, i.e. every element in $\rho_{new}(v)$ is set to 0.

The for-loop on lines 4 to 10 iterates through all w with (v,w) in E, and stores in $\rho_{new}(v)$ the maximum (respectively, minimum) $\rho(w)$ value seen so far

```
1   synchronized on ρ(w):
2       let ϱ(w) = ρ(w)
3   if ϱ(w) = ⊤ return ⊤
4   synchronized on ρ(v):
5       let ρ_new(v) = ρ(v)
6   if ρ_new(v) ≤_c(v) ϱ(w) then
7           let ρ_new(v) = zeroElements(ϱ(w),c(v))
8           if c(v) % 2 = 1 then
9                   ρ_new(v) = increment(ϱ(v),c(v))
10  return ρ_new(v)
```

Fig. 8. $prog(v,w)$

that makes $\rho(v)$ stable. Then $\rho(v)$ is set to the final value of $\rho_{new}(v)$, which is the only time the write lock is applied.

Method $prog(v, w)$ (see Fig. 8) returns a progress measure $\rho_{new}(v)$ that is stable for w only. The synchronized sections on line 2 and 5 take local copies of $\rho(w)$ and $\rho(v)$, and store them in $\varrho(w)$ and $\rho_{new}(v)$, respectively. Therefore, the rest of the method does not require further locking.

- If $\varrho(w)$ is $\top$, then return $\top$, as in this case, the only valid progress measure for v is $\top$.
- If $\rho(v)$ is greater than $\varrho(w)$, $\rho(v)$ is also stable for w, so we return $\rho_{new}(v)$.
- Otherwise, the output of $prog(v, w)$ needs to be greater or equal to, or strictly greater than $\varrho(w)$ (depending on the parity of $c(v)$, see Fig. 2) where elements higher than the $c(v)$th position are "zeroed out".

Method $zeroElements(\varrho(w), c(v))$ zeros out elements in $\varrho(w)$ above the $c(v)$th position, and $increment(\varrho(v), c(v))$ adds 1 to the $c(v)$th element in $\varrho(v)$.

We see that the progress measure update operation ($parallelLift(v)$) requires iterating through all v's successors, while there are opportunities to escape the full iteration in $stable(v)$. Therefore, CSPM checks the stability of a node v before an update is attempted to reduce the overall computation complexity.

Revisiting game G in Fig. 3, let us consider the following cases:

- Nodes v_0 and v_3 share no edge, so they can be processed in parallel.
- Note that v_0 is a V_1 node with odd color, so $\rho(v_0)$ has to be strictly greater than both $\rho(v_1)$ and $\rho(v_4)$ (according to SPM stability rules in Fig. 2). If the update to $\rho(v_0)$ happens before the update to $\rho(v_4)$, and if $\rho(v_4)$ has the stale data 0100 (with $\rho(v_1) = 0001$), then $\rho(v_0)$ is updated to 0101. The node v_0 is added to the $pendingQueue$ for reprocessing when v_4 is processed. This requires one additional iteration for $\rho(v_0)$ to reach expected value ($\top$).
- Similarly, v_1 and v_4 can be processed at the same time with no interference.
- However, if $\rho(v_4)$ is processed before $\rho(v_0)$, then $\rho(v_4)$ is first incremented to $\top$, and then $\rho(v_0)$ is subsequently updated to $\top$, thus saving one iteration for $\rho(v_0)$ to reach the expected value.

5   Experimental Results

The aim of our experiments is a relative comparison of the performance of different solvers under the same conditions, rather than measuring their maximal possible throughput. Hence, we implemented solvers in Scala for ease of programming and comprehension. Games, nodes, and progress measures are coded as domain objects which understand their roles and responsibilities. For example, a node object knows who its predecessors/successors are, and a progress measure object knows how to compare itself with other progress measures.

By the same token, we did not implement the hardware specific optimizations in [11] as they would blur relative comparisons of the algorithmic essence of solvers. We also did not implement ordering optimizations that exploit knowledge of game structure, as we seek comparisons across a wide spectrum of parity game types as alluded to in the introduction.

In [11], permutation approaches were suggested for the PW solver but none were identified as being uniformly better. So we only implemented one such approach, *swiping*, for PW and PW_e as it is the simplest heuristic to program. In it, each worker iterates through her partition. This approach aims to minimise the thread contentions at cost of higher computational complexity.

All experiments are run on a multi-core machine, a server with four Dual-Core AMD Opteron™ 8220 SE processors running at 2.8 GHz, and 16G of RAM. This effectively means the total number of CPU cores available is eight.

We measure the wall-clock time to solve different parity game types under various solver configurations. No prior analysis is carried out on the generated games to inform solver configurations. PGSolver was used to generate non-random games, detailed descriptions on the game types used in the experiments can be found in [3]. (As we do not control the node creation exploration order of the PGSolver, our PW_e implementation thus can not guarantee that successor nodes will always be processed before predecessors.)

Experiments include 5 iterations of tests for a solver configuration against each game type listed in Fig. 9. We show the average results of five iterations to allow for timing variations in running parallel programs on the same game. The notation $CSPMX$ is CSPM solver with X threads, and PW_eY is PW_e solver using Y partitions (hence Y worker threads). Similarly for the PWY notation.

Each game type is denoted by GameName [xx] $vv/ee/cc$, where xx is the game configuration option, and $vv/ee/cc$ describes internal structure of the game. Part vv is the number of total nodes, ee the total number of edges, and cc the index of the game. For example, a Jurdziński [25 50] 3850/10149/52 game is the worst case game defined in [5] of depth 25 and width 50, whose node count, edge count and index are 3850, 10149 and 52. Note that most of these games have large indices compared to the maximum index 4 for PW in [11].

Each test consists of the following sequence of activities:

1. PGSolver generates a parity game G with desired game configuration option.
2. For each configuration config listed in Fig. 9:
   (a) Solve parity game G with config to extract winning regions W_0 and W_1.
   (b) For config $= CSPM16$, verify that W_0 is correct by checking that W_0, after we removed all edges that are inconsistent with the computed winning strategy τ_{w0} for player 0, contains no cycle of nodes whose minimal color has odd parity. Then we save the solution $\{W_0, W_1\}$ as $\{W_0, W_1\}_{saved}$.
   (c) For other values of config, verify that $\{W_0, W_1\}$ equals $\{W_0, W_1\}_{saved}$.

The time taken to generate parity games (step 1), and to verify winning regions (step 2b and 2c) was excluded from the experimental results. Figure 9 shows the average wall-clock time only for solving 5 games of each type (step 2a). If one of the solutions fails the verification steps (step 2b or 2c), the whole experiment is aborted. This was useful for debugging code for our experiments.

For CSPM, 8 threads are optimal for most game types, to be expected for an 8 core test server. Each core can execute a thread effectively without resorting to time-sliced multiplexing. However, CSPM4 is optimal for games Jurdziński [25 50] suggesting a high degree of thread contention in their solving.

Solver Config	Clique [100] 100/ 9900/100	Ladder [400] 800/ 1600/2	Jur- dziński [25 50] 3850/ 10149/52	Recursive Ladder [100] 500/ 1097/303	Strategy Impr [10] 260/ 610/295	Model Checker Ladder [500] 1501/ 2001/1001	TowerOf- Hanoi [5] 972/ 1698/2
CSPM16	242	1541	331	156	453	861	3289
CSPM8	118	1575	256	109	362	601	3231
CSPM4	157	2152	198	140	442	1002	3498
CSPM2	271	4871	203	252	465	1946	3013
CSPM1	548	10419	301	446	1123	3882	3511
PW$_e$16	139	1465	461	2821	2076	1546	335
PW$_e$8	172	1269	775	2280	2354	1587	343
PW$_e$4	230	656	1647	2795	1802	2584	608
PW$_e$2	421	1941	3655	4357	1563	5325	1517
PW$_e$1	424	3753	10367	7297	2365	10045	4555
PW16	316	1455	865	2626	3082	1701	433
PW8	283	1198	1466	1501	3313	1378	444
PW4	421	430	2802	3000	2586	2474	751
PW2	689	1438	6120	5505	2855	4841	1727
PW1	1467	3402	13782	10802	4185	9866	4862

Fig. 9. Average times (in ms) for 5 runs of non-random games [3] with CSPM, PW$_e$, and PW

For most game types, CSPM8 consistently outperforms the optimal PW$_e$ and PW solver configurations under the constraints specified in our experiments. One exception is games with extremely small indices, e.g. the index-2 games Ladder [400] and TowerOfHanoi [5]. This is so since a small index implies a short progress measure and so there will be low computational load in each update. Therefore, the worker threads spend relatively more CPU cycles on node switching than on node processing. And the PW and PW$_e$ solvers favor the reduction of thread contention in this situation.

Within the constraints of our experimental setup, one of the contributing factors to performance gain of CSPM over PW$_e$ is the scheduling of its task delegation. The *pendingQueue* maintains only nodes likely to require updates, so worker threads can concentrate on performing "useful" tasks. As a result, we observed solver time reductions from 14% to 95% between the optimal thread counts of CSPM and PW$_e$ for most non-random game types (and with reasonable index sizes) in the experiments.

The added stability check can hinder or improve performance for non-random games. If the structure of the game promotes high probability of unstable nodes, PW$_e$ (and CSPM for that matter) needs to frequently perform $stable(v)$ and then $parallelLift(v)$ actions. This costs extra processing. In Fig. 9, we see that the optimal performance of PW$_e$ is better than PW for 4 out of 7 games (Clique [100], Jurdziński [25 50], Strategy Impr [10], and TowerOfHanoi [5]).

The combination of these two factors allows CSPM to exhibit 56% to 93% performance gain over PW under their optimal thread counts for most games, except for the two games with extremely small indices.

Solver Config	200/1/ 40/200	400/1/ 80/400	800/1/ 160/400	1000/1/ 200/400	1600/1/ 200/400	1600/1/ 320/400	2000/1/ 400/400
CSPM16	186	780	6668	11121	23277	148265	219514
CSPM8	139	610	5164	9336	21290	167359	229943
CSPM4	140	1043	9493	18195	35115	197345	288196
CSPM2	232	1992	18702	34129	77654	248926	411811
CSPM1	452	3966	36661	67723	145505	349815	617459
PW_e16	190	603	4138	7961	22185	190558	324805
PW_e8	126	550	4363	7526	28518	164139	265443
PW_e4	125	922	7805	14163	38833	183424	336146
PW_e2	200	1706	15157	27991	60620	214494	391561
PW_e1	386	3349	30325	56414	110731	307127	534214

Fig. 10. Average times (in ms) for 20 runs of $xx/yy/zz/cc$ games for CSPM and PW_e

We now discuss our experiments on random games. The notation used to describe randomly generated parity games is $xx/yy/zz/cc$, where xx is the number of nodes (node ownership is determined by a fair coin flip for each node independently), with between yy to zz out-going edges for each node, and with colors at nodes chosen at random from $\{0, \ldots, cc\}$. We then modify these games to ensure that they have no dead-ends (so $yy > 0$), no self-loops, and no color gaps (by reducing colors to eliminate gaps). The latter means that, e.g. a set of colors $\{0, 3, 4, 5, 8\}$ is being compressed to $\{0, 1, 2, 3, 4\}$.

Experiments include 20 iterations of tests to allow solver timing variations due to randomness of the game structures. The set of solver configurations and the game types used in the experiments are listed in Fig. 10. The indices of the random games are capped at 400, except for 200-node parity games. Test activities were as for non-random games, except step 1 now generates random games in the manner described previously.

We performed experiments on CSPM vs PW_e and on CSPM vs PW, separately. The results show that, using the optimal thread counts (8 or 16), CSPM is consistently 52% to 71% faster than PW, while the performance of PW_e is closer to that of CSPM. This indicates that the added stability check is effective in increasing overall efficiency in solving random games. The CSPM vs PW results are omitted in the discussion.

We analyze our experimental data in Fig. 10. The raw data (before averaging) suggest that run times for solving different games of the same type can vary quite significantly, especially for larger games. Run times of "harder" games can be orders of magnitude longer than those of "easier" games of similar size. We attribute this to the existence of large winning regions W_1 with high color nodes. Solvers then need to increment a greater and greater number of progress measures from a relatively low value all the way to $\top$. This update process can heavily increase the running time as the index may be as large as 400.

As these discrepancies apply to both CSPM and PW_e solver, it is still apt to compare their relative differences through the averaged statistics discussed already. These data then lead us to the following insights:

- For most game types, the best performance of CSPM solver are obtained with 8 worker threads.
- We noticed additional performance gains for larger parity games (for example, 1600/1/320/400 and 2000/1/400/400) using CSPM with 16 threads.
- As the number of nodes increases in parity games, the time required to solve these games using the CSPM and PW_e solvers grows exponentially.
- The optimal performance of PW_e is better than CSPM for smaller games.
- As game size increases above 1600 nodes, CSPM performs better than PW_e.

Eight threads are optimal for the reason discussed before. For larger games (1600/1/320/400 and 2000/1/400/400), we observed that 16 worker threads produced optimal performance (5% to 11% time reduction from 8 threads). We understand that the computational complexity for processing a node v is tied to the number of v's successors w. The value $\rho(v)$ can reach its fixed point only if all $\rho(w)$ values reach their fixed points. When the number of successors passes a certain threshold, the benefit of having extra threads to push a greater number of "areas" towards their least fixed points, begins to outweigh the additional context switching overhead due to handling of multiple threads per CPU. Hence, ρ may reach its least fixed point in less iterations and so in less wall-clock time.

This claim is corroborated by the experimental results on 1600/1/200/400 games. The performances of the solvers on this game type exhibit similar patterns as for smaller (200, 400, 800 nodes) games, where the CSPM8 remains optimal.

Our experimental data confirm that none of these solvers can avoid an exponential blowup in the size of games. But we do see a linear speed-up for the CSPM solver. For all the game types in the experiments, CSPM enjoys around 29% to 50% reduction in solver time from one to two threads (essentially the change from the generic SPM solver to using two workers), 21% to 55% reduction from two to four threads, and 1% to 49% reduction from four to eight threads. For larger games (1600/1/320/400 and 2000/1/400/400), sixteen workers achieved extra 5% to 11% solver time reduction over eight workers.

Experiments on games with more than 2000 nodes (and index capped at 400) did not complete in a reasonable amount of time, due to resource constraints imposed by our test server and programming model.

6   Correctness of CSPM Solution

For a parity game G, we now argue that our CSPM solver is correct and that this correctness depends neither on configuration details (such as the number of threads) nor on scheduling details.

Definition 2. *For a parity game G with node set V, let a state of G be a progress measure function $\rho: V \to M_G^\top$. We write S_G for the set of all states of G.*

The set of states S_G is a finite lattice, induced by the partial order $\rho_1 \leq \rho_2$ iff for all $v \in V$ we have $\rho_1(v) \leq_d \rho_2(v)$ in $M_G^\top$, where d is the maximal color. We now define a function $F \colon S_G \to S_G$ such that $F(\rho)$ captures all updates one could have made in state ρ. We then show that F is monotone, that its least fixed point is the state computed by SPM, and that our CSPM solver computes that same state.

To that end, we recall the formal definition of method $prog(v, w)$ in Figure 8. Note that when $prog(v, w)$ increases $\rho(w)$, elements above the $c(v)th$ position in $\rho(w)$ are set to 0. We denote by $\rho(w) +_c 1$ the increase of the cth element of $\rho(w)$ by 1. The definition of F is given in the same figure.

$$prog(v, w) = \begin{cases} \rho(v), & \text{if } \rho(v) >_{c(v)} \rho(w) \\ \rho(w), & \text{if } \rho(v) \leq_{c(v)} \rho(w) \text{ and } c(v) \text{ is even} \\ \rho(w) +_{c(v)} 1, & \text{if } \rho(v) \leq_{c(v)} \rho(w) \text{ and } c(v) \text{ is odd} \end{cases}$$

$$F(\rho)(v) = \begin{cases} \rho(v), & \text{if } v \text{ is stable} \\ min\{prog(v, w) \mid (v, w) \in E\}, & \text{if } v \text{ is unstable and } v \in V_0 \\ max\{prog(v, w) \mid (v, w) \in E\}, & \text{if } v \text{ is unstable and } v \in V_1 \end{cases}$$

Fig. 11. Definition of $prog(v, w)$ where (v, w) is in E, and of $F(\rho)$ for ρ in S_G

Now we can prove some key properties of the global update function F.

Lemma 1. *Let G be a parity game. Then we have:*
1. *For all ρ in S_G, $\rho \leq F(\rho)$, i.e. F is extensional.*
2. *For all $\rho_1 \leq \rho_2$ in S_G, $F(\rho_1) \leq F(\rho_2)$, i.e. F is monotone.*

Using that lemma, we can formally prove the correctness of our CSPM solver.

Theorem 2. *Let G be a parity game. Every function ρ computed by our CSPM solver is the least fixed point of F for game G.*

This theorem ensures that our CSPM solver always computes the correct final state, no matter how scheduling works or how many threads run.

7   Conclusions

We implemented a concurrent version of the Small Progress Measure solver for parity games (CSPM), and have formally proven its correctness. Our implementation of CSPM relies on the maintenance of a synchronized queue (*pendingQueue*), but tasks delegated require worker threads to process only *potentially* unstable nodes. The worker threads are only blocked when accessing the mutable property (i.e. progress measures) of nodes and the *pendingQueue*. They only become idle when *pendingQueue* is empty as there is then no more work to do.

Because of this, we believe CSPM achieves a good balance between computational complexity and thread contention, and should deliver better performance over SPM [5], PW_e, and a known parallel implementation of SPM in [11] (PW). Our experimental results on non-random games support this expectation:

- CSPM8 and CSPM16 have performance gain between 8% to 85% of solver time reduction, over the original version SPM (i.e. CSPM1) in a multi-core environment for all of seven, non-random game types studied here.
- CSPM4 has 44% time reduction over CSPM1 for Jurdziński [25 50] games.
- For games whose index is greater than 2, CSPM's solver time is 15% to 95% less over PW_e for their optimal thread counts.
- CSPM took 56% to 93% less time than PW under the same conditions.

We do observe better performances from PW_e and PW for Ladder [400] and TowerOfHanoi [10] due to their small indices of 2. The experimental results on random games give us similar insights. CSPM is better than PW_e for games with higher computational complexity, and has better performance for all random games we generated than the original PW.

We also argued that our CSPM solver is more flexible and generic as it won't rely on configuration details, e.g. a predefined partition of the game graph.

In conclusion, we think that our implementations and experimental results attest to the great potential that parallelization may bring to game solving.

References

[1] Etessami, K., Wilke, T., Schuller, R.A.: Fair Simulation Relations, Parity Games, and State Space Reduction for Büchi Automata. In: Yu, Y., Spirakis, P.G., van Leeuwen, J. (eds.) ICALP 2001. LNCS, vol. 2076, p. 694. Springer, Heidelberg (2001)

[2] Friedmann, O., Lange, M.: Solving Parity Games in Practice. In: Liu, Z., Ravn, A.P. (eds.) ATVA 2009. LNCS, vol. 5799, pp. 182–196. Springer, Heidelberg (2009)

[3] Friedmann, O., Lange, M.: The pgsolver Collection of Parity Game Solvers. Technical report, Institut für Informatik, LMU Munich (February 2010) Version 3

[4] Friedmann, O., Latte, M., Lange, M.: A Decision Procedure for CTL* Based on Tableaux and Automata. In: Giesl, J., Hähnle, R. (eds.) IJCAR 2010. LNCS, vol. 6173, pp. 331–345. Springer, Heidelberg (2010)

[5] Jurdziński, M.: Small Progress Measures for Solving Parity Games. In: Reichel, H., Tison, S. (eds.) STACS 2000. LNCS, vol. 1770, pp. 290–301. Springer, Heidelberg (2000)

[6] Jurdziński, M.: Deciding the winner in parity games is in UP∩co-UP. Inf. Process. Lett. 68, 119–124 (1998)

[7] Kozen, D.: Results on the propositional μ-calculus. In: ICALP 1982, pp. 348–359 (1982)

[8] Kress-Gazit, H., Fainekos, G.E., Pappas, G.J.: Where's waldo? sensor-based temporal logic motion planning. In: ICRA, pp. 3116–3121 (2007)

[9] Pnueli, A., Rosner, R.: On the synthesis of a reactive module. In: POPL, pp. 179–190 (1989)

[10] Stirling, C.: Local Model Checking Games. In: Lee, I., Smolka, S.A. (eds.) CONCUR 1995. LNCS, vol. 962, pp. 1–11. Springer, Heidelberg (1995)

[11] van de Pol, J., Weber, M.: A multi-core solver for parity games. In: PDMC. ENTCS, vol. 220(2), pp. 19–34 (2008)

[12] Zielonka, W.: Infinite games on finitely coloured graphs with applications to automata on infinite trees. Theoretical Computer Science 200(1-2), 135–183 (1998)

Specification and Quantitative Analysis of Probabilistic Cloud Deployment Patterns

Kenneth Johnson, Simon Reed, and Radu Calinescu

Computer Science Research Group, Aston University, Birmingham B4 7ET UK
{k.h.a.johnson,reeds,r.c.calinescu}@aston.ac.uk

> *The probable is what usually happens.*
>
> Aristotle

Abstract. Cloud computing is a new technological paradigm offering computing infrastructure, software and platforms as a pay-as-you-go, subscription-based service. Many potential customers of cloud services require essential cost assessments to be undertaken before transitioning to the cloud. Current assessment techniques are imprecise as they rely on simplified specifications of resource requirements that fail to account for probabilistic variations in usage. In this paper, we address these problems and propose a new *probabilistic pattern modelling* (PPM) approach to cloud costing and resource usage verification. Our approach is based on a concise expression of probabilistic resource usage patterns translated to *Markov decision processes* (MDPs). Key costing and usage queries are identified and expressed in a probabilistic variant of temporal logic and calculated to a high degree of precision using quantitative verification techniques. The PPM cost assessment approach has been implemented as a Java library and validated with a case study and scalability experiments.

Keywords: Cloud computing, formal verification methods, formal specification languages, formal modelling and specification, probabilistic model checking, Markov processes, costing analysis, resource usage patterns.

1 Introduction

Cloud computing can be succinctly described as *computing as a service* [1,22,20] where software, platforms and virtualised hardware are available on-demand on a pay-as-you-go basis. The elastic nature of the cloud enables customers to adapt service usage to meet fine-grained variations of their resource requirements by dynamically scaling their computing services up or down. This situation is economically favourable in comparison to making large initial investments on infrastructure based on requirements for peak demand. Despite the envisioned benefits of cloud computing, there are still barriers to its adoption. Alongside concerns such as cloud security [10], reliability and compliance with data protection laws [11], many potential customers are reticent due to an inability to accurately express and analyse their resource requirements.

K. Eder, J. Lourenço, and O. Shehory (Eds.): HVC 2011, LNCS 7261, pp. 145–159, 2012.

The most attractive feature of cloud computing is the ability to dynamically scale resources up or down over fine-grained time intervals. As a result, cloud requirements are often thought about in terms of *patterns of usage*, where resource requirements vary over time. Resource usage can change due to small variances in workload or changing economic situations such as fluctuations in a cloud provider's prices and the customer's capital income.

These types of resource usage patterns are inherently *probabilistic* in nature and involve potentially unknown or *non-deterministic* factors, making requirements specification difficult, and existing cost assessment methods less accurate. Current cost modelling tools employ cloud usage patterns that disregard the probabilistic nature of resource usages resulting from the cloud's dynamic scalability [13,3]. This leads to a naive cost assessment, where probabilistic behaviours do not play a role in determining cost. Instead, resource usage is simplified to follow either constant rates of change or variations over coarser time intervals. To overcome these limitations we propose a new *probabilistic pattern modelling* (PPM) approach for the expression of resource requirements as *probabilistic patterns*, and the application of *quantitative verification* techniques to analyse a wide range of cost-related characteristics of potential cloud deployments.

Probability has been used to model unreliable or unknown behaviour in both hardware and software systems. Thanks to the development of effective probabilistic modeller checkers such as PRISM [17], MRMC [12] and RAPTURE [9], quantitative verification has found applicability in a wide range of application domains. Typical applications include verification of QoS properties in service-based systems [5] and run-time model checking to guide self-optimisation strategies in software systems [6,4]. Most recently, probabilistic modelling was used for performance analysis of live migration of virtual machines between physical servers in a cloud data centre [15].

Our approach employs quantitative verification techniques [18,19] to enable potential customers of cloud services to check two classes of quantitative properties of a cloud deployment

- **costs:** to determine a deployment's variation of costs over time, and to calculate the maximum accumulated costs owed to a cloud provider at the end of a billing period, and
- **resource usage:** to determine the maximum and minimum probabilities that a deployment's resource usage exceeds a certain threshold.

The main contributions of our work are:

1. A high-level language for the specification of probabilistic and non-deterministic patterns of cloud resource usage.
2. Techniques to synthesise Markov decision process (MDP) models from resource usage patterns and to formalise resource usage and cost properties as rewards-augmented probabilistic computation tree logic (PCTL) formulae [8].
3. An implementation of our PPM approach as an open-source Java library.
4. A case study and scalability experiments to validate the approach.

The paper is organised as follows. Section 2 provides background information on Markovian models, property specification and probabilistic model checking. Section 3 presents the steps of the PPM approach in detail. A grammar for probabilistic patterns is given and we describe an algorithm for MDP synthesis. Properties for cost and resource usage analysis are formalised as probabilistic temporal logic. Section 4 introduces our prototype implementation of the PPM approach and presents a case study and scalability experiments. Section 5 discusses related research and Section 6 summarises our results and suggests directions for future work.

2   Background

A *Markov decision process* (MDP) is a tuple

$$M = (S, s_0, Act, Dist, step, L) \tag{1}$$

where $S = \{s_0, \ldots, s_n\}$ is a finite set of states, s_0 the initial state, Act a set of actions, $Dist$ a set of probability distributions over the states in S, $step :$ $S \to 2^{(Act \times Dist)}$ is a probabilistic transition function that maps the states in S to finite sets of action-distribution pairs, and $L : S \to 2^{AP}$ is a map labelling individual states with finite subsets of properties from an atomic proposition set AP.

Probabilistic model checking [18] is a technique for building specifications of systems exhibiting probabilistic behaviour and determining the satisfiability of their quantitative properties. For the analysis of MDP models, properties are specified in a probabilistic temporal logic PCTL extending computation tree logic CTL with a probabilistic operator $P_{\bowtie p}$, for $p \in [0,1]$ and $\bowtie \in \{<, \leq, \geq, >\}$. A wide range of quantitative properties for Markovian models can be specified in this logic. For example "the probability of a cloud deployment eventually requiring x or more resources is less than p" can be specified by the PCTL formula $P_{<p}[F\ res \geq x]$. For model checking MDPs, the operators $Pmin_{\bowtie p}$ and $Pmax_{\bowtie p}$ determine the minimum and maximum probabilities over all adversaries (all resolutions of the non-determinism induced by $Dist$ from (1)), respectively.

A *reward structure* for an MDP assigns values to states and transitions that are interpreted, for example, as resource usage. Formally, a rewards structure is a pair of functions (r_s, r_a) such that $r_s : S \to \mathbb{R}_{\geq 0}$ is a state-reward function, and $r_a : S \times S \times Act \to \mathbb{R}_{\geq 0}$ is a transition-reward function. PCTL is extended to include rewards-augmented operators: instantaneous rewards $R_{\bowtie r}[I = t]$ and cumulative rewards $R_{\bowtie r}[C \leq t]$, for $r, t \in \mathbb{R}_{\geq 0}$.

Our PPM approach uses the probabilistic model checker PRISM [17] developed at the Oxford University Computing Laboratory to verify quantitative properties of models that encode probabilistic cloud deployment patterns, and which are synthesised from these patterns automatically.

3   Approach

Our approach to assessing the cost and resource usage characteristics of cloud deployments (Figure 1) comprises the following steps:

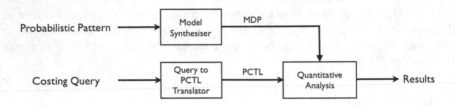

Fig. 1. Quantitative analysis of cloud deployments

1. Specification of the resource requirements for the cloud deployment as a high-level probabilistic pattern.
2. MDP Generation. Patterns from Step 1 are accepted as input to a *model synthesiser* that outputs an MDP model formalising probabilistic resource variations over a time interval associated, for example, with a particular day, week, or billing period.
3. PCTL generation. Queries relating to costs or other quantitative properties of the cloud deployment act as input to a *query-to-PCTL translator* that outputs the query formalised as a PCTL formula.
4. Quantitative Analysis. The MDP model generated in Step 2 and the PCTL formula from Step 3 act as input to a probabilistic model checker which performs quantitative analysis. The numerical results of the analysis are returned for further analysis or data visualisation.

3.1   A Language for Probabilistic Cloud Usage Patterns

PPM formalises the resource requirements of a cloud deployment as probabilistic patterns, expressed in terms of a simple language[1] based on the declaration of rules that specify elastic variations of cloud resource usage over time. Formally, a *probabilistic pattern*

$$P = BR^* \qquad (2)$$

is a high-level syntactic representation of a customer's hourly usage of cloud computing resources, beginning with a baseline declaration B, and optionally followed by a finite list of r rule declarations $R_1, \ldots, R_r$[2].

A baseline declaration B has the syntactic form

$$\texttt{Baseline } bl \qquad (3)$$

---

[1] We do not expect probabilistic patterns to be composed by hand but rather generated automatically through analysis of application resource usage and request logs.

[2] We list the syntactic form of each declaration in the language with terminals displayed in `fixed-width font`.

specifying that the user requires a constant amount b of cloud computing resources (e.g., virtual machines).

A rule declaration R has the syntactic form

$$\text{Rule Start } S \text{ Vary } V \tag{4}$$

which enables the specification of a variation V from the resource usage at a certain point in time S. For example, a rule might specify an increase in resources to meet computing requirements at peak times when more resources are needed. Such variations are probabilistic in nature to reflect the increase and decrease of resources depending on factors such as workload, capital, economies, and even the fluctuations in the pricing of cloud services themselves.

A variation V is a set of m discrete probability distributions

$$\{D_1, \ldots, D_m\} \tag{5}$$

each of which has the syntactic form

$$[p_1:Op_1(z_1) + \ldots + p_q:Op_q(z_q)] \tag{6}$$

to express the fact that change in resources involves

- a non-deterministic choice of a probability distribution $D_i \in V$, and
- a selection of a resource usage *variant* $Op(z)$ according to the probability distribution D_i, with probabilities $p_1, p_2, \ldots, p_q$, $\sum_{j=1}^{q} p_j = 1$.

A variant $Op(z)$ comprises a name Op of an operation and a numerical operand z. Variants perform arithmetical operations on the resource amount res at time S to yield a new resource usage value res' for time $S+1$. The types of variants that can be used in PPM patterns are given in Table 1, noting that the "baseline" variant bl does not require an operand.

Table 1. Pattern Variants

Variant $Op(z)$	Description	Resources res' at time $S+1$
add(z)		$res + z$
sub(z)	Apply arithmetical operation to	$res - z$
mult(z)	current resource usage amount	$res \times z$
div(z)		$res \div z$
bl	Set resource usage to baseline value	bl
bl-add(z)		$bl + z$
bl-sub(z)	Set resource usage to baseline value	$bl - z$
bl-mult(z)	and apply arithmetical operation.	$bl \times z$
bl-div(z)		$bl \div z$

Example 1. Consider a cloud deployment associated with a set of applications whose resource requirements follow a weekly (probabilistic) pattern. Assume, for instance, that less resources are required at the weekend than during the rest of the week as specified by the probabilistic pattern

```
Baseline 10
Rule1 Start Jun 2nd 0h  Vary {[0.6:sub(2) + 0.4:sub(5)],
                              [0.1:add(1) + 0.9:sub(3)]}
Rule2 Start Jun 3rd 23h Vary {[1:bl]}
```

that declares a baseline of 10 resource units followed by two rules. The first rule starts at the beginning of Saturday, June 2nd (2012), varying resource usage according to the two stated probability distributions. Variants in these distributions subtract resources from the baseline amount, suggesting that this rule generally decreases resource usage; there is a small probability of selecting the variant add(1). The second rule begins at the end of Sunday June 3rd, and consists of a single distribution setting the resource usage back to the baseline bl.

Of course, one might want to specify that less resources are required for *every* weekend during certain months in the year. To support this scenario, our language allows the specification of an optional repeat declaration for each rule (4):

$$\text{Rule Start } S \text{ Vary } V \text{ Repeat } F \text{ Until } U \tag{7}$$

where F is a keyword from the set {Day, WeekDay, Week, WeekEnd, Month} setting the frequency of the rule's application, and U specifies the last time the rule is to be applied.

Example 2. Using the repeat construct (7), the probabilistic pattern in Example 1 can be extended to

```
Baseline 10
Rule1 Start Jun 2nd  0h Vary {[0.6:sub(2) + 0.4:sub(5)],
                             [0.1:add(1) + 0.9:sub(3)]}
                    Repeat WeekEnds Until Aug 31
Rule2 Start Jun 3rd 23h Vary {[1:bl]}
                    Repeat WeekEnds Until Aug 31
```

This specifies that both rules apply every weekend during the summer months of June, July and August.

3.2   Markov Decision Process Synthesis

The model synthesiser takes as input a probabilistic pattern (2) in the form of the concrete syntax described in Section 3.1 and a time interval

$$T = [0, n], \tag{8}$$

and outputs an MDP model that allows the formal analysis of cost- and resource-related characteristics of the pattern.

We say that an MDP $M = (S, s_0, Act, Dist, step, L)$ *models* P over T if it satisfies the following properties:

1. The state space is $S \subseteq \{(res, t) \mid res \geq 0,\ t \in T\}$, contains a state $s = (res, t)$ for each resource amount $res \geq 0$ that the cloud deployment may assume at time instant t, and no other states.
2. The initial state is $s_0 = (bl, 0)$ according to the value bl specified in the baseline declaration B.
3. Act comprises an action a_{ij} for each rule R_i from P, $1 \leq i \leq r$ and each distribution D_{ij} from rule R_i.
4. $Dist$ represents the set of all distributions from rules $R_1, \ldots, R_r$ of P.
5. $step : S \to 2^{Act \times Dist}$ specifies state transitions of the form $(res, t) \overset{a_{ij}, p}{\to} (res', t+1)$ where $a_{ij} \in Act$ is the action corresponding to distribution D_{ij} and p the probability that D_{ij} associates with state $(res', t+1)$.
6. $AP = \{"resources \geq x" \mid x \in \mathbb{R}_{\geq 0}\}$ and $L(res, t) = \{"resources \geq x" \mid x \geq res\}$.

The remainder of the section describes the algorithm that PPM uses to determine S and *step*. First, we model the progression of time over (8) by the function $tick : S \to S$ defined by

$$tick((res, t)) = \begin{cases} (res, t+1) & \text{if } 0 \leq t < n, \\ (res, t) & \text{otherwise.} \end{cases} \tag{9}$$

We say that a rule R_i in P *applies* at time t if R_i is

- a rule declaration of the form (4) with start time t, or
- a repeat rule declaration of the form (7) with start time t or frequency F such that $t \bmod F = 0$,

with a possible change of resource usage occurring at time $t+1$. We model rule applications by the function $apply : Variant \times S \to S$ defined by

$$apply(Op(z), (res, t)) = tick((res', t)) \tag{10}$$

where res' is the new resource usage value at time $t+1$ defined according to Table 1.

Letting S^t denote the subset of all states in S associated with time t, the state space S of an MDP modelling a pattern over (8) is defined by the equations

$$S^0 = \{s_0\},$$

$$S^{t+1} = \begin{cases} \bigcup_{D_{ij} \in V} \bigcup_{p : Op(z) \in D_{ij}} \\ \quad \{apply(s, Op(z)) \mid s \in S^t\} & \text{if a rule applies at time } t, \\ \{tick(s) \mid s \in S^t\} & \text{otherwise,} \end{cases} \tag{11}$$

where $S = S^0 \cup S^1 \cup \cdots \cup S^n$ and $S^t \cap S^{t'} = \emptyset$, for $t \neq t'$. Equation 11 defines the states in S^{t+1} by applying variants $Op(z)$ to the states in S^t whenever a rule applies at time t. If no rule applies then resources remain unchanged and only t is updated by the *tick* function.

The transition function *step* is defined by the equation
For all $s \in S^t$:

$$step(s) = \begin{cases} \bigcup_{D_{ij} \in V} \bigcup_{p:Op(z) \in D_{ij}} \\ \quad \{(s \xrightarrow{a_{ij},p} apply(s, Op(z)))\} & \text{if a rule applies at time } t \\ \{s \xrightarrow{a,1} tick(s)\} & \text{otherwise,} \end{cases}$$

where $step(s)$ contains state transitions of the form $s \xrightarrow{a_{ij},p} apply(s, Op(z))$ whenever a rule applies at time t. If no rule applies then a unique action $a \in Act$ is chosen and $step(s)$ contains state transitions of the form $s \xrightarrow{a,1} tick(s)$.

3.3   Quantitative Analysis of Cloud Deployment Queries

Using the query-to-PCTL translator, high-level queries relating to cost and other quantitative properties are formalised as rewards-augmented PCTL formulae. In this section, we present a list of such queries and their specification in PCTL and we outline the verification of each property on an MDP pattern model M over time interval T from (8).

1. *What is the maximum probability of the cloud deployment's resource requirements equalling or exceeding the amount x?*

This resource usage query is specified by the PCTL formula $Pmax_{=?}[F \ res \geq x]$. Quantitative verification returns the maximum probability of eventually reaching a state in M satisfying the property $res \geq x$. Queries for minimum probabilities or those with probability bounds are also easily specified.

To perform cost analysis we augment M with a rewards structure $r_s : S \to \mathbb{R}_{\geq 0}$ defined by $r_s((res, t)) = res$, associating every state (res, t) with the value res. We interpret rewards as the *cost* of the deployment at time t. By using actual resource amounts the customer can scale values according to unit resource prices set by the provider. For example, the cost at time t of using Amazon's Standard On-Demand large instances is calculated $res \times 0.34¢.$[3]

2. *What is the expected maximum cost of a cloud deployment's resource requirements at any point t?*

Using MDPs with costs, this high-level cost analysis query is specified by the rewards-augmented PCTL formula $Rmax_{=?}[I = t]$, where $I = t$ denotes the instantaneous cost at time t.

3. *What is the expected maximum cumulative cost of a cloud deployment's resource requirements up to time t?*

This high-level cost analysis query is specified by the rewards-augmented PCTL formula $Rmax_{=?}[C \leq t]$, where $C \leq t$ denotes the cumulative reward up to time

---

[3] aws.amazon.com/ec2/pricing (Checked January 2012).

t. Quantitative verification returns the expected maximum cost of M accumulated over the time interval $[0, t] \subseteq T$.

4   Implementation and Validation

We developed a probabilistic pattern modelling tool PPM that implements our approach for the analysis of probabilistic cloud deployment patterns. PPM is an open-source Java class library[4] that supports the realisation of the workflow in Figure 1. The core component of PPM is a PatternProcessor class whose constructor takes as parameters the probabilistic pattern (2) to analyse, and the upper bound for (8). The PatternProcessor constructor implements the MDP synthesis technique described in Section 3.2 by means of a parser-generator built using the off-the-shelf language tool ANTLR[5]. The result of this model synthesis is an MDP expressed in the PRISM state-based language.

Table 2. Analysis methods provided by the PatternProcessor PPM class

Java	`double getMaxProbResourcesExceeds(int x)`
	`double getMinProbResourcesExceeds(int x)`
Input	$x \geq 0$
Output	max(min) probability of resource usage exceeding x at any time
PCTL	`Pmax=?[F res >= x]`, `Pmin=?[F res >= x]`
Java	`Double[] getMaxResources(int t1, int t2, int step)`
	`Double[] getMinResources(int t1, int t2, int step)`
Input	$t_1, t_2, step > 0$ such that $t_1 < t_2$
Output	List of expected max(min) resource usage over $[t_1, t_2]$ performed for each $t = t_1 + i \cdot step$, $i = 0, 1, 2, \ldots$ such that $t_1 \leq t \leq t_2$.
PCTL	`Rmax=?[I=t]`, `Rmin=?[I=t]`
Java	`Double[] getMinCumulativeResources(int t1, int t2, int step)`
	`Double[] getMaxCumulativeResources(int t1, int t2, int step)`
Input	$t_1, t_2, step > 0$ such that $t_1 < t_2$
Output	Expected max(min) cumulative resource usage over $[t1, t2]$ performed for each $t = t_1 + i \cdot step$, $i = 0, 1, 2, \ldots$ such that $t_1 \leq t \leq t_2$.
PCTL	`R=?[C<=t]`

The public methods of the PatternProcessor class (Table 2) enable the quantitative analysis of a range of cost and resource usage properties of the considered probabilistic pattern. Each such method synthesises the appropriate PCTL property as described in Section 3.3, and runs the probabilistic model checker PRISM in the background to analyse this PCTL property against the MDP model generated by the constructor. The result of the PRISM analysis is parsed and returned to the client that invoked the method.

---

[4] PPM is freely available from `http://www1.aston.ac.uk/eas/staff/dr-kenneth-johnson/ppm/`

[5] `http://www.antlr.org/`

To assess the effectiveness and scalability of PPM, we implemented a simple test tool that was used to carry out the case study and scalability experiments presented in the remainder of this section. The results of this validation exercise are being used to improve PPM, with a view to integrate it into an existing high-level tool for cloud adoption decision [13].

4.1 Case Study

The case study described in this section considers a potential cloud customer whose applications require at least three virtual machines at all times in order to maintain an acceptable system response time. This resource requirement can be formalised as a probabilistic pattern with a single baseline declaration:

Baseline 3.

Each weekday two or three more VMs above the baseline usage are required to be started at 7am. At 9am, four or five virtual machines above the baseline usage are required. These requirements are modelled by two rules:

```
Rule1 Start Jan,1,7 Vary {[0.8:bl-add(2) + 0.2:bl-add(3)]}
                Repeat WeekDay Until Dec,31
Rule2 Start Jan,1,9 Vary {[0.7:bl-add(4) + 0.3:bl-add(5)]}
                Repeat WeekDay Until Dec,31.
```

Resource usage is reduced at 5pm and again at 7pm where resources are set back to baseline. These requirements are modelled by two further rules:

```
Rule3 Start Jan,1,17 Vary {[0.8:bl-add(2) + 0.2:bl-add(3)]}
                Repeat WeekDay Until Dec,31
Rule4 Start Jan,1,19 Vary {[1:bl]}
                Repeat WeekDay Until Dec,31.
```

We used PPM to analyse the probabilistic cloud deployment pattern described above. The PRISM MDP model generated as a result of building the PPM Pattern Processor object for this pattern is depicted in an abbreviated form in Figure 2.

We display in Figure 3 the results of analysing the pattern's maximum expected resource usage over the time interval ($72 \leq t \leq 96$) representing the weekday of January 3rd. The figure labels each application of a rule by the rule name. As the pattern indicates, the number of VMs is 3 at the beginning of the day and peaks between 9am and 5pm (i.e., for $79 \leq t \leq 90$), when the expected maximum resource usage has value 7.3. The resource usage returns to the baseline outside working hours at 7pm (when $t \geq 91$). Figure 4 depicts the results of cost analysis performed to determine monthly maximum expected accumulated costs from January to April 2012. The four values on the graph are labeled with the cloud resource usage at the end of each month. These values can be used to determine the maximum expenditures for cloud computing services expected at the end of a provider's billing period. For example, supposing the customer uses Amazon's standard EC2 instance at a unit cost of 0.32¢ throughout January, the maximum expected expenditure at the end of January is 3024×0.32¢ = $967.68.

```
mdp
...
const BASELINE=3;
formula Rule1  = (m=Jan)&(d=3)&(h=6);
const double p1=0.8; const double p2=0.2;
const Amount1 = 2; const Amount2 = 3;
formula Vary1 = min(BASELINE+Amount1,MAXRES);
formula Vary2 = min(BASELINE+Amount2,MAXRES);
...
formula RuleStart = (Rule1| ... );

rewards true : res; endrewards
module pattern
    m : [0..11] init Jan; d : [1..31] init 1; h : [0..23] init 0;
    res: [0..Max] init BASELINE;

[] (!DayEnd)&(!RuleStart) -> (h'=h+1);
[] (!DayEnd)&(Rule1) -> p1:(res'=Vary1)&(h'=h+1)+p2:(res'=Vary2)&(h'=h+1);
...
[] (DayEnd)&(NotMonthEnd)&(!RuleStart) -> (h'=0)&(d'=d+1);
[] (DayEnd)&(NotMonthEnd)&(Rule1) -> p1:(res'=Vary1)&(h'=0)&(d'=d+1)+
                                     p2:(res'=Vary2)&(h'=0)&(d'=d+1);
...
[] (DayEnd)&(MonthEnd)&(m<Dec)&(!RuleStart) -> (m'=m+1)&(h'=0)&(d'=1);
[] (DayEnd)&(MonthEnd)&(m<Dec)&(Rule1)  ->
    p1:(res'=Variation1)&(m'=m+1)&(h'=0)&(d'=1) +
    p2:(res'=Variation2)&(m'=m+1)&(h'=0)&(d'=1);
...
[] (m=Dec)&(DecEnd)&(DayEnd)-> true;
endmodule
```

Fig. 2. Abbreviated PRISM file generated by analysis of the case study

4.2 Scalability

Experiments were performed on the PPM tool to test the scalability of our approach using a set of different patterns of increasing complexity defined over a single week beginning January 1st. Between one and five rules formed with the Repeat construct with WeekDay frequency increased resource amounts on each day in the week. Rules started from 12am staggered by four hours, and one or two probability distributions were specified in each rule.

The experiments recorded the number of states and transitions for each MDP model synthesised from the patterns. The analysis speed of PPM was tested by performing two method invocations from the Java library on each pattern:

- getMaxResources(0,168,1), calculating the maximum expected resource usage over a week with a step of one hour, and
- getMaxCumulativeResources(0,168,1), calculating the maximum expected cumulative cost over a week with a step of one hour.

Our experiments were performed using the PPM command-line interface on an Apple MacBook Pro operating on Mac OS X Version 10.7.2 with a 2.66Ghz Intel Core 2 Duo processor and 8GB of 1067MHz DDR3 memory. PRISM version 4.0.2 was used to perform the quantitative analysis on the synthesised MDPs using the sparse matrix PRISM engine [16]. The results of the experiments are listed in Table 3, where method invocation times are averages over several runs,

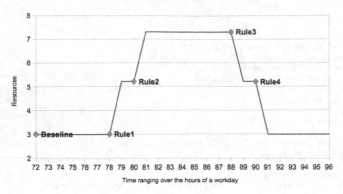

Fig. 3. Expected maximum resource usage for January 3rd (hours 72 to 96)

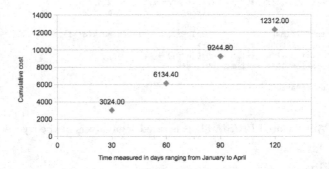

Fig. 4. End of month expected accumulated costs from January to April

and include all steps in processing the pattern: parsing, model synthesis and verification.

To analyse the size complexity of the state space S of an MDP modelling a pattern, we introduce the following notation. The *size* of a rule R with m probability distributions each with q_i probabilities, $1 \leq i \leq m$ is defined as $size(R) = q_1 + \cdots + q_m$. We assume that the maximum number of rule applications at time t is bounded by the value K. For a pattern with rules $R_1, \ldots, R_r$ we set this value to satisfy the inequality $size(R_1) + \cdots + size(R_r) \leq K$. We adapt Equation 11 to give the inequality

$$|S^{t+1}| \leq \begin{cases} |S^t| \cdot K & \text{if a rule applies at time } t, \\ |S^t| & \text{otherwise,} \end{cases} \tag{12}$$

for all $t \geq 1$ and $|S^0| = 1$. Using Inequality 12, and noting the inequality $|S| \leq |S^0| + |S^1| + |S^2| \cdots + |S^n|$ we calculate a bound on the size $|S|$ of the state space over the interval $[0, n]$. For patterns consisting of only a baseline declaration, we have $n + 1 \leq |S|$, e.g. a single state models each point in the time interval. Using the **Repeat** construct, rules can be applied repeated on a frequency F yielding an upper bound $|S| \leq \sum_{t=0}^{n} K^{\lceil \frac{t}{F} \rceil}$.

Table 3. Model size and method invocation time according to pattern complexity

Pattern size		Model size		Avg. analysis time (minutes)	
Rules	Dists	States	Transitions	Max. Usage	Max. Cost
1	1	654	669	3.67	2.81
2	1	1119	1174	3	6.22
3	1	1427	1532	7.41	6.23
4	1	1610	1763	13.47	4.94
5	1	1700	1890	10.54	4.21
1	2	1624	1729	7.96	7.85
2	2	3019	3454	15.58	16.22
3	2	3943	4804	18.29	19.47
4	2	4492	5767	26.81	27.11
5	2	4762	6358	29.87	25.58

5 Related Work

Several research projects focused on developing tools and techniques to assist organisations in assessing the cost-savings of transitioning to the cloud. Specific aspects of cloud technology such as Infrastructure as a Service (IaaS) have been formally modelled to analyse cost-savings of leasing virtualised hardware from remote data centres [21], while case studies assessing feasibility of cloud computing has been carried out for specific industries [14] and applications [7].

Advanced tools such as CloudSim [2] model components of cloud computing data centres for fine-tuning applications deployed on the cloud. CloudSim enables users to improve application performance by simulating resource provisioning policies, and work is in progress to extend support to include simulated costing-analysis of deployment on public clouds [3].

Research undertaken as part of the Large Scale Complex IT Systems (LSC-ITS)[6] initiative in the United Kingdom has developed the Cloud Adoption Toolkit [13] which is an organisational framework identifying key concerns of cloud services adoption, and comprising tools that support the decision making process of potential cloud customers. In particular, the framework's cost modelling tool allows cost-analysis of cloud deployments to be performed with resource requirements expressed in a notation similar to the language developed in our approach, but does not support the specification of probabilistic and non-deterministic characteristics.

Our work complements and improves upon these approaches by accounting for probabilistic behaviour of cloud deployments, and using precise techniques for cost and resource usage analysis.

---

[6] http://lscits.cs.bris.ac.uk/

6   Conclusion and Future Work

The results presented in this paper target the growing need for precise cost analysis techniques that address both uncertainty and probability in using cloud computing services. The probabilistic pattern modelling approach introduced in the paper formalises cloud computing resources as probabilistic patterns and synthesises Markov decision processes. Quantitative verification performed on the model providing accurate costing and usage results. The approach has been implemented as an open-source Java library using the probabilistic model checker PRISM. We have validated our approach with a case study, and carried out a number of preliminary scalability experiments.

Our future work aims at improving the PPM approach and tool in a number of ways. The scalability performance of the tool can be improved by exploiting the periodical nature of some patterns to eliminate redundant calculations when performing analysis. We plan to extend the PPM workflow to include software components to synthesises probabilistic cloud deployment patterns using data mining techniques on application resource request logs. Lastly, we plan to integrate the PPM tool with existing toolkits such as [13].

Acknowledgements. This work was partly supported by the UK Engineering and Physical Sciences Research Council grant EP/H042644/1.

References

1. Armbrust, M., Fox, A., Griffith, R., Joseph, A.D., Katz, R., Konwinski, A., Lee, G., Patterson, D., Rabkin, A., Stoica, I., Zaharia, M.: A view of cloud computing. Commun. ACM 53, 50–58 (2010)
2. Buyya, R., Ranjan, R., Calheiros, R.: Modeling and simulation of scalable cloud computing environments and the CloudSim toolkit: Challenges and opportunities. In: Intl. Conf. on High Performance Computing Simulation, pp. 1–11 (2009)
3. Calheiros, R.N., Ranjan, R., Beloglazov, A., De Rose, C.A.F., Buyya, R.: CloudSim: a toolkit for modeling and simulation of cloud computing environments and evaluation of resource provisioning algorithms. Software: Practice and Experience 41(1), 23–50 (2011)
4. Calinescu, R., Grunske, L., Kwiatkowska, M., Mirandola, R., Tamburrelli, G.: Dynamic QoS management and optimization in service-based systems. IEEE Transactions on Software Engineering 37, 387–409 (2011)
5. Calinescu, R., Johnson, K., Rafiq, Y.: Using observation ageing to improve Markovian model learning in QoS engineering. In: Proc. of the 2nd Joint Intl. Conf. on Performance Engineering, pp. 505–510. ACM (2011)
6. Calinescu, R., Kikuchi, S.: Formal Methods @ Runtime. In: Calinescu, R., Jackson, E. (eds.) Monterey Workshop 2010. LNCS, vol. 6662, pp. 122–135. Springer, Heidelberg (2011)
7. Deelman, E., Singh, G., Livny, M., Berriman, B., Good, J.: The cost of doing science on the cloud: the Montage example. In: Proc. of the 2008 ACM/IEEE Conf. on Supercomputing, pp. 50:1–50:12 (2008)

8. Hansson, H., Jonsson, B.: A logic for reasoning about time and reliability. Formal Aspects of Computing 6, 512–535 (1994)
9. Jeannet, B., D'Argenio, P., Larsen, K.: Rapture: a tool for verifying Markov decision processes. In: Cerna, I. (ed.) Proc. Tools Day, Affiliated to 13th Int. Conf. Concurrency Theory (CONCUR 2002). Technical Report FIMU-RS-2002-05, Faculty of Informatics, Masaryk University, pp. 84–98 (2002)
10. Jensen, M., Schwenk, J., Gruschka, N., Iacono, L.: On technical security issues in cloud computing. In: IEEE Intl. Conf. on Cloud Computing, pp. 109–116. IEEE Computer Society (2009)
11. Joint, A., Baker, E., Eccles, E.: Hey, you, get off of that cloud? Computer Law & Security Review 25(3), 270–274 (2009)
12. Katoen, J.P., Zapreev, I.S., Hahn, E.M., Hermanns, H., Jansen, D.N.: The ins and outs of the probabilistic model checker MRMC. In: Proc. of the 6th Intl. Conf. on the Quantitative Evaluation of Systems, QEST 2009, pp. 167–176. IEEE Computer Society Press, Los Alamitos (2009)
13. Khajeh-Hosseini, A., Greenwood, D., Smith, J.W., Sommerville, I.: The cloud adoption toolkit: supporting cloud adoption decisions in the enterprise. Software: Practice and Experience (2011)
14. Khajeh-Hosseini, A., Greenwood, D., Sommerville, I.: Cloud migration: A case study of migrating an enterprise IT system to IaaS. In: IEEE 3rd Intl. Conf. on Cloud Computing, pp. 450–457. IEEE Computer Society (2010)
15. Kikuchi, S., Matsumoto, Y.: Performance modeling of concurrent live migration operations in cloud computing systems using PRISM probabilistic model checker. In: Proc. 4th Intl. Conf. on Cloud Computing (2011)
16. Kwiatkowska, M., Norman, G., Parker, D.: PRISM: Probabilistic Symbolic Model Checker. In: Field, T., Harrison, P., Bradley, J., Harder, U. (eds.) TOOLS 2002. LNCS, vol. 2324, pp. 200–204. Springer, Heidelberg (2002)
17. Kwiatkowska, M., Norman, G., Parker, D.: PRISM 4.0: Verification of Probabilistic Real-Time Systems. In: Gopalakrishnan, G., Qadeer, S. (eds.) CAV 2011. LNCS, vol. 6806, pp. 585–591. Springer, Heidelberg (2011)
18. Kwiatkowska, M.: Quantitative verification: models techniques and tools. In: Proceedings of the the 6th Joint Meeting of the European Software Engineering Conference and the ACM SIGSOFT Symposium on the Foundations of Software Engineering, pp. 449–458 (2007)
19. Rutten, J., Kwiatkowska, M., Norman, G., Parker, D.: Mathematical Techniques for Analyzing Concurrent and Probabilistic Systems. In: Panangaden, P., van Breugel, F. (eds.) CRM Monograph Series, vol. 23. AMS (2004)
20. Vaquero, L.M., Rodero-Merino, L., Caceres, J., Lindner, M.: A break in the clouds: towards a cloud definition. SIGCOMM Comput. Commun. Rev. 39, 50–55 (2008)
21. Walker, E., Brisken, W., Romney, J.: To lease or not to lease from storage clouds. Computer 43(4), 44–50 (2010)
22. Youseff, L., Butrico, M., Da Silva, D.: Toward a unified ontology of cloud computing. In: Grid Computing Environments Workshop (GCE 2008), pp. 1–10 (2008)

Interpolation-Based Function Summaries in Bounded Model Checking*

Ondrej Sery, Grigory Fedyukovich, and Natasha Sharygina

Formal Verification Lab, University of Lugano, Switzerland
{ondrej.sery,grigory.fedyukovich,natasha.sharygina}@usi.ch
http://verify.inf.usi.ch/

Abstract. During model checking of software against various specifications, it is often the case that the same parts of the program have to be modeled/verified multiple times. To reduce the overall verification effort, this paper proposes a new technique that extracts function summaries after the initial successful verification run, and then uses them for more efficient subsequent analysis of the other specifications. Function summaries are computed as over-approximations using Craig interpolation, a mechanism which is well-known to preserve the most relevant information, and thus tend to be a good substitute for the functions that were examined in the previous verification runs. In our summarization-based verification approach, the spurious behaviors introduced as a side effect of the over-approximation, are ruled out automatically by means of the counter-example guided refinement of the function summaries. We implemented interpolation-based summarization in our FunFrog tool, and compared it with several state-of-the-art software model checking tools. Our experiments demonstrate the feasibility of the new technique and confirm its advantages on the large programs.

1 Introduction

Model checking is a popular technique for automated analysis of software. Due to the state explosion problem, it is usually infeasible to analyze a whole program in a single run starting from its entry point (e.g., the main function). Instead, the problem is often modularized and a model checker is used to exhaustively explore portions of the program for different properties. Typically, this means that the same code (e.g., same functions) of the original program is used in multiple model checker runs and it is analyzed multiple times. We observe that significant savings can be achieved if information concerning the already analyzed code is reused in the subsequent runs of the model checker.

We present a technique for extracting and reusing information about the already analyzed code, in the form of function summaries. The novelty of our work lies in the use of Craig interpolation [8] to extract function summaries after a

---

* This work is partially supported by the European Community under the call FP7-ICT-2009-5 — project PINCETTE 257647.

K. Eder, J. Lourenço, and O. Shehory (Eds.): HVC 2011, LNCS 7261, pp. 160–175, 2012.
© Springer-Verlag Berlin Heidelberg 2012

successful verification run. An interpolant-based function summary is an over-approximation of the actual function behavior and it symbolically captures all execution traces through the function. Since interpolants tend to contain mostly the relevant information, the computed function summaries are more compact than a precise representation of the function, and thus result in the overall verification efficiency gain. We prove that no errors are missed due to the use of the interpolation-based summaries. On the other hand, when spurious errors occur as a side-effect of over-approximation, our approach uses a counter-example guided strategy to automatically refine summaries.

The implementation of the proposed technique, the FunFrog tool, is based on the CBMC bounded model checker [6]. We use propositional encoding to get bit-precise reasoning. However, our approach is general and works also with SMT encodings for which an interpolation algorithm exists. To evaluate the new approach, we compared running times of FunFrog with the state-of-the-art model checkers CBMC, SATABS [7], and CPAchecker [4] on various benchmarks. The experimental results demonstrate feasibility and advantages of our approach.

2 Preliminaries

As customary in model checking, we use an adapted definition of interpolation:

Definition 1 (Craig interpolation). *Let A and B be formulas and $A \wedge B$ be unsatisfiable. Craig interpolant of (A, B) is a formula I such that $A \to I$, $I \wedge B$ is unsatisfiable, and I contains only free variables common to A and B.*

For an unsatisfiable pair of formulas (A, B), an interpolant always exists [8]. For many theories, an interpolant can be constructed from a proof of unsatisfiability [19]. In this work, interpolation is used to extract function summaries in the context of bounded model checking (BMC). Therefore, for the sake of simplicity but without a loss of generality, the paper refers to unwound programs without loops and recursion as an input of the summarization algorithm. Intuitively, such a program is created from the original one by unwinding all loops and recursive calls by the given number (bound). Note that in our implementation the unwinding is performed on-the-fly when needed.

Definition 2. *An* unwound program *for a bound ν is a tuple $P_\nu = (F, f_{main})$, s.t. F is a finite set of functions and $f_{main} \in F$ is an entry point.*

We use relations $child, subtree \subseteq F \times F$, where $child$ relates each function f to all the functions invoked by f, and $subtree$ is a transitive closure of $child$. In addition, we use $\hat{F}$ to denote the finite set of unique function calls, i.e., function call with a unique combination of a call stack, a program location, and a target function (denoted by $target : \hat{F} \to F$). $\hat{F}$ corresponds to the invocation tree of the unwound program. By $\hat{f}_{main}$ we denote the implicit call of the program entry point and $target(\hat{f}_{main}) = f_{main}$. We extend the relations $child$ and $subtree$ to $\hat{F}$ in a natural way, s.t. $\forall \hat{f}, \hat{g} \in \hat{F} : child(\hat{f}, \hat{g}) \to child(target(\hat{f}), target(\hat{g}))$ and $subtree$ is a transitive closure of the extended relation $child$.

```
f(int a) {
  if (a < 10)
    return a;
  return a - 10;
}

main() {
  int y = 1;
  int x = nondet();

  if (x > 0)
    y = f(x);

  assert(y >= 0);
}
```

```
// main
y0 = 1;
x0 = nondet();
if (x0 > 0) {
  a0 = x0;
  // f
  if (a0 < 10)
    ret0 = a0;
  else
    ret1 = a0 - 10;
  ret2 = phi(ret0, ret1);
  // end f
  y1 = ret2;
}
y2 = phi(y0, y1);
assert(y2 >= 0);
```

$y_0 = 1 \wedge$

$x_0 = nondet_0 \wedge$

$a_0 = x_0 \wedge$

$ret_0 = a_0 \wedge$

$ret_1 = a_0 - 10 \wedge$

$(x_0 > 0 \wedge a_0 < 10 \Rightarrow$
$\qquad ret_2 = ret_0) \wedge$

$(x_0 > 0 \wedge a_0 \geq 10 \Rightarrow$
$\qquad ret_2 = ret_1) \wedge$

$y_1 = ret_2 \wedge$

$(x_0 > 0 \Rightarrow y_2 = y_1) \wedge$

$(x_0 \leq 0 \Rightarrow y_2 = y_0) \wedge$

$y_2 < 0$

| (a) C code | (b) SSA form | (c) BMC formula |

Fig. 1. BMC formula generation

Standard BMC of software encodes an unwound program to a BMC formula in a way illustrated in Fig. 1 (more details on the encoding can be found in [6]). First, the unwound program is converted into the SSA form (Fig. 1b), where each variable is assigned at most once. A so called ϕ-function is used to merge values from different control-flow paths. Functions are expanded in the call site as if being inlined. Then a BMC formula (Fig. 1c) is constructed from the SSA form. Assignments are converted to equalities, path conditions are computed from branching conditions and used to encode ϕ-functions. Negation of the assertion condition guarded by its path condition (*true* in this case) is conjuncted with the BMC formula. The resulting BMC formula is unsatisfiable if the assertion holds. In the other case, a satisfying assignment identifies an error trace.

3   Function Summaries

This section first defines function summaries as a means to over-approximate functions in BMC. Then it shows how interpolation can be used as a way to extract function summaries after a successful verification run. Finally, it presents a BMC algorithm extended with the interpolation-based function summarization.

A function summary relates input and output arguments of a function. Therefore, a notion of arguments of a function is necessary. For this purpose, we expect to have a set of program variables $\mathbb{V}$ and a domain function $\mathbb{D}$ which assigns a domain (i.e., set of possible values) to every variable from $\mathbb{V}$.

Definition 3. *For a function f, sequences of variables $args_{in}^{f} = \langle in_1, \ldots, in_m \rangle$ and $args_{out}^{f} = \langle out_1, \ldots, out_n \rangle$ denote the input and output arguments of f,* *where* $in_i, out_j \in \mathbb{V}$ *for* $1 \le i \le m$ *and* $1 \le j \le n$. *In addition,* $args^f = \langle in_1, \ldots, in_m, out_1, \ldots, out_n \rangle$ *denotes all the arguments of* f. *As a shortcut, we use* $\mathbb{D}(f) = \mathbb{D}(in_1) \times \ldots \times \mathbb{D}(in_m) \times \mathbb{D}(out_1) \times \ldots \times \mathbb{D}(out_n)$.

In the following, we expect that functions do not have other than input and output arguments, which include also the return value. Note that an in-out argument[1] is split into one input and one output argument. Similarly, a global variable accessed by a function is rewritten into the corresponding input or/and output argument, depending on the mode of access (i.e., read or/and write).

Precise behavior of a function can be defined as a relation over values of input and output arguments of the function as follows.

Definition 4 (Relational Representation). *Let* f *be a function, then the relation* $R^f \subseteq \mathbb{D}(f)$ *is the* relational representation *of the function* f, *if* R^f *contains exactly all the tuples* $\bar{v} = \langle v_1, \ldots, v_{|args^f|} \rangle$ *such that the function* f *called with the input values* $\langle v_1, \ldots, v_{|args^f_{in}|} \rangle$ *can finish with the output values* $\langle v_{|args^f_{in}|+1}, \ldots, v_{|args^f|} \rangle$.

Note that Def. 4 admits multiple combinations of values of the output arguments for the same combination of values of the input arguments. This is useful to model nondeterministic behavior, and for abstraction of the precise behavior of a function. In this work, the summaries are applied in BMC. For this reason, the rest of the text will be restricted to the following bounded version of Def. 4.

Definition 5 (Bounded Relational Representation). *Let* f *be a function and* ν *be a bound, then the relation* $R^f_\nu \subseteq R^f$ *is the* bounded relational representation *of the function* f, *if* R^f_ν *contains only the tuples representing computations with all loops and recursive calls unwound up to* ν *times.*

Then a summary of a function is an over-approximation of the precise behavior of the given function under the given bound. In other words, a summary captures all the behaviors of the function and possibly more.

Definition 6 (Summary). *Let* f *be a function and* ν *be a bound, then a relation* S *such that* $R^f_\nu \subseteq S \subseteq \mathbb{D}(f)$ *is a* summary *of the function* f.

The relational view on a function behavior is intuitive but impractical for implementation. Typically, these relations are captured by means of logical formulas. Def. 7 makes a connection between these two views.

Definition 7 (Summary Formula). *Let* f *be a function,* ν *a bound,* σ *a formula with free variables only from* $args^f$, *and* S *a relation induced by* σ *as* $S = \{\bar{v} \in \mathbb{D}(f) \mid \sigma[\bar{v}/args^f] \models true\}$. *If* S *is a summary of the function* f *and bound* ν, *then* σ *is a* summary formula *of the function* f *and bound* ν.

A summary formula of a function can be directly used during construction of the BMC formula to represent a function call. This way, the part of the SSA form

---

[1] E.g., a parameter passed by reference.

$$y_0 = 1 \wedge$$
$$x_0 = nondet_0 \wedge$$
$$a_0 = x_0 \wedge$$
$$(\mathbf{a_0 > 0} \Rightarrow \mathbf{ret_0 > 0}) \wedge$$

$$y_1 = ret_0 \wedge$$
$$(x_0 > 0 \Rightarrow y_2 = y_1) \wedge$$
$$(x_0 \le 0 \Rightarrow y_2 = y_0) \wedge$$
$$y_2 < 0$$

Fig. 2. BMC formula created using summary $a > 0 \Rightarrow ret > 0$ for function f

corresponding to the called function does not have to be created and converted to a part of the BMC formula. Moreover, the summary formula tends to be smaller. Of course, the arguments have to be assigned the correct SSA version. Considering the example in Fig. 1, using the summary formula $a > 0 \Rightarrow ret > 0$ for the function f yields the BMC formula in Fig. 2.

The important property of the resulting BMC formula is that if it is unsatisfiable (as in Fig. 2) then also the formula without summaries (in Fig. 1c) is unsatisfiable. Therefore, no errors are missed due to the use of summaries.

Lemma 1. *Let ϕ be a BMC formula of an unwound program P for a given bound ν, and let ϕ' be a BMC formula of P and ν, with some function calls substituted by the corresponding summary formulas bounded by ν', $\nu' \ge \nu$. If ϕ' is unsatisfiable then ϕ is unsatisfiable as well.*

Proof. Without loss of generality, suppose that there is only one summary formula σ_f substituted in ϕ' for a call to a function f. If multiple summary formulas are substituted, we can apply the following reasoning for all of them.

For a contradiction, suppose that ϕ' is unsatisfiable and ϕ is satisfiable. From the satisfying assignment of ϕ, we get values $\langle v_1, \ldots, v_{|args^f|} \rangle$ of the arguments to the call to the function f. Assuming correctness of construction of the BMC formula ϕ, the function f given the input arguments $\langle v_1, \ldots, v_{|args_{in}^f|} \rangle$ can finish with the output arguments $\langle v_{|args_{in}^f|+1}, \ldots, v_{|args^f|} \rangle$ and with all loops and recursive calls unwound at most ν times. Therefore, by definition of the summary formula, the values $\langle v_1, \ldots, v_{|args^f|} \rangle$ also satisfy σ_f. Since the rest of the formulas ϕ and ϕ' is the same, the satisfying assignment of ϕ is also a satisfying assignment of ϕ' (up to SSA version renaming). □

3.1   Interpolation-Based Summaries

There may be multiple ways to obtain a summary formula. In this section, we present a way to extract summary formulas using Craig interpolation. To use interpolation, the BMC formula ϕ should have the form $\bigwedge_{\hat{f} \in \hat{F}} \phi_{\hat{f}}$ such that every $\phi_{\hat{f}}$ symbolically represents the function f, a target of the call $\hat{f}$. Moreover, the symbols of $\phi_{\hat{f}}$ shared with the rest of the formula are only the elements of $args^f$.

Note that the BMC formula is generally not in this form. Variables from the calling context tend to leak into the formulas of the called function as a part

$y_0 = 1 \wedge$

$x_0 = nondet_0 \wedge$

$a_0 = x_0 \wedge$

$\mathbf{x_0 > 0 \Leftrightarrow callstart_{\hat{f}}} \wedge$ (1)

$y_1 = ret_0 \wedge$

$(x_0 > 0 \Rightarrow y_2 = y_1) \wedge$

$(x_0 \leq 0 \Rightarrow y_2 = y_0) \wedge$

$(\mathbf{callend_{\hat{f}} \vee x_0 \leq 0) \wedge y_2 < 0}$ (2)

$ret_1 = a_0 \wedge$

$ret_2 = a_0 - 10 \wedge$

$(\mathbf{callstart_{\hat{f}}} \wedge a_0 < 10 \Rightarrow ret_0 = ret_1) \wedge$ (3)

$(\mathbf{callstart_{\hat{f}}} \wedge a_0 \geq 10 \Rightarrow ret_0 = ret_2) \wedge$ (4)

$(\mathbf{callend_{\hat{f}}} \Rightarrow \mathbf{callstart_{\hat{f}}})$ (5)

    (a) formula $\phi_{\hat{f}_{main}}$ (b) formula $\phi_{\hat{f}}$

Fig. 3. Partitioned bounded model checking formula

of the path condition. For example in Fig. 1c, the variable x_0 from the calling context of the function f appears in the bold part, which represents f itself. To achieve the desired form, we generate the parts of the formula corresponding to the individual functions in separation and bind them together using two boolean variables for every function call: $callstart_{\hat{f}}$ and $callend_{\hat{f}}$. We call the resulting formula a *partitioned bounded model checking* (PBMC) formula.

Fig. 3 demonstrates creation of a PBMC formula for the example from Fig. 1. Intuitively, $callstart_{\hat{f}}$ should be *true* when the corresponding function call is reached. Therefore, the formula of the calling context (Fig. 3a) makes it equivalent to the path condition of the call (1). The $callend_{\hat{f}}$ variable is *true* if the call returns. It is conjuncted with the path condition so it occurs in the guard of the assertion check (2). In the called function (Fig. 3b), $callstart_{\hat{f}}$ is taken as the initial path condition, and thus it appears in the expanded ϕ-function (3, 4). The value of $callend_{\hat{f}}$ is derived from the path conditions[2] at function exit points (5). The two helper variables are added to the set of function arguments $args^f$. Therefore, the variables shared between the individual formulas $\phi_{\hat{f}}$ and the rest of the PBMC formula (here $\phi_{\hat{f}_{main}}$) are only the variables from $args^f$.

If the resulting PBMC formula is unsatisfiable, we compute multiple Craig interpolants from a single proof of unsatisfiability to get function summaries.

Definition 8 (Interpolant summary formula). *Let $\hat{f}$ be a function call of an unwound program P, ν a bound, and $\phi \equiv \bigwedge_{\hat{g} \in \hat{F}} \phi_{\hat{g}}$ an unsatisfiable PBMC formula for P. Furthermore, let $I_\nu^{\hat{f}}$ be a Craig interpolant of (A, B) such that $A \equiv \bigwedge_{\hat{g} \in \hat{F}: subtree(\hat{f}, \hat{g})} \phi_{\hat{g}}$, and $B \equiv \bigwedge_{\hat{h} \in \hat{F}: \neg subtree(\hat{f}, \hat{h})} \phi_{\hat{h}}$. Then the interpolant $I_\nu^{\hat{f}}$ is an* interpolant summary formula.

Of course, an important property of the interpolant summary formula is that it is indeed a summary formula from Def. 7.

---

[2] Note that the implication may be more complicated, e.g., if the function can exit the program or if it contains user assumptions that prune some computational paths.

Lemma 2. *The interpolant $I_\nu^{\hat{f}}$ constructed by Def. 8 is a summary formula for the function f and the bound ν.*

Proof. By definition of Craig interpolation, the only free variables of $I_\nu^{\hat{f}}$ are from $args^f$. Moreover, we know that $A \Rightarrow I_\nu^{\hat{f}}$ and that A represents the call $\hat{f}$ with all function invocations within it. By construction of A and the PBMC formula ϕ, every tuple of values $\bar{v} \in R_\nu^f$ defines a partial valuation of A that can be extended to a satisfying valuation of A. Therefore by $A \Rightarrow I_\nu^{\hat{f}}$, all these partial valuations satisfy $I_\nu^{\hat{f}}$ as well. The relation S induced by the satisfying valuations of $I_\nu^{\hat{f}}$ thus satisfies $R_\nu^f \subseteq S \subseteq \mathbb{D}(f)$. $\square$

Another useful property of the interpolant summary formula is that $I_\nu^{\hat{f}} \wedge B$ is unsatisfiable (by Def. 1). In other words, the interpolant summary formula contains all the necessary information for showing that the program under analysis is safe with respect to the property being analyzed. Since the interpolant is created from a proof of unsatisfiablity of $A \wedge B$, it tends to contain only the relevant part and thus be smaller than A. An important consequence is that the interpolant summary formulas can be used to abstract function calls in BMC without missing errors that are reachable within the given bound.

Theorem 1. *Let ϕ be a BMC formula of an unwound program P for a given bound ν and let ϕ' be a BMC formula of P and ν, with some function calls substituted by the corresponding interpolant summary formulas bounded by ν', $\nu' \geq \nu$. If ϕ' is unsatisfiable then ϕ is unsatisfiable as well.*

Proof. The proof directly follows from Lemmas 1 and 2. $\square$

3.2   Algorithm

An overview of the BMC algorithm for creation of the PBMC formula and extraction of interpolant summaries is depicted in Alg. 1. First, the algorithm creates the PBMC formula. It takes one function at a time and creates the corresponding part of the formula (line 12) using the SSA encoding as sketched in Section 2. The difference lies in handling of function calls. When available, function summaries (line 8) are used instead of processing the function body (**ApplySummary** maps the symbols in the summary to the correct SSA version). Otherwise, the function is queued for later processing (line 10). In both cases, a glue part of the formula, which reserves the argument SSA versions and generates the $callstart_{\hat{f}}$ and $callend_{\hat{f}}$ bindings as described above, is created (line 6).

Having the PBMC formula, the algorithm calls a SAT or SMT solver. In the case of a successful verification (UNSAT answer), the algorithm extracts new function summaries (line 18-24). For many functions, the summary is just a trivial *true* formula, which means that the function is not relevant for validity of the property being verified. Note that the function **StoreSummary** (line 23) also does a simple filtering, i.e., if there are multiple summaries for a single function, it checks that none of them implies any other. Though this means a quadratic number of solver calls in general, in our experience, the actual cost is very small.

Algorithm 1. BMC algorithm with summary application and extraction.

Input: Unwound program $P_\nu = (F, f_{main})$ with function calls $\hat{F}$
Output: Verification result: $\{SAFE, UNSAFE\}$
Data: D: queued function calls, ϕ: PBMC formula

```
 1  D ← {f̂_main}, φ ← true ;                              // (1) formula creation
 2  while D ≠ ∅ do
 3      choose f̂ ∈ D, and D ← D \ {f̂};
 4      φ_f̂ ← true;
 5      foreach ĝ s.t. child(f̂, ĝ) do
 6          φ_f̂ ← φ_f̂ ∧ ReserveArguments(ĝ);
 7          if HasSummary(ĝ) then
 8              φ_f̂ ← φ_f̂ ∧ ApplySummary(ĝ) ;              // apply summaries
 9          else
10              D ← D ∪ {ĝ} ;                              // process ĝ later
11      end
12      φ_f̂ ← φ_f̂ ∧ CreateFormula(f̂);
13      φ ← φ ∧ φ_f̂
14  end
15  result ← Solve(φ) ;                                   // (2) run solver
16  if result = SAT then
17      return UNSAFE;
18  foreach f̂ ∈ F̂ do                                     // (3) extract summaries
19      A ← ⋀_{ĝ∈F̂:subtree(f̂,ĝ)} φ_ĝ;
20      B ← ⋀_{ĥ∈F̂:¬subtree(f̂,ĥ)} φ_ĥ;
21      I_f̂ ← Interpolate(A, B);
22      if I_f̂ ≠ true then
23          StoreSummary(I_f̂);
24  end
25  return SAFE;
```

4 Refinement

When the PBMC formula is satisfiable, the BMC algorithm reports an error (line 17 of Alg. 1), which can be either a real or a spurious violation since function summaries are computed using over-approximation. This section introduces an algorithm that iteratively refines the PBMC formula until either a real error is found or an unsatisfiable PBMC formula is detected. The refinement algorithm uses the generalized version of Alg. 1 that can be executed with a specified level of approximation.

Definition 9. *A substitution scenario for function calls is a function* $\Omega : \hat{F} \to \{inline, sum, havoc\}$.

For each function call, a substitution scenario determines a level of approximation as one of the following three options: *inline* when it processes the whole function body; *sum* when it substitutes the call by an existing summary, and *havoc* when it treats the call as a nondeterministic function. The *havoc* option abstracts from the call; it is equivalent to using a summary formula *true*. To employ these options, we replace lines 7-10 of Alg. 1 by the following code:

```
7 switch Ω(ĝ) do
8     case sum:  φ_f̂ ← φ_f̂∧ ApplySummary(ĝ) ; // apply summaries
9     case inline:  D ← D ∪ {ĝ} ;              // process ĝ later
10    case havoc:  skip;         // treat ĝ nondeterministically
11 endsw
```

For example, a substitution scenario that makes the generalized algorithm equivalent to Alg. 1 looks as follows:

$$\Omega_0(\hat{g}) = \begin{cases} sum, & \text{if } \texttt{HasSummary}(\hat{g}) = true \\ inline, & \text{otherwise} \end{cases}$$

The substitution scenario used as the initial approximation is called *initial scenario* and denoted as Ω_0. The above initial scenario is *eager*, since it eagerly processes bodies of functions without available summaries. Alternatively, one can use a *lazy* initial scenario to treat functions without available summaries as nondeterministic ones (by replacing the *inline* with *havoc* case). This results in a smaller initial PBMC formula and leaves identification of the important function calls to the refinement loop, possibly resulting in more refinement iterations.

When a substitution scenario Ω_i leads to a satisfiable PBMC formula, a *refinement strategy* either shows that the error is real or looks for another substitution scenario Ω_{i+1}. In the latter case, Ω_{i+1} represents a tighter approximation, i.e., it refines Ω_i.

Definition 10. *Given two substitution scenarios Ω_1, Ω_2, we say that Ω_2 refines Ω_1, if $\forall \hat{f} \in \hat{F} : \Omega_1(\hat{f}) = inline \rightarrow \Omega_2(\hat{f}) = inline$, and $\exists \hat{g} \in \hat{F} : \Omega_1(\hat{g}) \neq inline \wedge \Omega_2(\hat{g}) = inline$.*

Note, that due to a finite size of $\hat{F}$, the refinement loop terminates independently from the refinement strategy (i.e., the choice of Ω_{i+1}). Rephrasing Def. 10, we have $\{\hat{f} \in \hat{F} \mid \Omega_i(\hat{f}) = inline\} \subset \{\hat{f} \in \hat{F} \mid \Omega_{i+1}(\hat{f}) = inline\} \subseteq \hat{F}$. Therefore, the sequence of sets $\{\hat{f} \in \hat{F} \mid \Omega_i(\hat{f}) = inline\}$ grows strictly monotonically while being bounded by $\hat{F}$. If the refinement loop reaches a substituting scenario $\Omega_\top$ such that $\forall \hat{f} \in \hat{F} : \Omega_\top(\hat{f}) = inline$, the generalized algorithm using $\Omega_\top$ is equivalent to BMC without summarization, thus yielding the same precise answer. In the following, we call $\Omega_\top$ the *supreme scenario*.

Counter-Example Guided Refinement. We propose a refinement strategy based on analysis of an error trace. When refining a substitution scenario Ω_i, the counter-example guided refinement strategy refines the function calls that (1) are substituted by a summary or havoced in Ω_i and (2) are on the error trace corresponding to the given satisfying assignment of the current PBMC formula and (3) do influence validity of the assertion being analyzed.

The second point is deduced from the satisfying assignment of the PBMC formula. By construction of the PBMC formula, a variable $callstart_{\hat{f}}$ is valuated to true, if and only if the satisfying assignment represents a trace that includes the function call $\hat{f}$. Therefore, all function calls for which the $callstart$ variable is assigned $true$ are suspected. The third point is decided based on a path-sensitive dependency analysis over the SSA form. As a result, only the function calls that actually influence validity of the assertion are marked $inline$ in Ω_{i+1}. If no such function call exists, the error trace is real and it is reported to a user.

$$\Omega_{i+1}(\hat{g}) = \begin{cases} inline, \text{ if } \Omega_i(\hat{g}) \neq inline \wedge callstart_{\hat{g}} = true \wedge \texttt{InfluenceProp}(\hat{g}) \\ \Omega_i(\hat{g}), \text{ otherwise} \end{cases}$$

Note that we do not explicitly test whether the error trace is feasible. The error trace can be simulated exactly, where summaries are not used. However, a summary hides precise paths inside the substituted function and only the inputs and outputs of the functions are preserved in the satisfying assignment. Thus all the possible paths through the function would have to be considered to see whether this combination of inputs and outputs is indeed possible. This becomes costly for summaries of large functions and the advantage of having a simple abstraction might be lost.

For experimentation purposes, we define another simplistic refinement strategy, a *greedy* one. When the PBMC formula corresponding to the chosen initial scenario Ω_0 is satisfiable, the greedy strategy simply refines Ω_0 directly to the supreme scenario $\Omega_\top$. This way, the greedy strategy fallbacks to the standard BMC when the approximation is too coarse to prove the assertion being verified.

5   Evaluation

We implemented the interpolation-based function summarization and refinement in a tool called FunFrog, extending the CBMC model checker. Currently, there is a limited support for pointers. The OpenSMT solver [5] is used both for satisfiability checks and interpolation. Note that OpenSMT is used as a SAT solver, which gives us bit-precise reasoning[3]. FunFrog and the benchmarks used for its evaluation are available for other researchers[4].

We run FunFrog on industrial benchmarks to show that it works correctly for real-life purposes, and on artificial programs (artN), to stress-test the implementation. Three benchmarks are taken from the Versicec[5] suite (verisecN), small string manipulating programs. The most interesting benchmarks (kbfiltrN, diskperfN, floppyN) are taken from [18], which are three Windows device drivers, each of which contains user defined assertions. All the assertions hold, i.e., FunFrog may generate and reuse summaries.

---

[3] Specialized SAT solvers without proof construction generally outperform OpenSMT in the satisfiability checks though they lack the interpolant generation features.
[4] http://verify.inf.usi.ch/funfrog
[5] se.cs.toronto.edu/index.php/Verisec_Suite

Table 1. Verification times (sec.) of FunFrog, CBMC, SATABS, and CPAchecker. Number of assertions and lines of code in the benchmarks and interpolation time for FunFrog are shown. WA: wrong answer, TO: 1 hour timeout exceeded.

benchmark			FunFrog		CBMC	SATABS	CPAchecker
name	#assert	LoC	total time	itp. time			
verisec1	2	63	0.020	0.002	0.003	1.004	2.851
verisec2	2	101	0.515	0.005	0.016	0.003	0.896
verisec3	2	81	0.093	0.004	0.011	TO	1.91
art1	2	242	1.731	0.034	0.280	534.8	65.37
art2	2	63	3.327	0.030	0.408	881.2	WA
art3	4	120	1.811	0.076	2.112	TO	WA
kbfiltr1	8	12253	6.718	0.003	5.742	106.457	WA
kbfiltr2	5	12253	2.665	0.008	3.702	13.002	WA
diskperf1	9	6321	5.284	0.037	20.309	433.74	15.045
diskperf2	4	6321	43.486	2.005	11.620	1064.2	24.849
floppy1	2	10259	2.196	0.001	18.028	2735.4	15.246
floppy2	4	10259	2.283	0.003	53.801	1402.1	47.891
floppy3	11	10259	45.073	0.006	99.512	2208.5	97.436

To evaluate FunFrog, we compared it with CBMC (v3.9), SATABS (v2.4 with Cadence SMV v10-11-02p46), and CPAchecker (rev3901). SATABS and CPAchecker are CEGAR-based model checkers of C. Being a bounded model checker, CBMC is the closest tool to compare with. We used the same bounds for FunFrog and CBMC, sufficient to traverse the state space of the benchmarks. In order to make the results comparable, we manually unwound the benchmarks to represent the same verification task for SATABS and CPAchecker.

We expected reusability of the interpolation-based function summaries to be sensitive to the mutual relevance of the assertions in the code. Therefore, for the large benchmarks (kbfiltrN, diskperfN, floppyN), we experimented with multiple groups of assertions with a different level of mutual relevance, ignoring the other assertions.

The experimental results are captured in Table 1. The timings are in seconds and denote the whole verification process[6]. FunFrog performs very favorably on the larger benchmarks as it outperforms all other tools. In some cases, it outperforms CBMC, the second best tool, by an order of magnitude. However, as may be expected, the benefit is not general for all assertions. Clearly, when a set of unrelated assertions is checked, the generated function summaries are not reusable (see diskperf2). In this case, a number of refinement steps is needed to construct a precise approximation (which is close to the supreme substitution scenario). Since CBMC creates the full BMC formula right away without the iterative refinement, it outperforms FunFrog on this benchmark. Even in this case, running time of FunFrog is still comparable to the other tools.

---

[6] On some benchmarks, the simplified handling of pointers and the known implementation bug prevent CPAchecker from producing the correct results. We reported the problems to the developers of CPAchecker.

As expected, FunFrog is less competitive on the small benchmarks, as it, for example, is outperformed by CBMC. We identified several reasons for this. First, there is a rather small number of function calls in these benchmarks. Thus the benefit of function summarization is smaller compared to the overhead of using a slower solver and the extra work on partitioning the formula. Second, CBMC can prove trivially holding assertions using only constant propagation, which is currently not implemented in FunFrog.

Notably, the overhead of our technique is small as the actual interpolation time is very low (itp. time in Table 1). Still, some cost (not measured) is hidden in the need to create an unsatisfiability proof, which hinders the solver.

Comparison of Refinement Strategies. Table 2 compares verification times for different combinations of refinement strategies and initial scenarios. Due to their realistic size, only the benchmarks from [18] are considered.

We note that the counter-example guided refinement strategy (noted as CEG to prevent confusion with classical CEGAR) is better or comparable to the greedy one on almost all the benchmarks. The exception (`diskperf2`) is the case where CBMC outperforms FunFrog. In this case, the number of refinement iterations is quite large due to too coarse summaries. In general, however, the number of refinement iterations needed is small. Therefore, we conclude that the counter-example guided refinement strategy performs well.

Based on the experiments, neither initial scenario is universally better. Despite winning in some cases, the lazy initial scenario performs very poor on some others. The eager initial scenario tends to perform consistently well in general, even though loosing sometimes. Therefore, the eager initial scenario combined with counter-example based refinement strategy is a safer, less volatile choice.

6   Related Work

Function summaries date back to Hoare [13]. Now it is commonly used in program analysis to achieve scalable interprocedural analysis [1,9]. Each function is processed only once, its summary is created and applied for other calls of the function. To get more fine grained summaries, multiple summaries may be created for different input conditions [9]. In BMC, state exploration of the unwound symbolically encoded program is left to a SAT/SMT solver. Thus, the program analysis approaches using fixpoint computation are not directly applicable.

Another domain of function summaries is model checking of pushdown systems (PDS). Here the most related work is [2] proposing a method to create function summaries for bounded model checking of PDS using a QBF solver. As admitted in [2], QBF queries constitute a major bottleneck. In our case, we extract multiple function summaries from a single proof of unsatisfiability of a BMC formula, which is inexpensive in comparison.

Less frequently, the idea of function summaries is used in concolic execution [10] and explicit-state model checking [20]. For example, the model checker Zing records explicit summaries as a set of tuples of explicit input and output values that were observed on an execution trace during state space traversal [20]. Summaries used in Zing also contain lock-related information necessary

Table 2. Verification times (sec.) and refinement iterations (RI) per assertion

benchmark (assertion)	lazy/greedy		eager/greedy		lazy/CEG		eager/CEG	
	time	#RI	time	#RI	time	#RI	time	#RI
kbfiltr1 (1/5)	0.637	1	0.448	0	0.639	1	0.446	0
kbfiltr1 (2/5)	0.650	1	0.975	1	0.187	1	0.801	1
kbfiltr1 (3/5)	0.115	0	0.468	0	0.133	0	0.466	0
kbfiltr1 (4/5)	0.124	0	0.493	0	0.121	0	0.444	0
kbfiltr1 (5/5)	0.120	0	0.501	0	0.114	0	0.508	0
kbfiltr2 (1/8)	1.141	1	1.029	0	1.133	1	1.042	0
kbfiltr2 (2/8)	0.595	1	0.908	1	0.058	1	0.811	1
kbfiltr2 (3/8)	0.036	0	0.251	0	0.061	1	0.525	1
kbfiltr2 (4/8)	0.634	1	0.518	0	0.104	1	0.864	1
kbfiltr2 (5/8)	0.693	1	0.491	0	1.170	2	0.927	1
kbfiltr2 (6/8)	0.074	0	0.294	0	0.101	1	0.597	1
kbfiltr2 (7/8)	0.662	1	0.491	0	0.653	2	0.865	1
kbfiltr2 (8/8)	0.586	1	0.849	1	0.601	2	1.087	2
diskperf1 (1/9)	1.686	1	1.493	0	1.727	1	1.462	0
diskperf1 (2/9)	0.061	0	0.370	0	0.055	0	0.372	0
diskperf1 (3/9)	0.060	0	0.379	0	0.055	0	0.369	0
diskperf1 (4/9)	0.031	0	1.287	0	0.028	0	0.252	0
diskperf1 (5/9)	0.044	0	1.222	0	0.034	0	1.310	0
diskperf1 (6/9)	0.060	0	0.343	0	0.065	0	0.335	0
diskperf1 (7/9)	1.545	1	0.523	0	1.544	2	0.535	0
diskperf1 (8/9)	0.075	0	0.385	0	0.073	0	0.376	0
diskperf1 (9/9)	0.030	0	0.267	0	0.029	0	0.273	0
diskperf2 (1/4)	6.917	1	1.110	0	7.032	1	1.129	0
diskperf2 (2/4)	5.397	1	6.007	1	8.631	11	6.075	1
diskperf2 (3/4)	5.660	1	5.267	1	9.630	11	20.025	10
diskperf2 (4/4)	8.910	1	9.084	1	13.713	12	16.257	10
floppy1 (1/4)	0.284	0	1.346	0	0.285	0	1.334	0
floppy1 (2/4)	0.281	0	0.472	0	0.287	0	0.477	0
floppy1 (3/4)	149.401	1	0.485	0	151.163	1	0.509	0
floppy1 (4/4)	31.510	1	0.504	0	31.017	1	0.503	0
floppy2 (1/2)	155.741	1	1.088	0	154.174	1	1.080	0
floppy2 (2/2)	161.395	1	1.111	0	39.875	1	1.116	0
floppy3 (1/11)	160.323	1	6.549	0	161.108	1	6.508	0
floppy3 (2/11)	159.470	1	148.587	1	39.213	1	12.956	1
floppy3 (3/11)	144.195	1	1.747	0	9.346	1	2.238	0
floppy3 (4/11)	160.492	1	1.739	0	9.345	1	2.254	0
floppy3 (5/11)	0.328	0	1.904	0	9.355	1	2.354	0
floppy3 (6/11)	0.312	0	1.835	0	0.294	0	2.339	0
floppy3 (7/11)	0.313	0	1.870	0	0.291	0	2.393	0
floppy3 (8/11)	0.320	0	2.716	0	9.401	1	3.452	0
floppy3 (9/11)	166.772	1	2.877	0	9.402	1	4.246	0
floppy3 (10/11)	0.313	0	2.840	0	9.493	1	4.180	0
floppy3 (11/11)	0.149	0	1.537	0	2.335	1	2.153	0

for checking concurrent software. In contrast, in FunFrog each summary symbolically defines an over-approximation of *all* explicit execution traces through a function, but currently without concurrency related data.

Craig interpolation [8] is commonly used as a means of abstraction in model checking [16]. It was used to speed up convergence of BMC by iterative over-approximation of transition relation [15]. In the scope of predicate abstraction, interpolation was used [12] to derive new predicates in the abstraction refinement phase of CEGAR-based tools (e.g., Blast [3], CPAchecker [4]). In these tools, sets of predicates are extracted from interpolants of the formulas corresponding to a prefix and suffix of a spurious error trace. This results in predicates associated to program locations along the spurious error trace yielding a more fine grained abstraction [12]. The authors also propose reordering of a path formula to generate interpolants with local variables suitable for inter-procedural analysis. Focusing on predicates, these works ignore the boolean structure of interpolants. Others observed that interpolation can be directly used to create an inductive sequence of interpolants [17,21]. The authors of [17] envision interpolation-based function summaries that would be derived from a single spurious error trace. Unfortunately, the idea is not further refined. In comparison, our function summaries are derived from the whole BMC formula and thus they contain information about all the paths through the function. Moreover, we provide a refinement strategy to deal with too weak summaries. In [11], the authors extend the idea of finding an inductive sequence of interpolants [17] to programs with function calls and recursion. The work does not refine the idea of function summaries in any way.

Lazy annotation [18] also uses function summaries. It extends symbolic execution to remember a reason for infeasibility of an execution path, i.e., a blocking annotation. Blocking annotations are used to reject other execution paths as early as possible. Compared to our technique, lazy annotation uses interpolation to derive and propagate the blocking annotations backwards for every program instruction. If the annotation is to be propagated across a function call, a function summary merging blocking annotations from all paths through the function is generated and stored for a later use. Our technique uses interpolation on the whole BMC formula and creates one function summary from one interpolant.

7   Conclusion

This paper presented a new technique to speed up BMC by means of extracting and reusing over-approximating function summaries. Our function summaries are extracted from a successful verification run using Craig interpolation which symbolically captures all execution traces through the function. We provided a counter-example guided refinement strategy to automatically refine spurious behaviors which are possible due to over-approximation. The new approach was implemented in our tool FunFrog whose application to various benchmarks demonstrated feasibility and advantages of our approach. Although the presented technique is not strictly limited to BMC, it requires combining with another technique for dealing with loops and recursion. We are therefore investigating possible connection with an engine for loop invariant detection, e.g., the one used in LoopFrog [14]. Nevertheless, we restrict the presentation in this paper to the BMC case that is also covered by the implementation in FunFrog. Another restriction of our technique is that it is defined for sequential programs. We believe that the generated summaries may be extended by a locking related information in a similar way as in [20]. However, this is left for a future work.

References

1. Babic, D., Hu, A.J.: Calysto: scalable and precise extended static checking. In: Int. Conference on Software Engineering (ICSE 2008), pp. 211–220. ACM (2008)
2. Basler, G., Kroening, D., Weissenbacher, G.: SAT-Based Summarization for Boolean Programs. In: Bošnački, D., Edelkamp, S. (eds.) SPIN 2007. LNCS, vol. 4595, pp. 131–148. Springer, Heidelberg (2007)
3. Beyer, D., Henzinger, T.A., Jhala, R., Majumdar, R.: The software model checker Blast: Applications to software engineering. Int. J. STTT 9, 505–525 (2007)
4. Beyer, D., Keremoglu, M.E.: CPACHECKER: A Tool for Configurable Software Verification. In: Gopalakrishnan, G., Qadeer, S. (eds.) CAV 2011. LNCS, vol. 6806, pp. 184–190. Springer, Heidelberg (2011)
5. Bruttomesso, R., Pek, E., Sharygina, N., Tsitovich, A.: The OpenSMT Solver. In: Esparza, J., Majumdar, R. (eds.) TACAS 2010. LNCS, vol. 6015, pp. 150–153. Springer, Heidelberg (2010)
6. Clarke, E., Kroening, D., Lerda, F.: A Tool for Checking ANSI-C Programs. In: Jensen, K., Podelski, A. (eds.) TACAS 2004. LNCS, vol. 2988, pp. 168–176. Springer, Heidelberg (2004)
7. Clarke, E., Kroening, D., Sharygina, N., Yorav, K.: SATABS: SAT-Based Predicate Abstraction for ANSI-C. In: Halbwachs, N., Zuck, L.D. (eds.) TACAS 2005. LNCS, vol. 3440, pp. 570–574. Springer, Heidelberg (2005)
8. Craig, W.: Three uses of the Herbrand-Gentzen theorem in relating model theory and proof theory. J. of Symbolic Logic, 269–285 (1957)
9. Engler, D., Ashcraft, K.: RacerX: effective, static detection of race conditions and deadlocks. In: Symposium on OS Principles (SOSP 2003), pp. 237–252. ACM (2003)
10. Godefroid, P.: Compositional dynamic test generation. In: Principles of Prog. Languages (POPL 2007), pp. 47–54. ACM (2007)
11. Heizmann, M., Hoenicke, J., Podelski, A.: Nested interpolants. In: Principles of Prog. Languages (POPL 2010), pp. 471–482. ACM (2010)
12. Henzinger, T.A., Jhala, R., Majumdar, R., McMillan, K.L.: Abstractions from proofs. In: Principles of Prog. Languages (POPL 2004), pp. 232–244. ACM (2004)
13. Hoare, C.: Procedures and parameters: An axiomatic approach. In: Symposium on Semantics of Algorithmic Languages, pp. 102–116 (1971)
14. Kroening, D., Sharygina, N., Tonetta, S., Tsitovich, A., Wintersteiger, C.M.: Loopfrog: A Static Analyzer for ANSI-C Programs. In: Automated Software Engineering (ASE 2009), pp. 668–670. IEEE (2009)
15. McMillan, K.L.: Interpolation and SAT-Based Model Checking. In: Hunt Jr., W.A., Somenzi, F. (eds.) CAV 2003. LNCS, vol. 2725, pp. 1–13. Springer, Heidelberg (2003)
16. McMillan, K.L.: Applications of Craig Interpolation in Model Checking. In: Halbwachs, N., Zuck, L.D. (eds.) TACAS 2005. LNCS, vol. 3440, pp. 1–12. Springer, Heidelberg (2005)

17. McMillan, K.L.: Lazy Abstraction with Interpolants. In: Ball, T., Jones, R.B. (eds.) CAV 2006. LNCS, vol. 4144, pp. 123–136. Springer, Heidelberg (2006)
18. McMillan, K.L.: Lazy Annotation for Program Testing and Verification. In: Touili, T., Cook, B., Jackson, P. (eds.) CAV 2010. LNCS, vol. 6174, pp. 104–118. Springer, Heidelberg (2010)
19. Pudlák, P.: Lower bounds for resolution and cutting plane proofs and monotone computations. Journal of Symbolic Logic 62(3), 981–998 (1997)
20. Qadeer, S., Rajamani, S.K., Rehof, J.: Summarizing procedures in concurrent programs. In: Principles of Prog. Languages (POPL 2004), pp. 245–255. ACM (2004)
21. Weissenbacher, G.: Program analysis with interpolants. PhD thesis, Oxford (2010)

Can File Level Characteristics Help Identify System Level Fault-Proneness?

Thomas J. Ostrand and Elaine J. Weyuker

AT&T Labs - Research, Florham Park, NJ
180 Park Avenue
Florham Park, NJ 07932
{tostrand,weyuker}@gmail.com

Abstract. In earlier studies of multiple-release systems, we observed that the number of changes and the number of faults in a file in the past release, the size of a file, and the maturity of a file are all useful predictors of the file's fault proneness in the next release. In each case the data needed to make predictions have been extracted from a configuration management system which provides integrated change management and version control functionality. In this paper we investigate analogous questions for the system as a whole, rather than looking at its constituent files. Using two large industrial software systems, each with many field releases, we examine a number of questions relating defects to system maturity, how often the system has changed, the size difference of a release from the prior release, and the length of time a release has been under development before the start of system testing. Most of our observations match neither our intuition, nor the relations observed for these two systems when similar questions were asked at the file level.

Keywords: software fault prediction, fault density, system maturity, system size, system changes, elapsed development time.

1 Introduction

For the last several years, we have been developing highly accurate software fault prediction models to identify the files most likely to contain the largest numbers of defects in the next release of large systems. We have also designed and implemented an automated tool that allows practitioners to see the results of predictions without knowledge of the underlying data mining algorithms used or any expertise in statistics or modeling.

All of the information needed to make the predictions is obtained by extracting data from a configuration management system's repository in which every time a change to the software is deemed necessary for any reason, a modification request (MR) is made detailing such information as the reason for the change and the development stage at which the MR is being written. Since the configuration management system integrates a change management functionality with the version control system, it contains not only information directly entered by the person who initiates the MR, but also the code itself and history

K. Eder, J. Lourenço, and O. Shehory (Eds.): HVC 2011, LNCS 7261, pp. 176–189, 2012.

information such as how and when the code was changed, and which changes represent bug fixes. Both sorts of information have been used to make our predictions and jointly have yielded far more accurate results than using either type of characteristic alone.

In our previous work, we have constructed and evaluated predictions of fault-proneness of individual files in nine different large industrial systems. Each system has been through a number of releases and each has been in the field for multiple years, running continuously. Collectively predictions for more than 160 distinct releases have been made and evaluated. Together these systems have been in the field for almost 50 years.

In this paper, we use data from the repository to answer questions about the software at the system level. To our knowledge, this is the first paper that has considered whether the characteristics that have been used to make successful predictions at the method, file or module level, are also useful in making predictions at the system level.

Accurate prediction of the fault-proneness of the overall system can guide the allocation of testing resources, including the number and experience level of the assigned testers, and the time scheduled for testing. Similarly, it can be used to decide on the numbers and skill levels of developers needed to make changes at the next release. In addition, the predicted fault-proneness of a future release can be an input to help evaluate if the system is on track toward successful completion, or to decide whether major redesign or re-establishment of project goals are needed.

In this paper we pose the following questions, and observe trends as the system matures.

- Does a system's fault density increase, decrease, or remain relatively stable as the system matures?
- Is there a relationship between the number of changes made to a system during a release and the number of faults occurring in that release and in the next release?
- Is there a relationship between the amount of change in the size of a system during a release and the number of faults occurring in the system's next release?
- Is there a relationship between the length of time that a system release is in the coding, unit testing, and integration phases of development and the number of faults occurring in that release?

In our earliest studies [1], we considered these sorts of questions at the file level to determine which variables were likely to affect our predictions. For example, we found that files that were new to a system or had been changed in the previous release, were much more likely to contain defects than files that were in the previous release but were not changed. Based on these relations, we built negative binomial regression models that were able to identify most of the files that contained the largest numbers of defects in the next release. In this paper we consider the analogues of some of the file-level questions we studied, to see whether we can detect similar patterns for complete systems.

2   System Information

The two large industrial systems described below have been written and maintained by teams from two different companies.

System TS is a business maintenance support system that has been in the field for over 9 years and 35 releases. Its most recent release included in the study consists of 442,000 lines of code, mostly written in C. System IC is a service provisioning system that initializes a service for a customer. This system has been operational for over 4 years, and we have collected data from 16 releases for this study. The most recent release consists of 1,370,000 lines of code, primarily in Java. Both of these systems run continuously.

Tables 1 and 2 provide detailed information about the two systems on a release by release basis, including each release's size, the number of faults detected, the number of changes made, and the elapsed calendar days that the release was in development. A change refers to a check-out/check-in of the code for any reason. A fault is a check-out/check-in for the purpose of fixing a bug, and may consist of modifying or removing existing code, or adding new code. For the purpose of this paper, we consider that a release is in development during the coding, unit testing and integration stages. All of the necessary data was extracted from their respective repositories.

3   Observations

In this section we consider each of the four questions presented in the introduction to see whether we find any pattern either within a system or between systems.

3.1   Fault Density with Maturity

How does fault density change as a system matures? Our intuition might tell us that as a system matures, the number of faults per release should decrease, while the size of the system increases, and therefore the fault density should decrease as the system matures.

Although many researchers, including us, have observed that change of any type (sometimes referred to as *churn*), whether to add new functionality, to modify existing functionality, or to correct defects, often leads to new defects being inserted into a file, we nonetheless expect that a system will eventually stabilize with age and there will be fewer and fewer defects observed as the system matures. Surely it is not uncommon for newly released systems to be highly problematic, perhaps because they were rushed to market to get a competitive advantage or because they were released prematurely before sufficient testing had occurred for some other reason.

A look at Tables 1 and 2 shows that in each case studied, as expected, the systems almost always increase in size with age. The only exception is a slight decrease in size from Release 33 to Release 34 of System TS. However, we do not see the expected decrease in the number of faults as the system matures.

Table 1. Size, Faults, Changes and Development Time for System TS (Maintenance System)

Release	Files	LOC	Faults	Changes	Days in Development
1	354	144572	22	3147	256
2	362	191592	26	522	56
3	369	194884	24	168	40
4	382	201285	59	492	96
5	390	214730	131	556	103
6	412	239224	59	354	79
7	441	242549	63	361	90
8	485	268760	72	413	90
9	490	271227	59	527	90
10	500	284259	28	201	77
11	507	285365	44	162	77
12	510	287532	18	192	91
13	518	294261	51	194	84
14	530	303830	27	276	98
15	535	308740	4	166	108
16	574	310975	23	384	157
17	573	317416	35	206	109
18	578	324346	58	192	123
19	579	330360	39	59	91
20	596	342894	61	140	97
21	602	350909	36	177	125
22	611	364169	54	259	76
23	614	372958	61	147	92
24	614	377919	54	229	96
25	616	385467	58	338	106
26	624	404895	42	208	91
27	633	411926	74	352	114
28	636	425278	72	97	104
29	638	427511	64	188	126
30	648	429373	50	162	120
31	653	432929	22	142	89
32	663	438177	40	161	173
33	664	443099	8	32	87
34	667	441569	5	32	84
35	668	441888	6	29	NA

Table 2. Size, Faults, Changes and Development Time for System IC (Provisioning System)

Release	Files	LOC	Faults	Changes	Days in Development
1	1832	816,000	275	799	90
2	1847	842,000	161	451	64
3	1860	854,000	392	897	100
4	1913	872,000	238	1015	114
5	1933	892,000	182	592	105
6	2027	914,000	277	591	49
7	2190	960,000	569	2359	112
8	2320	1,005,000	347	1354	91
9	2460	1,044,000	438	2571	140
10	2798	1,150,000	678	2819	126
11	2843	1,206,000	563	1150	65
12	2809	1,212,000	161	295	51
13	3003	1,280,000	717	2458	130
14	3058	1,323,000	452	2019	119
15	3084	1,357,000	389	1133	91
16	3085	1,370,000	184	565	66

This is reflected in Figures 1 and 2 showing the fault density over time for Systems TS and IC, respectively. For neither system do we see any systematic decrease in the fault density.

Although Releases 4-9 of System TS have higher fault density than the following releases, and the last 3 releases have markedly lower density, the overall graph does not show a pattern of decrease. For System IC, the fault density again does not show any systematic decreasing trend. In fact two of the three highest values for fault density in this system occur well into the third and the fourth year that the system was in the field, contrary to our expectations. Although the density drops off after Release 13, the values are not substantially different from those of much earlier releases.

3.2   Number of Changes vs. Number of Faults

Is there a relationship between the number of changes made to a system during a release and the number of faults occurring in the system in the next release?

As the number of changes increases, it is reasonable to expect that the number of defects in the next release would also increase in some "reasonable" way. That is certainly what we have observed at the file level. Reasonable might mean linearly, in which case the graph showing the ratios of the number of changes in Release N to the number of defects in Release N+1 shown in Figures 3 and 4 should look approximately flat.

A more likely expectation would be that as the number of changes increases, the number of faults in the next release increases faster than linearly. In that

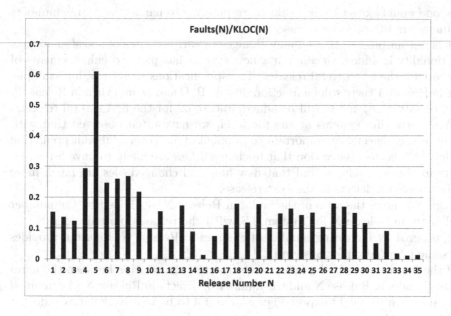

Fig. 1. Faults per KLOC - System TS

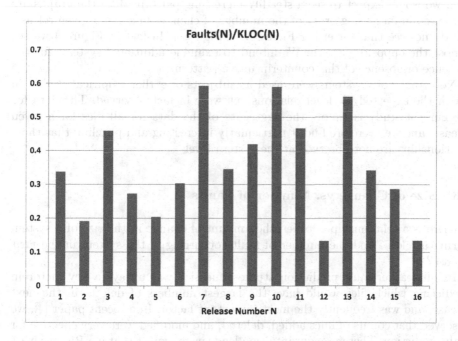

Fig. 2. Faults per KLOC - System IC

case, one would expect to see peaks corresponding to particularly large numbers of changes in the previous release.

It is not uncommon to see many changes in early releases of a system as new functionality is added, since often a new system has planned enhancements of this sort for the first several releases. The specifications might say, for example, that in Release 1 there will be functionality A, B, C and D, and then in Release 2, functionality E, F, and G will be added, and so on for the first several releases.

When studying systems at the file level, we have often observed that with change comes defects. An important component of our successful fault prediction models [2,3] is the observation that unchanged files are likely to have few or no faults in the next release, and that new files and changed files are much more likely to contain defects in the next release.

Figure 3 shows the ratio of the faults in Release N+1 divided by the number of changes in Release N for System TS, with the releases plotted along the x-axis, ordered by increasing number of changes in Release N. Figure 4 provides the same information for System IC.

If the first hypothesized relation were true and the relation between the number of changes in Release N and the number of defects in Release N+1 remained constant, then we might expect Figures 3 and 4 to be relatively flat. We do not see such a pattern for either system.

If on the other hand, the second hypothesized relation were true, that releases with many changes lead to subsequent releases with high numbers of defects, then we would expect to see a steadily increasing pattern, since the graphs are presented in increasing order of the number of changes made in a given release. We do not see that for either Figure 3 or Figure 4. In fact in Figure 4 we see almost the opposite pattern. We intend to examine additional systems for the presence or absence of this counterintuitive pattern.

Note that both systems were used as subjects of earlier empirical studies in which the expected file-level relationships were in fact observed. The data for the current study is simply the aggregate of the data for all files for a given release, and we therefore find it particularly interesting and puzzling that these relationships are not observed at the system level.

3.3   Size of Change vs. Number of Faults

Is there is a relationship between the amount of change in the size of a system during a release and the number of faults occurring in the system in the next release?

In our earlier fault prediction studies, file size was always a key factor in predicting which files would have the largest numbers of defects in the next release, and was frequently the most important factor. In a recent paper [4], we observed that counts of lines added, deleted, and modified were very effective for fault prediction. Therefore, our intuition leads us to expect that if a Release N+1 increases in size by a large amount over the size of the previous Release N, then Release N+1 would likely have many defects.

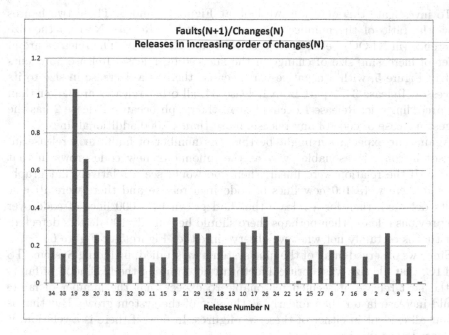

Fig. 3. Faults by changes in prior release - System TS

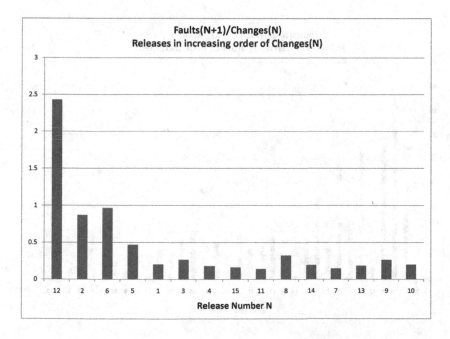

Fig. 4. Faults by changes in prior release - System IC

To investigate this question, we look at Figures 5 and 6. These two figures show the ratio of the number of faults detected in Release N+1 to the size difference (in KLOC) between Release N+1 and Release N. The releases are in order of increasing size of change in the succeeding release. Release 33 occurs first in Figure 5, with a negative bar, because there is a decrease in size to its successor, Release 34. Apart from Release 34, all other releases are larger than the preceding one. Release 1 occurs last in the graph because Release 2 has the largest increase of code of any release, more than 47,000 additional lines.

Again, our expectation might be that the number of faults in a release increases in some "reasonable" way as the amount of new code grows in that release. If the relation were linear, then one would see a relatively flat graph. Thus if there were 100 new lines of code in a release and there were 10 new faults detected, then for a release that had grown by 1,000 lines of code over the previous release, then perhaps there should be roughly 100 defects detected. But that is certainly not what we observe in either Figure 5 or Figure 6.

Since we observed in all of the nine systems we studied, including Systems TS and IC, that file size was a critical factor in determining the likelihood of faults in the next release, it seemed reasonable to expect that the number of faults would increase faster than linearly as the size of the system grows. But that is not at all evident in either of these two figures. In fact, if there is a relation, it is closer to the inverse.

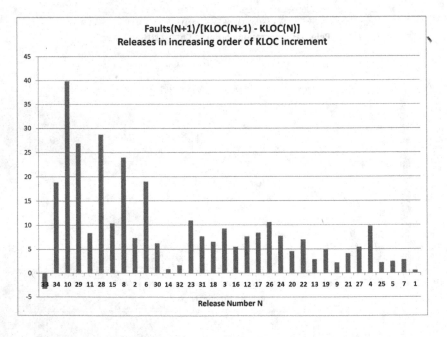

Fig. 5. Faults by KLOC difference - System TS

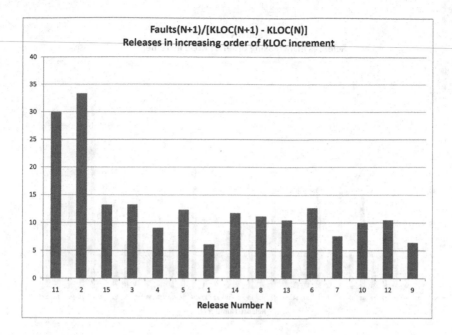

Fig. 6. Faults by KLOC difference - System IC

Another way of viewing this relation between size and faults involves looking at the absolute number of faults in Release N+1 rather than the ratio considered in Figures 5 and 6.

Figures 7 and 8 plot the absolute number of faults in a given release for each release. Again the releases are in order of increasing size of change in the succeeding release. We have typically seen that as the size of the file increased, the number of faults in the file also increased. Therefore, when sorting the files based on the amount of added code, one might expect a monotonically increasing graph or close to it. Clearly we do not see anything like that in either of these graphs. In Figure 7, we see no discernible pattern. In Figure 8, while we do not see a monotonically increasing graph, we do see that the seven releases that have the smallest amounts of increment often have fewer faults than the eight releases that have the largest amounts of increment, but even that is not always the case.

3.4   Development Time vs. Number of Faults

Is there is a relationship between the length of time that a release is in the coding, unit testing, and integration phases and the number of faults occurring in that release?

The systems we have investigated are all long-lived products, whose software is developed and released at roughly regular intervals, in well-defined stages. Generally, at any given time three versions or releases of the system are active. Release N-1 has been released to the field; Release N is undergoing system test-

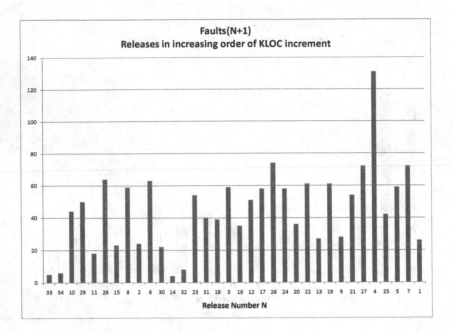

Fig. 7. Number of faults per release - System TS

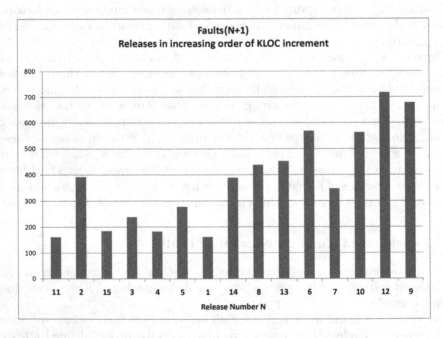

Fig. 8. Number of faults per release - System IC

ing; and Release N+1 is under development, including coding, unit testing and integration. The start time of a release is the date when coding for that release begins, and is usually the date when the previous release enters system testing. After the initial version, each subsequent Release N is usually started by copying all the code of the previous Release N-1 into a base version of N.

We refer to the period of elapsed calendar time between the start date of Release N and the start date of Release N+1 as the *development time* of N. The start date of Release N+1 usually corresponds to the end of the coding, unit testing, and integration testing phases of N, and the beginning of N's system testing phase. We can easily measure the development time of each release, and ask whether there is a relation between Release N's development time, and the number of faults that are detected in system testing of Release N.

Reasonable arguments in two directions could be given that fault count depends on the length of a release, with a longer development time leading to either more faults or fewer faults. A longer development time for Release N might mean that more code is being written for N, or that the functionality being implemented is more complex than the average. Both of those situations could plausibly lead to more faults in the code to be discovered during N's system testing.

On the other hand, one could also argue that a longer time in development of Release N means that more care is being taken for the design of new functionality, or that the release is being tested more thoroughly in the early stages of unit and integration testing. Both of those situations might lead to more stable code, with fewer faults to be discovered during system testing of Release N. Figures 9 and 10, showing faults per release with the releases ordered from shortest to longest development time, are inconclusive.

Although the development times for most releases of both systems are usually close to 90 days (as can be seen in Tables 1 and 2), there is substantial variation, especially for System TS. Its development times range from 40 days for Release 3 up to 256 days for Release 1. The average is 103 days. System IC's development times range from 49 to 140 days, with an average of 95. The two systems show significantly different relations between faults and development time.

The Spearman rank correlation between faults and development time for System TS is very low, at .131. Figure 9 shows the faults in each release, with releases in increasing order of their development time. There is no discernible pattern, even if the obvious outliers at Releases 34, 33, 5 and 15 are removed. Despite having the longest development time, and by far the largest number of changes, very few faults were detected during system testing of Release 1. The relative scarcity of faults continued through Releases 2 and 3, with a large number detected finally at Release 5.

The rank correlation for System IC is a much stronger .617, and the corresponding Figure 10 shows at least some indication that the faults frequently increase with an increased development time.

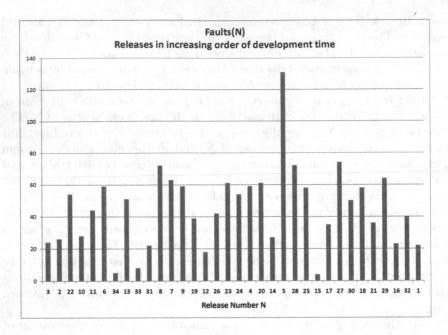

Fig. 9. Faults per release ordered by development time - System TS

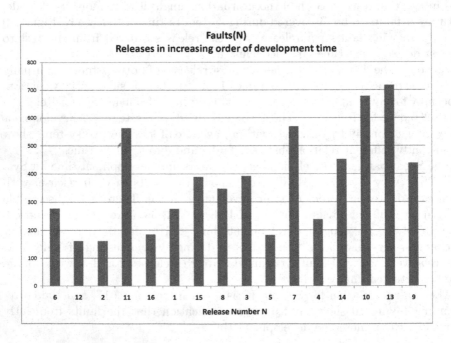

Fig. 10. Faults per release ordered by development time - System IC

4   Conclusions

We have presented and examined a number of intuitively plausible relations between defects and system history data, with the data extracted from a configuration management system for two large, mature software systems. Our expectation was that we would see patterns similar to those observed for these systems when we looked at analogous questions at the file level. Our reasoning was that software systems are simply the aggregate of their files, so that if many changes in a file indicate that it is likely to have many defects in the next release, then if a release has many changes, it should be likely to have many defects in the next release. We did not observe any of the expected relations for any of the questions we investigated for either of these systems.

What does that tell us? The most important thing we have learned is that it is not acceptable to rely on our intuition or software engineering folklore, even when questions addressed are at least superficially similar to ones already asked and observed in large industrial empirical studies. Specifically, we learned that the answer to each of the questions we posed is no, even though our expectation was that the answers would all be in the affirmative.

References

1. Weyuker, E.J., Ostrand, T.J.: The Distribution of Faults in a Large Industrial Software System. In: Proc. ACM/International Symposium on Software Testing and Analysis (ISSTA 2002), Rome, Italy, pp. 55–64 (July 2002)
2. Ostrand, T.J., Weyuker, E.J., Bell, R.M.: Predicting the Location and Number of Faults in Large Software Systems. IEEE Trans. on Software Engineering 31(4) (April 2005)
3. Weyuker, E.J., Ostrand, T.J., Bell, R.M.: Comparing the Effectiveness of Several Modeling Methods for Fault Prediction. Empirical Software Eng. (June 2009)
4. Bell, R.M., Ostrand, T.J., Weyuker, E.J.: Does Measuring Code Change Improve Fault Prediction? In: Proc. 7th International Conference on Predictive Models in Software Engineering (Promise 2011), Banff, Canada (September 2011)

Reverse Coverage Analysis

Ariel Birnbaum[1], Laurent Fournier[1], Steve Mittermaier[2], and Avi Ziv[1]

[1] IBM Research - Haifa, Israel
{arielb,laurent,aziv}@il.ibm.com
[2] IBM Server and Technology Group, Poughkeepsie, NY, USA
mitt@us.ibm.com

Abstract. Commonly used approaches for accumulating coverage data do not properly track events that have been covered in the past but not recently (stale events). They either treat stale events as covered events (global approach) or as uncovered events (window approach). We propose a new approach called reverse coverage analysis that is based on tracking the last time each coverage event was hit and looking at the coverage data backward in time from the present. With this approach, we can easily identify stale events and when the ability to cover them was lost. The reverse coverage approach was successfully used in the verification of two high-end IBM microprocessors and improved treatment of stale events and their causes.

1 Introduction

The size and complexity of modern hardware systems have turned the functional verification of these systems into a mammoth task [1]. Verifying such systems involves tens or hundreds of person years and requires the computing power of thousands of workstations. In current industrial practice, verification is a highly automated process that is based on autonomous verification environments. Such environments contain random stimuli generators [2] that generate a massive amount of tests, simulation engines, and sophisticated checking mechanisms [3].

Coverage [4] is one of the main vehicles for monitoring and controlling the verification process. Coverage analysis provides the means to track the progress of verification and identify weaknesses in it. To this extent, *coverage-driven verification* (CDV) methodology [5], which tightly connects the verification plan and its execution with coverage measures, is a commonly used verification methodology.

The goal of coverage analysis tools and techniques is to convert the huge amount of coverage data collected during the lifetime of a project into simple and concise reports that provide useful information to the users about the state and progress of the verification process. In general, coverage analysis tools provide users with two types of reports: progress reports that track the state of coverage (e.g., number of events covered) over time; and status reports that provide a description, at various levels of details, of the coverage state. Advanced analysis techniques, such as the ones described in [6, 7], are often used to improve the

K. Eder, J. Lourenço, and O. Shehory (Eds.): HVC 2011, LNCS 7261, pp. 190–202, 2012.

quality of the generated reports. For example, hole analysis [6] can be used to detect large uncovered areas and report these areas instead of large lists of uncovered events.

Usually, coverage analysis tools look at coverage data that is accumulated over time. Therefore, it is an interesting and important question to determine the timeframe in which coverage data is analyzed. There are two major approaches to answer this question. The first approach looks at all the data collected since the beginning of time; while the second approach looks at the coverage data in fixed windows (e.g., the coverage collected during the last seven days). These two approaches have significant drawbacks when handling *stale events*; that is, events that were covered in the past, but not recently. Both approaches do not properly treat these events properly. The global approach treats these events like other covered events, denying the users the important fact that these events have not been covered for a long time. This may prevent an investigation of why the events have not been covered recently, which may lead to the detection of problems in the design, its environment, or the verification process. In the window approach, stale events fall outside the window and look like any other uncovered events. This hides the fact that the events have been covered in the past and something (perhaps important) caused the loss of the ability to cover them.

Reverse coverage analysis is a new approach for accumulating and looking at coverage data. It is designed to overcome the drawbacks of the global and window approaches regarding stale events. This approach uses a global view of the coverage data, but it looks at the data in reverse chronological order. That is, instead of looking at the data from the beginning of time toward the present, it looks at the data from the present towards the beginning of time. The basis of this approach is the reverse progress report that plots for each time t, how many events, of those events that were covered in the past, are not covered after time t.

The reverse progress report can provide useful information about the state of the verification process. The time it takes the plot to flatten from the present backwards is an indicator of the time it takes to cover all the covered events again; the level of the plot when it flattens shows how many stale events exist; and sharp changes in the slope of the plot point to times when the ability to cover some events was lost. In addition to the reverse progress plot, the reverse analysis also allows status reports regarding the stale events, such as displaying all the stale events that have not been covered for the last two weeks.

We used the reverse analysis approach in the verification of two recent IBM high-end microprocessors, POWER7 and z196. The approach was implemented on top of two internal coverage tools: Meteor [6], a cross-product coverage tool that uses the global approach, and Bugspray [8], a designer-level discrete events tool that uses the window approach. The reverse progress and stale events reports helped the verification teams identify stale events and other problems in the verification processes and simplified the process of reaching the root cause of these problems.

The rest of the paper is organized as follows. In Section 2, we provide some background on coverage analysis and its importance. In Section 3, we explain the reverse coverage analysis approach and its advantages over other approaches for accumulating coverage data. Section 4 describes some of our experience in using reverse coverage analysis in two recent IBM projects. Finally, in Section 5, we present our conclusions and plans for the future.

2   Coverage Analysis

Coverage analysis is one of the important sources for information to the verification team regarding the status and progress of the verification process. For example, large uncovered areas may indicate that a feature is missing in the stimuli generator; and not hitting new events for a long time may indicate that the current set of test templates ran out of steam.

The goals of coverage analysis tools are to collect the coverage data that is created during the lifetime of the project, process and analyze the data, and provide the users with concise and meaningful reports. In general, this work is done in two steps. The first step includes processing the raw coverage data and storing it in coverage databases. The second step is to analyze the coverage data stored in the database and to produce coverage reports. In this work we consider a large verification project that produces a very large amount of raw coverage data. This large amount of data makes it impossible to keep all the data in the coverage database. Therefore, the coverage data kept in the database is a summary of the raw data fed to the coverage tool.

The amount of data saved in the coverage database determines the analysis tool's ability to provide useful information to its users. For rudimentary coverage analysis, simply recording which events occurred may be sufficient. Small additions to this information that still keep the database compact can significantly increase the analysis capabilities of the tool. For example, reporting the number of times an event has occurred can help discover lightly covered events; and recording the time an event was first covered allows coverage progress to be computed.

In this section we describe basic coverage analysis techniques and coverage reports. We use, as an example, a simple coverage model for floating-point data. The model is used throughout this paper to demonstrate various analysis techniques and reports, and to compare different approaches for accumulating coverage data. This model has been used to check the coverage of tests generated for the floating-point units of several processors in IBM [9]. Note that the model presented in the paper is a subset of the real coverage model (e.g., not all the floating-point instructions are included). The data presented in the reports below represent 12 weeks of coverage collection in an experimental work. The coverage collection period is June 10 through August 31 (this fact is important for dates shown in the reports).

Figure 1 shows the attributes of the coverage space and possible values for each attribute. The space consists of three attributes — Instr, Result, and Rounding

Attribute	Values
Instr	fadd, fadds, fsub, fmul, fdiv, fmadd,
	fmsub, fres, frsqrte, fabs, fneg, fsel, ...
Result	SNaN, QNaN, ±0, ±∞,
	±Norm, ±MinNorm, ±MaxNorm,
	±DeNorm,±MinDeNorm, ±MaxDeNorm,
RM	Near , 0, +∞, −∞

Fig. 1. Coverage space attributes for the floating-point model

Mode (RM) — each with the possible values shown. The semantic description of the coverage space is as follows: test that all *instructions* produce all possible *target results* in the various *rounding modes* supported by the processor.

A critical step in the coverage process is to define a coverage model that contains only the legal events in the coverage space. This is because not all events in the coverage space of the schema are legal. For example, the results of executing a floating-point absolute value instruction can never be negative.

Most coverage tools provide two types of reports — status reports that provide the state of coverage at a given time and progress reports that show how coverage progresses over time [4]. The actual reports vary in their level of detail and the way they present their data according to their specific goals and target users. For example, project management is usually interested in high-level status and progress of coverage, while a verification engineer may be interested in many details about small sets of coverage events assigned to her.

Status reports are designed to describe the status of coverage (or a specific coverage model) at a specific point in time. The reports can range in detail from a high-level summary of the coverage status to detailed reports that contain the status of each event. The high-level summary reports are useful for a quick overview of the coverage status. They can be used, for example, to determine which coverage models deserve more attention and deeper analysis. Detailed coverage reports can be used by the verification team to detect areas in the DUV that are unverified or lightly verified and direct the verification efforts to these areas.

Figure 2 shows some coverage reports for the floating-point coverage model. The summary of the coverage status is shown in Figure 2(a). The summary includes information about the size of the coverage space and model, how many events are covered and not covered, and the number of measured traces. On its own, it is hard to interpret the significance of the data in the report. This can be done only by comparing the data to previous reports and reports of other models or by looking at a more detailed report.

Figure 2(b) shows part of the detailed status. Because the model contains close to 1700 events, and not all of them can be displayed, only a small set of events is shown. The report shows, for each event, how many times it was hit and the first time it was hit. Note that a detailed report can include additional information about the events, such as a threshold under which they are considered lightly covered, their coverage status (uncovered, lightly covered, or covered),

Size of coverage space:	2104
Number of events in model:	1696
Number of covered events:	1599
Percent of covered events:	94.28%
Number of holes:	97
Number of illegal events:	0
Number of traces measured (total):	13973

(a) Summary report

Attributes			Coverage Data	
Instr	Result	RM	Count	First
fadd	+Norm	0	471	6/10
fsub	-∞	Near	193	6/11
fres	-DeNorm	0	219	6/14
fadd	-MaxNorm	+∞	153	6/27
fabs	+0	−∞	189	7/02
fdiv	QNaN	Near	48	7/16
fsqrt	+DeNorm	−∞	0	-

(b) Status report

Hole size	Instr	Result	RM
72	fctid	*	*
24	fsqrt, fsqrts	RES.DENORM	*
1	fdiv	-MaxDeNorm	−∞

(c) Holes report

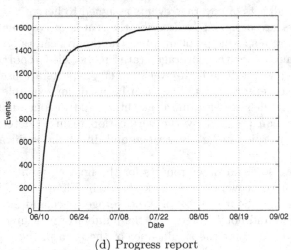

(d) Progress report

Fig. 2. Examples of coverage reports for the floating-point model

details about the first test that hit them, etc. To reduce the size of the report, the user can filter the presented events based on the coverage data of the events. For example, a user may ask for events that have not yet been covered. To further reduce the size of the reports and improve their usefulness, more advanced analysis techniques, such as the ones described in [6], can be used. For example, hole analysis can be used to detect large areas of uncovered events. Figure 2(c) shows the hole analysis report for the floating-point model. The report shows two large holes. The first hole corresponds to the `fctid` instruction that was not covered at all; this hole can be attributed to a problem in the stimuli generator. The second hole contains square root instructions with very small results; these events are actually impossible and should be removed from the model. Note that the '*' in the hole report represent a don't-care value for that attribute.

Progress reports display the progress of coverage over time, usually in terms of covered events. These reports are useful in showing if and how fast coverage is progressing and detecting when the verification is "running out of steam". Sharp changes in the slope of the coverage progress are good indicators for changes in the verification environment or its activation that caused an increase or decrease in the coverage improvement rate. In addition, statistical analysis techniques can be used to predict potential coverage levels [7].

Figure 2(d) displays the progress report for the floating-point model. The figure shows that progress has flattened and over the last three weeks no progress in coverage was made. The figure also shows a sharp increase in the coverage rate around Week 4. This improvement in the coverage rate was caused by coverage analysis that revealed a large hole in the coverage of the model. The root cause of the hole was a bug in the stimuli generator. When the bug was fixed, the events in the hole started to be covered and the coverage rate improved.

3   Reverse Coverage Analysis

In general, coverage analysis tools look at coverage data that accumulates over time. While looking at the coverage of single tests can be useful, most of the benefits of coverage analysis come from analysis of large sets of tests. Therefore, an interesting and important question is to determine the timeframe in which coverage data is analyzed.

There are two major approaches to answering this question. The first approach is to look at all the data that has been collected. The advantage of this approach is that it uses all the coverage data available. Therefore, it will not miss or ignore coverage events that are rarely seen. The disadvantage of the approach is that it does not distinguish between stale events (events that have not been covered for a long time) and other covered events. Regarding stale events as covered may hide problems such as losing the ability to cover an event because of changes in the design or its environment.

The second approach looks at the coverage data in fixed windows (e.g., the coverage collected during the last seven days). This approach ensures that only recent coverage data is viewed and considered in coverage analysis. On the other hand, this approach does not distinguish between stale events and uncovered events, as both types look like uncovered events. Another disadvantage of this approach is the difficulty in determining the size of the window.

Figure 3 compares a basic status report and a progress report for the global and window approaches of the floating-point coverage model. To illustrate the

Attributes			Global		Window	
Instr	Result	RM	Cnt	First	Cnt	First
fadd	+Norm	0	471	6/10	53	8/25
fsub	-∞	Near	193	6/11	27	8/25
fres	-DeNorm	0	219	6/14	0	-
fadd	-MaxNorm	+∞	153	6/27	21	8/27
fabs	+0	-∞	189	7/02	30	8/24
fdiv	QNaN	Near	48	7/16	0	-
fsqrt	+DeNorm	-∞	0	-	0	-

(a) Status report

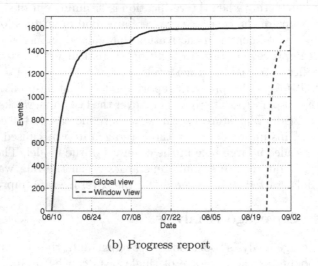

(b) Progress report

Fig. 3. Comparison of the global and window approaches

differences between the approaches, we have overlaid the figures. Look first at the progress report in Figure 3(b). The figure helps illustrate some of the disadvantages of the two approaches. First, the slope of the progress report of the window approach is still positive at the end, indicating that a larger window would improve the window coverage. Second, the total number of events covered in the window approach is less than the total number of events covered globally. This means there are some events that have not been covered recently. The third and sixth rows of the status report in Figure 3(a) are examples of such events. The <fres, -DeNorm, 0> event in the third row has been covered many times (more than its surrounding events in the report), but has not been covered in the last seven days. This raises the suspicion that something happened to the ability to cover the event. The <fdiv, QNaN, Near> event on the sixth row, on the other hand, was covered a small number of times, so the reason for not covering it during the last seven days may be caused by a difficulty of reaching it. Note that such events can not be detected by just the global or window approaches, and even the combined approach does not reveal if such events are not covered recently because the window is too small or because of a more serious problem in the verification process.

To address the disadvantages of the global and window approach, we propose a new way to accumulate and look at coverage data: the *reverse coverage analysis* approach. This approach uses a global view of the coverage data, but it looks at the data in reverse chronological order. That is, instead of looking at the data from the beginning of data collection to the present, it looks at the data from the present backwards. Note that the reverse coverage analysis approach should not replace the global or window approaches. Instead, it should be combined with one of these approaches to provide the benefits of forward and backward looking at the coverage data.

The reverse analysis approach is enabled by recording information on the last time each coverage event was hit. With this information we can generate a reverse progress report. This report shows, for each time t, how many covered events have their last hit at time less than t. In other words, the plot shows how many events, out of the events that have been covered in the past, are not covered after time t. Clearly, at the present time, all the covered events meet this criterion, so the reverse progress plot starts where the normal progress plots ends. As we move back in time (leftward) the number of events that meet the criterion drops and so does the plot, until it reaches a point in time when the number of events that meet the criterion is zero, or, in other words, all the covered events have been covered after that time.

We can describe the reverse analysis more formally. Let E be the set of all coverage events in the design, and **first**, **last** $: E \rightarrow \mathcal{T}$ denote the first and last times each event was covered (we take $\mathcal{T}$ to be the axis of time plus an additional point $\bot$ to indicate an event has never been covered). Now we can define, for any given point t in time, the following set of events:

$$S_t = \{e \in E \mid \mathbf{last}(e) \leq t \,\&\, \mathbf{last}(e) \neq \bot\}$$

This set includes the events that are "stale" since time t. We then refer to the analysis that refers to this set as the reverse coverage approach. For example, a reverse coverage plot shows the size of S_t versus the t axis.

For contrast, we can give a similar description of the global and window approaches. The global approach can be seen as the analysis of the set of events covered at any point in time:

$$C_t = \{e \in E \mid \mathbf{first}(e) \leq t \,\&\, \mathbf{first}(e) \neq \bot\}$$

The window approach requires some more information: if we take $\mathbf{first}_w(e)$ to be the first time event e was covered after time w (the earliest date in our window), we can define:

$$W_t = \{e \in E \mid \mathbf{first}_w(e) \leq t \,\&\, \mathbf{first}_w(e) \neq \bot\}$$

Figure 4 shows an example of progress and status reports for the floating-point coverage model with reverse coverage analysis. The status report in Figure 4(a)

Attributes			Coverage Data		
Instr	Result	RM	Count	First	Last
fadd	+Norm	0	471	6/10	8/31
fsub	-∞	Near	193	6/11	8/31
fres	-DeNorm	0	219	6/14	7/24
fadd	-MaxNorm	+∞	153	6/27	8/28
fabs	+0	-∞	189	7/02	8/30
fdiv	QNaN	Near	48	7/16	8/23
fsqrt	+DeNorm	-∞	0	-	-

(a) Status report

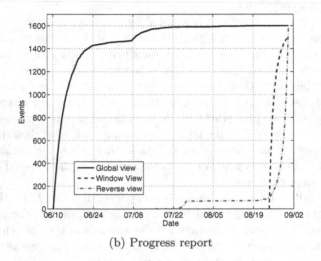

(b) Progress report

Fig. 4. Reverse coverage reports

is similar to the report in Figure 2(b), except for the added *Last* column that specifies when events are last hit. This column can be used to identify stale events, such as the third event that has not been hit in more than 30 days. The progress plot in Figure 4(b) shows the reverse progress plot in addition to the "normal" global progress and window progress.

Like the "normal" progress report, the reverse progress report can reveal useful information to its users about the state and progress of the verification process. The slope of the plot can be useful in determining the rate of covering events again. Specifically, the time it takes the plot to flatten is the time needed to cover again all the events that the current environment can cover. This time can be used to determine the size of the window in the window approach. For example, in Figure 4(b) it takes the reverse plot about $1\frac{1}{2}$ weeks to flatten, and therefore this value (or a slightly bigger one) should be used as the window size instead of the 1 week that is used in Figure 3(b).

Discontinuities and sharp changes in the slope indicate a sudden loss of the ability to cover a set of events. For example, in Figure 4(b) we see such a change around July 25. This change indicates that about 40 events that were hit early are suddenly no longer hit. A simple query to the coverage database regarding events that were last hit before July 25 yields a report like the one shown in Figure 5(a). This basic status report can be combined with more advanced coverage analysis techniques, such as the techniques described in [6], to provide more compact and meaningful reports. For example, clustering techniques such as hole analysis can be used to identify groups of events that have not been covered lately and indicate that a major area has been skipped. In our example, the hole analysis report produces the report in Figure 5(b) that contains only one line. This report quickly identifies that the `fres` instruction has not been used with negative results since July 25.

This kind of phenomenon cannot be seen with the global report alone, as this only looks at the time of first coverage. The window report does show a decrease in coverage when compared to the global one, but as stated before, it is hard to understand from this report alone if the decrease shows a true gap in coverage power or is just a measurement artifact and would go away with a wider window. The plateau in the reverse coverage plot tells us it is the former.

Attributes			Coverage Data		
Instr	Result	R.M	Count	First	Last
fres	-Norm	0	258	6/10	7/23
fres	-DeNorm	0	219	6/14	7/25
fres	-∞	Near	138	6/16	7/26
fres	-MaxNorm	+∞	113	6/17	7/22
fres	-MinNorm	-∞	148	6/18	7/26

(a) Simple list of stale events

Hole size	Instr	Result	R.M
36	fres	SIGN.NEG	*

(b) Large area of stale events

Fig. 5. Events not covered since July 25

Another advantage of the reverse coverage analysis is the creation of regression suites. Static, coverage-oriented regression suites are small sets of test cases that can cover all the covered events. Efficient algorithms for creating such regression suites exist [10], but they rely on obtaining coverage information of all test cases available. When this information is not available, such as the case in this paper, regression suites are created by saving to a database the test case that hit each coverage event for the first time. With the reverse coverage analysis approach, this method is replaced by saving the test cases that are the last to hit coverage events. The advantage of the reverse method is that it harvests newer test cases, and therefore, the chances that these test cases lose their coverage capabilities because of changes to the DUV or its verification environment are smaller. In addition, newer test cases are being generated by an improved and better tuned verification environment. Therefore, they cover events faster and result in smaller regression suites. For example, in the floating-point model, the size of a first hit based regression suite is 193 test cases, while the size of reverse regression suite is only 175 test cases.

Implementing the reverse coverage analysis requires saving the last time each event is hit. This adds small constant factor to the size of the coverage database. It also adds a small constant factor to the time needed for processing raw coverage data. Performing the reverse coverage analysis and producing its reports have similar complexity as global analysis. For example, both the normal and reverse progress reports require sorting the events according to coverage time (**first** for the normal report and **last** for the reverse report) followed by a scan of the sorted list to create the plot, which leads to a complexity of $o(n \log n)$ for n events.

4   Usage Example

The reverse coverage analysis was used in the verification of two high-end IBM microprocessors: POWER7 and z196. The support for reverse coverage was implemented on top of two IBM internal coverage tools, Meteor [6] and Bugspray [8].

Meteor is a cross-product coverage analysis tool used for architectural and microarchitectural coverage. It uses the global approach and it already keeps information about the last time coverage events are hit in its databases. However, its analysis engines do not support the reverse progress and stale events reports. We created the reverse progress reports by post-processing a detailed status report of covered events, sorted according to the last hit time. To generate stale reports, such as the one shown in Figure 5(b), we filtered the events based on the last hit time and fed the filtered events back to the tool analysis engines.

Figure 6 shows the reverse progress of the CoreExecute model. This model is designed to check that all aspects of the execute instructions (ex and exrl) are verified. The figure is similar in shape to Figure 4(b), although the effects in Figure 4(b) such as the flattening of slope and sudden changes in it are less noticeable here. This figure and similar figures for other models are produced as part of the daily coverage reports of the project. The plots are used to detect bad trends in the coverage, such as a large number of stale events and sharp changes in the ability to cover events again.

Bugspray is a designer-level coverage tool for discrete coverage events. It uses the window approach with a configurable window size. The POWER7 and z196 projects used windows of 14 and 21 days for their reports. To add support for reverse coverage analysis, we added a small, simple database that includes a summary of the coverage history for each event. This summary includes dates of when an event is defined and when it first and last hit. The history database is updated when the daily reports are generated. It reports stale events in two ways: it marks stale events in purple instead of red that is used for uncovered events, and it creates reports of the stale events like the one shown in Figure 7.

Reporting the stale events helped the verification teams in several ways. First, it ensured that the window time period was appropriate. This was done by ensuring that only a very small number of events fluctuated between the covered and stale states. In addition, the information on stale events combined with information on the test templates that contributed to the coverage of which

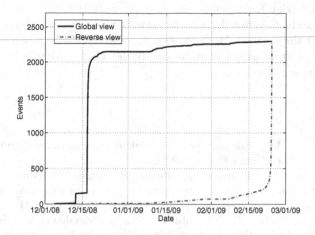

Fig. 6. Reverse progress report for the z196 CoreExecute model

Unit	Entity	Var	First Hit	Last Hit
L3	l3sdrtl	case-00951	May-1-08	Oct-27-08
L3	l3sdrtl	bad-hpc-dir-dis	Apr-15-08	Jul-19-09
MCU	mca-top	crc-w-idxmatch	Oct-6-08	Jun-28-09
IFU	pref-mac	squash-w-dmd	Apr-1-08	Jul-15-09
LSU	ls-srqs	lssrqs-count053	Nov-10-08	Feb-18-09
NCU	ncrccomc	bsr-rc-arc-s8-s8	Apr-22-08	Jul-25-09

Fig. 7. Sample of stale events report for POWER7 system verification

events helped fine-tune the execution policy of test templates and identify other problems in activating the verification environment.

5 Conclusions

Information about stale coverage events can be important to verification teams because it reveals problems in the verification process. This paper proposed the reversed coverage analysis approach to better handle stale events. By recording the last time coverage events are hit and looking backwards in time, reverse coverage analysis can easily detect and report stale events. In addition, it can provide users with other useful information about the state of the coverage process, such as the time it takes to re-cover all the covered events.

The reverse coverage analysis was implemented on top of two IBM coverage tools and was used in the verification of two high-end microprocessors. The reverse progress and stale events reports helped the verification teams in both projects to detect stale events, and through them, identify problems in the verification environments and processes.

Our current work is focused on extending the usefulness of the reverse coverage analysis approach. Specifically, we are investigating new methods to improve the analysis of the reverse data. For example, we examine how trend analysis techniques [11] can be used to automatically detect a sudden loss in the ability to cover a large set of events.

References

1. Wile, B., Goss, J.C., Roesner, W.: Comprehensive Functional Verification - The Complete Industry Cycle. Elsevier (2005)
2. Adir, A., Almog, E., Fournier, L., Marcus, E., Rimon, M., Vinov, M., Ziv, A.: Genesys-Pro: Innovations in test program generation for functional processor verification. IEEE Design and Test of Computers 21(2), 84–93 (2004)
3. Shacham, O., Wachs, M., Solomatnikov, A., Firoozshahian, A., Richardson, S., Horowitz, M.: Verification of chip multiprocessor memory systems using a relaxed scoreboard. In: Proceedings of the 41st IEEE/ACM International Symposium on Microarchitecture (MICRO-41), pp. 294–305 (2008)
4. Piziali, A.: Functional Verification Coverage Measurement and Analysis. Springer (2004)
5. Carter, H.B., Hemmady, S.G.: Metric Driven Design Verification: An Engineer's and Executive's Guide to First Pass Success. Springer (2007)
6. Azatchi, H., Fournier, L., Marcus, E., Ur, S., Ziv, A., Zohar, K.: Advanced analysis techniques for cross-product coverage. IEEE Transactions on Computers 55(11), 1367–1379 (2006)
7. Hajjar, A., Chen, T., Munn, I., Andrews, A., Bjorkman, M.: High quality behavioral verification using statistical stopping criteria. In: Proceedings of the 2001 Design, Automation and Test in Europe Conference, pp. 411–418 (2001)
8. Ludden, J.M., et al.: Functional verification of the POWER4 microprocessor and POWER4 multiprocessor systems. IBM Journal of Research and Development 46(1), 53–76 (2002)
9. Aharoni, M., Asaf, S., Fournier, L., Koyfman, A., Nagel, R.: FPgen - a deep-knowledge test generator for floating point verification. In: Proceedings of the 8th High-Level Design Validation and Test Workshop, pp. 17–22 (2003)
10. Buchnik, E., Ur, S.: Compacting regression-suites on-the-fly. In: Proceedings of the 4th Asia Pacific Software Engineering Conference, pp. 385–394 (1997)
11. Lyu, M.: The Handbook of Software Reliability Engineering. McGraw Hill (1996)

Symbolic Testing of OpenCL Code

Peter Collingbourne, Cristian Cadar, and Paul H.J. Kelly

Department of Computing,
Imperial College London
{peter.collingbourne03,c.cadar,p.kelly}@imperial.ac.uk

Abstract. We present an effective technique for crosschecking a C or C++ program against an accelerated OpenCL version, as well as a technique for detecting data races in OpenCL programs. Our techniques are implemented in KLEE-CL, a symbolic execution engine based on KLEE and KLEE-FP that supports symbolic reasoning on the equivalence between symbolic values.

Our approach is to symbolically model the OpenCL environment using an OpenCL runtime library targeted to symbolic execution. Using this model we are able to run OpenCL programs symbolically, keeping track of memory accesses for the purpose of race detection. We then compare the symbolic result against the plain C or C++ implementation in order to detect mismatches between the two versions.

We applied KLEE-CL to the Parboil benchmark suite, the Bullet physics library and the OP2 library, in which we were able to find a total of seven errors: two mismatches between the OpenCL and C implementations, three memory errors, one OpenCL compiler bug and one race condition.

1   Introduction

The Open Computing Language (OpenCL) [12] is an open standard for parallel computing architectures, such as Graphics Processing Units (GPUs). OpenCL includes a C API which provides the means for a developer to execute computational *kernels* in parallel on an OpenCL compatible device. Kernels are written in a variant of ISO C99 [11] referred to as OpenCL C.

The fundamental unit of execution in OpenCL is the *work-item*, which represents a single invocation of a specified kernel function. A kernel invocation constitutes the parallel execution of a set of work-items, optionally organised into *work-groups*, which can share common resources such as local memory. Each work-item conceptually resides at a point in the kernel invocation's iteration space, referred to as the *n*-dimensional range, or *NDRange*. Data-level parallelism is achieved by having the kernel function vary the data items accessed depending on the position of the work-item in the iteration space. Figure 1 shows an example of how *work-item functions* can be used for this purpose.

The translation of an existing C or C++ program to OpenCL can be a complex process, especially for those unfamiliar with the concurrency model and the relevant APIs. In the end, the developer has little confidence that their translated OpenCL code is equivalent to the original C or C++ code. Neither can the

K. Eder, J. Lourenço, and O. Shehory (Eds.): HVC 2011, LNCS 7261, pp. 203–218, 2012.
© Springer-Verlag Berlin Heidelberg 2012

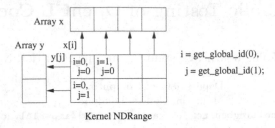

Fig. 1. Using a 2-dimensional NDRange iteration space to vary the data items accessed

developer easily determine that their code is compliant with the OpenCL specification, because he or she may unknowingly be using undocumented quirks of their particular implementation. For example, memory is generally not required to be consistent across work-items [12, § 3.3.1], and the actual behaviour generally depends on the underlying hardware memory model.

This paper presents a crosschecking and data race detection technique for OpenCL programs. Our approach is based on symbolic execution [13], which provides a systematic way of exploring all feasible paths in a program for inputs up to a certain size. On each explored path, our technique works by building the symbolic expressions associated with the C/C++ and OpenCL versions of the code, and proving their equivalence. During symbolic execution of OpenCL kernels, we also maintain a log of all memory accesses for use in race detection. We build on earlier work [5], in which we extended the KLEE symbolic execution engine with support for crosschecking floating point and SIMD code.

This paper makes the following contributions:

1. We present a symbolic execution based technique for crosschecking OpenCL programs against their original C or C++ implementations.
2. We present a technique for testing for the presence of data races in OpenCL programs using a memory access log.
3. We describe KLEE-CL, an open-source tool that implements our technique by extending KLEE-FP [5] (itself an extension to the open source symbolic execution tool KLEE) with a model of the OpenCL runtime library and our race detection algorithm.
4. We evaluate KLEE-CL by applying it to three Parboil benchmarks, the Bullet physics library and the OP2 library, and show that it can find real bugs, including memory errors, race conditions, and implementation mismatches.

2   Overview

Our approach for testing OpenCL code is illustrated graphically in Figure 2. Given an OpenCL and a C/C++ implementation of a given routine, our technique uses symbolic execution to explore all feasible pairs of paths (or as many as possible in a given time budget) through the given implementations (§3.1).

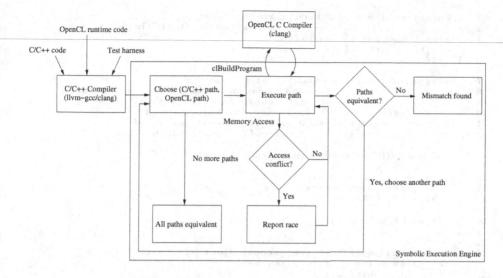

Fig. 2. Architecture diagram for KLEE-CL

Then, on each explored path it (1) symbolically checks whether the two implementations compute equivalent outputs (§3.2) and (2) checks whether there are any race conditions (§5). In order to be able to reason about OpenCL code, our technique implements a symbolic OpenCL model (§4).

To illustrate the main features of our technique, we walk the reader through a simple example in which we check the equivalence between a C and an OpenCL implementation of a simple routine. The code example shown in Listing 1 contains a function called `cpu_arr_sqrt`, a C implementation of a function that computes the square root of every element of an array `in`, storing it into an array `out`; as well as `gpu_arr_sqrt`, an OpenCL implementation of the same function that makes use of the OpenCL kernel `arr_sqrt_kern`.

Like the C implementation, `gpu_arr_sqrt` takes as arguments the input and output arrays `in` and `out` and their size `size`. However, `gpu_arr_sqrt` receives three additional arguments: a `context`, which is used to execute kernels on one or more devices and to manage objects such as memory and kernel objects; a `command_queue`, which is created on a specific device and is used to enqueue OpenCL commands to be executed by the device; and `kernel`, which represents the function to be executed on the device (in our case `arr_sqrt_kern`).

In order to run the `arr_sqrt_kern` kernel, the code first creates two *memory buffer* objects, `in_buf` and `out_buf`, which represent memory allocated on the device. The memory buffer objects are set up such that OpenCL will copy data between the host and the device when necessary (i.e. `in` will be copied to `in_buf` before kernel execution, and `out_buf` to `out` after execution).

On line 11 the code sets the first kernel function argument to `out_buf`, and on line 12 the second to `in_buf`. Then on line 14 it calls `clEnqueueNDRangeKernel`, which schedules the execution of `arr_sqrt_kern` on the device. Finally on line 20 it calls `clFinish`, which blocks until kernel execution terminates.

```
1   __kernel void arr_sqrt_kern(__global float *out,
2                               __global const float *in) {
3     size_t i = get_global_id(0);
4     out[i] = sqrt(in[i]);
5   }
6
7   void gpu_arr_sqrt(cl_context context,
8                     cl_command_queue cmd_queue, cl_kernel kernel,
9                     float *out, const float *in, size_t size) {
10    /* Initialisation of in_buf and out_buf: omitted */
11    clSetKernelArg(kernel, 0, sizeof(cl_mem), &out_buf);
12    clSetKernelArg(kernel, 1, sizeof(cl_mem), &in_buf);
13
14    clEnqueueNDRangeKernel(cmd_queue, kernel,
15      /* work_dim */ 1,
16      /* global_work_offset */ NULL,
17      /* global_work_size */ &size,
18      NULL, 0, NULL, NULL);
19
20    clFinish(cmd_queue);
21  }
22
23  void cpu_arr_sqrt(float *out, const float *in, size_t size) {
24    for (size_t i = 0; i != size; ++i)
25      out[i] = sqrt(in[i]);
26  }
27
28  int main(void) {
29    float in[64], cpuout[64], gpuout[64];
30    uint32_t *cpuouti = (uint32_t *) cpuout;
31    uint32_t *gpuouti = (uint32_t *) gpuout;
32    klee_make_symbolic(in, sizeof(in), "in");
33
34    cpu_arr_sqrt(cpuout, in, 64);
35
36    /* Initialisation of context, cq, kernel: omitted */
37    gpu_arr_sqrt(context, cq, kernel, gpuout, in, 64);
38
39    for (size_t i = 0; i != 64; ++i)
40      assert(gpuouti[i] == cpuouti[i]);
41  }
```

Listing 1. A simple test benchmark

The call to clEnqueueNDRangeKernel specifies the bounds of an implicit parallel loop around a call to arr_sqrt_kern. In this case, the work_dim argument is set to 1, so the loop has one dimension; global_work_size is a pointer to size, so the loop will have size iterations; and global_work_offset is NULL, so the lower bound of the loop index is 0.

The arr_sqrt_kern kernel function implements one iteration of the loop found in cpu_arr_sqrt. The get_global_id(0) function call on line 3 is used to retrieve the loop index, which indexes the in and out arrays in the same way as the loop index i in cpu_arr_sqrt. As with cpu_arr_sqrt, the loop index ranges between 0 and size-1 due to the loop bounds specified by the arguments to clEnqueueNDRangeKernel.

The `main` function constitutes the test harness, which is similar to the ones used to crosscheck scalar and SIMD implementations in KLEE-FP [5]. In order to use our KLEE-CL tool, developers have to identify the C/C++ and the OpenCL versions of the code being compared, and the inputs and outputs to these routines. In our example, we have one input, namely the array `in`. Thus, the first step is to mark this array as *symbolic*, meaning that its elements could initially have any value (see §3.1 for more details). This is accomplished on line 32 by calling the function `klee_make_symbolic()` provided by KLEE, which takes three arguments: the address of the memory region to be made symbolic, its size in bytes, and a name used for debugging purposes only. Then, on line 34 we call the C version of the code and store the result in `cpuout`, and on line 37 we call the OpenCL version and store the result in `gpuout` (the initialisation of the parameters `context`, `cq` and `kernel` are omitted for brevity). Finally, on lines 39–40 each element of `gpuout` is compared against the corresponding element of `cpuout`. As in KLEE-FP, we use bitcasting to integers via the pointers `gpuouti` and `cpuouti` for a bitwise comparison. This is necessary because in the presence of `NaN` (*Not a Number*) values, the C floating point comparison operator `==` does not always return `true` if its floating-point operands are the same, as distinguished from a bitwise comparison.

3   Crosschecking of OpenCL and C Implementations

Our technique uses symbolic execution to explore multiple paths through the OpenCL and C/C++ implementations being compared, in order to check, on each path, for output equivalence (§3.2) and race conditions (§5).

3.1   Symbolic Execution

At a high level, symbolic execution is a technique that allows the automatic exploration of paths in a program. It works by executing the program on *symbolic* input, which is initially unconstrained. As the programs runs, any operations that depend on the symbolic input add constraints on the input. For example, if the program input is represented by variable `x`, than the statement `y = x+3` would add the constraint that $y = x + 3$. Furthermore, whenever a branch that depends on the symbolic input is reached, the technique first checks if both sides are feasible, and if so, it forks execution and follows each side separately, adding the constraint that the branch condition is true on the true side and false on the other side. For example, given the symbolic input `x`, where `x` is unconstrained, the symbolic execution of the branch `if (x == 3)` would result in two paths being explored, one on which $x = 3$ and one on which $x \neq 3$.

In our work, we use symbolic execution to explore the different paths in the OpenCL and C/C++ implementations being tested, and for each pair of paths, we check whether (1) there are no memory errors (these checks are by default performed by KLEE); (2) the implementations are race free (§5) and (3) the outputs computed by the two implementations are equivalent (§3.2).

One fundamental limitation of symbolic execution is that it only handles objects of fixed size (e.g., each data structure in a program usually has to be assigned a concrete size, as in the normal execution of the program). For our work, this means that we can verify the equivalence of OpenCL and C/C++ programs only up to a certain input size and number of threads. In the rest of the paper, we discuss our experiments solely in terms of input size: this is because in a typical OpenCL program, the number of work-items depends linearly on the size of the input being processed.

3.2 Equivalence Checking

To verify the output equivalence on a pair of paths through the two implementations, our technique first constructs the symbolic expressions corresponding to the output of each implementation, applies a set of canonicalisation rules to bring the two expressions to a canonical form, and then compares the two expressions syntactically. The main advantages of this approach are performance and the ability to deal with floating-point expressions, for which there are no efficient constraint solvers currently available. On the other hand, this approach is prone to false positives, i.e., it can say that two expressions are not equivalent when in fact they are. For more details, we refer the reader to our previous work on KLEE-FP [5].

In addition to the canonicalisation rules already implemented in KLEE-FP, we added a set of new rules, some of which rely on certain *assumptions* about the floating point model. For example, it is generally unsound to simplify $x \times 0$ to 0 because if x is negative or infinite the result is respectively -0 or NaN. However, developers are often not interested in such edge cases, and therefore we added the option to enable such assumptions on demand (via command line arguments). We added a total of three assumptions with five associated rules:

- The *positive zero* assumption allows the simplifier to disregard the difference between positive and negative zero, which is usually inconsequential. If this assumption is enabled, $x + 0$ may be simplified to x.
- The *finite* assumption allows the simplifier to assume all results are finite. If this assumption together with the positive zero assumption is enabled, $x \times 0$ and $0 \times x$ may be simplified to 0.
- The *associativity* assumption allows the simplifier to assume that floating point operations are associative. If this assumption is enabled, $+$ and $\times$ operations are rearranged to be left-associative, so $x + (y + z)$ is normalised to $(x + y) + z$ and $x \times (y \times z)$ to $(x \times y) \times z$.

We also added two rules which do not rely on any assumptions being enabled. These rules allow $x \times 1$ and $1 \times x$ to be simplified to x.

4   Modelling the OpenCL Environment

Our OpenCL model presents a single OpenCL compliant device to the program under test. This device presents itself as a CPU-based device with support for the cl_khr_fp64 extension, which allows the kernel to use double-precision floating point arithmetic.

The OpenCL model is made up of two distinct parts: the runtime library, which is used by the host to manage the execution of OpenCL kernels, and the OpenCL C environment, which models the execution of a kernel on the device.

4.1   The OpenCL Runtime

The OpenCL runtime library is specified by two sections of the OpenCL specification: the OpenCL Platform Layer [12, § 4] and the OpenCL Runtime [12, § 5]. The Platform Layer is used to query the set of available OpenCL devices, while the Runtime is used to query and manipulate objects on a specific device or set of devices such as device-side memory buffers and compiled OpenCL programs. In total, our model implements 30 functions specified as part of the Platform Layer and Runtime. For example, the clEnqueueNDRangeKernel function discussed in Section 2 is implemented by starting one modelled POSIX thread for each work-item in the iteration space. Each thread sets up the environment appropriately (for example, by initialising thread local variables) and then calls the kernel function. In our implementation, we use the POSIX threading model added to KLEE by Cloud9 [2].

4.2   The OpenCL C Programming Language

OpenCL kernels are written in an extended version of ISO C99 [11] referred to as OpenCL C, which is specified as part of the OpenCL specification [12, § 6]. Among the language extensions provided by OpenCL C are vector data types, specialised memory address spaces and a set of built-in functions.

The vector data types provided by OpenCL are used to exploit the SIMD capabilities common among GPUs. For example, float4 is the name of a data type referring to a vector of four float values. KLEE-FP, which our technique extends, already includes support for vector data types [5].

The four disjoint address spaces provided by OpenCL are named __global, __local, __constant and __private. Globally available data resides in __global, data local to a work-group in __local, read-only data in __constant and function arguments and local variables in __private.

Three of these address spaces (__global, __constant and __private) can be modelled using the generic address space used by regular CPU implementations. The __local address space, however, needs special attention because __local data must be shared between work-items in the same work-group, and each work-group must have its own __local data. To model __local, we added a group-local address space, which is an address space shared between user-created thread groups. Each thread belongs to a single thread group. Before beginning kernel execution, we create one thread group for each work-group, and set each thread's group to match its work-group.

Our model implements 18 of the built-in functions specified by the OpenCL specification, which are enough to run our benchmarks. These include work-item functions, which are used by the kernel to query various properties of the current execution's index space; math functions, which perform various mathematical operations (including vectorised variants); and the `barrier` synchronisation function, which is used to introduce execution barriers into the kernel.

4.3   Runtime Compilation of OpenCL Kernels

Programs that use the OpenCL runtime library (written in languages such as C or C++) are compiled in the usual way, before they are run. By contrast, kernels written in OpenCL C are normally compiled at runtime by passing their source code as a string to the runtime library function `clCreateProgramWithSource`, and later compiling the program using the `clBuildProgram` function. This can pose a challenge for tools such as ours, which necessarily must incorporate a full OpenCL C compiler. Our implementation of `clBuildProgram` invokes a compiler based on the OpenCL C front-end provided by the Clang [3] compiler. Clang is designed to be used as a library, which made it easy to integrate into KLEE-CL. Clang produces an LLVM [14] module representing the compiled program which is then dynamically loaded into the current instance of KLEE-CL.

5   Race Detection

Our model implements race detection capable of detecting, on each path explored, read-write and write-write races across work-items. Note that our analysis is targeted towards detecting races between work-items in the same NDRange. In OpenCL, a command queue may be created in out-of-order mode [12, § 5.11]. By scheduling multiple kernel invocations on an out-of-order command queue, or by scheduling kernel invocations across multiple command queues, a client program may cause kernel NDRanges to run in parallel such that races may occur between NDRanges. In this work, we concern ourselves only with the more common in-order case where only one NDRange is executing at a time.

To detect data races, we keep for each byte in the generic and group-local address spaces a *memory access record (MAR)* of accesses to that byte by a work-item thread. Each item in the MAR consists of the thread identifier of the most recent work-item to access the byte, the work-group identifier of the most recent work-group to access the byte, and four flags indicating whether the byte was (1) written by one or more work-items, (2) read by one or more work-items, (3) read by multiple work-items (*many-read*), and (4) read by multiple work-groups (*wg-many-read*).

The MAR may be stored concretely or symbolically. The concrete representation of the MAR is an array of structs, each holding the MAR for one byte in the array. The symbolic representation of the MAR is a set of 6 symbolic arrays, each as large as the underlying array, and each representing one of the MAR attributes. For efficiency we store the MARs concretely by default, but if a symbolically indexed memory access is performed, the array's MARs are converted to the symbolic representation.

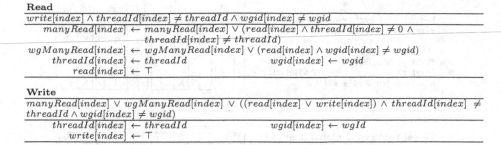

Fig. 3. Race condition test and MAR updates

Whenever a memory access occurs, the MAR is inspected for any race conditions, and then updated. A race condition can be a read-after-write, a write-after-write or a write-after-read performed by a work-item or work-group other than that identified by the corresponding entry in the MAR, or any write-after-read if either of the *many-read* or *wg-many-read* flags are set.

The race condition test, together with the required MAR updates, are shown in Figure 3. If the MAR is being stored concretely, we perform the test and the MAR updates directly. If the MAR is being stored symbolically, the test is performed by querying the constraint solver as to whether the symbolic expression representing the race condition test is feasible, and the MAR updates are performed by appending an update to the symbolic arrays.

The main intra-work-group synchronisation mechanism provided by OpenCL C is the `barrier` function, which acts as an execution barrier. `barrier` blocks until all work-items in the work-group have reached the call to `barrier`, at which point a memory fence is queued to ensure the correct ordering of memory operations between work-items, and all work-items resume execution.

To simulate this behaviour, when a work-item reaches a barrier we add it to a list of blocked work-items associated with the current work-group. When the size of this list becomes as large as the number of work-items in the work-group, the MAR is *locally reset* and the list emptied, resuming execution. We locally reset the MAR by removing the work-item identifier and clearing the many-read flag of each MAR whose work-group identifier matches the work-group performing the `barrier`. This has the effect of causing no intra-work-group accesses across the reset to be considered a race, while preserving inter-work-group race detection.

At the end of the execution of a kernel, we must perform a *full reset* of the MAR, to prevent access records from one kernel invocation from interfering with accesses from subsequent invocations (since we only support in-order kernel invocation, it is safe to do this). Similar to the case when a barrier is reached, we add the kernel to a list of inactive work-items, which is this time associated with the entire NDRange. When the list size becomes as large as the size of the NDRange, we reset the MAR by removing all identifiers and clearing all flags, and then resume execution.

To illustrate the race detection technique described above, we use the code in Figure 4. This code contains two simple kernels, `avg` and `avg2`, the purpose of

```
1 __kernel void avg(__global float *a) {
2   size_t lid = get_local_id (0),
3          lsize = get_local_size (0);
4   float r0 = lid > 0 ? a[lid-1] : 0;
5   float r1 = a[lid];
6   float r2 = lid+1 < lsize ? a[lid+1] : 0;
7   a[lid] = (r0 + r1 + r2) / 3;
8 }
```

Line	Work-item 1					Work-item 2				
	Tid	Wid	R	W	Con	Tid	Wid	R	W	Con
2						1	1	X	X	
3						1	1	X	X	
4						1	1	X	X	w/r
5	1	1	X			1	1	X	X	
6	1	1	X			1	1	X	X	
7	1	1	X	X		1	1	X	X	

```
1 __kernel void avg2(__global float *a) {
2   size_t lid = get_local_id (0),
3          lsize = get_local_size (0);
4   float r0 = lid > 0 ? a[lid-1] : 0;
5   float r1 = a[lid];
6   float r2 = lid+1 < lsize ? a[lid+1] : 0;
7   barrier(CLK_GLOBAL_MEM_FENCE);
8   a[lid] = (r0 + r1 + r2) / 3;
9 }
```

Line	Work-item 1					Work-item 2				
	Tid	Wid	R	W	Con	Tid	Wid	R	W	Con
2						1	1	X		
3						1	1	X		
4						1	1	X		
5	1	1	X			1	1	X		
6	1	1	X			1	1	X		
7	1		X			1	1	X	X	
8	1	1	X	X		1	1	X	X	

Fig. 4. Intermediate MARs for the memory location at a[0] during execution of work-items 1 and 2. Column Tid shows the byte's work-item identifier, Wid its work-group identifier, R the read flag, W the write flag, and Con (if present) the nature of the conflict detected at that line. Note that the many-read and wg-many-read flags are not shown here.

which is to store in each element of array a the mean of that element and the two adjacent elements.

The avg kernel contains a race condition, while avg2 uses an execution barrier to avoid the race. For each statement in the kernels, we show alongside it the state of the MAR for the first element of array a after execution of that statement. Note that in KLEE-CL we execute each work-item in its entirety until it reaches an execution barrier or terminates; however, our race detection algorithm would work with any other execution schedule. Thus, for avg the entirety of work-item 1 is executed before work-item 2, and the MAR persists from the end of execution of work-item 1 to the beginning of execution of work-item 2. For avg2 the first five lines of work-item 1 are executed (up to the barrier), then the first five lines of work-item 2, the memory access records are locally reset, the last two lines of work-item 1 are executed and finally the last two lines of work-item 2.

On line 4 of avg in work-item 2, we report a read-after-write race. This is due to the earlier write of work-item 1 on line 7 causing the write flag to be set. This race does not exist in avg2 because on line 4 of avg2 in work-item 2, line 8 in work-item 1 had not yet been reached, as it had been preempted by the barrier on line 7.

6   Evaluation

We evaluated our technique on a set of benchmarks that compare C/C++ and OpenCL variants of code developed independently by third parties. The codebases that we selected were the Parboil benchmark suite [10], the Bullet physics library [6] and the OP2 [8] library.

6.1   Parboil

Parboil [10] is a popular GPU benchmark suite, which contains C and CUDA [18] implementations of various algorithms. In order to be able to run Parboil benchmarks using KLEE-FP, we used Grewe et al's [9] translation of certain Parboil 1 benchmarks from CUDA to OpenCL. The translation comprised four benchmarks in total, and we tested three of these: cp (Coulombic Potential), mri-q (Magnetic Resonance Imaging – Q) and mri-fhd (Magnetic Resonance Imaging – FHD). We were unable to test the fourth benchmark, rpes (Rys Polynomial Equation Solver) because it created a very large number of work-items (> 30000) even for small problems, which KLEE-CL could not execute in a reasonable amount of time.

We modified the code for each benchmark to incorporate the C and OpenCL versions of the benchmarks into the same executable. This allowed us to construct simple test harnesses similar to the one in Listing 1 which invoke both versions of the benchmarks with the same symbolic arguments.

By running these benchmark programs using KLEE-CL, we detected two mismatches between the C and OpenCL implementations of cp. We also found three memory errors in mri-q and mri-fhd as a result of the memory bounds checking performed during symbolic execution.

Mismatches: The cp benchmark computes the Coulombic potential for a set of points on a grid. The computation of a Coulombic potential at a grid point involves the calculation of the Euclidean distance of the form $\sqrt{\delta x^2 + \delta y^2 + \delta z^2}$ between an electrically charged particle and that point.

The first mismatch for cp is due to an associativity issue. The OpenCL implementation uses an unrolled loop in which a set of adjacent grid points are computed during each iteration. Because only the x coordinate varies during an iteration, the values of δy and δz remain constant, allowing $\delta y^2 + \delta z^2$ to be precomputed at the start of each iteration. So the expression is evaluated as $\sqrt{\delta x^2 + (\delta y^2 + \delta z^2)}$. In the C implementation, the inner expression is left unbracketed and normal C associativity rules apply. Because $+$ is left-associative in C [11], the expression is evaluated as $\sqrt{(\delta x^2 + \delta y^2) + \delta z^2}$. Since $+$ in floating point is not associative, the two expressions do not match.

The second mismatch arises in the context of computing δx in the two implementations. In the C implementation, this is done by subtracting the atom's x coordinate from the grid's x coordinate. In the OpenCL implementation, δx for the iteration's first grid point is computed in the same way. However, for subsequent points in the iteration, δx is computed by adding the grid's spacing to the value of δx for the previous point. Since floating point $+$ and $\times$ are neither associative nor distributive, the expressions do not match.

Whether these mismatches are important or not depends on the specific application. KLEE-CL's job is to flag such mismatches, but it is up to the developer to assess whether strict equivalence should be enforced. Furthermore, developers can use the assumptions discussed in Section 3.2 to ignore the cause of different mismatches. For the current example, developers could add the assumption that floating point operations are associative and rerun KLEE-CL to find other problems. With this assumption enabled, KLEE-CL verifies a variant of this benchmark in which the second mismatch, but not the first, has been fixed.

Memory Errors: A non-obvious memory error was found in `mri-q`. After the OpenCL kernel is invoked, `mri-q` deallocates some OpenCL memory buffers and then copies some data from the GPU to the host. Because OpenCL kernel invocation is asynchronous, the memory buffers may be deallocated by the time that the kernel accesses them. KLEE-CL caught this error as a result of its thread scheduling behaviour—it will defer execution of code running in other threads (i.e. kernel code) until the current thread explicitly yields execution. This means that the deallocations (running in the main thread) were executed before the kernel code. We fixed this error by moving the data copies before the memory deallocations. Since the data copies were synchronous, they caused execution of the main thread to be preempted until after kernel execution.

A memory error found in both `mri-q` and `mri-fhd` was caused by a read beyond the end of a memory buffer used to store (x, y, z) coordinates. This memory buffer was indexed using the work-item identifier, which ranged between 0 and a multiple of the work-group size. This error was never caught, perhaps due to the fact that all benchmark data provided with Parboil had a size that was a multiple of the work-group size. We fixed these errors by enclosing the relevant part of the kernel inside an `if` statement.

A memory error found in `mri-fhd` is related to the use of uninitialised memory. This benchmark allocates a buffer of output data using `memalign`, which was assumed to be zero initialised. Since `memalign` buffers are uninitialised, and KLEE-CL models this, incorrect results were produced. The fix was simply to initialise the buffer using `memset`.

6.2 The Bullet Physics Library

Bullet [6] is a physics library primarily used in gaming and 3D applications. It incorporates a number of physics simulation algorithms, including a soft body simulation. This can be used to simulate objects such as cloths which are freely deformable within the environment. Bullet provides a C++ and an OpenCL implementation of the soft body simulation.

We implemented two benchmark programs which create a simulation with two soft body objects, each containing three vertices connected by three edges. The coordinates of the vertices are concrete values, but all other simulation parameters are symbolic. The program runs a single simulation step using both the C++ and the OpenCL implementations, and compares the results.

The first of our benchmarks (`softbody`) tests the soft body simulation in isolation, while the second benchmark (`dynworld`) tests the simulation using a soft rigid dynamics world, which exercises more of the soft body code.

For the `softbody` benchmark, KLEE-CL verified that the C++ and OpenCL code produce the same results. For `dynworld`, KLEE-CL was able to verify equivalence under the assumption that $x \times 0 = 0$ in floating point.

One important caveat is that we do not model inaccurate floating point operations, such as the single precision division operation in OpenCL (which need only be accurate to 2.5 ulp [12, § 7.4]), because the LLVM IR generated by the Clang compiler does not provide the accuracy of each individual operation. In fact, while running a test using real GPU hardware (an NVIDIA Tesla C1060), we found discrepancies between the C++ and OpenCL results, which were due to a single precision floating point division operation, caused by the incorrect modelling discussed above. We attempted to rectify this by casting the operands of the division operator to double precision ([12, § 9.3.9] requires double precision division to be correctly rounded).

OpenCL Compiler Bug: Of course, these equivalence results hold under the additional assumption that all the components involved in running the code—from compilers to hardware—are correct. The bug discussed below illustrates this point.

After fixing the single precision issue mentioned above, we were surprised to see that the test run on real GPU hardware still showed discrepancies between the OpenCL and C++ implementations, despite the fact that we were able to verify their equivalence. After further investigation, we found that the PTX assembly code produced by NVIDIA's OpenCL compiler continued to use a single precision division instruction (`div.full.f32`), despite the cast to double precision. If we disabled compiler optimisations, using the `-cl-opt-disable` flag to the OpenCL compiler, the double precision division instruction (`div.rn.f64`) was used. This suggested that the problem may lie in the optimiser.

We worked around this issue by postprocessing the PTX code to replace `div.full.f32` with `div.rn.f64` together with appropriate conversions, similar to the unoptimised code. After doing this, the results obtained were identical.

We reported the issue to NVIDIA who confirmed our bug report, and as of this writing had fixed the bug, but had not yet released a version of their OpenCL implementation with the fix.

6.3   OP2

OP2 [8] is a library for generating parallel executables of applications using unstructured grids. OP2 enables users to write a single program targeting multiple platforms. OP2 has four implementations: a serial reference (library) implementation and source-to-source transformations to CUDA, OpenCL and OpenMP.

Among the operations offered by OP2 is the *global reduction* operation, which is used to reduce a set of results computed across a set of grid nodes to a single result. We used KLEE-CL to test the correctness of the OpenCL implementation of the global reduction operation by extracting the relevant kernel from the OP2 source code and constructing a benchmark program which uses this kernel to perform a global reduction on an array of symbolic data.

KLEE-CL detected a race condition in this kernel, and the problematic code is shown in Listing 2. Each iteration of the `for` loop on lines 4–9 uses a result computed in an earlier iteration by another work-item (specifically, work-item `tid` uses a result computed by work-item `tid+d`) without using an execution barrier beforehand. Because of the lack of synchronisation, the behaviour of the kernel is undefined by the OpenCL specification.

```
1    int tid = get_local_id( 0 ), d = get_local_size( 0 )>>1;
2    __local volatile float *vtemp = temp;
3    ...
4    for ( ; d>0; d>>=1 ) {    /* d is at most 16 here */
5      if ( tid<d )
6        ...
7        vtemp[tid] = vtemp[tid] + vtemp[tid+d];
8        ...
9    }
```

Listing 2. OP2's unsynchronised loop (slightly modified for formatting purposes)

To understand why this loop was written in this way, one must consider the history of the code. The OpenCL implementation was heavily based on the CUDA implementation and was in many places developed by replacing CUDA constructs with the relevant OpenCL constructs. In CUDA (and the NVIDIA GPU architecture), each group of 32 work-items within a work-group (referred to as a *warp*) is executed in lockstep with implicit synchronisation between work-items [18]. However, no such feature is present in OpenCL, and OpenCL code relying on warps has implementation-defined behaviour. In the case of the NVIDIA implementation of OpenCL this happens to function correctly, however there is no requirement that it do so on other architectures.

We modified the kernel to introduce a local execution barrier using the `barrier` function before each iteration of the loop (between lines 4 and 5). With this modification in place, KLEE-CL does not report a race condition.

7   Related Work

Despite the growing popularity of GPU languages, there has been relatively little work on testing and verification techniques for code written in these languages. While we are not aware of any work directly targeting OpenCL, several relevant testing techniques exist for checking CUDA code.

Race Detection. Most previous work in this space has focused on race detection [1, 15, 24, 25]. Li and Gopalakrishnan [15] and Tripakis et al. [24] propose two static race detection techniques based on translating CUDA code into SMT constraints. The main advantage of a static analysis approach is coverage: our dynamic approach depends on the number of paths explored by symbolic execution in a given time budget and can only reason about objects with concrete bounds. On the other hand, static analysis suffers from false positives, due to various over-approximations resulting from, e.g., analysing kernels in isolation and loop unrolling.

A dynamic race detection approach similar to our technique is introduced by Boyer et al. in the context of CUDA programs [1]. A more recent technique from Zheng et al. [25] combines dynamic race detection with a static analysis pass that removes accesses that can be statically proven to be safe or unsafe, resulting in a system with a relatively small runtime overhead. The main weakness of these techniques is that they depend on the concrete inputs with which the program is run. Instead, our approach can check for symbolic race conditions on all the different paths explored via symbolic execution.

Our approach is also similar in spirit to previous dynamic race detection approaches for CPU code [7, 19, 21], although the barrier-based synchronisation model used in OpenCL allows for a simpler algorithm than in the case of traditional synchronisation primitives such as locks and semaphores.

Concurrently and independently with our work, GKLEE [16] has extended KLEE with the ability to find several categories of errors in CUDA programs, including race conditions and deadlocks caused by execution barrier divergence.

Equivalence Checking. As far as we know, this is the first technique that focuses on checking the equivalence between an OpenCL and a C or C++ implementation. Our work builds up on previous research on KLEE-FP [5], in which we have applied a similar approach to crosscheck SIMD and scalar implementations. To make this general crosschecking approach effective to OpenCL code, we had to construct an OpenCL model, and add support for concurrency, race detection and several additional rules and assumptions. In addition to our work on KLEE-FP, this approach has been successfully used in the past to verify code equivalence in other contexts, such as hardware verification [4], compiler optimisations [17], block cipher implementations [23] and parallel numerical programs [22]. The main advantages of normalizing symbolic expressions and then comparing them syntactically are that (1) the technique is lightweight compared to more precise symbolic analyses such as [20], and (2) it can deal with floating-point constraints, for which there are no efficient constraint solvers currently available. On the other hand, this approach is prone to false positives, i.e., it can say that two expressions are not equivalent when in fact they are.

8   Conclusion

We presented an effective technique for crosschecking OpenCL and C/C++ programs and for detecting race conditions in OpenCL code. We implemented our approach in the KLEE-CL tool, and applied it to three real OpenCL code bases, in which it found seven previously unknown errors: two mismatches between the OpenCL and C implementations, three memory errors, one OpenCL compiler bug and one race condition. The KLEE-CL tool is freely available from our website at http://www.pcc.me.uk/~peter/klee-cl/.

Acknowledgements. We would like to thank Stefan Bucur and the authors of Cloud9 [2] for providing the POSIX threading model; Lee Howes for assistance with the Bullet Physics library; Daniel Dunbar for helpful discussions; Guy Benyei, Tanya Lattner, Anton Lokhmotov and Alberto Magni for their contributions to the Clang OpenCL front-end; and Paul Marinescu for valuable comments on the text. This work was partially funded by an EPSRC DTA studentship and the EPSRC Platform Grant EP/I012036/1.

References

[1] Boyer, M., Skadron, K., Weimer, W.: Automated dynamic analysis of CUDA programs. In: STMCS 2008 (April 2008)

[2] Bucur, S., Ureche, V., Zamfir, C., Candea, G.: Parallel symbolic execution for automated real-world software testing. In: EuroSys 2011 (April 2011)

[3] clang: a C language family frontend for LLVM, http://clang.llvm.org/

[4] Clarke, E., Kroening, D.: Hardware verification using ANSI-C programs as a reference. In: ASP-DAC 2003 (January 2003)

[5] Collingbourne, P., Cadar, C., Kelly, P.H.: Symbolic crosschecking of floating-point and SIMD code. In: EuroSys 2011 (April 2011)

[6] Coumans, E., et al.: Bullet continuous collision detection and physics library, http://bulletphysics.org/

[7] Flanagan, C., Freund, S.N.: Fasttrack: Efficient and precise dynamic race detection. In: PLDI 2009 (June 2009)

[8] Giles, M.B., Mudalige, G.R., Sharif, Z., Markall, G.R., Kelly, P.H.J.: Performance analysis of the OP2 framework on many-core architectures. SIGMETRICS Performance Evaluation Review 38(4), 9–15 (2011)

[9] Grewe, D., O'Boyle, M.F.P.: A Static Task Partitioning Approach for Heterogeneous Systems Using OpenCL. In: Knoop, J. (ed.) CC 2011. LNCS, vol. 6601, pp. 286–305. Springer, Heidelberg (2011)

[10] IMPACT Research Group, UIUC. Parboil benchmark suite, http://impact.crhc.illinois.edu/parboil.php

[11] International Organization for Standardization. ISO/IEC 9899-1999: Programming Languages—C (December 1999)

[12] Khronos OpenCL Working Group. The OpenCL Specification, version 1.1, revision 36 (September 2010)

[13] King, J.C.: A new approach to program testing. In: ICRS 1975 (April 1975)

[14] Lattner, C., Adve, V.: LLVM: A compilation framework for lifelong program analysis & transformation. In: CGO 2004 (March 2004)

[15] Li, G., Gopalakrishnan, G.: Scalable SMT-based verification of GPU kernel functions. In: FSE 2010 (November 2010)

[16] Li, G., Li, P., Sawaya, G., Ghosh, I.: GKLEE: Concolic verification and test generation for GPUs. In: PPoPP 2012 (Februery 2012)

[17] Necula, G.C.: Translation validation for an optimizing compiler. In: PLDI 2000 (May 2000)

[18] NVIDIA. NVIDIA CUDA Programming Guide, Version 3.0 (February 2010)

[19] O'Callahan, R., Choi, J.-D.: Hybrid dynamic data race detection. In: PPoPP 2003 (June 2003)

[20] Person, S., Dwyer, M.B., Elbaum, S., Păsăreanu, C.S.: Differential symbolic execution. In: FSE 2008 (November 2008)

[21] Savage, S., Burrows, M., Nelson, G., Sobalvarro, P., Anderson, T.E.: Eraser: A dynamic data race detector for multithreaded programs. In: SOSP 1997 (October 1997)

[22] Siegel, S.F., Mironova, A., Avrunin, G.S., Clarke, L.A.: Using model checking with symbolic execution to verify parallel numerical programs. In: ISSTA 2006 (July 2006)

[23] Smith, E.W., Dill, D.L.: Automatic formal verification of block cipher implementations. In: FMCAD 2008 (November 2008)

[24] Tripakis, S., Stergiou, C., Lublinerman, R.: Checking non-interference in SPMD programs. In: HotPar 2010 (June 2010)

[25] Zheng, M., Ravi, V.T., Qin, F., Agrawal, G.: GRace: A low-overhead mechanism for detecting data races in GPU programs. In: PPoPP 2011 (February 2011)

Dynamic Test Data Generation for Data Intensive Applications

Allon Adir, Ronen Levy, and Tamer Salman

IBM Research - Haifa, Haifa, Israel
{adir,ronenl,tamers}@il.ibm.com

Abstract. There are many cases where the development and testing of data-intensive applications need to be supported without the prior existence of data. Our work presents a dynamic test data generation framework for testing such applications. This capability is important, when the data is confidential and cannot be given to the test person for security reasons or when the application is in its development phase and real data does not yet exist. The proposed solution dynamically intercepts queries made by the application under test and creates appropriate data based on user requirements. This approach does not require access to the source code of the application under test, which could also be confidential. Data generation can be controlled to achieve desired data and query result patterns, including realistic data or data with higher test quality. The paper concludes with experiments that demonstrate the coverage and performance aspects of the solution.

Keywords: Database applications, data privacy, query-aware data generation, constraint satisfaction problems.

1 Introduction

Test data needs to be prepared in advance for testing many data intensive applications. Many large data-intensive applications depend on and manipulate data that is stored in relational databases. These applications connect to the database(s) and read or write data from and into the database using SQL queries. In many cases, real data that the application uses is unavailable during the testing stage. This can be due to data privacy regulations, in which the application tester or even the developer might not have access to real data. Alternatively, testing may be carried out during an early development phase of the application when real data does not yet exist or is not structured in a way that the application assumes. Even when real data *is* available it might not have the required characteristics for thorough testing properties, such as covering rare corner cases.

We propose a solution that generates data on-the-fly while the application is running, without needing the source code of the application and without requiring access to real or masked data. In our solution, data generation can be constrained directly by the user or by a knowledge database to achieve the desired testing objectives.

K. Eder, J. Lourenço, and O. Shehory (Eds.): HVC 2011, LNCS 7261, pp. 219–233, 2012.

Existing solutions to this problem include various forms of data masking and scrambling, and the generation of new data. We briefly present these alternative solutions and the different set of conditions to which each solution applies.

1.1   Data Masking and Scrambling

Many industrial applications that manipulate large databases are developed and tested by a third party or even by different teams in the same organization - neither of whom have access privileges to real data. Access privileges to private information, such as in the banking, insurance, or health industries, is usually given to a limited group of individuals and cannot be transferred outside of the production environment. The problem also arises when the application development is outsourced to a different team with no access privileges to the data.

Testing such applications requires that an alternative database be supplied by the database owner. The alternative database is prepared by masking (hiding) a part or all of the data [1] in the real database. Masking is needed for many types of sensitive information, including the identities of people, credit card numbers, and more.

Masking usually incurs a large overhead of computation efforts when the databases are large. Moreover, any small changes to the structure of the database may require that the preparation process be done over again. The cost of such operations is a burden especially in the context of off-shore outsourced development or testing. The process requires access to secure data which naturally involves bureaucratic decisions and permits. Furthermore, in many high security situations, even the masking and scrambling of data could be deemed insufficient when non-reversibility, correctness, and security of these processes cannot be guaranteed.

1.2   Data Generation

A different approach to dealing with the absence of data during the application development and testing phases is the fabrication of alternative data. Off line approaches that are unaware of the usage of the generated data, such as DB2 test data generator [2] populate the database with consistent data according to its given schema. These methods require huge amounts of random data to ensure the existence of useful data. The work presented by Emmi et al. [3] shows how a software testing technique called concolic execution [4,5] can be used to generate test data. Concolic execution involves a simultaneous concrete and symbolic execution of the application. Concolic execution is usually applied for small unit tests (e.g. methods, functions, etc), in which full coverage of the unit under test is feasible [6,7,8]. Alternatively, a more realistic objective is to focus on specific functional coverage goals. Furthermore, testing applications using concolic execution requires access to the source code of the application, which could be unavailable or confidential (e.g., when the testing is carried out by a third party).

Other works focus on query-aware data generation [9,10,11], in which a query or a set of queries are given as input and the output is a database that answers all queries with non-empty answers. These works do not directly concern specific features of applications using databases, but nevertheless, can be used in such a paradigm. Some of these works are concerned with generating data for all coverage rules derived from a given query or a set of queries [12,13] and not only a non-empty answer. These works generate the data using the Alloy analyzer [14].

1.3 Proposed Solution

To overcome the shortcomings of existing techniques, we propose a solution that generates data on-the-fly while the application is running. The solution does not require access to real or masked data, to the tested application's source code, or to historic actual queries — all of which might involve some breach of security.

Data generation can be constrained directly by the user, who may be the tester or the developer, or by a knowledge database. These constraints can direct the generation towards desired testing objectives or to realistic database statistics and query behavior. The solution generates new data as needed to fulfill the test requirements while the application is running.

In the rest of the paper we present the solution framework. We elaborate on the central components of the solution and discuss aspects of its implementation. We also describe several experiments with our solution and then state our conclusions.

2 Dynamic Test Data Generation Framework

In this section, we outline how our solution enables interesting test cases to be run for a data intensive application, without previously available data. The solution needs the database schema, and can be driven by user requirements and a testing-knowledge base. The application's database is populated during the application run in an on-the-fly manner inducing a performance overhead that diminishes as the database is populated. A high-level description of the solution is depicted in Fig. 1.

From the application's point of view, the data generation process is transparent. This causes the application to run as if the data had already existed apriori. The user of the solution, whether developer or test person, equips the data-generation system with the schema of the database and can specify the requirements for the desired test properties. The data generation system also uses a testing-knowledge base that accumulates information on how to best test the database application through generated data. The user can then refer to or activate this testing-knowledge through user requirements. The testing-knowledge base may include information on interesting execution paths for the application as well as various sources of realistic data. Realistic data can be derived from publicly available data (e.g. lists of possible first names, formats of residence addresses, etc.) or can be modeled as software data generators that yield realistic

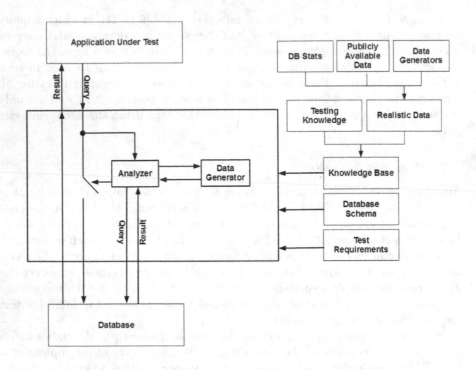

Fig. 1. A high level description of the dynamic data generation solution

data patterns when invoked. One especially interesting source for realistic data is database statistics automatically collected by most database servers. These statistics can provide information on the data (such as value distributions) in some actual database. This case is especially interesting when data already exists, but cannot be made available for the user at a certain stage due to confidentiality (proprietary data) or privacy regulations (health care records, banking industry data, governmental information, sensitive personal information) and when the data statistics are non or less confidential than the data itself.

The core of the data generation system is located between the application logic and the database. It consists of three main parts: an interception mechanism, a database analyzer, and a data generator. The interception mechanism catches queries from the application, pauses the execution of each query on the database, and passes it to the database analyzer. The analyzer queries the database and checks whether the test requirements are met for the current query. These requirements almost always imply that the database has enough data to return a non-empty result to the query. If the requirements are met by existing data in the database, the system lets the query pass through to the database. If, on the other hand, the requirements are not met, the analyzer sends the query to the data generator. The data generator parses the query and constructs a constraint-problem based on the query, the current state of the database, the test requirements, and the knowledge base. The constraint-problem [16,17] is solved using a constraint solver. The solution of the constraint-problem is used to construct the records needed to populate the database. These records are returned to the database analyzer which forms corresponding database commands to actually add the records to the database. These commands are in the form of Data-Modification-Language (DML) statements that are executed upon the database to change its state. When the records have been added to the database, the system lets the query pass from the application to the database. The application then receives the result from the database as if the data existed prior to the query execution. This entire generation scheme takes place "behind the scenes". Meanwhile, the application runs normally and receives answers to its queries as if the data had been in the database to begin with.

2.1 Database Schema

The data generation solution can create new data in an existing database or can start by creating an empty database; this is done by passing the appropriate SQL DDL commands to the database server. In both cases, the solution requires the database schema as one of its main inputs. The solution uses the schema to discover the structure of the database to be populated, its tables, and its columns, as well as rules that must be considered to make the data consistent.

There are various types of data consistency rules derived from the schema. For example, if a column is *not* allowed to be 'null', then null values must not be generated for it. A column might have some 'CHECK' constraint that must be taken into account while generating its values.

Consider the database schema in Fig. 2. Creating a record for the table t1 dictates some constraints: x should be an integer, y should be an integer between 1 and 99, x should be larger than y, z should be an integer of null, and idRef should be an integer for which a record with the same value must exist in table t2. Such 'referential integrity' constraints imply that when a record is generated for table t1, an additional record may need to be generated for t2 with the same value in the id field. The id field is a primary key of t2, which implies that different records generated for t2 cannot share the same id value. Additional constraints may be added due to the test requirements and the specific intercepted query. For example, if the query is a SELECT query from table t1 with the condition x > 30, then a constraint $x > 30$ is added to the list of constraints to be solved.

2.2 Test Requirements

The solution framework allows users to define requirements related to the desired test and ensure that the data leads to some interesting behavior in the tested application. Users state their requirements through directives to the data generation system.

There are two main types of test requirements. The first relates to queries executed by the application and the second relates to characteristics of the data in

```
CREATE TABLE t1 ( x      INT NOT NULL,
                  Y      INT NOT NULL CHECK (y > 0 AND y < 100),
                  idRef INT NOT NULL,
                  CHECK (x > y),
                  FOREIGN KEY (idRef) REFERENCES t2(id) );

CREATE TABLE t2 ( id     INT PRIMARY KEY NOT NULL,
                  z      INT );
```

Fig. 2. Simple database schema

the database. Requirements related to executed queries must identify the queries affected. This can be done using a query template in the form of a regular expression. Requirements related to executed queries can specify desired properties of the results including size, column distribution, maximal value, minimal value, average, etc. Requirements related to the database can specify the desired properties of the database including table sizes, column distribution, maximal value, minimal value, average, etc.

```
QUERY_TEMPLATE = SELECT $ FROM $ t1 $ WHERE $ x > $
AMOUNT_CONSTRAINT = [ >= 20 ]
```

Fig. 3. Query template with constrain for amount

Consider the database schema given in Fig. 2 and the user requirement in 3. This is an example for a requirement of the first type, relating to application queries. Here, the user identifies all queries that use a SELECT from the table t1 with an inequality constraint on x, x > $, where $ stands for a string of wild cards). The requirement in 3 then specifies that such queries must yield at least 20 records as a result.

Figure 4 gives an example for a user requirement of the second type, relating to the database. Here, the user specifies a desired distribution of values for some column in the database. The desired distribution could generally be expressed as either some formula or through quantile specifications. The requirement in Fig. 4 specifies that column z in table t2 be distributed normally with a bias of 100 and a standard deviation of 10.

The user can add test requirements that impose further conditions on the structure and relations of the database, such as conditions restricting the domains of some columns or the required relations between columns. These requirements are meant to impose conditions on the database that come from a

```
COLUMN = t2, z
DISTRIBUTION = normal(100,10)
```

Fig. 4. Distribution constraint

deeper understanding of the application and the different scenarios under which it is activated than what is expressed in the database schema. Such requirements should be used to help drive a specific test towards desired situations. For instance, the user might add a requirement constraining the column z of all records of table t2 to be either null or equal to the value of column x in the record in table t1 pointing to it.

Furthermore, test requirements might relate to various pieces of information provided in the knowledge base. For example, the user can add some specifically designed data generation functions for some column types into the knowledge base and then activate them through the tests directives.

2.3 The Knowledge Base

There are two categories of information accumulated in the knowledge base: testing-knowledge and realistic data. Testing knowledge generally embeds information that directs or biases the system to generate interesting test scenarios and corner test cases. Testing-knowledge includes common generic testing knowledge applicable to any application, such as knowledge about column data types, and also knowledge on the best way to test an application.

Information on realistic data is collected from external sources either for some specific needs of the application and the tester, or general information such as localized geographic knowledge. Using the knowledge base, one might dictate a set of predetermined values to be used for a certain column or column type when generating data. Equivalently, a data generation function might be written and entered into the knowledge base. For example, a useful external source for localization purposes might be a list of people's first names or a template for representing addresses, both of which may vary depending on the location of the application's usage and database origin. Alternatively, names could be generated according to a generation function that produces strings that sound like first names for the purpose of de-identification [15].

2.4 Database Statistics

One especially interesting type of information for the knowledge base are the database statistics generated by the database management system (DBMS) for some real databases – possibly even the confidential database to be used by the application. This is useful for cases where real data exists but is unavailable due to data privacy and confidentiality issues. For each column in the database, the distribution of values is given by various measures, such as the quantiles, cardinality, minimal value, maximal value, etc. When database statistics are given, the user can state a test requirement to generate data according to those statistics. In such cases, the solution can be viewed as a tool that attempts to mimic the behavior of the application for real data by populating the database with generated data that approximates the given statistics.

3   Building the Constraint-Problem

For a given relational database schema and a set of test requirements, we define a *satisfying set* of a certain SQL query as a set of records that comply with the given schema, and that satisfy the constraints originating from the conditions in the query and from the user requirements.

```
SELECT a.y FROM t1 AS a
WHERE
    EXISTS (
        SELECT * FROM t1 AS b
        WHERE b.x != a.x AND b.y = a.y)
AND
    a.y IN (
        SELECT z FROM t2 AS c
        WHERE c.z > 0 AND c.z < 100 AND
        c.id != a.idRef
        );
```

Fig. 5. Sample query

For example, consider the database schema in Fig. 2, the test requirements in Fig. 3 and Fig. 4, and the following complex (and artificial) query in Fig. 5. The SQL query is asking for y columns of records of t1 that occur in other records of t1 with different x columns. It also requires that the value of the selected y column be equal to a z column (in the range 0 through 100) in t2 records that don't share the id column with the t1 record.

Any satisfying set for this query must include at least two records of table t1, for which the y column is equal and the x column is not, and at least two records in table t2 – the first to conform with the referential integrity requirement of the id column in the selected t1 records, and the second to serve as the t2 record referred to in the query. An example satisfying set is depicted in Tab. 1.

Table 1. Satisfying set for the query in Fig. 5

t1				t2	
x	y	idRef		id	z
7	97	1		1	103
8	97	1		3	97

In general, the analyzer receives the query string and queries the database to see whether a satisfying set can be found in the database. If it is found, the query is allowed to pass through to the database and return the results. If no satisfying set is found in the database, the analyzer sends the query to the data generator, which formulates a constraint problem based on the query, the database schema, and the test requirements and knowledge base.

A constraint satisfaction problem (CSP) [16,17] is a triple $\langle X, D, C \rangle$, where X is a set of variables, D is a corresponding set of value domains for the variables, and C is a set of constraints. A constraint solver solves a CSP and produces an assignment for the variables in X with values from D, such that the constraints C are satisfied. Constraint solvers are extensively used in both software and hardware verification [6,13,18].

In our solution, the data generator formulates the CSP with different types of constraints hailing from the different inputs as depicted in Fig. 6.

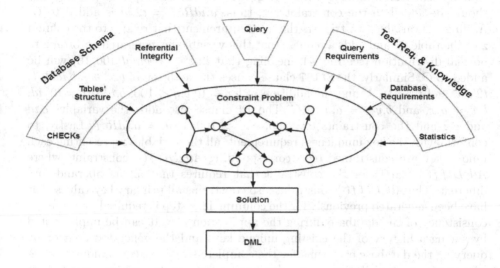

Fig. 6. A high level description of the CSP creation process. The constraints are taken from the query, the database schema, and the test requirements and knowledge base. The CSP is solved and the solution is then translated into a set of DML instructions to alter the database.

The set of variables X corresponds to all the columns of all the records needed to satisfy the query. A variable name is represented uniquely by either the table alias and the column name or by the table name and the column name. If the variable is not identified by an alias, and there are multiple occurrences of such variables belonging to the same table and the same column, then they are identified by the order of their integration in the CSP. For instance, for some column z of the table t2, the variables would be $t2.z$, $t2'.z$, $t2''.z$ and so on.

For each variable added to X, an appropriate domain is added to D that corresponds to the domain defined for the corresponding column in the database schema. If a foreign key is added to X, then all the referred columns are also added to X and a constraint stating equality between the foreign key and the referenced primary key is added to C. Furthermore, the condition that appears in the WHERE clause of the query is added to C. If the WHERE clause includes subqueries then the subquery is treated similarly by adding all the columns of all its joins to X and so on.

We demonstrate the CSP formulation process for the SELECT query given in Fig. 5. In the beginning, the SELECT query addresses a single table, namely t1 as a, therefore $a.x$, $a.y$, and $a.idRef$ are added to X with domains of $\mathbb{Z}$ for all, where $\mathbb{Z}$ stands for the integer domain. Since y is constrained in the schema, then $a.y > 0$ and $a.y < 100$ are added to C. Furthermore, for each foreign key variable, the referred columns are added. Then, $t2.id$ and $t2.z$ will be added to X due to $a.idRef$. Once the referenced table's columns are added, equality constraints linking each foreign key to the appropriate primary key should be added to the constraint list, thus, $a.idRef = t2.id$ is added to C. Adding the variable $t2.z$ triggers the test requirement that relates to the column z of the table t2 and adds a request that this variable be generated according to normal distribution (see Fig. 4), meaning that $t2.z \in Normal(100, 10)$ will be added to C. Similarly, the EXIST clause causes the addition of $b.x$, $b.y$, $b.idRef$, $t2'.id$, and $t2'.z$ to X and the addition of $b.y > 0$, $b.y < 100$, $b.idRef = t2'.id$, $b.x \neq a.x$, and $b.y == a.y$ to C. The IN clause also adds the variables $c.id$ and $c.z$ and the constraints $c.z > 0$, $c.z < 100$, $c.id \neq a.idRef$. Lastly, to conform with the key uniqueness requirement, all the variables representing each unique key are constrained by a corresponding $All\_Diff(\cdot)$ constraint, where $All\_Diff(\cdot)$ stands for the constraint that requires that all its operands are different. The $All\_Diff(\cdot)$ constraint also constrains all primary key values that have been generated previously for the column. This step is required preserve the consistency of the database during the application run. It can be implemented by saving a history of the existing unique keys and the generated ones or by querying the database each time for the complete set of existing unique keys. A more accurate, but also more complex to manage, constraint can demand that every pair of records in the query must either use different key values or be completely identical in all their columns. This can be formulated as follows:

$$X = \{ \, a.x, a.y, a.idRef, b.x, b.y, a.idRef, t2.id, t2.z, t2'.id, t2'.z, c.id, c.z \, \}, \ (1)$$

$$D = \{ \, \mathbb{Z}, \mathbb{Z}, \mathbb{Z}, \mathbb{Z}, \mathbb{Z}, \mathbb{Z}, \mathbb{Z}, \mathbb{Z} \cup \{null\}, \mathbb{Z}, \mathbb{Z} \cup \{null\}, \mathbb{Z}, \mathbb{Z} \cup \{null\} \, \}, \qquad (2)$$

$$C = \{ \, a.y > 0, \ a.y < 100, \ b.y > 0, \ b.y < 100, \qquad\qquad\qquad (3)$$
$$a.idRef = t2.id, \ b.idRef = t2'.id,$$
$$b.x \neq a.x, \ b.y == a.y,$$
$$c.z > 0, \ c.z < 100, \ c.id \neq a.idRef,$$
$$(t2.id \neq t2'.id) || (t2.z == t2'.z),$$
$$(t2.id \neq c.id) || (t2.z == c.z),$$
$$(t2'.id \neq c.id) || (t2'.z == t2'.z),$$
$$t2.z \in Normal(100, 10),$$
$$t2'.z \in Normal(100, 10),$$
$$c.z \in Normal(100, 10) \, \} \, .$$

A possible solution to the CSP stated in (1)-(3) is the solution depicted in Tab. 1.

If a QUERY_TEMPLATE with an AMOUNT_CONSTRAINT matches the query, then all variables are duplicated into arrays with the appropriate size. If the AMOUNT _CONSTRAINT states that more than a single record is needed for some table, then an $All\_Diff(\cdot)$ constraint is added to the constraints' set for each unique key. For example, the AMOUNT_CONSTRAINT in Fig. 3 causes each variable in Eq. 1 to be duplicated into an array of a size larger or equal to 20 (a random number can be chosen) and adds consistency constraints ensuring that all generated primary keys are unique.

4   Implementation and Experiments

We implemented the solution in a Java-based environment, exploiting the Java class loading mechanism. The query interception was implemented by overriding the Java class loader and tracking the classes being loaded by the application under test. Once the application causes the loading of the Java database connectivity (JDBC) driver classes, the overriding class loader loads the respective class and instruments it with dedicated code using byte code injection techniques. Within the instrumented class, appropriate methods that normally execute SQL queries are changed to redirect the calls to the analyzer. The analyzer, in turn, checks whether new data needs to be generated and manages the generation procedure as presented in Sect. 2. The constraint solver we used for the data generation was the IBM ILOG CPLEX Optimization Studio [19] and the database management system was MySQL [20].

The data generation system is given the database schema, the test requirements, and the knowledge base. The application under test is in Java bytecode and no source code is needed by the solution. We tested the solution with an application that runs queries against a synthetic database schema consisting of 30 tables with a total of 180 columns that include primary and foreign keys. The application ran 100 queries with multiple joins, each containing a set of conditions that involve 30 different columns. The data generation system caused the generation and insertion of 3000 new records to the database. The experiments were carried out on an Intel(R) Core(TM)2 Duo CPU E6550@2.33GHz personal computer with 3GB of RAM.

Figure 7 depicts the time consumption, in seconds, of the data generation for each query. The time period grows as the database grows due to the unique-key constraints. As can be observed, the time consumption of the data generation grows from $\sim 0.1sec$ for the first queries up to $\sim 1.4sec$ for the 100'th query. In practice the latter queries are much less likely to require data generation, because the database would already include most of the required data.

We also performed an experiment to show that the data generation overhead is diminished as more and more data is added to the database. We applied the dynamic data generation solution to an application running random queries with multiple constraints and plotted the time intervals between each 100 queries. Figure 8 depicts the data generation overhead in seconds for each 100 queries

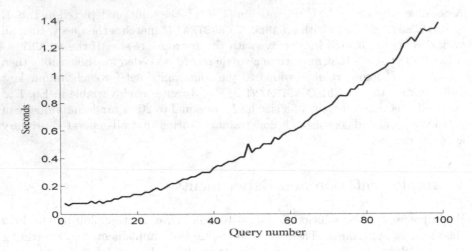

Fig. 7. Time consumption of the data generation of each query

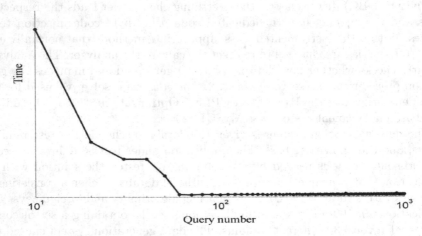

Fig. 8. The time consumption of the execution of the queries including data generation vs. the number of queries performed by the application

along the duration of the application's execution. The figure shows that most of the time overhead is spent at the beginning of the application run and the overhead per query is decreased as the database is populated.

Another experiment we conducted measured the application's method coverage, a simple case of code coverage [21] of the application under test. In our experiment, a coverage point was defined to be a method in the application. The coverage point belonging to a method is met during a test when the test executes the method. We created an application with 100 methods and marked them as coverage goals. The 100 methods all receive as input a record that came back from some query. The methods were divided into 50 pairs of methods: the

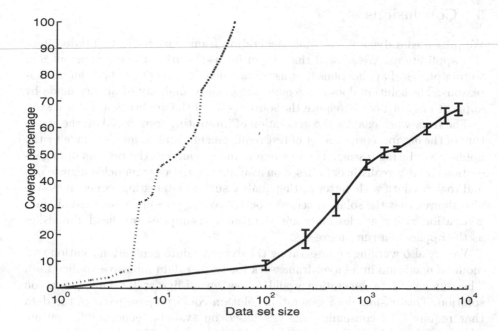

Fig. 9. Coverage percentage vs. the size of randomly generated testing data (*log* scale) averaged over 10 experiments (solid line with bars) and coverage percentage of the dynamic data generation solution (dashed line with circles)

first method of the pair is invoked for every record resulting from some SQL query. This method then used another internal SQL query that was based on the information in the input record. It then invoked the second method of the pair for every record resulting from the second query. The first set of queries was a set of simple SELECT statements with 5 simple random WHERE conditions, each relating to a different column of the same table. On average, the condition for each column could be satisfied for half of the possible values in the domain of the column. The second set of queries was a set of SELECT statements with one WHERE condition that could be satisfied only for one value in the domain of a column in a different table. In other words, the second set of queries was much harder to satisfy with random generation of data.

We tested our dynamic data generation on the above mentioned application and reached all the marked coverage goals, while generating a total of 49 records for the two tables (44 for the first table and 5 for the second table). We also measured the coverage with random generation of consistent data sets of different sizes. Figure 9 depicts the coverage percentage results achieved with our proposed dynamic generation solution and with random data vs. the size of the generated data set (*log* scale). The results obtained by the random data generator precisely correspond to the expected probability calculations.

5   Conclusions

We presented a dynamic test data generation framework for testing data intensive applications. We showed that it can be used during the development and
testing phases of applications that use data when data is not available for various
reasons. The solution does not require the prior availability of queries made by
applications nor does it require the source code of the application under test.

The framework enables the generation of interesting tests based on the structure of the database(s), on a set of test requirements, and on queries made by the
application during testing. The test requirements can bias the random data generation towards realistic data based on available statistics or modeled knowledge,
and towards data with better testing quality such as interesting corner cases. We
also showed that the solution achieves better coverage results than random data
generation with much less data and the time consumption overhead diminishes
as the application run progresses.

We are also working on integrating the dynamic data generation solution as a
mode of operation in a larger framework for testing data intensive applications.
The dynamic data generation would follow an off-line static data generation
solution. This off-line data generation solution could prepare parts of the data
that require time consuming analysis based on available generic information,
while the dynamic data generation would attempt to drive the tests towards
interesting cases based on the properties of the specific test. We believe that
such a hybrid solution should yield a good trade-off between systematic coverage
and user-guided scenarios with workload testing.

References

1. http://www.ibm.com/software/data/optim/core/data-privacy-solution/
2. IBM DB2 Test Data generator,
   http://www.ibm.com/software/data/optim/protect-data-privacy/
3. Emmi, M., Majumdar, R., Sen, K.: Dynamic Test Input Generation for Database
   Applications. In: Proceedings of the 2007 International Symposium on Software
   Testing and Analysis (ISSTA 2007), pp. 151–162. ACM, New York (2007)
4. Sen, K., Marinov, D., Agha, G.: CUTE: a Concolic Unit Testing Engine for C. In:
   Proceedings of the 10th European Software Engineering Conference Held Jointly
   with 13th ACM SIGSOFT International Symposium on Foundations of Software
   Engineering (ESEC/FSE-13). ACM, New York (2005)
5. Sen, K.: DART: Directed Automated Random Testing. In: Namjoshi, K.,
   Zeller, A., Ziv, A. (eds.) HVC 2009. LNCS, vol. 6405, p. 4. Springer, Heidelberg
   (2011)
6. Păsăreanu, C., Mehlitz, P., Bushnell, D., Gundy-Burlet, K., Lowry, M., Person, S.,
   Pape, M.: Combining Unit-Level Symbolic Execution and System-Level Concrete
   Execution for Testing Nasa Software. In: Proceedings of the 2008 International
   Symposium on Software Testing and Analysis (ISSTA 2008), ACM, New York
   (2008)
7. Veanes, M., Grigorenko, P., Halleux, P., Tillmann, N.: Symbolic Query Exploration.
   In: Breitman, K., Cavalcanti, A. (eds.) ICFEM 2009. LNCS, vol. 5885, pp. 49–68.
   Springer, Heidelberg (2009)

8. Taneja, K., Zhang, Y., Xie, T.: MODA: Automated Test Generation for Database Applications via Mock Objects. In: Proceedings of the IEEE/ACM International Conference on Automated Software Engineering (ASE 2010), pp. 289–292. ACM, New York (2010)
9. Binnig, C., Kossmann, D., Lo, E., Özsu, T.: QAGen: Generating Query-Aware Test Databases. In: Proceedings of the 2007 ACM SIGMOD International Conference on Management of Data (SIGMOD 2007), pp. 341–352. ACM, New York (2007)
10. Khalek, S., Elkarablieh, B., Laleye, Y., Khurshid, S.: Query-Aware Test Generation Using a Relational Constraint Solver. In: Proceedings of the 2008 23rd IEEE/ACM International Conference on Automated Software Engineering (ASE 2008), pp. 238–247. IEEE Computer Society, Washington, DC (2008)
11. Bruno, N., Chaudhuri, S., Thomas, D.: Generating Queries with Cardinality Constraints for DBMS Testing. IEEE Trans. on Knowl. and Data Eng. 18(12), 1721–1725
12. Tuya, J., Suárez-Cabal, M., De la Riva, C.: Full Predicate Coverage for Testing SQL Database Queries. Software. Test. Verif. Reliab. 20(3), 237–288 (2010)
13. De la Riva, C., Suárez-Cabal, M., Tuya, J.: Constraint-Based Test Database Generation for SQL Queries. In: Proceedings of the 5th Workshop on Automation of Software Test (AST 2010). ACM, New York (2010)
14. Jackson, D.: Alloy: A Lightweight Object Modeling Notation. ACM Trans. Softw. Eng. Methodol. 11(2), 256–290 (2002)
15. Grandison, T., Liu, K., Domany, T.: End-to-End Data De-identification (EDDI): Capitalizing on an Emerging Market. In: IBM Academy of Technology Security and Privacy Symposium, Yorktown, New York (2007)
16. Apt, K.: Principles of Constraint Programming. Cambridge University Press, New York (2003)
17. Rossi, F., Van Beek, P., Walsh, T. (eds.): Handbook of Constraint Programming. Elsevier (2006)
18. Naveh, Y., Rimon, M., Jaeger, I., Katz, Y., Vinov, M., Marcus, E., Shurek, G.: Constraint-Based Random Stimuli Generation for Hardware Verification. AI Magazine 28(3) (2006)
19. http://www.ibm.com/software/integration/optimization/cplex-optimization-studio/
20. MySQL open source database, http://www.mysql.com/
21. Marick, B.: The Craft of Software Testing, Subsystem Testing Including Object-Based and Object-Oriented Testing. Prentice-Hall (1985)

Injecting Floating-Point Testing Knowledge into Test Generators

Merav Aharony, Emanuel Gofman, Elena Guralnik, and Anatoly Koyfman

IBM Research Laboratory, Haifa Israel

Abstract. Floating-point unit (FPU) verification is a known challenge, due to the variety of corner cases both in its data path and control flow. We have identified a gap in the coverage of FP corner cases that combine special data and control scenarios. We propose a solution based on combining the deep FP knowledge of a special FP test generator with the strength of a general-purpose test generator. We present a novel FP testing knowledge package (FPTK) that consists of a weighted set of FP scenarios. We explain the flow of combining the existing tools with the FPTK and demonstrate its effect.

1 Introduction

Both formal and simulation methods have been developed to deal with floating-point unit (FPU) verification. Verification by simulation involves executing a subset of tests assumed to be a representative sample of the entire test space. Two major types of stimuli generators that address the floating-point (FP) realm exist. General-purpose generators, such as [5,6], can produce multi-instruction scenarios. However, they usually lack internal knowledge of the FP domain and thus do not apply for the verification of FP data path logic. FP test generators, such as [7], target the particular intricacies of FP data. Particular cases of such generators are directed test generators [8,9,10], which verify specific areas in the FP design, such as the rounding mechanism. Static FP test suites [1,2] are also used in simulation. Using all these methods, unit verification achieves high confidence in the validity of the FP data path. However, these techniques are all limited to handling single FP instructions.

FP verification still has a gap regarding combinations of data corner cases with control flow. This gap is particularly vulnerable in designs that have aggressive control features such as early forwarding of intermediate results. To systematically cover this gap, we would need to combine all coverage cases of interesting FP data with all interesting control flow cases, thus creating a large cross-product coverage space. No existing tools target this space.

We analyzed certain FP bugs found during verification and concluded that the scenarios that reveal such problems cannot be characterized in a single instruction. One example of such a bug is the following scenario. The first instruction produced an intermediate result of the form 1.11...1 and exponent equal to 1023 (max norm exponent), which led to overflow and to an infinite final result due

K. Eder, J. Lourenço, and O. Shehory (Eds.): HVC 2011, LNCS 7261, pp. 234–241, 2012.

to the rounding mode. The intermediate result before rounding was forwarded to another instruction, which also resulted in overflow. After overflow detection in the first instruction, the pipeline was flushed, and the second instruction was performed again, but the overflow flag was not reset.

A straightforward method to cover this gap is to inject interesting FP data into the general-purpose test generator, by having the test generator randomly select FP data from a static test suite every time it generates an FP instruction. Although we use this method during later stages of verification, it is not rigorous enough for core verification. This solution lacks the ability of the designer to specify a data-control scenario in general terms, and to have the test generator provide a suitable test.

In this paper, we propose combining the deep understanding of FP present in special FP-generators with the simulation abilities of general-purpose generators. For this purpose, we created an FP testing knowledge (FPTK) package that can be invoked by an external test generator. We constructed a system comprising three components: Genesys-Pro (GPro), IBM's processor level stimuli generator; FPgen, IBM's deep-knowledge coverage-driven FP test generator; and an FPTK package. The first two components are existing tools, and the third is new.

In subsequent sections we explain how this mechanism is constructed, and how it is used to target the cross-product coverage space created by control-data combinations. The proposed mechanism also provides flexibility over the level of coverage case selection. The user can, on one hand, target a specific combination corner, or on the other hand, randomly run tests out of the entire coverage space. Moreover, a user can focus on a certain slice of the coverage space. In Section 2, we provide background for this work and an overview of the tools we used. In Section 3, we describe the FPTK package we built. Section 4 presents application use and experimental results, and we conclude the paper in Section 5.

2 Background

Over the last two decades, IBM Haifa Research Labs has developed a large set of verification tools for processors, used within IBM as well as externally [11]. The predecessor of GPro, Genesys [3,4], contained an FP testing knowledge package, in which interesting FP data scenarios were implemented in C code. Our package is based on this approach. When generating an FP instruction, the test generator selects an interesting FP scenario using the FPTK package. Our idea was to use FPgen for generating operands of FP instructions as a part of the test generation process of GPro. Our implementation takes advantage of the state-of-the-art tools GPro and FPgen and combines their test generation abilities. In addition, we added a new FPTK package that directs the tools as to which FP scenarios to generate and over which the user has control.

2.1 FPgen Overview

FPgen is a random test generator that receives a list of tasks to be fulfilled (a coverage model) as input and then outputs a set of random tests covering the model. Coverage models are sets of FP instructions, with sets of constraints on the input, intermediate result(s), and result operands of the participating instructions. The constraints on FP operands are described in a language that allows domain definition (e.g., ranges of numbers, bit vectors, and number of leading zeros) and operations (set operations and relations between the values of the operand fields). Each operand field (sign, exponent, and fraction) can be constrained separately.

FPgen can be used by verification engineers to construct test cases by specifying constraints on the instructions. However, since interesting FP scenarios are common to all FP designs, a generic test plan (GTP) was written. This plan has been used for verification of all IBM FP designs over the last decade. It is composed of a large collection of coverage models implemented as input files for FPgen. This GTP is based on the experience accumulated during the verification of several processors along with a deep understanding of FPU algorithms and design. In addition to generic models, some tasks target implementation-specific features. In particular, the IBM's FP Test Suite for IEEE 754R Standard [2] was constructed by running FPgen on a part of GTP referring to the IEEE compliance.

2.2   Genesys-Pro Overview

GPro was specifically designed to address the challenges of test case generation for processor verification. The tool is based on a generic engine. Its inputs are a test specification describing a verification scenario and a design model that describes the design architecture and micro-architecture. It then outputs a test fitting the input requirements. The design model is specified in a declarative language containing special constructs for describing the architecture and micro-architecture. The test scenario is specified in a programming-like language. The restrictions specified by the test template and the design model are automatically translated into constraints on the output test. In the domain of FP, the GPro design model includes the description of FP instructions including the operands and a limited testing knowledge. This information is used to bias the chosen FP data toward special cases.

3   FPTK

The general idea is to assign the responsibility of defining control scenarios to a general-purpose test generator (GPro) and the responsibility for choosing meaningful data to an FP test generator (FPgen), with a software layer (FPTK) responsible for the connection between them. The crucial point is that the general-purpose test generator can bias the data chosen by the FP test generator via this layer, based on the control state chosen. This is implemented in FPTK through predefined weighted trees of different FP data cases, in which the weights can be changed by the general-purpose test generator in such a way that the desired data will be chosen by the FP test generator. Conceptually, FPTK consists of two components: an API between the two tools and a description of FP scenarios in a modeling language. Whereas the first component is specific code for our tools, the second component is generic and not tool-based.

At each stage of test generation, GPro decides (according to the specification of the test template) which instruction to generate and which source and target registers to use. In the normal flow of GPro, it also generates the data for the operands. However, when FPTK is enabled, if an FP instruction is selected, then GPro will call upon FPTK to provide the operand data. GPro sends a request, including the name of the instruction (mandatory), the constraints on the operands derived from the source and target registers' content (mandatory), new weights on the decision trees of FPTK (optional), and the constraints on the content of relevant control registers, such as specifying the rounding mode or enable bits (mandatory).

FPTK chooses a biasing for the operand/instruction and produces an FPgen task that contains the requested instruction and the data constraints derived from the original request, along with an FP bias request. FPgen solves the task to generate data that complies with all requests. This data is returned to GPro, which injects it as operand data for the current instruction and then continues with its regular flow.

The strategy for choosing a biasing for the instruction is based on an internal reservoir of scenarios. This reservoir was constructed based on the generic test plan (see Section 2.1), and consists of several weighted decision trees. The most basic distinction is between trees for operand and trees for instruction biasing. For each of these, separate trees exist for binary, decimal, and hexadecimal FP.

The nodes of an operand tree represent the possible biases for the input operands. Each edge from a parent node to a child node has a weight representing the probability of selecting the child node, given that the parent node was selected. Thus the biasing on each of the generated operands is selected from the operand tree, with probabilities determined by the weight of each edge in the operand tree. For example, the root of the binary operand tree has two children: "basic types" and "special values". The "basic types" has several children: "norm", "denorm", and so forth. The "norm" node has several children: "large norm", "max norm", and so on. The probability of selecting the "large norm" bias is the product of the weights of the edges to "basic types", "norm" and "large norm".

As for instruction biasing, a unique tree exists for every instruction type, such as a binary AddSub tree or a decimal Div tree. The biases resulted from the instruction tree are on the entire instruction, rather than on the operands. More specifically, biases can be on the final or intermediate result(s), or on some relationship involving input operands or/and output operands. Some of these biases are generic to all instructions, such as, "final result is overflow". Other biases are instruction-specific, such as, "divide: zero divisor exception". Figure 1 portrays a small section of the binary FPAdd instruction tree.

The list of all scenarios is visible to the user who has control over the relative probability of selecting each scenario. The edge weights can be changed during

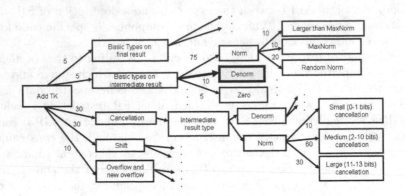

Fig. 1. Binary FPAdd instruction tree decision tree

test generation via directives passed to FPTK with other request attributes. For example, a user can exclude denormalized intermediate results of FPAdd instruction by changing the weight on the highlighted edge from 10 to 0 (see Figure 1).

FPTK stores a general TK model containing all the biasing trees. To use FPTK for choosing FP data, GPro calls FPTK in the beginning of test generation to create the FPTK model for the specified design. FPTK creates an operand tree for each format supported in the design and an instruction tree for each instruction implemented. At each call from GPro, FPTK creates an instance for the specified instruction, meaning that the relevant operand and instruction trees are prepared and that all environment fields are set, such as the rounding mode or enable bits. Then the edge weights of the instance's trees are updated in accordance with the directives received, and one leaf is chosen on each tree. These leaves define a constraint on the instruction's operands that FPgen will solve. The FPTK model currently contains approximately 2,000 leaves.

The three possible modes of operation are explained below:

1. Tailored cases: In this mode, a specific data-control scenario can be defined by the user. An appropriate control sequence is specified in GPro, and the desired data is chosen by setting zero weights on all other nodes in the FPTK decision tree. This mode is useful for bug reconstruction and verification of bug fixes.

2. Bias toward certain cases: In this mode, the user selects preferred scenarios, such as a denormalized intermediate result, and then requests FPTK to increase the probability of this case. This mode can also be used to exclude certain simulation events at different verification stages. For instance, if exceptions should be excluded, then the user can request FPTK not to generate intermediate results outside of the range of normalized numbers.

3. Completely random: This mode depends on the default strategy of choosing biases. In this case, FPTK runs in the background and generates interesting FP data without the user having to be aware of it.

4   Application Use and Experimental Results

The FPTK was used in the FP verification of IBM processor designs for about five years. The tailored cases mode was used mostly for bug reconstruction and bug fix verification. We have discovered that producing the desired stimuli with FPTK is significantly easier than manually writing the appropriate tests. The bias toward certain cases was widely used to prevent exceptions during early verification stages (when exception handling is not yet implemented) and to stress areas of the implementation not sufficiently otherwise exercised (for example, denormalized numbers treatment). This allowed the verification engineers to start the verification process earlier and easily focus on the desired areas. However, the largest impact was achieved when FPTK was used in the completely random mode. This mode of operation allowed us to significantly improve the FP coverage, as illustrated with the following experiment.

We used one of the recent IBM Power designs as a vehicle for the experiment. We fed two identical regression suites into GPro. One was generated with FPTK turned off, and the other with it turned on. We used two types of scenarios: specific (containing FP instructions only, in which each instruction had an equal probability of being selected), and general-purpose (actually used in verification, containing all processor instructions). The generated test cases contained 200 instructions each to provide greater interaction among FP instructions, as well as on encircling FP unit control logic. A total of 25,000 instructions per group were generated, and the coverage was evaluated. The list of coverage events used in the experiment is the list used for regression, containing 4,773 FP tasks. Although this number of instructions is far from sufficient for providing full coverage of all FP events, it allows for comparison of the tendencies of coverage with and without FPTK.

As we illustrated in Figure 2, better coverage (up to a 10% improvement) was achieved when running both test suites with FPTK turned on. As expected, FPTK led to better results while running the test suite containing only FP instructions.

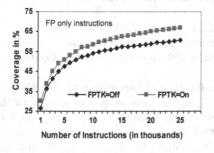
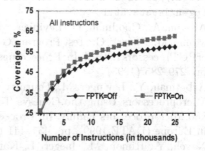

Fig. 2. Coverage by the set of instructions

GPro has its own embedded biasing, applied at each stage of decision making. When it comes to operand data biasing, special values such as all zeros, all ones, or denorm, have reasonable probabilities to be selected. This explains the relatively good coverage achieved by GPro, even without FPTK. However, GPro is not capable of creating test cases with more specialized FP scenarios, such as cases of dependency among FP operands. Generating such tests is important, not only to verify the correct implementation of an instruction, but also to verify its interaction with other instructions and with control logic, whose behavior may vary depending on the instruction result.

5   Conclusion and Future Work

FPTK is a package of interesting FP scenarios that can be invoked by an external test generator. It has been used in the verification of several FP units and has assisted in uncovering many interesting bugs. Our experiments have shown clear advantages to using FPTK in FPU verification. FPTK has achieved better coverage in less time than traditional methods and has generated control-data corner cases that would have otherwise required intensive manual efforts. Although we tested this approach using particular general-purpose and FP specific generators, the underlying ideas may be applied to any pair of the appropriate generators.

FPTK has been successfully integrated into existing verification processes, providing a means to easily address the coverage targets. The next step is to observe whether, given the new powers of scenario description and test generation offered by FPTK, test plans themselves can be extended to include additional microarchitectural corner cases.

References

1. Nelson, H.F.: Beebe's IEEE754 Floating-Point test software,
   http://www.math.utah.edu/~beebe/software/ieee
2. Floating-Point Test Suite for IEEE 754R Standard,
   https://www.research.ibm.com/haifa/projects/verification/fpgen/ieeets.html
3. Aharon, A., Goodman, D., Levinger, M., Lichtenstein, Y., Malka, Y., Metzger, C., Molho, M., Shurek, G.: Test Program Generation for Functional Verification of PowerPC Processors in IBM. In: Proceedings of the 32th Design Automation Conference, pp. 279–285 (1995)
4. Arbetman, Y., Levinger, M., Fournier, L.: Functional Verification Methodology of Microprocessors Using the Genesys Test Program Generator. Application to the x86 Microprocessors Family. In: Proceedings of the Design, Automation, and Test in Europe (DATE 1999), pp. 434–441 (1999)
5. Naveh, Y., Rimon, M., Jaeger, I., Katz, Y., Vinov, M., Marcus, E., Shurek, G.: Constraint-biased Random Stimuli Generation for Hardware Verification. AI Magazine 28(2), 13–30 (2007)

6. Chandra, A., Iyengar, V., Jameson, D., Jawalekar, R., Nair, I., Rosen, B., Mullen, M., Yoon, J., Armoni, R., Geist, D., Wolfsthal, Y.: AVPGEN - a test generator for architecture verification. IEEE Transaction on Very Large Scale Integration (VLSI) Systems 3(2), 157–172 (1995)
7. Aharoni, M., Asaf, S., Fournier, L., Koyfman, A., Nagel, R.: FPgen - A Test Generation Framework for Datapath Floating-Point Verification. In: Proc. IEEE International High Level Design Validation and Test Workshop 2003, HLDVT 2003 (2003)
8. Parks, M.: Number-theoretic Test Generation for Directed Rounding. In: Proc. Computer Arithmetic, pp. 241–248 (1999)
9. Kahan, W.: A test for Correctly Rouned SQRT, http://www.eecs.berkeley.edu/~wkahan/SQRT.ps
10. McFearin, L., Matula, D.: Generation and Analisys of Hard to Round Cases for Binary FP Division. In: Proc. Computer Arithmetic, pp. 119–126 (2001)
11. Rimon, M., Lichtenstein, Y., Adir, A., Jaeger, I., Vinov, M., Johnson, S., Jani, D.: Addressing Test Generation Challenges for Configurable Processor Verification. In: 2006 IEEE International High-Level Design Validation and Test Workshop (2006)

Combining Theorem Proving
and Symbolic Trajectory Evaluation in THM&STE

Yongjian Li[1], Naiju Zeng[1], William N.N. Hung[2], and Xiaoyu Song[3]

[1] Chinese Academy of Sciences, Beijing, China
[2] Synopsys Inc., Mountain View, California, USA
[3] Portland State University, Portland, Oregon, USA

Abstract. In this paper, we present a tool THM&STE, which combines theorem proving with symbolic trajectory evaluation. With the help of theorem proving, a large property is decomposed into smaller properties, which can be handled directly by running STE. Besides the support of decomposition by the classical STE laws, some novel techniques such as simplification on the assertions based on causal dependency between nodes, symmetry reduction, tacticals are provided in THM&STE.

1 Introduction

Symbolic trajectory evaluation (STE) is an efficient formal verification method that has grown from a combination of multi-valued simulation and symbolic simulation [10,2]. It has shown great promise in verifying medium to large scale industrial hardware designs with substantial automation. STE has been actively used by Intel, Motorola, and IBM. For example, STE was used at Intel to verify a floating point arithmetic unit against IEEE standard 754 and a complex IA instruction length decoder unit [9,1]. There were prior attempts to combine symbolic simulation with theorem provers such as ACL2 [3]. In addition, the FORTE formal hardware verification tool, which combines STE and theorem proving with higher-order logic, has been developed at Intel [4].

Tackling state space explosion is a central task of formal verification such as STE. Despite strategies such as X-abstraction and symbolic indexing techniques in STE, it is not sufficient for us to only rely on STE to solve this task. A promising approach is to combine STE with theorem proving [11,1,3]. The motivation of this hybrid approach is to harness the power and flexibility of theorem prover to decompose and transform large problems into tasks that can be tractably handled by STE.

The main motivation of ours is to build a practical tool, which combines theorem proving and STE, on top of the trial version of Forte. We provide a free tool which introduce some new tactics such as symmetry reduction, causal dependency-based simplification, etc. Tacticals can introduce control structure to compose proofs. These are powerful techniques to handle complex real-world verification problems.

2 An Overview of the THM&STE Framework

The overall framework of our tool is shown in Fig. 1. The tool takes a circuit netlist description such as EXLIF and automatically extracts a finite state machine model. Users

K. Eder, J. Lourenço, and O. Shehory (Eds.): HVC 2011, LNCS 7261, pp. 242–246, 2012.
© Springer-Verlag Berlin Heidelberg 2012

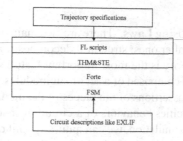

Fig. 1. Framework of THM&STE

interacts with the system by providing specifications and proof scripts for these specifications. Both specifications and proofs are written in FL. The proof scripts comprises a
series of tactics. The tool THM&STE accepts the specifications as a goal, and execute
the proof scripts to reach the goal. Once a proof tactic is applied to a goal, the goal is
reduced to some subgoals. The remaining subgoals are refined by further applications
of tactics until the remaining subgoals can be immediately solved by transforming them
to a STE assertion which can be verified by the STE engine.

3 Illustrating Example

In this section, we demonstrate our tool and our symmetry reduction method by verifying a Content-Addressable Memory (CAM). CAMs are hardware implementations of
lookup tables. A CAM stores a number of tags, each of which is linked to a specific
data-entry. A CAM circuit typically consists of two memory blocks, one containing tag
entries, and the other the same number of corresponding data entries, Given an input
tag, the associative-read operation consists of searching all tags in the CAM to determine if there is a match to the input tag, and if so sending the associated data-entry to
the output. The overall FL verification script can be found in [8].

3.1 Writing the STE Assertion

A natural account of the tag match operation of a CAM is as follows:
$entries = (0 \text{ upto } 15)$,
$ant = \mathsf{AndList}$
$[(\mathsf{ls1}\ aread), (tagin\ \mathsf{bvAre}\ vOfTagin), (tagmem\ \mathsf{memAre}\ vOfTagmem)]$
$matchCond\ i \equiv vOfTagin\ \mathsf{bvEq}\ (vOfTagmem_i)$
$consOfHit = \mathsf{AndList}\ (\mathsf{map}\ (\lambda i.\mathsf{When}\ (matchCond\ i)\ Is1\ hit)\ entries)$
$assertion = ant \rightsquigarrow consOfHit$
where $tagmem$ is a memory for stored tag nodes, $tagin$ a vector of input tag nodes,
$vOfTagmem$ a vector of vector of symbolic boolean variables, $vOfTagin$ a vector
of symbolic boolean variables. This specification says that once one line of stored tags
is matched with the input tag, the hit node becomes high.

3.2   Writing the Proof

Property Decomposition Using Laws. There are two main ways to decompose a complex STE assertion into smaller ones: structural decomposition and case split over data (input) space. Now modularity is the most important features in modern hardware design. A hardware module is composed of a set of submodules. Naturally an assertion on a module can boil down to assertions of the pieces of the modules. On the other hand, a complex STE assertion specifies behaviors of a circuit over some kinds of legal values of input nodes in symbolic simulation, we can naturally split cases over the legal values to decompose a complex assertion into a set of smaller assertions. The split cases are usually hinted by the boolean guards in the assertions.

The proof steps are backward-style reasoning steps combined with STE runs. After applying rule steConjI to the main goal cktSat cam $assertion$, we have 16 subgoals.

(1) cktSat cam $ant \rightsquigarrow$ When $(matchCond\ 0)$ $(\mathsf{ls1}\ hit)$

...

(16) cktSat cam $ant \rightsquigarrow$ When $(matchCond\ 15)$ $(\mathsf{ls1}\ hit)$

For (1), we apply rule steImpI to it, we have a new goal:

(1') $(matchCond\ 0) \implies$ cktSat cam $ant \rightsquigarrow (\mathsf{ls1}\ hit)$.

Let $B = (\mathsf{ls1}\ match_0)$, we use rule steTrans to reduce (1') into two subgoals:

(1-1) $(matchCond\ 0) \implies$ cktSat cam $ant \rightsquigarrow B$;
(1-2) $(matchCond\ 0) \implies$ cktSat cam $B \rightsquigarrow (\mathsf{ls1}\ hit)$.

Simplifying Assertions Based on Causal Dependency. For goal (1-1), we can remove all useless antecedents which assign symbolic values to memory lines $tagmem_i$ where $i \neq 0$, because only the memory line mem_0 and input tags will affect the value of $match_0$ after the symbolic simulation. The tool THM&STE supports an automatical simplification tactic steSimpByDelAnt for assertions such as (1-1) based on the causal dependency between nodes specified in the consequents and antecedents.

For instance, for the goal (1-1), the bounded cone of inputs of $match_0$ is the set of $tagmem_0$ and $tagin$, while the other memory lines has nothing with $match_0$. Then only the conjuncts $tagmem_0$ and $tagin$ in the ant are needed, and other antecedents are eliminated. Let $antf\ i =$ AndList $[(\mathsf{ls1}\ aread), (tagin\ \mathsf{bvAre}\ vOfTagin), (tagmem_i\ \mathsf{bvAre}\ vOfTagmem_i)]$, the renaming goal will be as follows after we use a command steSimpByDelAnt to simplify the the goal (1-1):

(1-1') $(matchCond\ 0) \implies$ cktSat cam $(antf\ 0) \rightsquigarrow (\mathsf{ls1}\ match_0)$

Running STE Engine. For goal (1-1') and (1-2), we can use STE symbolic simulation tactic steSymbSim to directly verify it, which in turn calls STE engine supported by FORTE . For a goal $P \implies$ cktSat ckt $A \rightsquigarrow C$, THM&STE transforms A and When $P\ C$ into two lists of 5-tuples $antL$ and $consL$ respectively, then runs Forte command STE "" $ckt\ []\ antL\ consL\ []$ to check the goal directly. If the result is returned as T, the goal is solved; otherwise the result is the condition where the assertion holds.

Symmetry Reduction. After solving the goal (1-1) by solving (1-1') and (1-2), now our task is to solve the remaining unsolved goals (2)-(16). For instance, for goal (2), we can use similar techniques to decompose it into subgoals: (2-1')($matchCond$ 1) $\Longrightarrow$ cktSat cam ($antf$ 1) $\rightsquigarrow$ (ls1 $match!$1). Our solution to (2-1') is to use symmetry reduction, instead of repeating an STE run.

THM&STE provides symmetry reduction tactic steSymReduce to solve the goal from the proved lemma. Roughly speaking, our symmetry reduction procedure is divided into four steps: (1) the matching procedure of two consequents C and C'; (2) exploring the symmetry between two causal parts of the circuit ckt on $A \rightsquigarrow C$ and $A' \rightsquigarrow C'$; the bijection computed in (1) is used as the heuristics to find symmetry; (3) checking whether the symmetry between nodes in step (2) is a swap function; if thus, then the function is used to transform the assertion $P' \Longrightarrow$ cktSat ckt $A' \rightsquigarrow C'$. (4) checking whether the transformed assertion in (3) can be unified with the proved Lemma. In THM&STE, we can first introduce a lemma of the form (1-1'), and name it "oneLineHit". For goal (2-1'), we can use the following command to solve: steSymReduce "oneLineHit" (\n.is_input n OR is_latch n)

Tacticals. A main goal can be decomposed into similar subgoals, which can be solved by similar proof procedures. For instance, subgoals (2)-(16) in CAM case study can be solved by repeating similar proof steps. Therefore a respectable proof procedure can be composed of tactics with the help of a few control structures. Such a control structure is called a tactical, which is formally a higher-order functor operating on tactics. Properly using tacticals make proof as automatically as possible.

For subgoals (i) in CAM case where $1 < i \leq 16$, we can define a general $taci$ i to solve it, then we can call tactical forTact $[2, ..., 16]$ $taci$ to solve all the remaining goals. Here tactical forTact $list$ $tacPara$ st starts from proof state st, and applies a tactic ($tacParac$ i) repeatedly to solve all remaining goals, where i is in the integer list $list$. This process will be repeated until all the elements of L are used or the tactic ($tacParac$ i) fails.

4   Experiments

Besides the combination of STE with the aforementioned techniques, we also combine GSTE with these techniques. More experiments are done including ring-buffer based FIFO, shift registers based FIFO, shift memory, and round-robin arbiters. The detail experiment codes and data can be found in [5,7,6].

5   Conclusion

Our case studies on FIFOs and CAMs are typical examples to illustrate the guiding principle of THM&STE. Instead of symbolic indexing, theorem proving and STE are combined in THM&STE. The formal verification results are proof scripts, which use deductive inference rules to handle property decomposition, which is similar to the approach used in [11,1]. Necessary simplification are done to delete useless antecedents by the analysis on the causal dependency between nodes specified in the assertions. Deleting unnecessary antecedents means that the nodes, which specified by these antecedents are set X, and symbolic variables used in them are also not needed. Symmetry between some decomposed smaller properties *w.r.t.* the parts of the circuit under verification is exploited, a representative property from the equivalence class is verified in the STE simulator, and the others are solved by symmetry reduction. Tacticals can be used to compose proof scripts to handle the complex problem, and make proof developments as program developments. In our study on CAMs, we use laws to decompose the overall assertions on the tag matching to each match cases, then we simplify all assertions of each matching cases. We try to find the symmetry relation between assertions on each matching cases, thus only need one STE run for a matching case, and the others can be solved by symmetry reduction. Tactical forTact is used to repeat the similar proofs for each assertion on one match case.

Acknowledgments. This work was supported by grants (61170073, 60833001, 60603001, 60721061, 60973016, 60496321, 61050002, 60421001, 60903030) from the National Natural Science Foundation of China.

References

1. Aagaard, M.D., Jones, R.B., Seger, C.J.H.: Combining theorem proving and trajectory evaluation in an industrial environment. In: Design Automation Conference, pp. 538–541. ACM, San Francisco (1998)
2. Hazelhurst, S., Seger, C.J.: Symbolic Trajectory Evaluation. In: Kropf, T. (ed.) Formal Hardware Verification. LNCS, vol. 1287, pp. 3–78. Springer, Heidelberg (1997)
3. Hunt Jr., W.A., Swords, S., Davis, J., Slobodova, A.: Use of Formal Verification at Centaur Technology. In: Hardin, D.S. (ed.) Design and Verification of Microprocessor Systems for High Assurance Applications, pp. 65–88. Springer (2010)
4. Intel Corporation: Forte/fl user guide, 2003 edn. (2003)
5. Li, Y.: Formalization of symbolic trajectory semantics (2009),
   http://lcs.ios.ac.cn/~lyj238/steSymmetry.html
6. Li, Y., Zeng, N.: Enhanced symbolic simulation of a round-robin arbiter (2011),
   http://lcs.ios.ac.cn/~lyj238/roundRobin.html
7. Li, Y., Zeng, N.: Symmetry reduction in enhanced symbolic simulation (2011),
   http://lcs.ios.ac.cn/~lyj238/gsteSymmetry.html
8. Li, Y.: Case study of cam (2011),
   http://lcs.ios.ac.cn/~lyj238/papers/cam.fl
9. O'Leary, J., Zhao, X., Gerth, R., Seger, C.J.H.: Formally verifying IEEE compliance of floating-point hardware. Intel Technology Journal Q1, 147–190 (1999)
10. Seger, C.J.H., Bryant, R.E.: Formal verification by symbolic evaluation of partially-ordered trajectories. Formal Methods in System Design 6(2), 147–189 (1995)
11. Seger, C.J.H., Jones, R.B., O'Leary, J.W., Melham, T., Aagaard, M.D., Barrett, C., Syme, D.: An industrially effective environment for formal hardware verification. IEEE Transactions on Computer-Aided Design 24(9), 1381–1405 (2005)

HAVEN: An Open Framework for FPGA-Accelerated Functional Verification of Hardware*

Marcela Šimková, Ondřej Lengál, and Michal Kajan

FIT, Brno University of Technology, Czech Republic

Abstract. Functional verification is a widespread technique to check whether a hardware system satisfies a given correctness specification. As the complexity of modern hardware systems rises rapidly, it is a challenging task to find appropriate techniques for acceleration of this process. In this paper we present HAVEN, a freely available open functional verification framework that exploits the field-programmable gate array (FPGA) technology for cycle-accurate acceleration of simulation-based verification runs. HAVEN takes advantage of the inherent parallelism of hardware systems and moves the verified system together with transaction-based interface components of the functional verification environment from software into an FPGA. The presented framework is written in SystemVerilog and complies with the principles of functional verification methodologies (OVM, UVM), assertion-based verification, and also provides adequate debugging visibility, making its application range quite large. Our experiments confirm the assumption that the achieved acceleration is proportional to the complexity of the verified system, with the peak acceleration ratio being over 1,000.

1 Introduction

Today's highly competitive market of consumer electronics is very sensitive to the time it takes to introduce a new product (the so-called *time to market*). This has driven the demand for fast, efficient and cost-effective methods of *verification* of hardware systems. There are several options applicable to this issue, with *functional verification* currently being one of the most popular.

Functional verification is a simulation-based method that generates a set of constrained-random test vectors and compares the behaviour of the verified hardware system for these vectors with the dynamically predicted behaviour specified by a *transfer function*, which is called *scoreboarding*. In order to achieve a high level of coverage of a system's state space, it is necessary to (*i*) find a way how to generate test vectors that cover critical parts of the state space, and (*ii*) maximise the number of vectors tested. The generation of appropriate scenarios can be fully automated by an intelligent program that controls coverage results and chooses parameters or a pseudo-random number

* This work was supported by the Czech Science Foundation (projects P103/10/0306 and 102/09/1668), the Czech Ministry of Education (projects COST OC10009 and MSM 0021630528), Reduced Certification Costs Using Trusted Multi-core Platforms project, Artemis JU, RECOMP #100202 and the BUT FIT project FIT-S-11-1. An extended version of this paper is available as the technical report [1].

K. Eder, J. Lourenço, and O. Shehory (Eds.): HVC 2011, LNCS 7261, pp. 247–253, 2012.

generator seed according to the achieved coverage. This approach is called *coverage-driven verification*. To facilitate the process of verification and to formally express the intended behaviour, internal synchronization, and expected operations of the system, *assertions* may be used. Assertions create monitors at critical points of the system without the need to create separate testbenches where these points would be externally visible.

Simulation-based verification approaches including functional verification provide great opportunity to inspect the internal behaviour of a running system, but they suffer from the fact that software simulation of inherently parallel hardware is extremely slow when compared to the speed of real hardware. To address this issue, we introduce **HAVEN** (**H**ardware-**A**ccelerated **V**erification **EN**vironment), an open framework that exploits the inherent parallelism of hardware systems to accelerate their functional verification by moving the verified system together with several necessary components of the verification environment to a *field-programmable gate array* (FPGA). To provide advanced level of debugging capabilities, the framework adopts some formal techniques (assertion-based verification) and functional verification techniques (constrained-random stimulus generation, self-checking mechanisms) and enables partial signal observability to achieve appropriate debugging visibility while running in the FPGA. HAVEN is freely available and *open source*[1], and we welcome collaboration on its further development.

Currently, there already exist several approaches to acceleration of functional verification. Mentor Graphics' Veloce technology [2] accelerates simulation by synthesising the *design under test* (DUT) and placing it into a proprietary emulator. This provides simulation speed-up while maintaining full signal visibility. The maximum frequency of the emulator is claimed to be 1.5 MHz, which may still not be sufficient for some applications (e.g., applications that need to communicate using a high-speed interface). From the same deficit suffers also the Cadence's Transaction-Based Acceleration (TBA) environment [3] with the performance of a proprietary accelerator/emulator being up to 1 MHz. TBA supports a reusable accelerated verification environment and benefits from a direct transaction-based interface (based on the SCE-MI standard [7]) for the desired testbench language. TBA ensures the same results in simulation and acceleration without needing to change any design or testbench models and also guarantees access to all design components and signals throughout the whole runtime session. SEmulator [5] is a system that enables acceleration of simulation of a DUT using FPGA while sacrificing observability of the DUT's signals. Our approach is in many aspects similar to the work of Huang *et al* [4] who also place the DUT with necessary components to an FPGA, and in addition provide limited observability of the DUT's signals. Nevertheless, to the best of our knowledge, there is currently still no available working implementation based on their proposal. Unfortunately, we could not perform a detailed comparison of these solutions as they are not available to us.

2 Design of the Verification Framework

HAVEN is a SystemVerilog verification framework that allows users to run either a *non-accelerated* or an *accelerated* version of the same testbench with a cycle-accurate time behaviour.

---
[1] http://www.fit.vutbr.cz/~isimkova/haven/

The non-accelerated version of the framework presents a similar approach to functional verification that is commonly used in verification methodologies. This version is highly efficient in the initial phase of the verification process when testing basic system functionality with a small number of transactions (up to thousands). In this phase it is desirable to have a quick access to the values of all signals of the system and to monitor the verification process in a simulator. Coverage statistics (code coverage, functional coverage, path coverage, etc.) provide a feedback about the state space exploration and allows the user to arrange constrained-random test cases properly to achieve even higher level of coverage. Despite all these advantages the application of the non-accelerated version is very inefficient for verification of complex systems and/or large number of test vectors.

The accelerated version of the framework moves the DUT to a verification environment in the FPGA. As RTL simulation takes the biggest portion of verification time, this approach may yield a significant acceleration of the overall process. Complex systems can be verified very quickly and with much higher number of transactions (in the order of millions and more). Behavioural parts of the testbench, such as planning of test sequences, generation of constrained-random stimuli, and scoreboarding, remain in the software simulator. This partitioning is possible because the generic nature of currently prevalent verification methodologies, such as *Open Verification Methodology* (OVM) or its extension *Universal Verification Methodology* (UVM), and transaction-based communication among their subcomponents enable to transparently move some of these components to a specialized hardware. The communication between the software and the hardware part of the verification environment is mediated using a generic protocol. Nevertheless, the readability for verification engineers remains the same and the tests can be assembled at a high level of abstraction without the need to change any hardware-level code.

As illustrated in Fig. 1 some components of the framework are shared in both versions. On the other hand, the use of other components strictly depends on the selected version of the framework.

Testcases, written by the user, hold parameters such as settings of generics of the system, the number of tested transaction, or options for the generator of random transactions. *Generator* produces constrained-random stimuli, which are typically random data and random delays generated in the ranges specified in the Testcase. *Scoreboard* dynamically predicts the response of the DUT and compares it with received transactions. The remaining blocks were designed in order to create an innovative architecture that supports fast and easy switching between the two versions, which is as easy as changing a single parameter of the verification. These blocks are briefly described below and more details can be found in [1].

Input Controller interprets instructions from testcases. For the successive processing of transactions, the Input Controller hands over the control to Software Driver or to Hardware Driver according to the selected version.

Driver breaks down data transactions received from Input Controller into individual signal changes and supplies them either on the input interface of the simulated DUT in the non-accelerated version (Software Driver) or on the input interface of the synthesised DUT in the FPGA in the accelerated version (Hardware Driver).

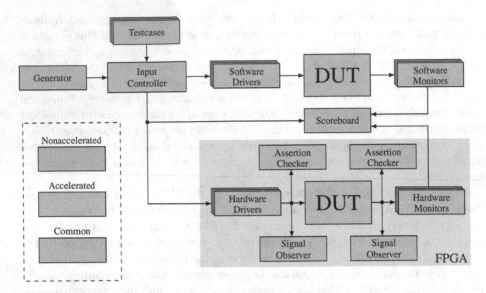

Fig. 1. The architecture of the HAVEN framework

Monitor observes signal transitions from the output interface of the simulated DUT in the non-accelerated version (Software Monitor) or from the output interface of the synthesised DUT placed in the FPGA in the accelerated version (Hardware Monitor). Subsequently, it groups signals together into high-level transactions and passes them to Scoreboard for comparison.

Assertion Checker is used to check validity of assertions inside or on the interfaces of the DUT. SystemVerilog uses the linear-time assertion language *SystemVerilog Assertions* (SVA) as its internal part. Given its linear nature, any assertion in the language can be effectively transformed into a Büchi automaton, which can in turn be easily implemented as a finite state machine in the FPGA (see [6]).

Signal Observer monitors values of signals in the system during a verification run. The values are sampled in each clock cycle and stored into the standardised *Value Change Dump* (VCD) format and streamed into software using the generic protocol. Later they can be inspected using any compliant waveform viewer, e.g., Model-Sim or GTKWave. When functional verification of a system detects an error, Signal Observer allows to observe internal states of the verified system in order to localise the source of the erroneous behaviour. There is no limit on the number of observed signals, however, observing a high number of signals may decrease the performance of a verification run, as the transport of observed signal values and test data share the same communication channel.

HAVEN is built upon NetCOPE[2], a free and open source platform for development of applications in FPGAs. NetCOPE provides abstraction over the type of the FPGA and the used acceleration card by defining a uniform interface for data transfers between the

---

[2] http://www.liberouter.org/netcope/

FPGA and the CPU. Although NetCOPE focuses primarily on network applications, it was successfully used for our purpose as well. Moreover, because NetCOPE provides a uniform interface over several protocols, its use makes it very easy to change the framework to use Ethernet or other supported communication protocol for data transfers instead of a system bus without any change to the verification environment itself.

In order to achieve cycle-accurate time behaviour of verification runs, simply placing the DUT into an FPGA is not sufficient, as the transfer of data through the system bus may be delayed, thus yielding behaviour different from the one obtained from the simulator. We solve this issue by placing the DUT into a separate clock domain in the FPGA and enabling/disabling the clock signal for this domain depending on the state of DMA buffers for the input and output transactions. The communication between the main and the DUT clock domain is accomplished using input and output internal asynchronous FIFO buffers (see [1] for further details). Thus the run of the DUT in the FPGA is guaranteed to result in the same waveform as the run in the simulator.

The framework monitors two types of errors: assertion failures and conflicts in Scoreboard such as missing or corrupted data or incorrect order of received transactions. If a bug is detected, the framework provides a short report about the nature of the failure, the simulation time when it occurred and the number of the received transaction which caused the inconsistency in Scoreboard.

3   Experimental Results

We performed a set of experiments using the COMBOv2 LXT155 acceleration card equipped with the Xilinx Virtex-5 FPGA in a server with two quad-core Intel Xeon E5420@2.50 GHz processors and 10 GiB of RAM. The data throughput between the acceleration card and the CPU was measured to be over 10 Gbps for this configuration and the clock frequency of the acceleration environment was 125 MHz. We used Mentor Graphics' ModelSim SE-64 6.6a as the SystemVerilog interpreter and in the case of the non-accelerated version also as the DUT simulator. Unfortunately, we were not able to compare HAVEN to other solutions for acceleration of functional verification, because these are mostly not freely available commercial products.

We evaluated the performance of HAVEN on two hardware components: a simple FIFO buffer and a hash generator (HGEN) which computes the hash value of input data. In order to fully exploit the capabilities of the accelerated version of HAVEN it is necessary to verify a complex system. For this purpose we also built systems with 2, 4, 8, and 16 parallelly working HGEN units.

The results of our measurements are shown in Table 1. The average acceleration ratio of the accelerated version computed from all verification runs for every verified system is given in the row **Acceleration**, whereas the row **Acceleration w/o trans.** represents the average acceleration ratio without the time of transaction generation (as this is the same for both versions). Rows **Slices** and **Slices %** describe the total consumed amount of resources at the FPGA (in Virtex-5 slices and percent respectively); the total number of slices on the used FPGA is 24,320 and the overhead of NetCOPE is about 35 % of FPGA resources. The resource consumption of overhead modules (driver, monitor, etc.) is negligible (below 2 %). The row **Build time** gives the time it took to build the

Table 1. Results of experiments with HAVEN

Component	FIFO	HGEN	HGENx2	HGENx4	HGENx8	HGENx16
Acceleration	2.38	4.73	12.47	17.11	35.68	142.26
Acceleration w/o trans.	38.25	27.51	81.97	116.39	243.09	1,008.00
Slices	9,362	9,787	11,315	12,938	16,304	22,096
Slices %	38.5	40.2	46.5	53.2	67.0	90.9
Build time [s]	1,473	1,724	1,895	2,340	3,390	7,909
B-E transactions	3,116,000	622,000	222,000	196,000	131,000	75,000

firmware of the accelerated version and the row **B-E transactions** holds the number of transactions for which the accelerated version starts to be beneficial (i.e., when the acceleration compensates for the build time of the firmware). Details about the experiments and further discussion can be found in [1].

4   Conclusion

We presented an open framework for FPGA-accelerated functional verification of hardware systems, which is to the best of our knowledge currently the only open and free solution available. The framework allows users to easily accelerate SystemVerilog testbenches by moving the verified DUT from the simulator into FPGA. The frequency of the acceleration environment achieved in our experiments was 125 MHz, which is significantly higher than the frequency of emulation-based commercial solutions (currently up to 1.5 MHz). However, the use of HAVEN is limited by available resources of current FPGA technology, thus it is more appropriate for verification of stand-alone IP cores than for verification of full industrial-size circuits. The components of the framework can be easily incorporated as blocks into testbenches that use OVM, UVM or any other transaction-based verification methodology. The experiments and their results show that by mapping the RTL logic into an FPGA instead of using a software simulator the acceleration ratio of over 1,000 can be achieved.

In the future, we wish to continue improving HAVEN. As currently only manual creation of Assertion Checkers is supported, we believe that implementing (and perhaps improving) the procedure proposed in [6] for synthesis of SVA assertions, both on interfaces and inside systems, is a reasonable step. The results of our experiments show that another challenging issue is hardware-accelerated generation of test vectors, which requires solving often quite complex constraints. In order to verify more complex and industrial-sized circuits, we wish to seek a less complex but sufficient platform for data transfers to use instead of NetCOPE. Moreover, to comply with current industry standards, providing the SCE-MI [7] interface for the accelerated testbench is desirable. In addition, our future effort will lead also to integration of HAVEN into various research areas, especially into diagnostics, where we wish to explore the capability of functional verification to improve the quality of fault-tolerant systems. We welcome collaboration on any of these issues and hope that the community can benefit from our contribution.

References

1. Šimková, M., Lengál, O., Kajan, M.: HAVEN: An Open Framework for FPGA-Accelerated Functional Verification of Hardware. Technical Report FIT-TR-2011-05, FIT BUT (2011), http://www.fit.vutbr.cz/~ilengal/pub/FIT-TR-2011-05.pdf
2. Mentor Graphics. Veloce (2011), http://www.mentor.com/products/fv/emulation-systems/veloce/
3. Cadence. Transaction-based Acceleration (TBA) (2011), http://www.cadence.com/products/sd/pages/transactionacc.aspx
4. Huang, C.-Y., Yin, Y.-F., Hsu, C.-J., Huang, T.B., Chang, T.M.: SoC HW/SW Verification and Validation. In: Proc. of ASPDAC 2011. IEEE (2011)
5. Schwarztrauber, A.: SEmulation: Use Your Emulation Board as a Hardware Accelerator for ModelSim SE. Verification Horizons 5, 31–34 (2009)
6. Das, S., Mohanty, R., Dasgupta, P., Chakrabarti, P.P.: Synthesis of System Verilog Assertions. In: Proc. of DATE 2006. EDAA (2006)
7. Accelera Interface Technical Committee. SCE-MI (2011), http://www.accellera.org/activities/itc/

On-Line Detection and Prediction of Temporal Patterns*

Shlomi Dolev[1,2], Jonathan Goldfeld[1,2], and Rami Puzis[2,3]

[1] Ben-Gurion University, Department of Computer Science, Beer-Sheva, Israel
[2] Deutsche Telekom Laboratories, Ben-Gurion University, Beer-Sheva, Israel
[3] Ben-Gurion University, Department of Information Systems Engineering, Beer-Sheva, Israel

Identifying a temporal pattern of events is a fundamental task of on-line (real-time) verification. In this work we present efficient schemes for on-line monitoring of events for identifying predefined patterns of events. The schemes use preprocessing to ensure that the number of comparisons during run-time is minimized. In particular, obsoloete sub-sequences are discarded to avoid unnecessary comparisons. We use our monitoring scheme for estimating the probability that a random suffix of a given execution will contain the pattern.

Many complex systems, both hardware and software, require a sound verification of their operation, usually in the form of safety and liveness properties. One of the prominent formal verification methods used today is model-checking [7]. The major drawback of model checking is the state explosion due to the exponential number of system states (w.r.t. the number of system variables) [3]. In addition, model checking can only be as accurate as the model is, compared to the actual system. A more accurate verification method in system specifications is testing. Unfortunately, an exhaustive search for specifications' violation is not feasible. It cannot tackle implementation flaws that materialize only during specific and rare executions.

In order to detect such flaws, a run-time verification of system execution is required [9,4]. We focus on a variant of run-time system verification, namely the detection of predefined temporal patterns in a given stream of system events. These temporal patterns are described by a sequence of system events and temporal constraints semantics.

Temporal patterns are defined as a triplet $TP = (A, CMax, CMin)$ where A is the sequence of events ($A = (a_1, a_2, ..., a_n)$) while $CMax$ and $CMin$ are sets of temporal constraints. A maximum temporal constraint is a tuple (a_i, a_j, t), where t is the maximum time allowed between a_i and a_j. Symmetrically, a minimum temporal constraint (a_i, a_j, t) defines the minimum time allowed between a_i and a_j. Note that the time interval bound (t) in a temporal constraint may also be 0 or ∞.

We design an algorithm that, given a set of temporal patterns, analyzes the stream of system events. In order to detect desired/undesired system behavior we employ methods similar to string matching solutions [6], however we deal with the added difficulty of

* Partially supported by Deutsche Telekom, Rita Altura Trust Chair in Computer Sciences, Lynne and William Frankel Center for Computer Sciences, Israel Science Foundation (grant number 428/11), Cabarnit Cyber Security MAGNET Consortium, Grant from the Institute for Future Defense Technologies Research named for the Medvedi of the Technion, Israeli Internet Association, and Israeli Defense Secretary (MAFAT).

K. Eder, J. Lourenço, and O. Shehory (Eds.): HVC 2011, LNCS 7261, pp. 254–256, 2012.
© Springer-Verlag Berlin Heidelberg 2012

the timing constraints. Our algorithm detects the first instance (and all subsequent ones) of the pattern's appearance during system execution.

The number of comparisons required for such patterns to be detected is minimized by a preprocessing phase that computes the temporal semantics closure of the constraints. The preprocessing resembles results in Temporal Constraint Networks [8] where, unfortunately, the on-line monitoring task and its composition with the preprocessing phase are not considered.

An approach of extending Computation Tree Logic (CTL) to include timing constraints appears in [2]. In [11] transitional durations are added to timed temporal formulae as an extension of Kripke Structures, and timed versions of CTL are considered. These frameworks however, do not address real-time verification.

Tools for real-time verification exist in the form of assertion checking, some of which follow the PSL IEEE standard, notably [1] and [5]. Whereas these allow the specification of quite general properties and employ an automaton for detecting a single property, we focus on patterns with timing constraints, and employ an automaton to detect all pattern instances.

Furthermore, we conduct an analysis to estimate the chances of a token representing a partial pattern to complete to a pattern match. We assume all events have some equal probability p to occur at any time point, however our approach is easily extended to arbitrary probabilities per event type. For each event, all possibilities of the next event occurring in the time window derived from the temporal constraints are examined.

We maintain a tree of partial executions which we call a *probability tree*. Each execution is a path from the root down to a leaf. The root represents the relative zero-time of a pattern match, i.e. the time from which we wish to compute the pattern match probability. An edge P_{x_i} to a node in the tree represents a time point with a shift of x_i time points relative to the beginning of the current time window, contributing a factor of $p_{x_i} = p(1-p)^{x_i}$ to the current probability path. The set of a node's children in the tree represents the different possibilities of the current history's continuation. In other words, suppose the current probability path counts the factors $p_{x_1} p_{x_2} \cdots p_{x_d} = p^d(1-p)^{\sum_{i=1}^{d} x_i}$. If we denote $x = \sum_{i=1}^{d} x_i$, we have $\prod_{i=1}^{d} p_{x_i} = p^*_{d,x}$. Suppose the next time window is of size k'. Then the edges to the current node's children are $P_0, P_1, \ldots, P_{k'}$, and continuing along an edge $P_{x_{d+1}}, 0 \le x_{d+1} \le k'$ adds the factor $p_{x_{d+1}}$ to the above multiple, yielding $p^{d+1}(1-p)^{\sum_{i=1}^{d+1} x_i} = p^*_{d+1, x+x_{d+1}}$.

In fact, we get here multiple paths that lead to the same probability. Let T be a probability tree, and let $Paths(T)$ be the set of rooted paths in T ending in a leaf. Then the pattern's completion probability equals $\sum_{P \in Paths(T)} p^*_{\rho(P)}$, where $\rho(P)$ denotes the value of the last node in P. Furthermore, if k is the size of the maximal time window for some event to occur, then the maximal value of a leaf is $k \cdot l$ where l is the number of events in the pattern. Hence, there are at most $k \cdot l + 1$ leaves and we can use an array of size $k \cdot l + 1$ to count the instances of every $p^*_j, 0 \le j \le k \cdot l$.

More details can be found in [10].

References

1. Abarbanel, Y., Beer, I., Glushovsky, L., Keidar, S., Wolfsthal, Y.: FoCs: Automatic Generation of Simulation Checkers from Formal Specifications. In: Conference on Computer Aided Verification, pp. 538–542 (2000)
2. Alur, R., Courcoubetis, C., Dill, D.: Model-Checking in Dense Real-Time. Information and Computation 104(1), 2–34 (1993)
3. Burch, J.R., Clarke, E.M., McMillan, K.L., Dill, D.L., Hwang, L.J.: Symbolic Model checking: 10^{20} States and beyond. Information and Computation 98(2), 142–170 (1992)
4. Brukman, O., Dolev, S., Kolodner, E.: Self-Stabilizing Autonomic Recoverer for Eventual Byzantine Software. Journal of Systems and Software 81, 2315–2327 (2008)
5. Boul'e, M., Zilic, Z.: Efficient automata-based assertion-checker synthesis of PSL properties. In: Proceedings of the IEEE International High Level Design Validation and TestWorkshop (HLDVT), pp. 69–76 (2006)
6. Crochemore, M.: String Matching with Constraints. In: Chytil, M.P., Janiga, L., Koubek, V. (eds.) MFCS 1988. LNCS, vol. 324, pp. 44–58. Springer, Heidelberg (1988)
7. Clarke, E.M., Grumberg, O., Peled, D.A.: Model Checking. MIT Press (1999)
8. Dechter, R., Meiri, I., Pearl, J.: Temporal Constraint Networks. Artificial Intelligence 49, 61–95 (1991)
9. Dolev, S., Stomp, F.: Safety Assurance via On-Line Monitoring. Distributed Computing 16(4), 269–277 (2003)
10. Goldfeld, J.: Efficient On-line Detection of Temporal Patterns, MSc Thesis, BGU-CS (2011)
11. Laroussinie, F., Markey, N., Schnoebelen, P.: Efficient Timed Model Checking for Discrete-Time Systems. Theor. Comput. Sci. 353(1), 249–271

Function Summaries
in Software Upgrade Checking*

Grigory Fedyukovich, Ondrej Sery, and Natasha Sharygina

University of Lugano, Formal Verification and Security Lab, Lugano, Switzerland
{grigory.fedyukovich,ondrej.sery,natasha.sharygina}@usi.ch
http://verify.inf.usi.ch/

We propose a new technique for checking of software upgrades based on an optimization of bounded model checking (BMC) with interpolation-based function summaries. In general, function summaries avoid duplicate actions during the verification process. We extract function summaries as an over-approximation of the actual function behavior after a successful model checker run and use it in the consecutive runs. It is useful in real life, when the same code gets analyzed multiple times for different properties. As a practical example of this situation, consider SLAM [1] which is used in a Static Driver Verifier to verify Windows device drivers. There the same code of the device driver is model checked repeatedly for different sets of predefined properties. In every run, function summaries could be generated and reused in the others to reduce the computational burden.

For generation of function summaries with respect to a given property (e.g., a user supplied or automatically generated assertion), we use Craig Interpolation [3]. As in the standard BMC, we transform the program into a logical formula, via unwinding, conversion into the SSA form, followed by addition of the negated property, and bit-blasting. Then we check satisfiability of the resulting formula, passing it to a SAT solver. From UNSAT result (i.e., the property holds), the solver generates an interpolant for each function call, occurring in the formula. By construction, the interpolant is an over-approximation of the corresponding function, i.e., its summary. To use the extracted summary later, we substitute it in the formula instead of processing the entire function again.

Consider we check the program with respect to a different property. Since the summary is an over-approximation of a function, made for a specific property, it may contain spurious behaviors. These behaviors may be crucial for checking another properties, leading to spurious errors. In such a case, our method requires refinement, in which we analyze the spurious error trace. It aims at identifying function calls substituted by summaries that occur on the error trace and influence the assertion (determined by dependency analysis). We repeat the check again without using these summaries, but keeping the rest. If no such summary is identified, the error is real. We describe the extraction, use, and refinement of summaries in details in [5], and implement the process in a tool called FunFrog[1].

As our contribution to upgrade checking, we propose to reuse the already extracted summaries to prevent re-verification of the entire code. Our upgrade

---

* This work is partially supported by the European Community under the call FP7-ICT-2009-5 — project PINCETTE 257647.
[1] http://verify.inf.usi.ch/funfrog

K. Eder, J. Lourenço, and O. Shehory (Eds.): HVC 2011, LNCS 7261, pp. 257–258, 2012.

checking procedure verifies that a property of a program still holds after the program is modified. The proposed method is based on the following observation. There are two possibilities for the modified functions, either their old summaries are still a valid over-approximation or not. If they are valid, properties of the old version, for which the summaries are relevant, still hold also in the new version.

Our method identifies the functions that were modified using syntactic comparison of different versions. Then, for all modified functions, it checks if the summaries are still valid. If the check fails, we detect the calling context of the function and try again. It is important to note two things. First, the check compares the function with its summary and ignores the rest of the system. So the check is local and thus relatively cheap. Second, we can reuse the summaries of the unmodified functions when performing the check. Of course, this implies that refinement may be necessary.

Obviously, the cost of the upgrade check would depend on the extend of the change both syntactical (number of modified functions) and semantical (number of invalid summaries). Thus our approach is likely to benefit for smaller changes that do not violated the properties. In the worst case, the problem is refined to checking of the entire upgraded program, which, however, is rare in practice.

In [2], the authors propose an algorithm for containment and compatibility checks for upgrades of software components. They use predicate abstraction and the CEGAR loop to create and refine models of the new and old components. Though the goal is the same, the means are different. In the context of dynamic test generation, the authors of [4] purpose to use function summaries for testing upgrades. Their notion of a summary is a collection of concrete pairs of inputs and outputs, i.e., an under-approximation, and thus their check can be not sound.

In future work, we will implement the proposed upgrade checker in the Fun-Frog tool. In collaboration with the PINCETTE project validators, we plan to apply the tool to verify real-world applications. As shown in [5], the current release of FunFrog, despite not being final, was already applied to industrial benchmarks. Enlarging the set of benchmarks, will help us to analyze experimentally the benefits of our approach and to reveal directions for further optimizations. We expect to confirm experimentally that interpolant-based upgrade checking outperforms model checking of the entire upgraded program.

References

1. Ball, T., Rajamani, S.K.: The SLAM Project: Debugging System Software via Static Analysis. In: POPL 2002, pp. 1–3 (January 2002)
2. Chaki, S., Clarke, E., Sharygina, N., Sinha, N.: Dynamic Component Substitutability Analysis. In: Fitzgerald, J.S., Hayes, I.J., Tarlecki, A. (eds.) FM 2005. LNCS, vol. 3582, pp. 512–528. Springer, Heidelberg (2005)
3. Craig, W.: Three uses of the Herbrand-Gentzen theorem in relating model theory and proof theory. J. of Symbolic Logic, 269–285 (1957)
4. Godefroid, P., Lahiri, S., Rubio-González, C.: Statically Validating Must Summaries for Incremental Compositional Dynamic Test Generation. In: Yahav, E. (ed.) SAS 2011. LNCS, vol. 6887, pp. 112–128. Springer, Heidelberg (2011)
5. Sery, O., Fedyukovich, G., Sharygina, N.: Interpolation-Based Function Summaries in Bounded Model Checking. In: Eder, K., Lourenço, J., Shehory, O. (eds.) HVC 2011. LNCS, vol. 7261, pp. 160–175. Springer, Heidelberg (2012)

The Rabin Index of Parity Games
(Extended Abstract)

Michael Huth[1], Jim Huan-Pu Kuo[1], and Nir Piterman[2]

[1] Department of Computing
Imperial College London
London, SW7 2AZ, United Kingdom
{m.huth,jimhkuo}@imperial.ac.uk
[2] Department of Computer Science
University of Leicester
Leicester, LE1 7RH, United Kingdom
nir.piterman@leicester.ac.uk

Abstract. We study the descriptive complexity of parity games by taking into account the coloring of their game graphs whilst ignoring their ownership structure. Different colorings of the same graph are identified if they determine the same winning regions and strategies, for *all* ownership structures of nodes. The Rabin index of a parity game is the minimum of the maximal color taken over all equivalent coloring functions. We show that deciding whether the Rabin index is at least k is in P for $k = 1$ but NP-hard for all *fixed* $k \geq 2$. We present an EXP-TIME algorithm that computes the Rabin index by simplifying its input coloring function. When replacing simple cycle with cycle detection in that algorithm, its output over-approximates the Rabin index in polynomial time. Experimental results show that this approximation yields good values in practice.

Parity games (see e.g. [1]) are infinite, 2-person, 0-sum, graph-based games that are hard to solve. Their nodes are colored with natural numbers, controlled by different players, and the winning condition of plays depends on the minimal color occurring in cycles. The condition for winning a node, therefore, is an alternation of existential and universal quantification. In practice, this means that the maximal color of its coloring function is the only exponential source for the worst-case complexity of most parity game solvers, e.g. for those in [1,2,3].

One approach taken in analyzing the complexity of such games is through the study of the descriptive complexity of their underlying game graph. This method therefore ignores the ownership structure on parity games.

An example of this approach is the notion of DAG-width in [4]. Every directed graph has a DAG-width, a natural number that specifies how well that graph can be decomposed into a directed acyclic graph (DAG). The decision problem for DAG-width, whether the DAG-width of a directed graph is at most k, is NP-complete [4] in k. But parity games whose DAG-width is below a given threshold have polynomial-time solutions [4]. The latter is a non-trivial result since DAG-width also ignores the colors of a parity game.

K. Eder, J. Lourenço, and O. Shehory (Eds.): HVC 2011, LNCS 7261, pp. 259–260, 2012.
© Springer-Verlag Berlin Heidelberg 2012

In this abstract, we report a similar measure of the descriptive complexity of parity games, their *Rabin index*, a natural number that ignores the ownership of nodes, but does take into account the colors of a parity game.

The name for this measure is inspired by related work on the Wagner hierarchy for automata on infinite words [5]: Carton and Maceiras use similar ideas to compute and minimize the Rabin index of deterministic parity automata on infinite words [6]. To the best of our knowledge, our work is the first to study this notion in the realm of infinite, 2-person games.

The idea behind our Rabin index is that one may change the coloring function of a parity game to another one if that change neither affects the winning regions nor the choices of winning strategies. This yields an equivalence relation between coloring functions. For the coloring function of a parity game, we then seek an equivalent coloring function with the smallest possible maximal color, and call that minimal maximum the Rabin index of the respective parity game.

The results we report here about this Rabin index are similar in spirit to those developed for DAG-width in [4] but there are important differences:

- We propose a measure of descriptive complexity that is closer to the structure of the parity game as it only forgets ownership of nodes and not their colors.
- We prove that for every *fixed* $k \geq 2$, deciding whether the Rabin index of a parity game is at least k is NP-hard.
- We can characterize the above equivalence relation in terms of the parities of minimal colors on simple cycles in the game graph.
- We use that characterization to design an algorithm that computes the Rabin index and a witnessing coloring function in exponential time.
- We define an approximation of the Rabin index by replacing simple cycles in the definition of Rabin index by cycles.
- We show how to efficiently compute this approximation by replacing the search for simple cycles by search for cycles in the same algorithm.
- We conduct detailed experimental studies that corroborate the utility of that approximation, also as a preprocessor for solvers.

References

1. Zielonka, W.: Infinite games on finitely coloured graphs with applications to automata on infinite trees. Theoretical Computer Science 200(1-2), 135–183 (1998)
2. Jurdziński, M.: Small Progress Measures for Solving Parity Games. In: Reichel, H., Tison, S. (eds.) STACS 2000. LNCS, vol. 1770, pp. 290–301. Springer, Heidelberg (2000)
3. Vöge, J., Jurdziński, M.: A Discrete Strategy Improvement Algorithm for Solving Parity Games. In: Emerson, E.A., Sistla, A.P. (eds.) CAV 2000. LNCS, vol. 1855, pp. 202–215. Springer, Heidelberg (2000)
4. Berwanger, D., Dawar, A., Hunter, P., Kreutzer, S.: DAG-Width and Parity Games. In: Durand, B., Thomas, W. (eds.) STACS 2006. LNCS, vol. 3884, pp. 524–536. Springer, Heidelberg (2006)
5. Wagner, K.: On ω-regular sets. Information and Computation 43, 123–177 (1979)
6. Carton, O., Maceiras, R.: Computing the Rabin Index of a Parity Automaton. Informatique Théorique et Applications 33(6), 495–506 (1999)

Using Computational Biology Methods to Improve Post-silicon Microprocessor Testing

Ron Zeira[1], Dmitry Korchemny[2], and Ron Shamir[1]

[1] Blavatnik School of Computer Science, Tel Aviv University
69978 Ramat Aviv, Tel Aviv, Israel
ronzeira@post.tau.ac.il, rshamir@tau.ac.il
[2] Intel, Haifa, Israel
dmitry.korchemny@intel.com

Abstract. Hardware testing is an expensive process at different stages of hardware design and manufacturing. It includes pre-silicon, post-silicon and production testing. Testing is expensive both in terms of manpower and in computing resources, and it directly affects the hardware profitability and the time to market. This problem is especially acute for Systems on Chip (SoC) where both manpower and timing constraints are very tight. Therefore it is important to reduce the total number of tests without sacrificing testing quality.

To learn the behavior of a large test set smart algorithms are needed. In addition, visualization techniques can provide a bird's-eye view of the total test coverage data.

Our goal is to optimize post-silicon hardware test suites based on coverage metrics and to provide test coverage visualization. We utilize ideas and methods developed in machine learning and bioinformatics, and develop new biology-inspired methods to analyze and visualize post-silicon data. In a different effort, we are exploring combinatorial methods of covering and domination for the same problem.

Mathematically, the results of post-silicon tests can be presented as a matrix whose rows correspond to the tests performed on the chip and columns correspond to certain events of interest occurring during the test's runs. The matrix values are the number of times the event occurred in the test. Such a matrix can then be used to define a similarity measure between tests and analyze their relations.

In computational biology (bioinformatics), advanced methods were developed to handle gene expression microarray data [1], which has a similar structure. The result of a set of microarray experiments is a gene expression values matrix where rows are genes and columns are conditions. A rich spectrum of methods was developed for analysis of such data [2], and we adapt them for the post-silicon analysis. For example, clustering techniques divide the tests into similarity groups, identifying subsets of tests that cover similar events. The identified groups can then be analyzed by the hardware validation engineers in order to identify coverage holes and to improve the test suite quality. In addition, similar test groups can be investigated for enrichment of certain chip properties as done for gene groups with biological properties. This

K. Eder, J. Lourenço, and O. Shehory (Eds.): HVC 2011, LNCS 7261, pp. 261–262, 2012.
© Springer-Verlag Berlin Heidelberg 2012

can give further insight on the chip's operation and the tests scope. Gene expression software tools that combine advanced analysis and visualization can assist in visual comprehension of the post silicon validation process. We are using for this task the Expander tool developed in Prof. Shamir's group [3-5].

We describe initial results obtained by applying computational biology methods to post-Si test suite optimization and visualization. Though we experimented only with post-silicon test data, most of the developed methods should be applicable with appropriate modifications also to pre-silicon, production, and even to software testing.

Keywords: Post-silicon, SoC, microprocessor testing, cluster analysis.

References

1. Quackenbush, J.: Computational analysis of microarray data. Nature Reviews Genetics (2001)
2. Handl, J., Knowles, J., Kell, D.B.: Computational Cluster Validation in Post-genomic Data Analysis. Bioinformatics 21(15), 3201–3212 (2005)
3. Sharan, R., Maron-Katz, A., Shamir, R.: CLICK and EXPANDER: a system for clustering and visualizing gene expression data. Bioinformatics 19(14), 1787–1799 (2003)
4. Shamir, R., et al.: EXPANDER–an integrative program suite for microarray data analysis. BMC Bioinformatics 6, 232 (2005)
5. Ulitsky, I., Maron-Katz, A., Shavit, S., Sagir, D., Linhart, C., Elkon, R., Tanay, A., Sharan, R., Shiloh, Y., Shamir, R.: Expander: from expression microarrays to networks and functions. Nature Protocols 5, 303–322 (2010)

Author Index